Petersburg

Andrei Bely

PETERSBURG

Translated, annotated, and introduced by
Robert A. Maguire and John E. Malmstad

BLOOMINGTON
INDIANA UNIVERSITY PRESS

Sources and Translation Series of the Russian Institute,
Columbia University

Manufactured in the United States of America

Library of Congress Cataloging in Publication Data

Bugaev, Boris Nikolaevich, 1880–1934.
  Petersburg.

  (Sources and translation series of the Russian Institute, Columbia
University)
  I. Title. II. Series: Columbia University.
Russian Institute. Sources and translation series of
the Russian Institute, Columbia University.
PZ3.B8647Pe 1977 [PG3453.B84] 891.7'3'42 77-74442
ISBN 0-253-34410-7   3 4 5 6 7 88 87 86 85 84 83

Contents

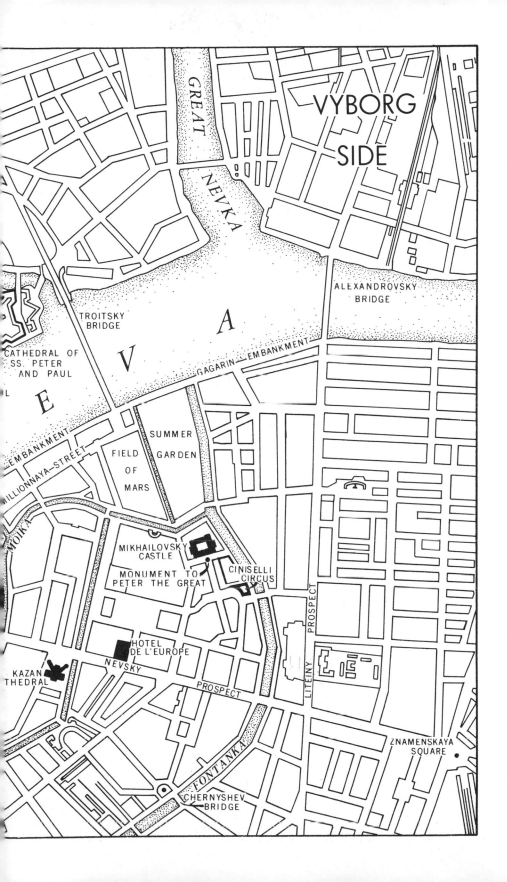

Translators' Introduction

"My greatest masterpieces of twentieth century prose," Vladimir Nabokov has said, "are, in this order: Joyce's *Ulysses*; Kafka's *Transformation*; Biely's *Petersburg*; and the first half of Proust's fairy tale *In Search of Lost Time*."[1] He puts the matter provocatively and puts it well. The order of ranking might be open to dispute; the presence of *Petersburg* on any list of this kind is not.

What entitles this novel to a place in such eminent company? Certainly it invites admiration as a skillful and effective piece of workmanship. But more than that is involved, as it must be for any truly significant work of art. *Petersburg* is firmly rooted in Russian soil, yet it speaks in a voice that is powerful and original, and that carries across national boundaries to the hearing of us all.

At the heart of *Petersburg* lies a question that has agitated Russians for generations: the national identity. Perhaps only the Germans and the Americans, among modern western peoples, have been so obsessed with finding out who they are, and so given to questioning their own reality and authenticity. The Russian version has been shaped as much by geography as anything else. As a nation straddling Europe and Asia, Russians have sought to define a vision of themselves that would amount to more than merely a sum of "western" and "eastern" traits. This in turn has provided a context in which the great writers have explored the individual's quest for identity and meaning with an intensity and earnestness that seem quintessentially Russian. *Petersburg* represents the culmination of this tradition.

At the same time, the problem has had larger dimensions. For Russians also conceive of "west" and "east" in ways that mark the human experience generally. "West" stands for reason, order, symmetry; "east" for the irrational, the impalpable, the intuitive. At given times one may outweigh the other in society at large or in the individual consciousness; or the two may even coexist more or less harmoniously. But in the twentieth century, as Bely clearly sees, these two principles, inside Russia and out, have more often been in open conflict, with neither gaining preponderance. We have developed a characteristically "modern" terminology to express our reaction to this conflict: anxiety, apprehension, alienation, isolation.

These also describe the moods that move Bely's great novel from beginning to end.

When writers of our century have not explored the consequences of this conflict on the battlefield or in the concentration camp, they have often turned to the city. Here Joyce's *Ulysses* is, of course, the most distinguished instance. Critics have sometimes compared Bely's novel to it, although the two are fundamentally different. Among works with urban settings, *Petersburg* is virtually unique in that the city is not merely the arena of the action, but itself becomes the main character, as rich both in experience and in meaning as any of the human characters in other great novels. (Significantly, Joyce did not name his novel *Dublin*.) And Bely creates this character by defining a unique vision and devising a unique language through which to explore it. The result is one of the most inventive works of literature ever written.

Despite its power, complexity, and freshness, *Petersburg* remains relatively unknown and unappreciated, both in its native land and abroad. The reasons for this are different on each side of the border.

Bely was born in Moscow in 1880, as Boris Nikolaevich Bugaev. He began to publish in 1902, while still a student at the university, adopting the pseudonym Andrei Bely ("Andrew White") to spare his prominent father the embarrassment of public association with the still-scandalous Symbolists, whose camp he immediately joined. Throughout his relatively brief career (he died in 1934) he was a poet, an essayist, and a theoretician of literature and culture. He was also a prolific novelist: besides *Petersburg*, he wrote *The Silver Dove* (1909), *Kotik Letaev* (1922), and, in the 1920s and 1930s, a series of novels with the generic title *Moscow*. His earliest efforts in prose fiction were four short works he designated as "symphonies." They departed from the nineteenth-century narrative tradition by cultivating a "musical" structure and diction that reflected, among other things, Symbolism's attempt to eradicate the boundaries among the various arts. In 1909 he tried his hand at a more conventional kind of novel, *The Silver Dove* (*Serebryanyi golub'*). Its hero, Daryalsky, is a young intellectual of occidental bent who has grown tired of the life of the mind and has gone to seek a new truth, largely mystical and non-western, among peasants belonging to a sect called the Doves. He encounters only frustration and ultimately death at the hands of the sectarians, who represent the darkest side of the "dark folk," as the peasantry is sometimes called in Russia. *Petersburg* was first intended as a continuation of this novel; but in the writing, it developed into something far different.[2]

It first appeared in book form in 1916, and was immediately recognized as a work of major literary importance. Yet so radically did it depart from the great tradition of the Russian novel that no one quite knew how to approach it. It became one of those works that are routinely praised without being understood or read. Before it could be subjected to proper study, the Bolsheviks came to power, and with them, a view of the nature and purposes of literature that was fundamentally hostile to the entire modernist outlook. To be sure, Bely's 1922 revision of the novel was twice reprinted in Soviet Russia (with major cuts by the censors); but with the growing demand that literature must conform to the standards of Socialist Realism, *Petersburg* was pronounced "decadent" and therefore inimical to the interests of the "new" reader. It was consigned to virtual oblivion, along with all of Bely's *oeuvre*, as indeed were most of the achievements of that brilliant generation of writers, painters, and composers who came to prominence before 1917. The result led Igor Stravinsky, as late as 1960, to remark of music in Russia: "It was new just *before* the Soviets."[3] The same could be said of every other form of art.

The passage of time and the easing of official strictures in the two decades since Stalin's death have conferred a measure of acceptability (if not always respectability) on many of the important Symbolists. A carefully controlled and highly selective "reclaiming" of the Russian past is under way. In 1966, a collection of Bely's verses and long poems (*Stikhotvoreniya i poemy*) was published. And a new critical edition of *Petersburg* has been prepared. But publication has been delayed indefinitely, for reasons that are not entirely clear. As of this writing, the novel has not been reprinted in its native land for more than forty years.

In many ways the reception of Bely's work in the west has followed a parallel course. Our far more open societies have shown themselves curiously prone to ape the Soviets by allowing political criteria to determine what belongs in the canon of "interesting" Russian literature and what does not. Attention focuses on "acceptable" writers like Leonid Leonov or Valentin Kataev for the picture they supposedly provide of Soviet life, and conversely, on writers who are completely unacceptable, like Solzhenitsyn and the Pasternak of *Doctor Zhivago*, for their exposure of gross defects in the moral fabric of their country. Those writers of real talent whom the Soviets have simply neglected tend to suffer the same fate here. Isaac Babel and Yury Olesha are significant cases in point. Both ran afoul of the official ideologues. For two decades their writings were not republished. Even their names all but disappeared from public mention. And western translators and critics took almost no interest in them either. It was only after their "rehabilitation" in the mid-1950s and the publication of new editions of their work that their "significance" was rediscovered abroad. A similar pattern can be traced for the Symbolists. For decades the Soviets treated them as a minor aberration and refused to reissue their works (Alexander Blok being the notable exception); they were known to only a handful of connoisseurs in the west. As they were slowly restored to a modicum of favor during the 1950s, they began to attract notice outside Russia. One of the first signs was a new translation of Fyodor Sologub's famous novel *The Petty Demon* in 1962, some five years after it had been republished in the provincial Soviet town of Kemerovo (and had cost its editors their jobs). By now translators are opening up the Symbolist period as a whole, and it is finally becoming the target of considerable scholarly endeavor as well.

In the case of Andrei Bely, we are for once ahead of the Soviets in the strictly chronological sense. His major works have been reprinted in the Russian language outside the Soviet Union. *Kotik Letaev* and *The Silver Dove* can now be read in English. A German version of *Petersburg* appeared in 1919, and another in 1959; an Italian translation came out in 1961, a French in 1967, an English in 1959. Yet the familiar pattern holds. Nearly all this activity is of very recent vintage, too recent for the scholarly industry to have started full-scale production, though it is gearing itself up. For English readers, a major obstacle to the appreciation of *Petersburg* has been that 1959 version, which bears only incidental resemblance to the original. Apart from gross misreadings, it makes numerous cuts, which eliminate, among other things, virtually the entire persona of the narrator, whose presence is essential to any real understanding of what Bely is up to. The translator, John Cournos, deserves our respect as a pioneer, but his work conveys little of the intricacy and subtlety of the original. It is also devoid of annotation, and therefore supplies none of the cultural context which Bely, like any writer, takes for granted in his audience and which by and large is unfamiliar to western readers. Even the great nineteenth-century Russian "realist" classics still strike most foreigners as exotic. How much truer that is of *Petersburg*, with its cultivation of the grotesque and its invocation of an epoch of Russian cultural and political history which, though not so remote in time, is still little known to the English-speaking world. One of the reasons why Joyce, Kafka, and Proust—to take just the writers mentioned above by Nabokov—have achieved such enormous popularity is that an elaborate critical and scholarly literature has grown up to elucidate the texture, the feel, and the facts of the times and places in which their works are set.

The present translation aims at removing these impediments to a deeper understanding and appreciation of one of the masterpieces of twentieth-century literature. We offer here the first full version of the definitive 1922 text of the novel, along with the kind of annotation we deem essential for anyone who wishes to get below the surface.

II.

Petersburg paints a vivid picture of the capital of the world's largest land empire during the autumn of 1905. Russian culture was then at its most brilliant and innovative. Literature, music, theater, and ballet were beginning to win fame throughout the world. But the society from which they sprang seemed shaky. Japan had just proved victorious in a war that Russia was supposed to have won easily. Political agitation and social unrest were on the rise. Outright revolution was being preached and prepared; and from January 1905 on, the country was shaken by a series of mutinies, uprisings, assassinations, and strikes. There was a widespread feeling among those who witnessed such events that the old values were no longer adequate to the new realities, and that Russia teetered on the edge of some dreadful catastrophe. This ominous feeling, with the attendant moods of anxiety, apprehension, and disorientation, permeates Bely's *Petersburg* from the first page to the last.

Appropriately enough, conspiracy and terror are the forces that move the novel. The story looks like simplicity itself. Nikolai Apollonovich, an impressionable university student, has gotten entangled with a revolutionary terrorist organization, which plans to assassinate a high government official with a time bomb. The twist is that the official is Nikolai's father, Apollon Apollonovich, and that Nikolai himself is entrusted with planting the bomb. It is duly delivered to him, the clock mechanism is set to explode within twenty-four hours, and———. But we must not give away the ending: *Petersburg* is a novel of suspense. It is also a social novel, a family novel, a philosophical, political, psychological, historical novel—and even then we do not begin to exhaust the possible approaches to it. One has to go back in Russian literature at least to *Crime and Punishment* to find a work in which so many plots and subplots are as intricately and subtly interwoven, with no loose ends protruding. Yet Bely ranges much farther afield than does Dostoevsky. It is relatively easy to account for the main lines of *Crime and Punishment*, tangled though they be, whereas to do that for *Petersburg* would be to rewrite the novel: it is all but immune to paraphrase.

All these planes, levels, and dimensions come together in the characters of the novel, who are at the same time engaged in moving the story line ahead. Through the characters themselves—and not through any raisonneur-figure, or through any of those grand panoramic statements to which the nineteenth-century novelists were addicted—Bely creates a picture of Petersburg society. He focuses on the two extremes—the powerful and privileged (Apollon Apollonovich and his circle) and the poor and disaffected (Dudkin and the peasant Styopka). But he creates an impression of fullness and completeness by bringing in, if only fleetingly, representatives of other classes and groups, such as merchants and servants, and by constantly invoking the gray faceless masses of the metropolis. Through the characters he also introduces the intellectual and cultural fashions that held sway in Petersburg at the time: Apollon Apollonovich and his son cherish Comte and Kant respectively; Sofia Petrovna's enthusiasm for the nonexistent "Henri Besançon" suggests that the rage for Henri Bergson and Annie Besant had infected even muddled society ladies; Dudkin's mind is a virtual compendium of anarchist theories popular at the turn of the century, in which Nietzsche and mysticism admixed powerfully. Characters also provide the means by which Bely saturates the novel with literary allusions. For instance, Nikolai Apollonovich's adulterous mother has the same given name as Tolstoy's Anna Karenina, and is also married to an unloving man with oversized ears. The encounter between Nikolai and Morkovin in the seedy restaurant, with the heavy hints at possible blood kinship, suggests the relationship between Ivan and Smerdyakov in Dostoevsky's *The Brothers Karamazov*. Apollon Apollonovich is, among other things, a composite of two characters in Gogol's "The Overcoat": the lowly Akaky Akakievich and the haughty Person of Consequence (who is Akaky's alter ego). Many of the characters also transfer universally recognizable social and psychological types into the Petersburg of 1905: Apollon Apollonovich, for one, is the quintessential bureaucrat and the quintessential anal erotic. Even the excursions into the timeless and dimensionless realm of myth and the "cosmos" are shown as the experiences of specific characters.

Such a multiplicity of functions tends to pull the characters out of themselves. Like many modern writers, Bely does not attempt anything resembling full psychological portraits. Ultimately there are no private thoughts or private actions; all are reflexes of larger realities, which in turn are experienced by all the characters. Even something as concrete as a tic or a gesture may be shared by a number of otherwise seemingly different personages. For instance, Dudkin's favorite posture, when alone in his garret and unable to sleep, is to flatten himself against the wall with arms outstretched; Lippanchenko does the same just before he is killed by Dudkin, who then mimics the statue of Peter the Great (an important character in the novel) by straddling the corpse, as Peter does his horse. Yet it is Bely's great achievement to make these characters seem real and memorable as individuals. He endows each with certain striking physical traits which he repeats again and again by way of imprinting them on our memories: Apollon Apollonovich has large greenish ears, a bald head, and a puny physique; Sofia Petrovna possesses luxuriant tresses and an incipient mustache; Lippanchenko is obese and has a low, narrow forehead. Nearly all the characters bear "meaningful" names as well: Apollon is the Russian for "Apollo"; Ableukhov contains the word for "ear" (*ukho*); Lippanchenko draws on the morpheme *lip–*, which can make the word for "sticky." Each character has his own skew of temperament, which helps determine which aspects of the vast reality of the novel he will tend to see. And Bely surrounds him with an array of objects that serve as correlatives to his outlook. Apollon Apollonovich relishes the icy symmetries of the formal rooms of his mansion, which reflect his passion for the abstractions of geometry. His son lives in three very different rooms, which suggests greater temperamental complexity: the study, with its bookshelves and its bust of Kant, mirrors his yearning for systems and his penchant for abstraction (both "western" traits); the sleeping room, which is almost entirely taken up by a huge bed, objectifies and is meant to exorcise his Oedipal obsession with the "sin" of his conception; and the reception room, with its oriental motifs, gratifies the "eastern" side of his character which emerges after his mother runs off with her lover. For many of these devices Bely is heavily indebted to his great predecessors; but he has achieved a synthesis that is unmistakably personal.

Bely's characters, then, are both general and particular, abstract and concrete, unreal and real, at one and the same time. This unity in duality is characteristic of every aspect of the novel. Consider the matter of time. The novel as a whole unfolds between September 30 and October 9, 1905. Although these dates are not specified, they can readily be established if we note the wealth of detail Bely introduces (much of it from the daily press) on current events and the vagaries of the weather. Once the bomb begins ticking, in Chapter V, we are forced to think in terms of the twenty-four-hour period within which it is set to explode. All this gives us a sense of being firmly planted in time and in space. Yet the chronology is constantly warped: characters and events from the literature and history of the past move into 1905; there are sudden shifts into a distant unspecified future time, and even into the timeless realm of myth. We come to see that time and timelessness are both "real" in this novel; the one does not exclude the other.

The same point can be made about the city itself. As Bely recreates it, it is as familiar to any Russian as London or Paris is to an Englishman or Frenchman. Through a careful and lavish specification of the peculiarities of climate, geography, and prominent architectural features, Bely manages to convey a sense of the actual physical presence of the city, making it so vivid and "real" that sometimes we almost think we are reading a gloss on Baedeker. (At the same time, we understand that Petersburg represents the modern city generally.) Yet it has a curiously elusive quality. To be sure, the great public buildings and the famous monuments are all located where they should be, and remain fixed throughout. But other external, man-made features tend to be as fluid as the waters that run through, around, and beneath the city itself: when we try to plot them on a map, we find, for instance, that the Ableukhov house occupies three very different locations, that the Likhutin house is an "impossible" composite of several others, and that the government institution headed by the senator cannot be even approximately situated, even though all three of these buildings are described in considerable detail.[4]

In fact, Bely readily acknowledges his debt to the version of Petersburg that has been shaped by Russian literature. Writers of the eighteenth century tended to see Petersburg as a magnificent monument to the power of human reason and will: it was a planned city, founded in 1703 and built on a trackless bog. Part I of Pushkin's "The Bronze Horseman" (1833) honors this point of view; but Part II strikes a new note that came to predominate in virtually all literary treatments of Petersburg well into the twentieth century: beneath the "western" facade lay a shadowy world of intangibilities and unrealities, alien to man's reason and apprehensible only to his unconscious being—an "eastern" world, in the Russian terminology. It was Petersburg, with its uneasy coexistence of "west" and "east," that appealed to the Russian mind as being emblematic of the larger problem of national identity. Readers of Gogol and Dostoevsky are familiar with this double view. It characterizes Bely's novel too. He takes all the literary myths of Petersburg, which Dostoevsky called "the most fantastic and intentional city in the world," and brings them to culmination.

Each of the characters in *Petersburg* participates in the enactment and perpetuation of the myth of the city—none more vigorously and meaningfully than the Bronze Horseman. The subject of the statue, Peter the Great, was a real man and a historical figure. In his efforts to shatter and update the Russia he inherited, he was a revolutionary; yet at the same time he created the bureaucracy by which the reforms were rigidified into the self-perpetuating authority of the state. In the single-minded tyranny with which he acted, he was an "eastern" despot; but in his vision of a modern state he was "western." As the "father" of Russia, he is the ultimate symbol of the paternal authority against which the "sons" rebel in various ways. At the same time, he has a literary dimension, as the main subject of Pushkin's "The Bronze Horseman," which is constantly invoked throughout Bely's novel; the Horseman, in turn, is the most famous monument in Petersburg, and is in effect a symbol of the city. In the novel, Peter is alive and ever-present in all these manifestations—a point Bely reinforces not only by bringing the statue to life (Pushkin does that too), but also by tying Peter in with the all-pervasive theme of generational conflict and revolution, with the literary myth of the city, and with the apocalyptic destiny he sees awaiting Russia.

The Bronze Horseman is the most perceptive character in the novel. But most of the others are intelligent enough to see that they are not self-contained, that they participate, whether wishing to or not, in the workings of a larger reality that exists independent of them. This reality is sometimes referred to in the novel as "abyss" or "void." Occasionally a character is vouchsafed a disturbing glimpse into it, in dreams, at the moment of death, or at times of great stress which pull him out of his routines and, in the words of a recent critic, "bring him into contact with the universe [literally, 'world-structure,' *mirozdanie*] and turn him into a 'particle' of the universe too. There, beyond the bounds of the visible world, man falls into the powers of a 'timeless' stream of time, in which are grouped events and persons of not only past but also future epochs."[5] Such an experience is profoundly unsettling to Bely's characters, for it threatens to undo their identities as individuals. By way of resistance, they construct a world of objects with definite shapes and functions, whether the city itself, representing Peter's attempt at self-assertion and self-definition, or the more modest houses, apartments, and rooms that his heirs inhabit. All relish what they can touch and see—the visible, the finite, the specific—or what they can construct out of their own heads—systems, categories, propositions. But the narrator treats all such attempts with irony; they represent no more than a partial and provisional reality, and therefore serve only to perpetuate self-deception. Where, for instance, is the line really to be drawn between the natural and the man-made? Nature lives, as the many personifications in the novel indicate; but so do the objects man creates in trying to deny nature: the statue of Peter the Great gallops through the streets and speaks; the caryatid adorning Apollon Apollonovich's government institution witnesses and muses on the events of Russian history. And the urge to make mental constructs is constantly sabotaged by the workings of "cerebral play," that sudden, unexpected explosion of mental forces which bursts out into the world and creates new realities entirely beyond the understanding and control of the individual.

What the characters fail to see is that the whole world, natural and man-made, visible and invisible, is a living entity, composed of parts which interconnect and thereby acquire their true meaning. To isolate one or more of these parts, physically or intellectually, is to diminish and damage the whole, much as the removal of an arm or a leg from the body detracts from the beauty, the efficiency, and even the health of the entire organism. But that is precisely what the characters in *Petersburg* attempt to do. Gogol was Bely's great predecessor in seeing the urge to fragment as a modern sickness. He deemed it the work of the devil. For Bely, the devil is modern urban man himself, whose obsession with the fragment is not so much an evil as a compulsion born of the fear of losing his individuality.

Language, as Bely sees it, is especially subject to the depredations of self-deception, perhaps because it is a wholly human construct. Apollon Apollonovich's habit of calling all flowers "bluebells" regardless of their variety divorces the word from living reality and turns it into an abstraction. All the other characters indulge in the same operation, to varying degrees. As a result, verbal exchanges in *Petersburg*, when not merely trivial, tend to be irrelevant and fatuous. Gestures can often be more expressive of true intentions and desires. In written form, words can be just as inadequate to deeper understanding and meaningful communication—perhaps even more so than spoken words, for they are fixed and motionless, and we tend to worship them as we worship artifacts generally. Whether spoken or written, however, language as modern man uses it is yet another of the abstractions he makes in an effort to deny the vitality, energy, and change that characterize real life. The consequences are grave, in Bely's view; for language—or, as he often calls it, "the word"—is our only means of knowing the world and ourselves. The living word, for Bely, is sound, or speech. Without it, "there is neither nature, nor the world, nor anyone cognizing them."[6] If modern thought and modern society are in a state of crisis, as Bely believes, then that is because language, as modern man employs it, is dying. Here his position is just the opposite of Emerson's, who wrote: "The corruption of man is followed by the corruption of language" (*Nature*, Chapter IV).

One of Bely's tasks as a literary artist is to convey a sense of the word as sound through the static medium of print. In *Petersburg*, as in several of his other works, he constantly tries to confound all our habits as visually-oriented readers for whom words are immobile, unobtrusive, and as silent as the type that encases them.

For one thing, he does violence to the accepted usages and the traditional strategies of "literary" language. He breaks his page up into small units with a profusion of dashes, dots, and new paragraphs. The result is a nervous and disjointed-looking discourse which does not flow in the majestic and seemingly effortless manner of the nineteenth-century novel. He is also addicted to catachresis: the expected word simply does not turn up in the expected place. Thus we find, to take a simple example, "thought train" (*myslennyi khod*) instead of the usual "train of thought" (*khod myslei*). Although there are comparatively few outright neologisms, Bely does devise unusual combinations of elements taken from standard Russian, particularly for abstract nouns, whose meaning is more or less clear, but which are not listed in any dictionary.

For another thing, he aims at creating a world of sound. Dialogue is prominent; in fact, *Petersburg* would lend itself well to adaptation for the stage or cinema (Bely himself made a play out of it in 1925). From the very beginning of the novel, we are confronted with a *speaking* narrator, whose voice rings in our ears throughout the novel. And we quickly become aware that this narrator also strives after certain sound effects. One of the many instances goes this way (in much abbreviated form): "I o něm rasprostranyát'sya ne búdem. Rasprostranímsya bólee o Peterbúrge: est' Peterbúrg íli Sankt-Peterbúrg íli Píter . . . Névskii Prospékt est' peterbúrgskii Prospékt . . . ," and so on. ("And we shall not expatiate on it. Let us expatiate at greater length on Petersburg: there is a Petersburg, or Saint Petersburg, or Pieter . . . Nevsky Prospect is a Petersburg Prospect . . ." ("Prologue"). If read purely for content, this strikes us as silly babble; but if we listen to it with our mind's ear, as it were, or even better, read it aloud, we realize that the words have been chosen for the purpose of clustering certain sounds (p-b-r-k-l-s-t). Sound play—much of it far more sophisticated than this—pervades the novel. Much later, in fact, Bely even claimed that *Petersburg* had been built on a system of sound. "I have the impression that 'll' is the smoothness of form: Apo-*lll*-on; 'pp' is the pressure created by covering surfaces (walls, the bomb); 'kk' is the height of insincerity: Ni-*kkk*-olái . . . *kkk*-lányalsya na, *kk*-a-*kk* la-*kk*, par-*kk*-éta-khkh ('Nikolai . . . bowed on the varnish-like parquet floor'); 'sss' are reflections; 'rr' is the energy of the explosion (beneath the covering surfaces): *prr*-o-*rr*-ývv v *brr*-ed ('a breakthrough into delirium')."

Bely went on to say in effect that in the composition of the novel, sound was preexistent, and "content" formed around it: "Later I myself stumbled on the connection—which surprised me—between the verbal instrumentation and the story line (*which came into being involuntarily*)."[7] We do not in fact know whether Bely actually created the novel in this way. But certainly sheer sound is so prominent as to constitute yet another level of reality with which we must reckon. From the very first page, we are conditioned to listen as well as look. We find it difficult to read rapidly or silently; our lips tend to move; and we pay closer attention than might otherwise be the case to the word itself and its components.

As a result, many otherwise common words take on new meanings. One handy example is *shárik*. Its primary dictionary meaning is "corpuscle"; and it is a "neutral" word in the sense that in ordinary contexts, no Russian stops for a moment to think of its literal meaning, "little sphere." But in the context of this particular novel, the reader is bombarded with other words made up of the same or very similar sounds: *shar* (sphere), *shírit'sya* (expand), *rasshirénie* (expansion, dilatation). Typically, spheres are shown as expanding—a point made as much by the phonic similarity of the roots *shar—/shir—*(they are not related otherwise), as by outright statement. The ear pulls *shárik* into this same phonic pattern; and then we are likely to remember that the primary component is *shar*. But of course the dictionary meaning of "corpuscle" still remains. The result is a certain tension between the phonic and semantic elements, as is the case with many other words in this novel. Any great writer, of course, renews the language. Bely invents as well, and compels his readers to participate in the invention, as few other writers do.

III.

How are we to approach a novel so complex and richly textured as *Petersburg*? No reader will get very far along without seeing that in theme, in personages, and in a whole array of specific techniques, *Petersburg* owes much to the tradition of the great Russian novels. At the same time, he is immediately aware that it is radically different from anything that has gone before. And in trying to account for the differences, he will to a large extent be defining not only its uniqueness, but also its special properties as a Symbolist novel. Nothing like a definitive interpretation can of course be essayed here.[8] We can only hint at some strategies and attitudes of mind that a good reader is advised to take with him as he sets out on his journey through the text.

Certainly we can say that Bely expects us to be more perceptive than his characters. We must resist a natural inclination to simplify, categorize, paraphrase, abstract, and fragment, that is, to treat the reality of the novel in the same way the characters do. We will not get very far if we succumb to the temptation, as some readers have done, of assuming that Bely's world is built on a system of dualities that amounts to a set of viable alternatives: east/west, animate/inanimate, revolutionary/reactionary, present/past, Christ/Satan, and so on. There are no real alternatives for Bely. Revolution and reaction are equally incompetent to deal with reality: both are constructs of the mind that end in mindless despotism; east and west are so intermingled in the Russian character that they cannot possibly be separated; there is no meaningful division between present and past, or present and future. The most useful rhetorical model for this novel is not either/or, but both/and.

Bely once remarked that "every novel is a game of hide and seek with the reader."[9] This is particularly true of *Petersburg*. And once we realize that the game lies in the seeking itself, that there are no firm answers or final solutions, we will have begun to grasp what Bely is aiming at. Constant uncertainty, constant tension, constant change are the normal modes here. We must bend to the will of the narrator, and allow that it is highly capricious. He ironizes and he bumbles; he lyricizes and he prattles; he plays the sophisticate, he plays the fool; he identifies himself with this or that character, only to draw back and mock all the characters, the reader, and himself. At times he appears omniscient, like a typical nineteenth-century literary narrator; at times he admits to being as baffled as anyone else. Such swings of tone, manner, and posture can occur with bewildering speed, often within a single sentence. We are kept constantly off guard, never knowing what the narrator will say next, or how he will say it. Although the novel is posited entirely in the narrator's mind, we do not really know when it is a projection of his consciousness and when his consciousness is itself a reflection of other realities. We can never safely generalize, evaluate, or predict, if only because the narrator shows us the folly of attempting to do so. We find no anchor in the world of this novel, no ethical ballast: we never know where we ought to stand on any given question, as we nearly always do in nineteenth-century novels.

We must, then, learn to endure a sense of insecurity as we read *Petersburg*. Nevertheless, it does help to keep constantly in mind that the world of this novel is ultimately a closed world, in which every part bears on every other. One of the ways in which Bely makes that point is through the repetition of words, sentences, and even entire paragraphs. The reader might be well advised to make a list. Among the items he will notice—and this is a very small sampling indeed—are the Ableukhov coat of arms (a unicorn goring a knight), the great black bridge, the greenish waters of the Neva, the red domino, the rectilineal prospects, the caryatid, the mists and clouds, various tints and hues, and of course the Bronze Horseman. Many repetitions serve as tags that make situations and characters unforgettably vivid, such as the senator's large greenish ears. Many serve as what one critic has called "compositional leitmotifs," which "indicate and tie together important points in the narrative structure."[10] A great many, however, contain a multiplicity of meanings which arise out of the various contexts in which they appear. Each repetition brings all the other meanings into play, and creates new ones. Such words both denote and suggest. In this respect, their function is symbolic.

Let us touch briefly upon one prominent instance, which will also suggest how the process works in general. We have already mentioned *shárik* as a phenomenon of sound and semantics. Its component, the sphere (*shar*), also has a symbolic function. It strikes our attention with particular force in Chapter I ("And Catching Sight, They Dilated . . ."). Apollon Apollonovich is riding in his carriage on the Nevsky Prospect, and looking out the window. "Contemplating the flowing silhouettes, Apollon Apollonovich likened them to shining *dots* (*tóchki*). One of these *dots* broke loose from its *orbit* (*orbíta*) and hurtled at him with dizzying speed, taking the form of an immense crimson *sphere* (*shar*) . . . among the *bowlers* (*kotelkí*) on the corner, he caught sight of a pair of *eyes* (*glazá*) . . . they grew rabid, *dilated* (*rasshírilis'*). . . ." In one brief passage, the basic images of sphericality are set down: dot, orbit, sphere, bowler, eyes, dilate. The senator's terrified reaction is described in related images: "His *heart* (*sérdtse*) pounded and *expanded* (*shírilos'*), while in his breast arose the sensation of a crimson *sphere* (*shar*) about to burst into pieces . . . Apollon Apollonovich, you see, suffered from *dilatation* (*rasshirénie*) of the heart." (Stresses supplied in both passages.)

Established here is the pattern that underlies the entire novel: a sphere, or circle, that widens and brings about disintegration and death. At this point we probably do not know that we are dealing with a symbol. But as the novel unfolds, the sphere image recurs again and again, in various manifestations, in association with various characters, and as embroidery on the basic pattern. In Chapter V, for instance, it provides the material for Nikolai's dream: "In the night, a little elastic *blob* would sometimes materialize before him and bounce about. . . . *Bloating* horribly, it would often assume the form of a *spherical fat* fellow. This *fat* fellow, having become a *harassing sphere*, kept on *expanding, expanding*, and *expanding*, and *threatened* to *come crashing down* upon him . . . it would *burst into pieces*." (Stresses supplied.)

At the end of this same scene, Nikolai "understood that he himself was a bomb. And he burst with a boom." This connects his fantasy with the actual bomb in the sardine tin (whose shape is sphere-like, and whose explosion is described as a series of expanding concentric circles), with the plot against his father, and through that, with what the senator sees from his carriage on the Nevsky Prospect. "Cerebral play" is also a component of the sphere symbol. It is often likened to an explosion that bursts forth from the skull and moves out in circles. At the same time, it always returns to its point of origin, only in a different form, thereby describing a kind of circle: "And one fugitive thought was the thought that the stranger really existed. The thought fled back into the senatorial brain. . . . *The circle closed*." (Chapter I, "The Writing Table Stood There," stresses supplied.) Gradually we become aware of many other items that go into the developing symbolism of the sphere, such as the "zero" into which all chronology turns in the dream-dialogue between Nikolai and his father (Chapter V), or even the play on the word "Saturn," whose Russian pronunciation—*sa-tóorn*—suggests to Nikolai's racing brain the French *ça tourne*, "it turns." We come to see that the "circle," "dots," and "point" that are used to characterize the city of Petersburg in the Prologue belong to the same symbol system, though we are not aware of it on first encounter. The sphere or circle also underlies the behavior patterns of the characters themselves. Time and again they return compulsively to the same places, as, for example, to the Senate Square, where the Bronze Horseman stands. And we realize eventually that the structure of the novel as a whole is circular. In Chapter VIII, Anna Petrovna comes back to the Ableukhov household; the family is reunited; everything suggests that a fresh start is being made. The senator and his wife recall their honeymoon in Venice; father and son experience true reconciliation ("they retraced their steps"). In the Epilogue, Apollon Apollonovich has lapsed into the second childhood of senility; we are also told, for the first time, the names of his mother and father; Nikolai returns to Russia from Nazareth, the childhood home of Jesus. In short, we find ourselves moving further and further back in time and space, only to experience other beginnings and other returns.

The ending of the novel seems ambiguous, as do the endings in many other notable works of Russian literature. But there can be no real endings for Bely. The world of his novel is a living organism, which constantly renews itself and which makes mockery of man's efforts to cut it to his own limited horizons. As an affirmation of the life principle, it is ever-dynamic. In that sense, it stands virtually alone among the great works of the twentieth century.

1. *Strong Opinions*, New York, 1973, p. 57. "Biely" is one way of transliterating the name, but we have stuck to the simpler and commoner "Bely" throughout.

2. For a fuller version of the origins of *Petersburg*, see "A Note on Text and Translation."

3. "Igor Stravinsky: Obiter Dicta," *New York Review of Books*, March 17, 1977, p. 31. Stravinsky made the remark in an interview in *The Washington Post*, December 24, 1960.

4. Cf. L. K. Dolgopolov, "Obraz goroda v romane A. Belogo 'Peterburg,'" *Izvestiya Akademii Nauk SSSR*, Seriya literatury i yazyka, Vol. 34, No. 1, 1975, esp. pp. 50–57.

5. Dolgopolov, "Obraz goroda . . . ," p. 47.

6. "Magiya slov," *Simvolizm*, Moscow, 1910; reprinted by Wilhelm Fink Verlag, Slavische Propyläen, Vol. 62, Munich, 1969, p. 430.

7. *Masterstvo Gogolya*, Moscow, 1934, p. 306. The italics are ours. The quote about the sound system in the preceding paragraph is from the same source (pp. 306–307), and is only part of a much longer statement in the original.

8. We are now preparing a critical study of the novel.

9. *Zapiski chudaka*, I, Berlin, 1922, p. 63.

10. Dagmar Burkhart, "Leitmotivik und Symbolik in Andrej Belyjs Roman 'Peterburg,'" *Die Welt der Slaven*, IX, No. 3, 1964, p. 280.

A Note on Text and Translation

Bely published his first novel, *The Silver Dove*, in 1909. He intended to follow it with two others. All would make a trilogy, to be entitled *East or West* (*Vostok ili zapad*).[1] But he put writing aside in favor of a trip to Italy, North Africa, and the Near East, for which he set out in 1910 on an advance from the Musaget Publishing House. After returning to Russia in the spring of the following year, he found himself unable to work. Not only had he now no clear idea of just how to proceed with the sequel to *The Silver Dove*, but he also lacked the peace of mind essential to concentrating on a major project: with the advance used up, he was forced to find lodgings with one indulgent acquaintance after another, and to make ends meet by churning out journalistic pieces.

By this time, Valery Bryusov had become the literary editor of *Russian Thought* (*Russkaya mysl'*), a leading semi-popular journal. He was a prolific and proficient writer himself, though not of the first rank, and an indefatigable literary entrepreneur as well. In the mid-1890s he had been responsible, almost single-handedly, for launching the Russian Symbolist movement, which Bely joined a few years later. Both writers had worked together on *The Balance* (*Vesy*, the most important of the Symbolist journals, which had closed down in 1909), and, along with Alexander Blok and Vyacheslav Ivanov, were considered the mainstays of Symbolism. Now Bely, impoverished and dispirited, turned to Bryusov with the proposal that he should write reviews and articles for *Russian Thought*. Bryusov gave cautious consent, and also asked him for a new novel. Heartened, Bely made the first sketches in July of 1911, and set to work in earnest that October. He continued to refer to his manuscript as "the second part of *The Silver Dove*," with the working title of "The Lacquered Carriage." (Other possibilities, all ultimately important themes in *Petersburg*, were "The Admiralty Needle," "Evil Shadows," "The Red Domino," and "Wayfarers.") But he already realized that what now engaged his attention was not and could not be a continuation of his earlier novel.

After three months of intensive work, he submitted his manuscript to *Russian Thought* in January of 1912. To his astonishment and dismay, the general editor, P. B. Struve, refused to accept it, and declined to pay the 1000-rouble advance that he had been expecting. Struve had never agreed to publish the novel sight unseen, as Bely seemed to believe; and when he did see it, he was indignant, deeming it "pretentiously and carelessly" written, "immature," and replete with "nonsense." Bely felt betrayed, and his predicament generated considerable sympathy in literary circles. Meanwhile, Vyacheslav Ivanov read the manuscript, and insisted that the only title it could possibly bear was *Petersburg*, inasmuch as the city was the real hero. It was then accepted for publication by the firm of K. F. Nekrasov in the provincial town of Yaroslavl, and much of it was actually set in type; but fresh problems arose, and it was simply abandoned. Finally, the prestigious Petersburg house of Sirin, which specialized in the work of Russia's leading modernist writers, took the manuscript, which by then had been completely reworked, and published it between 1913 and 1914 in installments in its literary miscellany (also called *Sirin*), and then in book form in 1916.

Bely was obviously dissatisfied with this first complete edition, for he began tinkering with it almost immediately. Throughout the years of revolution and civil war in Russia, he could find no one interested in committing the results to print. In 1921 he emigrated temporarily to Berlin; there he found a willing publisher and resumed revisions. Working more by massive cutting than by actual rewriting, he subjected the text to such changes that the result was virtually a new novel, which appeared in 1922.

Bely's enthusiasm for revision could get out of hand. Haste and carelessness left their mark: sometimes he failed to adjust the punctuation to conform to the demands of the new text; sometimes he excised just that word or phrase which would make his meaning (or at least its direction) clear to the reader. Linguistic intuition often enables us to fill in the ellipses created by radical cutting, but at times we must consult the 1916 edition. In such cases, we have not hesitated to add (always noting where) a word or two from that earlier text by way of clarification. Gone are some vivid scenes which any reader of the "Sirin" version can only regret, such as the political rally, which is talked about but not actually shown in any detail in the "Berlin" text.

All in all, however, the 1922 version is far stronger than its predecessor. Indeed, Bely thought of it as "merely a return to my basic conception." He regarded the "Sirin" text of 1916 as "a rough draft, which fate (the pressure of meeting a deadline) did not allow to be worked up into fair copy; in the rough draft, terseness, brevity, and compactness of exposition (this was how the author of *Petersburg* had originally envisaged it) had been turned into a hazy ornateness."[2] Certainly the "Berlin" text does in large measure restore those qualities. Bely threw out masses of superfluous detail, numerous repetitions, many grating inconsistencies, and certain sections whose only purpose was the settling of old scores with literary enemies. He also muted the anthroposophical element, which had figured so prominently in the first edition. The reader of the "Berlin" text has to work far harder than his predecessor at discovering the meaning of the world into which he is plunged. But Bely expects us to be zealous, and the clues to understanding are there if we are sufficiently attentive. Certainly the tighter structure and the faster pace heighten the sense of mystery and puzzlement, and make the novel a more effective vehicle for a story of plots and intrigues in a world that is never quite tangible.

The Berlin edition of 1922 was reprinted in Soviet Russia in 1928, with minor changes made by Bely himself and major changes that were unquestionably the work of the censors. That same version came out again in 1935, a year after the author's death. Since then, the novel has gone through three reprintings abroad in Russian: one of the 1916 version, and two of the 1928/1935 version. None of the texts have been reissued in Russia since 1935 (in fact, the "Berlin" text has never been reprinted anywhere at any time).

What follows is the first complete translation of the definitive 1922 text. One hesitates to use the word "definitive" when speaking of any work by Bely, given his habit of incessant revision in quest of perfection. But the 1922 text does represent the last version of the novel that Bely himself created before censorship intervened; and that fact has determined our choice of it as the text that merits translation.

The peculiarities of Bely's style that we have noted in the Introduction pose formidable problems for the translator. Shifted grammatical categories, assaults on conventional syntax, quirky (some would say "impossible") combinations of words, sudden compressions and ellipses, manipulations of sounds and semantics—in these and many other ways Bely creates a highly idiosyncratic verbal texture, which offers constant surprises to Russian readers, delighting the adventuresome and horrifying the conservative. We have attempted to convey some sense of this texture in our translation, at least in the spirit if not always in the letter. This means that we have eschewed "smooth" English as consciously and deliberately as Bely did "smooth" Russian. Everywhere we have resisted any urge to paraphrase or to inflict other "normalizations" on his style.

Our translation is literal in the sense that we have tried to find the most appropriate equivalent for a given word and have stuck to it throughout, bearing in mind the vital importance of repetition as one of Bely's principal devices. In another sense, no translation of *Petersburg*, or of any other Symbolist novel, can be "literal," for words as Symbolists use them do not have fixed meanings but instead take on a variety of meanings in the context of a work as whole. All we can hope is that our equivalents will do the same within the English context we have created. Naturally, the sound play and the rhythm of Bely's prose are impossible to render "literally." Occasionally there are happy coincidences between Russian and English. By and large, however, we have had to content ourselves with suggestion, sometimes even creating instances of sound play where none exist at precisely that point in the Russian text. Thus, our "jumpy Japanese ju-jitsu teacher," or our "trashy humor rags—whose bloody covers in those days were spawned with staggering swiftness on prospects swarming with people" are alliterative where the original is not. But we hereby honor the principle of alliteration that saturates the novel and creates many passages for which no ready English equivalent could be found. As for the verse passages: they are an important part of the verbal texture of the novel. We therefore decided that simple prose paraphrases would not do.

Bely claimed that the individualism of writers could be seen in their favorite punctuation marks. "The period is Pushkin's mark; the semicolon is Tolstoy's; the colon is mine; the dash is the mark beloved by the modernists."[3] In fact, *Petersburg* does abound in colons and dashes. They serve to break up sentences and create an effect of jerkiness or choppiness. We reproduced these punctuation marks faithfully in our first version, and discovered that the profusion proved disorienting and even baffling to a number of English readers, whereas they are not especially outlandish to the Russian eye. So we eliminated most of them, and substituted short sentences and phrases, which suggest something of the effect Bely intended. (Also, the dash in Russian often substitutes, in "normal" style as well as in Bely's, for the verb "to be," whereas it can rarely do that in English.) On the other hand, Bely's system of paragraphing is not confusing to English sensibilities, and we have observed it scrupulously, even when the paragraphs are extremely brief (sometimes the result of overenthusiastic cutting of the 1916 version), or radically indented by way of setting off what Bely regards as key sections.

A dagger (†) in the text indicates the presence of a corresponding note in the back of the book. Bely's own footnotes, of which there are only two in the entire novel, are marked with an asterisk.

R.A.M.
J.E.M.

Notes

1. The following account of the origins of *Petersburg* (including Bely's experiences with *Russian Thought*) is based largely on L. K. Dolgopolov, "Andrei Belyi v rabote nad 'Peterburgom' (Epizod iz istorii sozdaniya

romana)," *Russkaya literatura*, No. 1, 1972, pp. 157–167. The complex course of Bely's revisions or plans for a new edition of *Petersburg* between 1917 and 1922 is described by his widow, Klavdiya Nikolaevna Bugaeva (with A. Petrovsky) in *Literaturnoe nasledstvo*, Vol. 27–28, Moscow, 1937, pp. 600–603. These changes are discussed in detail in two essays on the novel by Ivanov-Razumnik, in *Vershiny. A. Blok. A. Belyi*, Petrograd, 1923. He is the only critic to have seen all the texts, both printed and in manuscript, and to have published his comparisons of them. He argues that the changes create a more positive image of the city and of the revolution in the 1922 version. We cannot agree.

2. "In Place of a Foreword" ("Vmesto predisloviya") to the 1935 edition of *Petersburg*.

3. Introduction to *Posle razluki*, Berlin, 1922, p. 11.

Acknowledgments

Given the special problems involved in this novel, any translator is well advised to avail himself of opportunities to consult other scholars who have worked in the literature and culture of Bely's time.

It has been our good fortune to be acquainted with several such people, who have generously agreed to share their talents and insights with us. At the inception of this project, Nina Berberova helped solve numerous problems, and she has given us constant encouragement and friendly counsel throughout. Robert and Olga Hughes read sections of the manuscript and made useful suggestions for revision. Carol Anschuetz discussed with us some aspects of Bely's theory of language and his use of anthroposophy, and contributed to our understanding of them. Franklin Sciacca, while a student in our seminar on the novel, presented a paper on some of the anthroposophical elements, which helped us in the preparation of the notes on Nikolai's dream in Chapter V. William E. Harkins, a sensitive translator of Russian and Czech literature, provided English readings of all the poems in the text which made our final versions far better than they would otherwise have been.

Our greatest debt of gratitude goes to Simon Karlinsky. He took time from a busy writing and teaching schedule to subject the entire manuscript to a careful comparison with the original Russian, and made countless suggestions for improvement, most of which we have incorporated. His masterful command of Russian and English, his extensive experience as a translator, and his expert knowledge of Russian literature have all contributed to strengthening our text immeasurably.

PETERSBURG

Prologue

Your Excellencies, Your Worships, Your Honors, and Citizens!

·   ·   ·   ·   ·   ·   ·

What is this Russian Empire of ours?

This Russian Empire of ours is a geographical entity, which means: part of a certain planet. And this Russian Empire includes: in the first place—Great, Little, White, and Red Rus; in the second place—the Kingdoms of Georgia, Poland, Kazan, and Astrakhan; in the third place, it includes. . . . But—et cetera, et cetera, et cetera.†

This Russian Empire of ours consists of a multitude of cities: capital, provincial, district, downgraded;† and further—of the original capital city and of the mother of Russian cities.

The original capital city is Moscow, and the mother of Russian cities is Kiev.†

Petersburg, or Saint Petersburg, or Pieter (which are the same)† actually does belong to the Russian Empire. And Tsargrad, Konstantinograd (or, as they say, Constantinople),† belongs to it by right of inheritance. And we shall not expatiate on it.

Let us expatiate at greater length on Petersburg: there is a Petersburg, or Saint Petersburg, or Pieter (which are the same). On the basis of these same judgments, Nevsky Prospect is a Petersburg prospect.†

1

Nevsky Prospect possesses a striking attribute: it consists of a space for the circulation of the public. It is delimited by numbered houses.† The numeration proceeds house by house, which considerably facilitates the finding of the house one needs. Nevsky Prospect, like any prospect, is a public prospect, that is: a prospect for the circulation of the public (not of air, for instance). The houses that form its lateral limits are—hmmm . . . yes: . . . for the public.† Nevsky Prospect in the evening is illuminated by electricity. But during the day Nevsky Prospect requires no illumination.

Nevsky Prospect is rectilineal (just between us), because it is a European prospect; and any European prospect is not merely a prospect, but (as I have already said) a prospect that is European, because . . . yes. . . .

For this very reason, Nevsky Prospect is a rectilineal prospect.†

Nevsky Prospect is a prospect of no small importance in this un-Russian—but nonetheless—capital city. Other Russian cities are a wooden heap of hovels.†

And strikingly different from them all is Petersburg.

But if you continue to insist on the utterly preposterous legend about the existence of a Moscow population of a million-and-a-half,† then you will have to admit that the capital is Moscow, for only capitals have a population of a million-and-a-half; but as for provincial cities, they do not, never have had, and never will have a population of a million-and-a-half. And in conformance with this preposterous legend, it will be apparent that the capital is not Petersburg.

But if Petersburg is not the capital, then there is no Petersburg. It only appears to exist.

However that may be, Petersburg not only appears to us, but actually does appear—on maps: in the form of two small circles, one set inside the other, with a black dot in the center; and from precisely this mathematical point, which has no dimension, it proclaims forcefully that it exists: from here, from this very point surges and swarms the printed book;† from this invisible point speeds the official circular.

Chapter the First

*in which an account is given of a certain worthy
person, his mental games, and the
ephemerality of being*

*It was a dreadful time, in truth,
Of it still fresh the recollection . . .
Of it, my friends, I now for you
Begin my comfortless narration.
Lugubrious will be my tale . . .†*

Pushkin

Apollon Apollonovich Ableukhov

Apollon Apollonovich Ableukhov was of venerable stock: he had
Adam as his ancestor. But that is not the main thing: it is more
important that one member of this venerable stock was Shem, pro-
genitor of the Semitic, Hessitic, and red-skinned peoples.†

Here let us make a transition to ancestors of an age not so remote.

Their place of residence was the Kirghiz-Kaisak Horde,† whence,
in the reign of the Empress Anna Ioannovna, Mirza Ab-Lai, the
great-great-grandfather of the senator, valiantly entered the Russian
service, having received, upon Christian baptism, the name Andrei
and the sobriquet Ukhov.† For brevity's sake, Ab-Lai-Ukhov was
later changed to Ableukhov, plain and simple.

This was the great-great-grandfather who was the source of the
stock.

.   .   .   .

A lackey in gray with gold braid was flicking the dust off the
writing table with a feather duster. A cook's cap peeped through
the open door.

"Looks like himself's already up. . . ."

"He's rubbing himself down with eau de cologne, he'll be taking
his coffee pretty soon. . . ."

"This morning the fellow who brings the mail was saying there
was a letter for the master all the way from Spain, with a Spanish
stamp on it."

"I'm going to tell you something: you shouldn't stick your nose
in other people's letters. . . ."

The cook's head suddenly vanished. Apollon Apollonovich Ableukhov proceeded into the study.

.　.　.　.　.　.　.　.

A pencil lying on the table struck the attention of Apollon Apollonovich. Apollon Apollonovich formed the intention: of imparting a sharpness of form to the pencil point. He quickly walked up to the writing table and snatched . . . a paperweight, which he long turned this way and that, deep in thought.

His abstraction stemmed from the fact that at this instant a profound thought dawned on him, and straightaway, at this inopportune time, it unfolded into a fleeting thought train.

Apollon Apollonovich quickly began jotting down this unfolded thought train. Having jotted down the train, he thought: "Now it's time for the office." And he passed into the dining room to partake of his coffee.

By way of preliminaries, he undertook an insistent questioning of the old valet.

"Is Nikolai Apollonovich up yet?"

"No indeed, sir, he's not up yet. . . ."

Apollon Apollonovich rubbed the bridge of his nose in dissatisfaction:

"Er . . . tell me: when, tell me, when does Nikolai Apollonovich, so to speak. . . ."

And, immediately, without awaiting an answer, he looked at the clock and proceeded to his coffee.

It was precisely half past nine.

Every morning the senator inquired about the times of his awakening. And every morning he made a face.

Nikolai Apollonovich was the senator's son.

In a Word, He Was Head of a Government Institution . . .

What, then, was the social position of the person who has arisen here from non-being?

I think the question is rather out of place: Ableukhov was known by all Russia for the eminent expansiveness of the speeches that he delivered. These speeches noiselessly effused certain poisons, as a result of which the proposals of an opposing camp were rejected in the appropriate place. With Ableukhov's installation in a responsible position, the Ninth Department became inactive.† With this particular Department Apollon Apollonovich did dogged battle, both through official papers and, where necessary, through speeches, in an effort to promote the import of American haybalers into Russia. (The Ninth Department did not favor their import.)

Apollon Apollonovich was head of a Government Institution. Oh, uhhh, what was its name?

Were one to compare the wizened and utterly unprepossessing little figure of my elder statesman with the immeasurable immensity of the mechanisms managed by him, one might perhaps lapse into naive astonishment for quite some time. But then, after all, absolutely everyone was astonished at the explosion of the mental forces which poured forth from this particular cranium in defiance of all Russia.

My senator† had just turned sixty-eight. And his pallid face recalled a gray paperweight (in a moment of triumph), and papier-mâché (in an hour of leisure). The stony senatorial eyes, surrounded by blackish green hollows, looked more blue and more immense in moments of fatigue.

On our part let us add: Apollon Apollonovich was not in the least agitated when he contemplated his ears, green all over and enlarged to immense size, against the bloody background of a Russia in flames. Thus had he recently been portrayed on the title page of a gutter rag,† one of those trashy humor rags put out by the kikes, whose bloody covers in those days were spawned with staggering swiftness on prospects swarming with people. . . .

Northeast

In the oak dining room the wall cuckoo clock had already cuckooed. Apollon Apollonovich had sat down before his porcelain cup and was breaking off warm crusts of bread. Over coffee—even then, even then—he would have his little joke:

"Who is the most respected of them all, Semyonych?"†

"I suppose, Apollon Apollonovich, that the most respected of them all is an Actual Privy Councilor."†

Apollon Apollonovich smiled with his lips only:

"You suppose incorrectly: a chimney sweep. . . ."

The valet already knew the way the riddle ended, but he kept quiet about it.

"But why, if I may venture to ask?"

"People make way for an Actual Privy Councilor, Semyonych. . . ."

"I suppose that's so. . . ."

"A chimney sweep. . . . Even an Actual Privy Councilor will make way for him: a chimney sweep can get you all dirty."

"So that's what it is, sir."

"Yes, precisely. Except that there is an even more respected occupation. . . ."

And then and there he added:

"A cesspool cleaner. . . ."

"Ugh. . . ."

And a gulp of coffee.

"Well, Apollon Apollonovich, there were times when Anna Petrovna . . ."

But with the word "Anna Petrovna" the gray-haired valet stopped short.

.   .   .   .

"The gray coat, sir?"

"Yes. . . ."

"And the gloves, sir?"

"Let me have the suede gloves. . . ."

"Kindly wait a moment, sir. Your Excellency, your gloves are in the chiffonier: Shelf B—northwest."

Only once had Apollon Apollonovich taken note of the trivia of life: he had made an audit of the household inventory. The inventory was registered in proper order and a nomenclature for all the shelves, large and small, was established: there appeared shelves labelled with the Latin letters A, B, C. And the four corners of each shelf received the designation of the four corners of the earth.

Putting away his spectacles, Apollon Apollonovich would note in the register, in a fine, minute hand: spectacles, shelf B and NE, that is, northeast. As for the valet, he was given a copy of the register.

.   .   .   .

In the lacquered house the storms of life flowed noiselessly on; here, nonetheless, the storms of life did flow destructively on.

Harrowing, Harrow

A long-legged bronze rose up from the table. The lampshade did not glow in a delicately decorated violet-rose color (our age has lost the secret of this tint): the glass had darkened with time, and so had the delicate painting thereon.

From all sides golden pier glasses swallowed the drawing room in greenish mirror surfaces. They were crowned by the wings of cute little golden-cheeked cupids. A small mother-of-pearl table glittered.

Apollon Apollonovich flung open the door, resting his hand on the faceted, cut-glass knob. His step tapped along the gleaming panels of parquetry. From all sides leaped cabinets with porcelain baubles. They had brought these bibelots from Venice, he and Anna Petrovna, some thirty years earlier. The remembrance of the misty lagoon, the gondola, and an aria sobbing in the distance flashed inappropriately through the senator's head.

He immediately shifted his eyes to the grand piano.

There, from the yellow lacquered lid, sparkled tiny leaves of bronze incrustation. And again (oh, tiresome memory!) Apollon Apollonovich recalled: a white Petersburg night;† in the windows the racing river; and the motionless moon; and the thunder of a Chopin roulade: the memory that Anna Petrovna now and then used to play Chopin (never Schumann). . . .

Tiny leaves of incrustation—mother-of-pearl and bronze—sparkled on the little boxes and on the little shelves that stood out from the walls. Apollon Apollonovich seated himself in an Empire armchair, where tiny garlands curled their way over the pale azure satin of the seat. And from a small Chinese tray his hand seized a packet of letters, still sealed. His bald head inclined over the envelopes.

And the envelopes were torn open one after the other: an ordinary one delivered by mail, with the stamp stuck on askew:

"I see, I see, fine . . .

"A petition . . .

"A petition, another petition. . . ."

In due time, later, sometime or other . . .

An envelope of heavy paper, and with a monogram, with a seal on the wax.

"Hmmm . . . Count W.† . . . What's this?

"Hmmm . . . ."

Count W. was head of the Ninth Department.

Next, a tiny pale pink envelope. The senator's hand trembled; he recognized this script. He scrutinized the Spanish stamp, but did not unseal the envelope.

"But wasn't the money sent?

"The money *will* be sent!!!"

And Apollon Apollonovich, thinking it was a pencil, extracted an ivory nailbrush from his waistcoat and was preparing to make a notation with it. . . .

"?"

"The carriage is here, sir."

Apollon Apollonovich raised his bald head and departed from the room.

.   .   .   .

Over the grand piano hung a reduced copy of David's "Distribution des aigles par Napoléon Premier."

The picture represented the imperious Emperor in laurel wreath and ermine-trimmed royal mantle.

Cold was the magnificence of the drawing room, because of the total absence of rugs. The parquetry gleamed. Had the sun illumined it for even an instant, one would have squinted involuntarily.

But having things cold was elevated into a principle by Senator Ableukhov.†

It left its imprint on the master of the house, on the statues, on the servants, even on the dark brindle bulldog, who made his residence somewhere in the vicinity of the kitchen. In this house everyone felt ill at ease, deferring to the parquetry, pictures, and statues, smiling, ill at ease, and holding their tongues. Everyone bowed and scraped and wrung cold hands in an access of sterile obsequiousness.

With the departure of Anna Petrovna the drawing room grew still, the piano lid was lowered; no more the thunder of roulades.

· · · · · · ·

When Apollon Apollonovich descended to the vestibule, his gray-haired valet, descending to the vestibule as well, kept glancing at the venerable ears, while gripping a snuffbox, the Minister's gift.

Apollon Apollonovich stopped on the staircase.

Apollon Apollonovich searched for the right word:

"What has, well, you know who, been up to . . . been up to?"

"?"

"Nikolai Apollonovich."

"He's getting along just fine."

"And what else?"

"It's his pleasure to shut himself up in his room and read books."

"And read books?"

"He walks around his rooms, sir."

"Walks around? And? How so?"

"In a dressing gown, sir."

"I see. Go on."

"Yesterday he was waiting for . . ."

"Whom?"

"A costumer."

"What do you mean, a costumer?"

"A costumer, sir."

· · · · · · ·

Apollon Apollonovich rubbed the bridge of his nose. His face lit up and suddenly became senile.

"Mmm. Did you ever have a harrowing experience?"†

"?"

"But you were brought up on a farm, weren't you? So you must have had a harrow."

"Yes, sir, my parents had one."
"There, you see, and you didn't even know."

The Carriage Flew into the Fog

An icy drizzle sprayed streets and prospects, sidewalks and roofs.†

It sprayed pedestrians and rewarded them with the grippe.† Along with the fine dust of rain, influenza and grippe crawled under the raised collars of a schoolboy, a student, a clerk, an officer, a shady type. The shady type cast a dismal eye about him. He looked at the prospect. He circulated, without the slightest murmur, into an infinity of prospects—in a stream of others exactly like him —amidst the flight and din, listening to the voice of automobile roulades.

And—he stumbled on the embankment,† where everything came to an end: the voice of the roulades and the shady type himself.

From far, far away, as though farther off than they should have been, the islands† sank and cowered in fright; and the buildings cowered; it seemed that the waters would sink and that at that instant the depths, the greenish murk would surge over them. And over this greenish murk the Nikolaevsky Bridge† thundered and trembled in the fog.

On this sullen morning the doors of a yellow house† flew open. The windows of the house gave onto the Neva. And a gold-braided lackey rushed to beckon the coachman. Gray horses bounded forward and drew up a carriage on which was depicted a coat of arms: a unicorn goring a knight.

A jaunty police officer passing by the carriage porch gave a stupid look and snapped to attention when Apollon Apollonovich Ableukhov, in a gray coat and a tall black top hat, with a stony face resembling a paperweight, ran rapidly out of the entryway and still more rapidly ran onto the footboard of the carriage, drawing on a black suede glove as he ran.

Apollon Apollonovich Ableukhov cast a momentary, perplexed glance at the police officer, the carriage, the coachman, the great black bridge, the expanse of the Neva, where the foggy, many-chimneyed distances were so wanly etched, and whence Vasilievsky Island† looked back at him in fright.

The lackey in gray hastily slammed the carriage door. The carriage flew headlong into the fog; and the police officer who had happened by glanced over his shoulder into the dingy fog, where the carriage had flown headlong. He sighed and moved on. The lackey looked there too: at the expanse of the Neva, where the foggy, many-chimneyed distances were so wanly etched, and whence Vasilievsky Island looked back at him in fright.

Here, at the very beginning, I must break the thread of my narrative, in order to introduce the reader to the scene of action of a certain drama.

Squares, Parallelepipeds, Cubes

There, where nothing but a foggy damp hung suspended, at first appeared the dull outline, then descended from heaven to earth the dingy, blackish gray St. Isaac's Cathedral:† at first appeared the outline and then the full shape of the equestrian monument of Emperor Nicholas I.† At its base the shaggy hat of a Nicholas grenadier thrust out of the fog.

The carriage† was flying toward Nevsky Prospect.

Apollon Apollonovich Ableukhov was gently rocking on the satin seat cushions. He was cut off from the scum of the streets by four perpendicular walls. Thus he was isolated from people and from the red covers of the damp trashy rags on sale right there at this intersection.

Proportionality and symmetry soothed the senator's nerves, which had been irritated both by the irregularity of his domestic life and by the futile rotation of our wheel of state.

His tastes were distinguished by their harmonious simplicity.

Most of all he loved the rectilineal prospect; this prospect reminded him of the flow of time between the two points of life.

There the houses merged cubelike into a regular, five-story row. This row differed from the line of life: for many a wearer of diamond-studded decorations, as for so many other dignitaries, the middle of life's road had proven to be the termination of life's journey.†

Inspiration took possession of the senator's soul whenever the lacquered cube cut along the line of the Nevsky: there the numeration of the houses was visible. And the circulation went on. There, from there, on clear days, from far, far away, came the blinding blaze of the gold needle,† the clouds, the crimson ray of the sunset. There, from there, on foggy days—nothing, no one.

And what was there were lines: the Neva and the islands. Probably in those distant days, when out of the mossy marshes rose high roofs and masts and spires, piercing the dank greenish fog in jags—

—on his shadowy sails the Flying Dutchman† winged his way toward Petersburg from there, from the leaden expanses of the Baltic and German Seas,† in order here to erect, by delusion,† his misty lands and to give the name of islands to the wave of onrushing clouds.

Apollon Apollonovich did not like the islands: the population there was industrial and coarse. There the many-thousand human swarm shuffled in the morning to the many-chimneyed factories. The inhabitants of the islands are reckoned among the population of the Empire; the general census has been introduced among them as well.†

Apollon Apollonovich did not wish to think further. The islands must be crushed! Riveted with the iron of the enormous bridge, skewered by the arrows of the prospects. . . .

While gazing dreamily into that illimitability of mists, the statesman suddenly expanded out of the black cube of the carriage in all directions and soared above it. And he wanted the carriage to fly forward, the prospects to fly to meet him—prospect after prospect, so that the entire spherical surface of the planet should be embraced, as in serpent coils,† by blackish gray cubes of houses; so that all the earth, crushed by prospects, in its lineal cosmic flight should intersect, with its rectilineal principle, unembraceable infinity; so that the network of parallel prospects, intersected by a network of prospects, should expand into the abysses of the universe in planes of squares and cubes: one square per "solid citizen,"† so that. . . .

After the line, the figure which soothed him more than all other symmetries was the square.

At times, for hours on end, he would lapse into an unthinking contemplation of pyramids, triangles, parallelepipeds, cubes, and trapezoids.

While dwelling in the center of the black, perfect, satin-lined cube, Apollon Apollonovich revelled at length in the quadrangular walls. Apollon Apollonovich was born for solitary confinement. Only his love for the plane geometry of the state had invested him in the polyhedrality of a responsible position.

.   .   .   .

The wet, slippery prospect was intersected by another wet prospect at a ninety-degree right angle. At the point of intersection stood a policeman.

And exactly the same kind of houses rose up, and the same kind of gray human streams† passed by there, and the same kind of yellow-green fog hung there.

But parallel with the rushing prospect was another rushing prospect with the same row of boxes, with the same numeration, with the same clouds.

There is an infinity of rushing prospects with an infinity of rushing, intersecting shadows.† All of Petersburg is an infinity of the prospect raised to the nth degree.

Beyond Petersburg, there is nothing.

The Inhabitants of the Islands Startle You

It was the last day of September.

On Vasilievsky Island, in the depths of the Seventeenth Line,† a house enormous and gray looked out of the fog. A dingy staircase led to the floors. There were doors and more doors. One opened.

And a stranger with the blackest of small mustaches appeared on its threshold.

Rhythmically swinging in his hand was a not exactly small and yet not very large bundle tied up in a dirty napkin with a red border design of faded pheasants.

The staircase was black, strewn with cucumber peels and a cabbage leaf crushed under foot. The stranger slipped on it.

He then grasped the railing with one hand; the other hand (with the bundle) described a zigzag. The stranger wished to protect the bundle from a distressing accident, from falling onto the stone step, because the movement of his elbow mimicked a tightrope walker's turn.

Then, meeting the porter, who was climbing the stairs with a load of aspen wood over his shoulder, the stranger began to show increased concern about the fate of the bundle, which might catch against a log.

When the stranger reached the bottom, a black cat underfoot hitched up its tail and cut across his path, dropping chicken innards at the stranger's feet. And a spasm contorted his face.

Such movements are peculiar to young ladies.

And movements of precisely this same kind sometimes mark those of our contemporaries who are exhausted by insomnia. The stranger suffered from insomnia: his smoke-redolent habitation hinted at that. And the bluish tinge of the delicate skin of his face also bore witness.

The stranger remained standing in the courtyard, a quadrangle completely paved with asphalt and pressed in from all sides by the five stories of the many-windowed colossus. Stacked in the middle of the courtyard were damp cords of aspen wood. And visible through the gate was a section of the windswept Seventeenth Line.

Oh, you lines!

In you has remained the memory of Petrine Petersburg.†

The parallel lines were once laid out by Peter. And some of them came to be enclosed with granite, others with low fences of stone, still others with fences of wood. Peter's line turned into the line of a later age: the rounded one of Catherine, the regular ranks of colonnades.†

Left among the colossi were small Petrine houses:† here a timbered one, there a green one, there a blue, single-storied one, with the bright red sign "Dinners Served." Sundry odors hit you right in the nose: the smell of sea salt, of herring, of hawsers, of leather jacket and of pipe, and of nautical tarpaulin.

Oh, lines!

How they have changed: how grim days have changed them!

The stranger recalled: on a summer evening, in the window of that gleaming little house, an old woman was chewing her lips. Since August the window had been shut. In September a brocade-lined coffin was brought.

He was thinking it was getting more and more expensive to live. Life was hard for working folk. From over there pierced Petersburg, both with the arrows of prospects and with a gang of stone giants.

From over there rose Petersburg: there buildings blazed out of a wave of clouds. There, it seemed, hovered someone spiteful, cold. From over there, out of the howling chaos someone stared with stony gaze, skull and ears protruding into the fog.

All of that was in the mind of the stranger. He clenched his fist in his pocket. And he remembered that the leaves were falling.

He knew it all by heart. These fallen leaves were the last leaves for many. He became a bluish shadow.

.   .   .   .

And as for us, here's what we'll say: oh, Russian people, oh, Russian people! Don't let the crowd of shadows in from the islands! Black and damp bridges are already thrown across the waters of Lethe. If only they could be dismantled. . . .†

Too late. . . .

And the shadows thronged across the bridge. And the dark shadow of the stranger.

Rhythmically swinging in his hand was a not exactly small, yet not very large bundle.

And, Catching Sight, They Dilated, Lit Up, and Flashed . . .

The aged senator communicated with the crowd that flowed in front of him by means of wires (telegraph and telephone). The shadowy stream seemed to him like the calmly current news of the world. Apollon Apollonovich was thinking: about the stars. Rocking on the black cushions, he was calculating the power of the light perceived from Saturn.

Suddenly—

—his face grimaced and began to twitch. His blue-rimmed eyes rolled back convulsively. His hands flew up to his chest. And his torso reeled back, while the top hat struck the wall and fell on his lap.

The involuntary nature of his movement was not subject to explanation. The senator's code of rules had not foreseen. . . .

Contemplating the flowing silhouettes, Apollon Apollonovich likened them to shining dots. One of these dots broke loose from its orbit and hurtled at him with dizzying speed, taking the form of an immense crimson sphere—

—among the bowlers on the corner, he caught sight of a pair of eyes. And the eyes expressed the inadmissible. They recognized the senator, and, having recognized him, they grew rabid, dilated, lit up, and flashed.

Subsequently, on delving into the details of the matter, Apollon Apollonovich understood, rather than remembered, that the upstart intellectual† was holding a bundle in his hand.

Hemmed in by a stream of vehicles,† the carriage had stopped at an intersection. A stream of upstart intellectuals had pressed against the senator's carriage, destroying the illusion that he, Apollon Apollonovich, in flying along the Nevsky, was flying billions of miles away from the human myriapod. Perturbed, Apollon Apollonovich had moved closer to the window. At that point he had caught sight of the upstart intellectual. Later he had remembered that face, and was perplexed by the difficulty of assigning it to any of the existing categories.

It was at just that moment that the stranger's eyes had dilated, lit up, and flashed.

In the swarms of dingy smoke, leaning back against the wall of the carriage, he was still seeing the same thing in his eyes. His heart pounded and expanded, while in his breast arose the sensation of a crimson sphere about to burst into pieces.

Apollon Apollonovich, you see, suffered from dilatation of the heart.

Automatically putting on his top hat and pressing his hand to his racing heart, Apollon Apollonovich had abandoned himself to his favorite contemplation, cubes, in order to give himself a calm account of what had occurred.

· · · · · · · ·

The horses came to a halt. The policeman saluted. Behind the glass of the entryway, beneath the bearded caryatid† supporting the stones of a little balcony, Apollon Apollonovich saw the same thing as always. The heavy-headed bronze mace gleamed there;

the dark tricorne had fallen onto the shoulder there: the octogenarian doorman dozed over *The Stock Exchange Register*.† Thus he had dozed the day before yesterday and yesterday.

Thus he had been sleeping for the past five years. Thus he would sleep on.

Since the time that Apollon Apollonovich had driven up to the Government Institution as head of the Government Institution, more than five years had gone by. And there had been events: there had been turmoil in China, and Port Arthur had fallen.†

.   .   .   .

The door flew open. The bronze mace rang out. From the carriage door Apollon Apollonovich transferred his gaze into the entryway.

"Your Excellency. . . . Do sit down, sir. . . . Heavens, you're all out of breath. . . .

"You're always running like a little boy. . . .

"Maybe you'd like some water?"

But the eminent statesman's face became all wrinkles:

"Tell me, if you will: who is the husband of the countess?"†

"Which countess, may I ask?"

"Oh, just any countess."

"?"

"The counter."

.   .   .   .

"Heh, heh, heh, sir. . . ."

.   .   .   .

Of Two Shabbily Dressed but Sweet Girl Students . . .†

Amidst the crowds that slowly flowed past, the stranger was flowing past. Or rather, he was flowing away in utter confusion from the intersection where he had been pressed against a carriage, from which had stared an ear, a top hat.

He had seen this ear before!

He broke into a run.

Cutting across columns of conversations, he caught fragments, and sentences took form.

"Do you know?" was heard from somewhere on the right. And died away.

And then surfaced:

"They're planning . . ."

"To throw . . ."

A whisper from behind:

"At who?"
And then an indistinct couple said:
"Abl . . ."
They passed by:
"At Ableukhov?!"
The couple completed the sentence somewhere far away:
"Abl–ution is not the sol–u–tion for what . . ."†
And the couple hiccuped.
And the stranger stopped, shaken by all he had heard:
"They're planning . . ."
"To throw . . .?"
Whispering began all around:
"Probable . . . proof . . ."
The stranger heard not "prob" but "prov," and finished it himself:
"Prov–ocation?!"†
Provocation began its revelry all along the Nevsky. Provocation had changed the meaning of the words that had been heard.
He had simply, on his own, added the preposition "at." With the addition of the letters "a" and "t" an innocent verbal scrap had changed into a scrap with horrible contents. And, most important: the preposition had been added by the stranger.
Provocation, accordingly, had its seat within him.
Oh, Russian people!
You are becoming shadows of swirling whorls of mist. From time immemorial the mists have been swirling out of the leaden expanses of the seething Baltic. Into the mists stared cannons.
At noon a muffled cannon-shot† triumphally filled all of Petersburg, the magnificent capital of the Empire. And the mists were rent asunder, and the shadows dispersed.
Only one shadow, a young man, was not shaken and did not disintegrate from the shot, as he continued his run to the Neva unhindered.
Suddenly he saw, fastened upon him, the eyes of two shabbily dressed but sweet girl students.

Why Don't You Keep Quiet!

"We–me . . ."
But it sounded like:
"Me–me."
And a scraggly bunch of gents in suitcoats would start squealing:
"A–aha–ha, aha–ha!"

. . . .

A Petersburg street in autumn is piercing; it both chills you to the marrow, and tickles. As soon as you leave it and go indoors, the street flows in your veins like a fever.

The stranger experienced all that when he came into the sweaty and steamy vestibule, jam-packed with every which kind of black, blue, gray, yellow coat, with lop-eared caps, and with every conceivable kind of overshoe. A steamy pancake smell hung everywhere:

"Aaa! . . ."

.   .   .   .

The restaurant premises consisted of a small grimy room. The floor was waxed. The walls had been decorated by some amateur painter, and depicted remnants of a flotilla, from above which Peter was pointing off into space.

"A little picon in it?"

"No, no picon!"

He was thinking: why had there been a frightened look behind the carriage window? The eyes had bulged, gone petrified, and shut. The head had reeled back and disappeared. A hand had trembled impotently there; it was not a hand but . . . a tiny paw.

And in the meantime snacks were drying up on the counter; and wilted leaves of some kind were turning sour under a mound of overdone meat patties.

.   .   .   .

Lingering there at a distance was an idle sweating stalwart with a coachman's beard, a blue jacket, and blacked boots. He was knocking back glass after glass. Now and then he would summon the waiter:

"How's about a little somethin'?"

"Some melon, sir?"

"Your melon, it tastes like soap with sugar on it."

"Perhaps a banana, sir."

"That's a dirty-sounding fruit."

.   .   .   .

Thrice had my stranger swallowed the acerbic poison. And his consciousness, detaching itself from his body, like the handle on the lever of a mechanism, began revolving around the organism.

And the stranger's consciousness became clear for an instant. Yes: where's the bundle? Here it is, right beside me, here. . . .

The encounter had knocked his memory out.

.   .   .   .

"A nice piece of watermelon, sir?"

"The heck with your watermelon. All it does is crunch between your teeth, and there's nothin' left in your mouth. . . ."

"All right, how 'bout some vodka. . . ."

.   .   .   .

"Buy you a drink, pal?"

The idle sweating stalwart with a beard gave a wink.

"But why not?"

"I've already had enough."

"Come on, have a little drink, just to keep me cumpaneee. . . ."

My stranger realized something: he looked at him suspiciously, clutched at the damp bundle, at a sheet (of newspaper). He covered the bundle with it.

"Hey, you from Tula, pal?"

"Not at all."

.   .   .   .

He was thinking, and he wasn't. His thoughts were thinking themselves, and they produced a picture: tarpaulins, hawsers, herring, sacks crammed full of something; amidst the sacks a workman dressed in blackest leather, and standing out distinctly in a fog of fleeting surfaces, kept hoisting sacks onto his back; and the sacks thudded dully into a barge overloaded with beams; the workman (something familiar about him) was standing over the sacks and was taking out a pipe.

.   .   .   .

"Here on business?"

                    (Oh, Lord!)

"No!"

"O–ho, and me, I'm a coachman."

.   .   .   .

"Now my wife's brother, *he* drives for Konstantin Konstantinych. . . ."†

"Well, so what?"

"So what? So nothin'!"

.   .   .   .

Suddenly . . .

But about suddenly, we shall speak later.

The Writing Table Stood There

Apollon Apollonovich was taking aim at the current business day. And there arose: reports from the previous day; he pictured papers on the table in his office, their sequence, and the pencil notations he had made: the blue *"expedite,"* with a curlicue on the silent *"e,"* the red *"further information,"* with a flourish on the *"n."*

While between the staircase of the department and the doors to his office, Apollon Apollonovich, by an act of his will, shifted the center of his consciousness. Cerebral play was retreating to the edge of the field of vision, as were the whitish patterns of wallpaper: a small pile of dossiers placed parallel shifted to the center of the field, as had the portrait.

The portrait? That is:

"He's gone—and Rus he has deserted. . . ."†

Who? The senator? He? Apollon Apollonovich Ableukhov? Why, no: Vyacheslav Konstantinovich.† And what about him, Apollon Apollonovich?

"My turn has come, in very truth . . .
Beloved Delvig calls for me. . . ."†

My turn is my turn: there comes a turn for everyone—

"And o'er the earth new thunderclouds have gathered,
The hurricane . . ."†

The small pile of papers leaped to the surface of his consciousness. Apollon Apollonovich took aim at the current business day.

"Hermann Hermannovich, be so good as to prepare that, oh, what's it called . . .

"The dossier on the deacon Zrakov's pupil!"†

Now he recalled (he had completely forgotten): yes, the eyes. They had been astonished, they had grown rabid. . . . And why that zigzag? A most unpleasant one. And he seemed to have seen that upstart intellectual at some time or other. Or maybe—nowhere, never.

Apollon Apollonovich opened the door to his office.†

The writing table stood there, and the logs in the fireplace crackled away. Apollon Apollonovich was warming his frozen hands at the fireplace, while his cerebral play went on constructing misty planes:

"Nikolai Apollonovich . . ."

At this point Apollon Apollonovich . . .

"?"

Apollon Apollonovich stopped at the door.

His innocent cerebral play again moved spontaneously into his brain, that is, into the pile of papers and petitions. Apollon Apollonovich perhaps would have considered cerebral play on the same plane as the wallpaper of the room; the plane, however, in moving apart at times, admitted a surprise into the center of his mental life.

Apollon Apollonovich recalled:

Once before he had seen that upstart intellectual—just imagine—in his very own house.

One time he had happened to be descending the staircase. Nikolai Apollonovich, leaning over the balustrade, was chatting with someone. The statesman did not consider that he had the right to make inquiries about Nikolai Apollonovich's acquaintances. His sense of tact naturally prevented him from asking:

"Kolenka, my dear boy, who is it that's visiting you?"†

Nikolai Apollonovich would have lowered his eyes:

"Nobody special, papa: people come to see me."

That was precisely why Apollon Apollonovich had not taken the slightest interest at that time in the identity of the upstart intellectual wearing an overcoat and looking in from the vestibule. The stranger had the very same small mustache and startling eyes (such as you would encounter at night in the Moscow chapel of the Martyr Panteleimon,† which is by the Nikolsky Gate; such as you would encounter in the portrait of a great man appended to his biography; and further: in a neuropathological clinic).

Even then the eyes had dilated, gleamed, and flashed. Therefore, it had already happened once and, perhaps, would be repeated.

.   .   .   .

Apollon Apollonovich suddenly looked beyond the door: tables and more tables! Piles of dossiers! And, inclined heads! What a bustling and mighty paper mill!

.   .   .   .

The cerebral play of the wearer of diamond-studded decorations was distinguished by strange, very strange, extremely strange qualities: his cranium was becoming the womb of thought-images, which at once became incarnate in this spectral world.

Oh, better that Apollon Apollonovich should never have cast off a single idle thought, but should have continued to carry each and every thought in his head, for every thought stubbornly evolved into a spatiotemporal image, and continued its uncontrolled activities outside the senatorial head.

Apollon Apollonovich was like Zeus: out of his head flowed goddesses and genii. One of these genii (the stranger with the small black mustache), arising as an image, had already *begun to live and breathe* in the yellowish spaces. And he maintained that he had emerged from there, not from the senatorial head. This stranger turned out to have idle thoughts too. And they also possessed the same qualities.

They would escape and take on substance.

And one fugitive thought was the thought that the stranger really existed. The thought fled back into the senatorial brain.

The circle closed.

Apollon Apollonovich was like Zeus. Thus, scarcely had the Stranger-Pallas been born out of his head when from there another Pallas, exactly like it, came crawling out.†

This Pallas was the senator's house.

.   .   .   .

The lackey was climbing the staircase. Oh, most beautiful staircase! And the steps: soft, like the convolutions of the brain, over which cabinet ministers had climbed more than once. The lackey was already in the hall. . . .

And then again the hall: most beautiful. Windows and walls, somewhat cold. . . .

We have cast an eye over this habitation, guided by the general characteristics which the senator was wont to bestow on all objects. Thus:—

> —having found himself on one rare occasion in the flowering bosom of nature, Apollon Apollonovich saw: the flowering bosom of nature. For us this bosom would immediately break down into its characteristics: into violets, buttercups, pinks; the senator would again reduce the particulars to a unity. We would say, of course:
>
> "There's a buttercup!"
>
> "There's a nice little forget-me-not. . . ."
>
> But Apollon Apollonovich would say simply and succinctly:
>
> "A flower. . . ."

Just between us: for some reason, Apollon Apollonovich considered all flowers the same, bluebells.

He would have characterized even his own house with laconic brevity, as consisting, for him, of walls (forming squares and cubes) into which windows were cut, of parquetry, of tables. Beyond that were details.

But we would do well to remember: what has flickered by (pictures, grand piano, mirrors, mother-of-pearl, small incrusted tables) —everything that has flickered by—was only an irritation of the cerebral membrane, if not an indisposition of the cerebellum.

An illusion of a room would be constructed, and it would then fly apart, leaving no trace. And when the door to the small hollow-echoing corridor slammed shut, it was only a hammering in the temples.

There proved to be no drawing room behind the slammed door but rather, cerebral spaces: convolutions, gray and white matter, the pineal gland; while the heavy walls of sparkling spurts (due to the afflux of blood) were a leaden and painful sensation: of the occipital, frontal, temporal, and sincipital bones.

Apollon Apollonovich was sitting at the table, busy with dossiers; he had the sensation that his head was six times larger than it should be, and twelve times heavier than it should be.

Our Role

Petersburg streets possess one indubitable quality: they transform passersby into shadows.

This we have seen in the case of the mysterious stranger.

Having arisen as a thought, he somehow became connected with the senator's house. He surfaced there on the prospect, immediately following the senator in our story.

From the intersection to that restaurant on Millionnaya Street† we have obligingly described the route of the stranger as far as that notorious word "suddenly,"† which interrupted everything.

Let us investigate his soul. But first, let us investigate that restaurant, and even the vicinity of that restaurant. There are grounds for this.

In the investigation that we have quite naturally undertaken, we have merely anticipated Senator Ableukhov's desire that an agent of the secret police† should doggedly follow the steps of the stranger. While the insouciant agent is still inactive back in his office, we ourselves will be this agent.

But haven't we made fools of ourselves? Now what sort of agent are we? The real one does exist. And he's on the alert, so help me, he is.

When the stranger disappeared through the doors of that restaurant, we turned and spied two silhouettes cutting through the fog. One was both fat and tall and conspicuous for his build. But we could not make out his face (silhouettes, after all, have no faces). And yet we did discern an open umbrella and galoshes and a hat, half sealskin, with ear-flaps.

The mangy little figure of an utterly undersized gentleman was what largely comprised the second silhouette. His face was visible: we did not manage to see his face, for we were astonished by the enormous size of a wart. Thus facial substance had been obscured by insolent accidentality (which is as it should be in the world of shadows).

Pretending to be looking into the clouds, we let the indistinct pair pass ahead. The pair paused in front of the restaurant door.

"Hmmm?"

"Here. . . ."

"That's what I thought."

"What measures have you taken?"

"I've placed a man there, inside the restaurant."

.   .   .   .

"Hmmm . . . I'll have to . . . Hmmm! . . . wish you success. . . ."

The undertaking had been set like a clock mechanism.

"Hmmmm?"

"What's wrong?"

"Damned head cold."

"Listen: you should accept some remuneration. . . ."

"No, you just won't understand me!"

"Yes, I will: you're definitely out of handkerchiefs."

"What?"

"But you have a cold!"

"I'm not working for remuneration: I am an artist!"

"In a manner of speaking."

"What?"

"I'm using the tallow candle cure."

The little figure took out its snotty handkerchief:

"Be sure to report it: Nikolai Apollonovich has given a promise. . . ."

"A tallow candle is a wonderful remedy!"

"Tell them everything!"

"At night you smear your nostrils with it and in the morning you're fit as a fiddle."

Again the handkerchief began its work beneath the wart. The two shadows were already flowing off into the brain-chilling murk. Soon the shadow of the fat man reemerged from the fog, and looked distractedly at the spire of Peter and Paul.†

And it went into that restaurant.

And Besides, the Face Glistened

"Suddenlys" are familiar to you. Why, then, do you bury your head like an ostrich at the approach of the inexorable "suddenly"?

"It" sneaks up behind your back. Sometimes it even precedes your appearance in a room. You feel horribly uneasy. In your back grows the sensation that a gang of things invisible has shoved its way in through your back, as through a door. You turn, you ask your hostess:

"Madam, would you mind if I close the door? I have a peculiar kind of nervous sensation: I can't bear to sit with my back to the door."

They laugh. You also laugh: as if there were no "suddenly."

"It" feeds on cerebral play. It gladly devours all vileness of thought. And it swells up, while you melt like a candle. "Suddenly," like a fattened yet unseen dog, begins to precede you, producing in an observer the impression that you are screened from view by an invisible cloud. This is what your "suddenly" is.

.   .   .   .

We left the stranger in that restaurant. *Suddenly* he turned around. It seemed to him that slime had gotten under his collar and had begun to ooze. He turned around. But there was nobody behind his back. And from there, from the door, something invisible shoved its way in.

At that very moment when my stranger turned away from the door, an unpleasant fat man came in through it. And as he walked toward the stranger, he set a floorboard creaking. His yellowish, clean-shaven face, inclined slightly to the side, smoothly floated on its own double chin. And besides, the face glistened.

At this point our stranger turned around. *The person* was waving a hat at him, half sealskin, with ear-flaps:

"Alexander Ivanych . . ."

"Lippanchenko!"†

Round *the person's* shirt collar was a necktie, satin-red, loud, and fastened with a large paste jewel. A dark yellow striped suit enveloped *the person*. Polish gleamed on his yellow shoes.

Taking a seat at the stranger's table, *the person* yelled:

"A pot of coffee! And listen, some cognac. My bottle's there, under my . . ."

And around them was heard:

"What about you? Did you have something to drink?"

"I did."

"Something to eat?"

"I did."

"Then permit me to say you're a pig."

.   .   .   .

"Careful!" exclaimed the stranger. The fat man, called Lippanchenko by the stranger, was about to set his dark yellow elbow on the sheet of newspaper covering the bundle.

"What?" Here Lippanchenko, lifting the paper, saw the bundle. His lips quivered.

"Is that the . . . the? . . ."

His lips still quivered, resembling pieces of sliced salmon,† not yellowish red, but oily and yellow.

"How careless you are, Alexander Ivanovich, if I do say so." Lippanchenko reached his clumsy thick fingers toward the bundle,

all aglitter with the fake stones of his rings, all swollen, nails gnawed
(and on the nails showed dark traces of brown dye, of a color identical to that of his hair; an attentive observer could draw the conclusion: why, this person dyes his hair).

"After all, the slightest movement (if I'd just set down my
elbow), after all, there might have been a catastrophe."

And with special caution *the person* now transferred the bundle
to the chair.

"Well, yes, we would both have been splattered all over the
walls," the stranger joked unpleasantly.†

    ·   ·   ·   ·   ·   ·   ·

And around them was heard:

"Don't you dare call me a pig."

"I didn't mean anything by that."

"Yes, you did. You're mad you had to pay."

"All right, go on and eat, let's forget it."

    ·   ·   ·   ·   ·   ·   ·

"Well then, Alexander Ivanovich, well then, my dear fellow, as
for this bundle"—and Lippanchenko looked out of the corner of his
eye—"take it to Nikolai Apollonovich right away."

"Now wait a minute. The bundle will certainly be safe at my
place."

"That's not convenient. You might be arrested. *There* it will be
safe."

And the fat man, leaning over, began whispering something in
his ear:

"Pss–pss–pss . . ."

"Ableukhov's?"

"Pss . . ."

"To Ableukhov? . . ."

"Pss . . ."

"With Ableukhov? . . ."

"No, not with the senator, with the son. Deliver this letter to
him along with the bundle, here it is."

Lippanchenko's low narrow forehead was practically touching
the stranger's face. His searching little eyes were guarded, his lips
quivered slightly and sucked at the air. The stranger lent a close
ear to the whispering of the fat gentleman, carefully trying to make
out the contents of the whispering, which was almost drowned out
by the voices in the restaurant. And from the repugnant lips came
a rustling (like the rustle of ants' legs on a dug-up anthill). And it
seemed as if the whispering had horrible contents, as though worlds
and planetary systems were being whispered about here. But it was

worthwhile listening closely, because the dreadful contents of the
whispering were disintegrating into something humdrum.

"Be sure to deliver the letter."

.   .   .   .

Around them was heard:

"What is Man?"

"Man is what he eats."

"I know."

"Well, since you know, grab a plate and eat."†

.   .   .   .

Lippanchenko's suit reminded the stranger of the color of the
yellow wallpaper in his habitation on Vasilievsky Island, a color
associated with insomnia. That insomnia evoked the memory of a
fateful face† with very narrow little Mongol eyes. The face had
looked repeatedly at him from the wallpaper. When he examined
this place during the day, he could make out only a damp spot,
over which crawled a sow bug. In order to distract himself from
memories of the tormenting hallucination, he grew garrulous, to his
own surprise:

"Listen carefully to the noise."

"They're noisy, all right."

"You think you hear 's–s–s,' but you really hear 'SH'. . . ."

Lippanchenko, in a daze, had retreated into his own thoughts.

"You can hear something dull and slimy in the sound 'sh.' Or am
I mistaken?"

"No, not at all," and Lippanchenko tore himself away from his
thoughts.

"All words with 'sh' are outrageously trivial.† 'S' isn't like that.
'S–s–s': sky, concept, crystal. The sound 's–s–s' evokes in me the
image of the curve of an eagle's beak. But words with 'sh' are
trivial. For example: the word *fish*. Listen: *fi–sh–sh–sh*, that is,
something with cold blood. And again: *slu–sh–sh–sh*: something
slimy; mu*sh*, something shapeless; ra*sh*, something diseased."

The stranger broke off. Lippanchenko was sitting before him
like utterly shapeless mush. And the ash from his cigarette slushed
up the grayish atmosphere. Lippanchenko was sitting in a cloud.
The stranger then looked at him and thought: "Ptui, what filth,
how Tartarish." Sitting before him was simply some kind of "SH."

.   .   .   .

From the next table someone hiccuped and shouted: "Don't you
shush me, you!"

.   .   .   .

"Excuse me, Lippanchenko: are you by any chance a Mongol?"
"Why such a strange question?"
"Every Russian has some Mongol blood."

.   .   .   .

What Costumer?

Nikolai Apollonovich's quarters consisted of a bedroom, a study,
and a reception room.

The whole of the bedroom was occupied by an enormous bed.
It was covered by a satin spread, with pillow covers.

The study was lined with oak shelves crammed with books, before which silk could be slid back on rings to reveal rows of leather
bindings.

The furniture in the study was upholstered in dark green. There
was a handsome bust of—it stands to reason—Kant.

For two years Nikolai Apollonovich had not risen before noon.
For two and a half years before that, however, he had awakened
at nine o'clock, and had appeared in a student uniform buttoned up
to the neck.†

Then he did not walk around the house in a Bukhara dressing
gown. A skullcap did not grace his oriental drawing room. Two
and a half years ago Anna Petrovna, the mother of Nikolai Apollonovich and the spouse of Apollon Apollonovich, had abandoned
the family hearth, inspired by an Italian singer.† It was after her
flight with the singer that Nikolai Apollonovich appeared on the
parquetry of the domestic hearth in a Bukhara dressing gown. The
daily encounters over morning coffee broke off by themselves.

The senator partook of his coffee considerably earlier than did
his son.

A dressing gown began to appear on Nikolai Apollonovich. Tartar slippers were introduced. A skullcap made its appearance.

Thus was a brilliant student transformed into an Oriental.

Nikolai Apollonovich had just received a letter in an unfamiliar
hand, some pathetic doggerel with the striking signature: "A Soul
Aflame."

Nikolai Apollonovich began rushing about the room, looking for
his spectacles, rummaging among books, quills, and pens.

"Oh!

"Damn it all!"

Nikolai Apollonovich, just like Apollon Apollonovich, talked to
himself.

His movements were abrupt, like his papa's movements. Like
Apollon Apollonovich, he was distinguished by an unprepossessing
stature and by restless eyes set in a smiling face. Whenever he sank

into serious contemplation, his gaze grew rigid: the lines of his totally white countenance stood out dry, sharp and cold, iconlike. His most noble feature was his forehead, finely chiselled, with tiny swollen veins. The pulsation of the veins on his forehead was a sign of sclerosis.

The bluish veins matched the circles around his immense dark cornflower blue eyes (in moments of agitation, his eyes grew black: from dilation of the pupils).

Nikolai Apollonovich was wearing a Tartar skullcap. Were he to remove it, there would appear a thatch of fine flaxen white hair, which softened his cold, severe exterior, with its stamp of stubbornness. It is rare to find hair of such a shade on a grown man. This shade is often to be seen on infants, especially in White Russia.

Here, in his own room, Nikolai Apollonovich would truly grow into a self-contained center, into a series of logical premises that flowed from the center and predetermined thought, soul, and this very table. Here he was the sole center of the universe, conceivable as well as inconceivable.

This center made deductions.

But no sooner had Nikolai Apollonovich managed to set aside the trivia of daily life and the abysm of inapprehensibilities called the world and life, than inapprehensibility again burst in.

Nikolai Apollonovich tore himself away from his book:

"Well? . . ."

A muffled and deferential voice was heard:

"Someone is asking for you, sir."

After locking himself in, and while reviewing the tenets of his system, which was being reduced to a unity step by step, he felt his body poured into "*all*," while his head was displaced into the light bulb's potbellied sphere of glass.

And having thus displaced himself, Nikolai Apollonovich would become a truly creative being.

He loved to lock himself in. And the rustle and tread of any intruder would shatter his consciousness.

So it was now.

"What is it?"

But a voice answered from afar:

"Someone has come."

.   .   .   .

At this, Nikolai Apollonovich's face assumed a satisfied expression:

"Ah, it's someone from the costumer. The costumer has brought me my costume. . . ."

And gathering up the skirts of his dressing gown, he strode off
in the direction of the door. At the balustrade of the staircase, he
leaned over and shouted:

"Is that you?

"The costumer?"

What is this costumer business?

. . . .

In Nikolai Apollonovich's room a box appeared. Nikolai Apollonovich locked the door. He cut the string with great fuss. He
lifted the top and took out of the box: a half-mask with a black
lace beard, and after the mask, a luxuriant bright red domino† with
folds that rustled.

Soon he was standing before the mirror, all satiny and red, holding the miniature half-mask over his face. The black lace of the
beard fell away and back onto his shoulders, forming a fantastic
wing on each side, right and left.

After this masquerade, Nikolai Apollonovich, an extremely satisfied expression on his face, put first the red domino and then the
black half-mask back in the box.

Wet Autumn

Tufts of cloud scudded by in a greenish swarm. The greenish
swarm rose ceaselessly over the interminable remoteness of the prospects of the Neva; into the greenish swarm stretched a spire . . .
from the Petersburg Side.†

Describing a funereal arc in the sky, a dark ribbon, a ribbon of
soot, rose from the chimneys; and it tailed off onto the waters.

The Neva seethed and shrieked with the high-pitched whistle of
a small steamboat, it smashed steely, watery shields against the piers
of the bridges, and it lapped at the granite.

And against this glooming background of hanging soot tailing
above the damp stones of the embankment railing, eyes staring into
the turbid germ-infested waters of the Neva, there stood, in sharp
outline, the silhouette of Nikolai Apollonovich.

At the great black bridge† he stopped.

An unpleasant smile flared on his face. He was gripped by memories of an unhappy love affair. Nikolai Apollonovich recalled a
certain foggy night. That night he had leaned over the railing. He
had turned around and raised his leg. He had lifted it, in shiny
overshoe, over the railing. It would seem that further consequences
ought to have ensued, but . . . Nikolai Apollonovich had lowered
his leg.

Recalling this unsuccessful act of his now, Nikolai Apollonovich smiled in a highly unpleasant manner, cutting a rather comic figure. Wrapped up in a greatcoat, he seemed stooped and somehow armless, with the long wing of the greatcoat flapping in the wind.

"How handsome," was heard all around Nikolai Apollonovich.

"An ancient mask . . ."

"Ah, how pale the face . . ."

"That marble profile . . ."

But had Nikolai Apollonovich burst out laughing, the ladies would have said:

"What an ugly monster . . ."

At a porch where two lions mockingly place paw on gray granite paw† he stopped, having spied the back of a passing officer. All entangled in the skirts of his greatcoat, he tried to overtake the officer:

"Sergei Sergeyevich?"

For a moment some thought or other flickered over the officer's face. From the expression on his trembling lips one might have supposed that the officer was hesitating: should he recognize him or not:

"Ah . . . hello. . . ."

"Where are you going?" asked Nikolai Apollonovich, so that he might walk along the Moika† with the officer.

"Home."

"That means we're going the same way."

Above the two of them, alternating with rows of windows on a yellow building, were rows of lion faces, each over a coat of arms entwined with a stone garland.

As if trying not to touch on something that was past, the two of them, interrupting each other, talked about how the disturbances of recent weeks had affected Nikolai Apollonovich's philosophical labors.

Above the two of them, alternating with rows of windows on a yellow government building, were rows of lion faces, each over a coat of arms entwined with a garland.

There's the Moika, and that same light-colored, three-storied, five-columned building; and the narrow strips of ornamented moulding above the third story: ring after ring; inside each ring was a Roman helmet on two crossed swords. They had already passed the building. And there's *the* house. And there are *the* windows. . . .

"Goodbye. Are you going further?"

Nikolai Apollonovich's heart began to pound. He was on the verge of asking something. But no, he did not ask. He stood all alone before the door that had just been slammed. He was gripped by memories of an unhappy love affair, or rather, of a sensual attraction.

That same light-colored, five-columned building with a strip of ornamental moulding: inside each ring a Roman helmet on two crossed swords.

.   .   .   .

Of an evening the Prospect is flooded with fiery obfuscation.† Down the middle, at regular intervals, hang the apples of electric lights.† While along the sides plays the changeable glitter of shop signs. Here the sudden flare of ruby lights, there the flare of emeralds. A moment later the rubies are there, and the emeralds are here.

.   .   .   .

Nikolai Apollonovich was not seeing the Nevsky; before his eyes was that same house; windows and shadows behind the windows; perhaps merry voices: of the yellow cuirassier, Baron Ommau-Ommergau; and *her* voice, *her* voice.

Apollon Apollonovich Recalled

Yes, Apollon Apollonovich recalled: recently he had overheard an inoffensive joke told by the clerks about himself:

"He harps on the same note: disdain. . . ."

His defenders intervened:

"Gentlemen, that comes from hemorrhoids. . . ."†

At that point the door flew open. Apollon Apollonovich entered. The joke broke off (thus does a nimble baby mouse scamper off into a crack). Apollon Apollonovich did not take offense at jokes.

Apollon Apollonovich then went up to the window. Two heads in the windows across the way saw opposite them the blur of the face of an unknown little old man behind a pane.

.   .   .   .

Here, in the office of a high Government Institution, Apollon Apollonovich would grow into a kind of center of governmental institutions and green-topped tables. Here he was a point of radiating energy, a grid, an impulse. He was a force in the Newtonian sense, and a force in the Newtonian sense is an occult force.

Consciousness would detach itself from individuality, becoming incredibly clear and concentrating in a single point (between the eyes and the forehead). A flame, flaring between the eyes and the forehead, would scatter sheaves of lightning bolts. His lightning-bolt thoughts would fly from his bald head in every direction like snakes; a clairvoyant would doubtless have seen the head of the Gorgon–Medusa.

Consciousness would detach itself from individuality: and individuality presented itself to the senator's imagination as a cranium and as a container that had been utterly emptied.

From this armchair he would intersect his life by means of his consciousness. From this place circulars sliced up the patchwork field of humdrum life, which he would equate with sexual, vegetable, or other kinds of needs.

Only from here did he loom and hover madly over Russia, and in his foes evoke a fateful comparison (with a bat).†

Apollon Apollonovich was particularly sharp today. Not once did his head nod over a report. Lord knows why, Apollon Apollonovich had come to the conclusion that his very own son, Nikolai Apollonovich, was a scoundrel.

.   .   .   .

At the entryway the caryatid was visible: a bearded man of stone.

The bearded man of stone rose above the noise of the street, above the seasons. The year eighteen hundred and twelve saw him freed from his scaffolding. The year eighteen hundred and twenty-five saw the crowds rage beneath him.† The crowd passed by even now, in the year nineteen hundred and five. For more than five years Apollon Apollonovich had been looking daily from here at the smile carved in stone. The tooth of time was gnawing it away. During those five years events had flown by: Anna Petrovna was in Spain; Vyacheslav Konstantinovich was no more; the yellow heel had brazenly mounted the ridges above Port Arthur; there had been turmoil in China, and Port Arthur had fallen.

The door opened. The secretary, a young man with a medal flapping on his chest, flew up to the high personage, the over-starched edge of his cuff crackling deferentially. And to his timid question Apollon Apollonovich droned back:

"No, no! Do as I said. And you'd better do it . . ." said Apollon Apollonovich; but he stopped and corrected himself:

"I mean . . ."

He had wanted to say "be so good as" to the secretary, but it came out "you'd better do it."†

The tales of his absentmindedness were legion.

Cold Fingers†

Apollon Apollonovich Ableukhov, in a gray coat and a tall black top hat, with a stony face resembling a paperweight, ran rapidly out of the carriage, and ran up the steps of the entryway, removing a glove as he ran.

He entered the vestibule. The top hat was handed to the lackey.

"Would you be so kind: does a young man often come here?"

"Young people do visit, Your Excellency."

"Yes, but . . . with a small mustache?"

"With a small mustache, sir?"

"Well, yes, and . . . wearing a coat . . . with a turned-up collar?"†

Suddenly something dawned on the doorman:

"One such-like did come once, sir . . . he dropped in to see the young master."

"With a small mustache?"

"That's right, sir!"

Apollon Apollonovich paused for a moment. And suddenly, Apollon Apollonovich moved on.

The staircases were covered by a gray velvet carpet. This gray carpet also covered the walls. On the walls glittered a display of antique weapons: a Lithuanian helmet glittered beneath a rusty green shield; the hilt of a knight's sword sparkled; here were rusting swords, there halberds fixed at an angle; and a pistol and a battle mace hung at a tilt.

The top of the staircase gave onto a balustrade. Here from a matte-white pedestal a Niobe,† forever frozen, raised her alabaster eyes heavenward.

Resting his bony hand on the faceted knob, Apollon Apollonovich briskly flung open the door.

Thus It Is Always

A phosphorescent blot raced across the sky, misty and deathlike. The heavens gradually misted over in a phosphorescent glow, making iron roofs and chimneys flicker. Here flowed the waters of the Moika. On one side loomed that same three-storied building, with projections on top.

Wrapped in furs, Nikolai Apollonovich was making his way along the Moika, his head sunk in his overcoat. Nameless tremors arose in his heart. Something awful, something sweet. . . .†

He thought: could *this* too be love? He recalled.

He shuddered.

A shaft of light flew by: a black court carriage flew by. Past window recesses it bore blood red lamps that seemed drenched in blood. They played and shimmered on the black waters of the Moika. The spectral outline of a footman's tricorne and the outline of the wings of his greatcoat flew, with the light, out of the fog and into the fog.

Nikolai Apollonovich stood for a while in front of the house. He kept standing and then suddenly disappeared in the entryway.

The entryway door flew open before him; and the sound struck him in the back. Darkness enveloped him, as though all had fallen away (this is most likely how it is the first instant after death). Nikolai Apollonovich was not thinking about death now; he was thinking about his own gestures. And in the darkness his actions took on a fantastic stamp. He seated himself on the cold step by the door, his face buried in fur, listening to the beating of his heart.

Nikolai Apollonovich sat in the darkness.

.   .   .   .

The stone curve of the Winter Canal† showed its plangent expanse. The Neva was buffeted by the onslaught of a damp wind. The soundlessly flying surfaces glimmered, the walls that formed the side of the four-storied palace† gleamed in the moonlight.

No one, nothing.

Only the Canal streaming its waters. Was that shadow of a woman darting onto the little bridge to throw itself off? Was it Liza?† No, just the shadow of a woman of Petersburg. And having traversed the Canal, it was still running away from the yellow house on the Gagarin Embankment,† beneath which it stood every evening and looked long at the window.

Ahead the Square† was now widening out. Greenish bronze statues emerged one after another from everywhere. Hercules and Poseidon looked on as always. Beyond the Neva rose an immense mass—the outlines of islands and houses. And it cast its amber eyes into the fog, and it seemed to be weeping.

Higher up, ragged arms mournfully stretched vague outlines across the sky. Swarm upon swarm they rose above the Neva's waves, coursing off toward the zenith. And when they touched the zenith, the phosphorescent blot would precipitously attack them, flinging itself upon them from the heavens.

The shadow of a woman, face buried in a muff, darted along the Moika to that same entryway from which it would dart out every evening, and where now, on the cold step, below the door, sat Nikolai Apollonovich. The entryway door closed in front of it; the entryway door slammed shut in front of it.† Darkness enveloped the shadow, as though all had fallen away behind it. In the entryway, the black little lady thought about simple and earthly things. She had already reached her hand toward the bell, and it was then that she saw an outline, apparently masked, rise up before her from the step.

And when the door opened and a shaft of light illuminated the darkness of the entryway for an instant, the exclamation of a terri-

fied maid confirmed it all for her, because first there appeared in
the open door an apron and an overstarched cap; then the apron
and cap recoiled from the door. In the sudden flash a picture of
indescribable strangeness was revealed. The black outline of the
little lady flung itself through the open door.

Behind her back, out of the gloom, rose a rustling clown in a
bearded, trembling half-mask.

One could see how, out of the gloom, the fur of the caped great-
coat† soundlessly and slowly slid from the shoulders, and two red
arms reached toward the door. The door closed, cutting off the
shaft of light and plunging the entryway stairs once more into utter
darkness.

.   .   .   .

In a second Nikolai Apollonovich sprang out into the street.
From beneath the skirts of his greatcoat dangled a piece of red
silk. His nose buried in the greatcoat, he raced in the direction of
the bridge.

.   .   .   .

On the iron bridge he turned. And saw nothing. Above the damp
railing, above the greenish waters teeming with germs, bowler, cane,
coat, ears, nose, and mustache rushed by into the gusts of Neva
wind.

You Will Never Ever Forget Him!

In this chapter we have seen Senator Ableukhov. We have also
seen the idle thoughts of the senator in the form of the senator's
house and in the form of the senator's son, who also carries his own
idle thoughts in his head. Finally, we have seen another idle shadow
—the stranger.

This shadow arose by chance in the consciousness of Senator
Ableukhov and acquired its ephemeral being there. But the consciousness of Apollon Apollonovich is a shadowy consciousness
because he too is the possessor of an ephemeral being and the fruit
of the author's fantasy: unnecessary, idle cerebral play.

The author, having hung pictures of illusions all over, really
should take them down as quickly as possible, breaking the thread
of the narrative, if only with this very sentence. But the author will
not do so: he has sufficient right not to.

Cerebral play is only a mask. Under way beneath this mask is the
invasion of the brain by forces unknown to us. And granting that
Apollon Apollonovich is spun from our brain, nonetheless he will
manage to inspire fear with another, a stupendous state of being

which attacks in the night. Apollon Apollonovich is endowed with
the attributes of this state of being. All his cerebral play is endowed
with the attributes of this state of being.

Once his brain has playfully engendered the mysterious stranger,
that stranger exists, really exists. He will not vanish from the Petersburg prospects as long as the senator with such thoughts exists,
because thought exists too.

So let our stranger be a real stranger! And let the two shadows
of my stranger be real shadows!

Those dark shadows will, oh yes, they will, follow on the heels
of the stranger, just as the stranger himself is closely following the
senator. The aged senator will, oh yes, he will, pursue you too, dear
reader, in his black carriage. And henceforth you will never ever
forget him!

End of the First Chapter

Chapter the Second

*in which an account is given of a certain rendezvous,
fraught with consequences*

> *My critics, pedants of the word,*
> *Have oft reproached me for hauteur;*
> *But I, you surely must have heard,*
> *Am just a simple commoner.†*
>
> Pushkin

The "Daily Chronicle"

Our citizens do not read the "Daily Chronicle" section of the newspapers. In October of nineteen hundred and five our respected citizens most likely were reading the editorials in *The Comrade,†* provided they were not subscribers to the most recent type of newspapers.

But all other truly Russian "solid citizens," as though nothing at all were going on, pounced on their "Daily Chronicle." I too pounced on it. And because I read the "Chronicle" I am thoroughly informed. Who else was bothering to read accounts of robberies, witches, and spirits? They were reading editorials. The account set forth here no one will remember.

Here are clippings from the newspapers of that time (the author will keep quiet): along with notices of robberies, rape, stolen diamonds, the disappearance of some writer or other from a small provincial town with diamonds worth a respectable sum,† we have sheer fantasy that would make the head of a reader of Conan Doyle spin.

"Daily Chronicle."

"*October 1.* According to the eyewitness account of a doctor's assistant, Miss N. N., we report on a puzzling event. On the evening of October 1, Miss N. N. was walking by the Chernyshev Bridge.† There, by the bridge, she noticed a strange spectacle: on the bridge over the canal a red domino was dancing. The face of the domino was covered by a black mask."

"*October 2.* According to the eyewitness account of the schoolteacher Miss M. M., we inform our respected readers of a puzzling event. The teacher Miss M. M. was giving her morning lesson. The school windows looked out on the street. Suddenly out the window a pillar of dust began swirling.† The teacher and her lively young charges rushed to the window. Imagine the confusion of the class and the schoolmistress, when a red domino, from the midst of the dust it had raised, glued a black mask to the window. Classes were suspended in the O. O. School."

"*October 3*. At a spiritualist seance in the apartment of Baroness R. R., the assembled spiritualists formed a chain. In the center of the chain a red domino then appeared and touched the tip of councilor S.'s nose with the folds of its mantle. A surgeon in the G. Hospital has already certified the presence of a burn on S.'s nose. Rumor has it that the tip of the nose is covered with purple spots."

Finally: "*October 4*. The population of the suburb of I. has fled because of the appearance of a red domino. A number of protests are being drafted. A squadron of Cossacks has been called in."

Who is N. N., who is M. M. the schoolmistress, R. R. and so on?

What is a contributor to a newspaper? He is a working member of the periodical press. As a working member of the press (of one sixth of the world), he receives, for each line, five copecks, seven copecks, ten, fifteen, twenty.

Such then are the respected qualities of contributors to rightist, centrist, moderate-liberal, and revolutionary newspapers. And the key that opens the truth of the year nineteen hundred and five—the truth of the "Daily Chronicle"—is found under the heading "The Red Domino." Here's the point: a contributor to a respected newspaper made use of a fact that had been communicated to him in a certain house by the mistress of the house. And accordingly, the point now is no longer the respected contributor, who is paid by the line. The point, accordingly, is the lady.

Who is the lady?

There was a certain lady.

The lady once announced with a laugh that she had just come across a red domino in an unlighted entryway. The lady's statement got into the columns of the "Daily Chronicle" section; after getting into the "Chronicle," it rapidly unravelled into a series of events that never happened.

What did happen?

Sofia Petrovna Likhutina†

Sofia Petrovna Likhutina was distinguished by the extraordinary luxuriance of her hair.† And she was unusually lissome. Had Sofia Petrovna Likhutina let down her black hair, the hair would have enveloped her entire torso and fallen to her calves. Speaking frankly, she did not know what to do with this hair of hers, so black that, perhaps . . . because of the hair, or because of its blackness . . . but in any event: a fine down was appearing above Sofia Petrovna's lip which threatened to turn into a mustache in her old age. She was possessed of an unusual complexion; the hue was, well, that of pearl iridescent with the rosy whiteness of delicate apple blossom petals. If anything agitated the bashful Sofia Petrovna, she turned poppy red.

Sofia Petrovna Likhutina's sweet little eyes were not sweet little eyes at all, but simply eyes: enormous eyes of a dark, blue—of a dark blue color (let us call them orbs). And the orbs now sparkled, now dimmed, at times seemed vacant, somehow washed out, sunk in their hollow, bluishly sinister orbits. They were slightly crossed. Her bright red lips were lips too large, but . . . her pretty little teeth (ah, her pretty little teeth!), her pretty little pearly teeth! And what's more, there was her childlike laugh. That laugh lent her pretty pouting little lips a certain charm. And then again her figure was very lissome. Every movement of her figure and her nervous back was now impetuous, now sluggish.

A black dress fastened at the back was wont to invest her splendid shape. If I speak of a "splendid shape," that means my vocabulary has been exhausted. And the banal expression "splendid shape" represents a threat to Sofia Petrovna: a premature filling out by age thirty. Sofia Petrovna Likhutina was only in the twenty-third year of her life.

Ah, Sofia Petrovna!

She resided in a small apartment on the Moika. From the walls tumbled cascades of the brightest, most irrepressible colors: there, very fiery; and here, sky blue. On the walls were Japanese fans, lace, tiny pendants, and bows, and on the lamps from satin shades fluttered wings of cotton fabric like tropical butterflies. And it seemed that a swarm of these butterflies, if they should fly off the walls, might unfold their sky blue wings here. The officers of her acquaintance always called her Angel Peri, distractedly merging two notions—"Angel" and "Peri"—into one.†

Sofia Petrovna Likhutina had hung small Japanese landscapes, all of them, without exception, depicting a view of Mt. Fujiyama. The landscapes had no perspective. And the rooms, jam-packed with divans, armchairs, sofas, fans, and live Japanese chrysanthemums, had no perspective either. Perspective was provided by a satiny alcove, from which Sofia Petrovna would emerge in a flutter, and by a rustling reed portiere hanging in the doorway, from which Sofia Petrovna would emerge in a flutter, with Fujiyama as the background for her marvelous hair. It must be said that when of a morning Sofia Petrovna Likhutina, wearing a pink kimono, flew from behind the door to the alcove, she was the perfect image of a real Japanese girl. Still, there was no perspective.

The rooms were small. Each was occupied by only one absolutely enormous object. In the minute bedroom the enormous object was the bed; in the minute bathroom, the bathtub; in the living room, the bluish alcove; in the dining room, the table and the sideboard; the enormous object in her husband's room was, it stands to reason, the husband.

Well then, how could there possibly be any perspective?

All six tiny little rooms were steam heated, as a result of which you were suffocated by moist heat in the apartment. The window panes sweated; the visitors sweated; the maid and the husband sweated; Sofia Petrovna Likhutina herself was covered with perspiration, like warm dew on a chrysanthemum. How could there possibly be any perspective?

And so, there was none.

Sofia Petrovna's Visitors

A visitor to Angel Peri's little hothouse had an obligation to furnish chrysanthemums, and he would praise her Japanese landscapes, adding his own opinions on painting. And knitting her little black brows, Angel Peri would blurt out: "The landscape is from the brush of Hadusai."* This captivating angel positively muddled all proper names and all words. A visitor who was an artist always took offense when this happened, and thereafter he would never address any comments on painting to Angel Peri. Nonetheless, the Angel kept using her last copeck to buy up landscapes. For long stretches of time she was lost in admiration of them.

Sofia Petrovna made no effort to entertain a visitor. If her admirer was a man about town, she laughed loudly apropos of every joking, nonjoking, and serious remark made. She laughed loudly at everything. And she would turn poppy red with laughter. And perspiration would stand out on her tiny little nose. The young man would turn poppy red; he would be covered with perspiration. The young man was surprised by her youthful laughter, which was so out of place in good society. He was so surprised that he relegated her to the demimonde. Meanwhile, a collection box would make its appearance, bearing the inscription "Charity Fund." And Sofia Petrovna Likhutina, the Angel Peri, would exclaim to him: "You've made a little 'phoophoo' again, now pay up." (Every "phoophoo" made by a visitor from good society went into a fund that Sofia Petrovna had set up for charity; "phoophoos" were her name for anything stupid said on purpose: she derived the word from "phoo.") And Baron Ommau-Ommergau, of Her Majesty's Yellow

*Hokusai.†

Cuirassiers, Count Aven, a Blue Cuirassier, and Life Hussar Shporyshev, and Verhefden,† a civil servant on special assignment to Ableukhov's office, young men about town, uttered "phoophoo" after
"phoophoo," dropping copeck after copeck into the tin collection
box.

If her visitor proved to be a musician, a music critic, or merely a
music lover, then Sofia Petrovna would explain to him that her idols
were Dun-CAN and Ni-KISCH.† With enthusiastic expressions,
not so much verbal as gesticulatory, she would explain that she intended to make a thorough study of meloplastics† and to perform
the dance of the Ride of the Valkyries at Bayreuth. And the musician, music critic or mere music lover, staggered by her inaccurate
pronunciation of names, concluded that Sofia Petrovna Likhutina
was an empty-headed female; he would then become more playful.
Sofia Petrovna Likhutina did not miss a single fashionable opera.
Musicians who performed for good society were rare in the little
hothouse. But Count Aven, Baron Ommau-Ommergau, Shporyshev,
and Verhefden came often. Likewise a student, Nikolenka Ableukhov, had at one time moved in their circle fairly often. Then he
suddenly disappeared.

Sofia Petrovna's visitors naturally fell into two categories: into
the category of guests from good society and *guests so to speak*.
These so-to-speak guests were welcome visitors . . . for pouring out
her soul. These visitors had made no effort to be received in the
little hothouse. The Angel dragged them there forcibly, and she
returned their visits. In their presence Angel Peri sat with tightly
pursed little lips. She did not laugh loudly, did not act capriciously,
did not play the flirt, but deported herself timidly and mutely. And
the so-to-speak guests constantly argued; one heard "revolution-
evolution." And then again, "revolution-evolution." They were neither gilded, nor even silvered, but just poor coppered youth who
had gotten an education with their hard-earned small change and
who paraded a lot of words on "social revolution." And then again,
"social evolution." Angel Peri kept getting all this mixed up.

An Officer: Sergei Sergeyevich Likhutin

Among the young students who frequented the Likhutins there
was a certain Varvara Evgrafovna, who was considered a shining
example.

Under the influence of this shining example, the Angel, if you
can imagine it, graced a mass meeting with her presence. Under
her influence the Angel set out the copper collection box† with the
vague inscription: "Charity Fund." Needless to say, the collection
box was intended for the *guests*. Individuals belonging to the *guests*

so to speak category were exempted from the extortions. Extortions were exacted from Count Aven, Baron Ommau-Ommergau, Shporyshev, and Verhefden. Under the influence of the shining example Angel Peri ground away at the "Manifesto" of Karl Marx. In those days the Angel was being visited daily by Nikolenka Ableukhov, whom she could introduce without risk to Varvara Evgrafovna (who was in love with Nikolenka) and to Her Majesty's Yellow Cuirassier.

Since the time Nikolenka had suddenly stopped coming to visit, the Angel, in secret from her guests, had suddenly fluttered off to the spiritualists. A magnificently bound book now lay prominently displayed on a small table in front of Sofia Petrovna: *Man and His Bodies*, by Madame Henri Besançon (Sofia Petrovna once again was getting everything all muddled).†

Sofia Petrovna concealed her new enthusiasm from both Baron Ommau-Ommergau and Varvara Evgrafovna. Despite her tiny little brow, the Angel's secretiveness reached incredible proportions: not once did Varvara Evgrafovna meet Count Aven; on one occasion she did accidentally glimpse the plumed hat of a Life Hussar in the vestibule.

There was yet another visitor at Likhutina's: an officer, Sergei Sergeyevich Likhutin. Properly speaking, this was her husband.† He was in charge of provisions somewhere out there. He left the house early in the morning; he appeared no earlier than midnight. He made a simple exchange of greetings with the guests; for propriety's sake he meekly uttered a "phoophoo," dropping in a twenty-copeck piece (if Count Aven or Ommau-Ommergau was there), or modestly nodded his head at the words "revolution-evolution," drank a cup of tea, and—off he went to his room. The men about town called him *that army type*, and the young students, the Prussian. Sergei Sergeyevich Likhutin would gladly have done without both "phoophoos" and the words "revolution-evolution." He would not have been averse to going to the Baroness for some spiritualism, but he did not use his position as a husband to insist on it: he was no despot with Sofia Petrovna. Two and a half years earlier he had married her against the wishes of his parents, very wealthy landowners. As a result, he had been cursed by his father and deprived of his inheritance.

There was yet another visitor: a Ukrainian type† named Prilippanchenko, or simply Lippanchenko. This one was lecherous. He did not call Sofia Petrovna an angel but . . . sweetie-pie. Lippanchenko kept within the bounds of propriety, and for that reason had entree to the house.

Her exceedingly good-natured husband, Sergei Sergeyevich Likhutin, a second lieutenant in the Gr–gorian Regiment of His

Majesty the King of Siam,† took a meek attitude toward the circle
of revolutionary acquaintances of his better half. Toward the representatives of the circle from good society he took merely an indulgent attitude. And the Ukrainian type Lippanchenko he just barely
tolerated. That crafty Ukrainian type resembled more a cross between a Semite and a Mongol,† although he passed for pure Russian.
Lippanchenko wore a red necktie, fastened with a paste jewel, and
he unblushingly dyed his hair brown. Of himself Lippanchenko
said that he exported Russian pigs abroad.

Be that as it may, Second Lieutenant Likhutin was not overly
fond of Lippanchenko (shady rumors were circulating about Lippanchenko). But what is the point in asking whom Second Lieutenant Likhutin did not like? It goes without saying that Second
Lieutenant Likhutin liked everyone. But there was one person Likhutin had especially liked at one time, and that was Nikolai Apollonovich Ableukhov. They had known each other since adolescence.
Nikolai Apollonovich had been best man at Likhutin's wedding and
a daily visitor to the apartment on the Moika. He had disappeared
without a trace.

All that was not Sergei Sergeyevich's fault.

The Trim, Handsome Best Man

Even on the first day of "marital bliss," when Nikolai Apollonovich held the solemn nuptial crown over Sergei Sergeyevich's head,
Sofia Petrovna Likhutina had been struck by the trim, handsome best
man, by the color of his eyes, the pallor of his face and the fairness
of his hair. His eyes did not peer, as they often did later, from behind the lenses of a pince-nez, and the face was propped up by a
gold collar (the likes of which not everybody has). And . . . Nikolai Apollonovich became a regular visitor: at first once every two
weeks; then, once a week; and, finally, he began to visit daily. Soon
Sofia Petrovna noticed that Nikolai Apollonovich's face had turned
into a mask. The aimless rubbing of his sweaty hands and the froglike look of his smile, alas, screened the face from her. And as soon
as Sofia Petrovna noticed that, she understood she had been in love
with that face, that other one, not this one. From behind the froglike lips she unconsciously tried to summon up her lost infatuation,
and she tormented Ableukhov. But hiding what she was doing from
herself, she began dogging his steps, she tried to ascertain his tastes
and inclinations, she followed them herself, hoping in them to re-
cover her loss. She started putting on airs: first meloplastics appeared
on the scene, and then the cuirassier. Varvara Evgrafovna appeared
with the tin box for the collection of "phoophoos."

From that time on Sergei Sergeyevich Likhutin had become merely a visitor to the apartment on the Moika. He took charge of provisions somewhere out there. He left the house early in the morning; he reappeared about midnight.

Freedom was more than Sofia Petrovna could endure. She had a tiny little brow. Along with the tiny little brow, she had hidden feelings. She was a lady, and chaos must not be awakened in ladies. In a lady lurks a criminal, but should a crime actually be committed, nothing would remain in a lady's soul but saintliness.

Soon without a doubt we shall prove to the reader that the soul of Nikolai Apollonovich is actually divided into two halves. Duality is the attribute of a lady. Duality is the attribute not of a man but of a lady. Verily, the symbol of a man is unity. Only thus does a triality result, and without this, can a domestic hearth exist?

Had Sergei Sergeyevich Likhutin or Nikolai Apollonovich been true unities, and not dualities, there would surely have been a triality. Sofia Petrovna would have found harmony in union with a man. The gramophone, meloplastics, Henri Besançon, and Lippanchenko would have gone straight to the devil.

But no unitary Ableukhov existed. That is just why everything had happened.

Just what had happened?

The Red Buffoon

Strictly speaking, in the last few months Sofia Petrovna had been acting very provocatively. In front of the gramophone horn belching forth "Siegfried's Death," she practiced various movements, raising her rustling skirt almost to her knees. And more than once her foot touched Ableukhov. Not surprisingly, the latter did his best to embrace the Angel, but she would slip away, throwing the cold water of indifference on her admirer, and resume what she had been doing. On one occasion Nikolai Apollonovich could bear it no longer. Passion rushed to his head (Nikolai Apollonovich threw her on the sofa), and she bit his searching lips until the blood came. When Nikolai Apollonovich pulled back in bewilderment from the pain, a slap resounded through the Japanese room.

"Ooo, you . . . monster, ooo, you . . . frog . . . ooo, you red buffoon."†

Nikolai Apollonovich answered calmly:

"You Japanese doll. . . ."

He straightened up with dignity. His face assumed that distant expression she had once caught, and remembering it, she fell in love again. And when he left, she crashed to the floor, clawing and biting the carpet. Suddenly she jumped up, and reached her arms out to the door:

"Come back!"

The door slammed in reply. Nikolai Apollonovich ran to the Petersburg Bridge.† At the Bridge he made a fateful decision (to destroy his own life on completion of a certain act). The expression "red buffoon" had touched him to the quick.

Sofia Petrovna Likhutina saw him no more. In unwitting protest against Ableukhov's enthusiasm for revolution-evolution, Angel Peri dropped the young students. Varvara Evgrafovna came by less often, and once again her regular visitors were Count Aven, Ommau-Ommergau, Shporyshev, and Verhefden, and even . . . Lippanchenko—more often than the others. With Count Aven, with Ommau-Ommergau, with Shporyshev, with Verhefden, and even with Lippanchenko she laughed loudly and incessantly. Suddenly she would ask piquantly:

"I'm a doll, aren't I?"

And they answered her with "phoophoos." And Lippanchenko said to her: "You're a sweetie-pie, a honey-bun, a sugar-puss." He gave her a small doll with a yellow face, a hand puppet.

When she said the same thing to her husband, her husband made no reply at all, and he pretended to go to bed. He was in charge of provisions somewhere out there. He sat down to write Nikolai Apollonovich a letter: he, Sergei Sergeyevich, Second Lieutenant in the Gr–gorian Regiment, insistently requests (the word "insistently" was underlined) that he cease visiting their house. His conduct did not change one iota: as before, he left very early and returned about midnight; uttered a "phoophoo" for propriety's sake, if he saw Baron Ommau-Ommergau; frowned ever so slightly if he saw Lippanchenko; nodded his head most indulgently at the words "evolution-revolution"; drank a cup of tea; and quietly vanished.

He was tall of stature, had a blond beard, possessed a nose, mouth, hair, ears, and eyes. Unfortunately, he wore dark blue spectacles, and no one knew the color of his eyes, nor their marvelous expression.

Base, Base, Base!

In those icy days of early October, Sofia Petrovna was unusually agitated. When by herself, she would wrinkle her little brow, and become flushed. She would go up to the window to wipe the steamed-up pane with her dainty fine-batiste handkerchief. The pane began to squeak. A view of the canal and a gentleman in a top hat was revealed—that and nothing more. Disappointed in her expectation, Angel Peri began to worry the damp handkerchief with her tiny teeth, ran to put on her plush coat and her hat, so as to wander aimlessly from the Moika to the Embankment with her muff pressed to her nose. Once she even dropped in at the Ciniselli Circus,[†] and saw a wonder of nature: a bearded lady. But more often she dropped into the kitchen, and exchanged whispers with the housemaid Mavrushka, a young girl in apron and cap. And in these agitated moments her eyes would cross.

Once, with a loud laugh, she snatched a pin from her hat in Lippanchenko's presence. She stuck it into her little finger:

"Look: it doesn't hurt. I'm . . . a doll."

Lippanchenko understood nothing, and said:

"You aren't a doll, you're a sweetie-pie."

In a rage, the Angel drove him away. Grabbing his hat with the ear-flaps, Lippanchenko withdrew.

She rushed around in the little hothouse and wiped the window pane. Into view came the canal and a carriage flying past—that and nothing more.

What more could there be?

Several days earlier Sofia Petrovna Likhutina was returning home from Baroness R. R.'s. At Baroness R. R.'s there had been table rappings, and the table had jumped—that and nothing more. But Sofia Petrovna's nerves naturally had been on edge (after the seance she had wandered the streets aimlessly). There was no light in the entryway of her house. Inside the entrance she very distinctly saw a black spot, like a mask, staring at her. There was something red beneath the mask, and Sofia Petrovna tugged at the bell. And when the door flew open and a stream of light fell on the stairs, Mavrushka let out a shriek and flung up her hands. Sofia Petrovna flew headlong into the apartment. Mavrushka saw: behind her mistress was a red domino extending a black mask with a fan of lace, which was, it goes without saying, black too. Luckily she did not turn her head. The red domino extended toward Mavrushka a bloody sleeve, from which a calling card protruded. Sofia Petrovna scrutinized the calling card on which was engraved a skull and crossbones, not a nobleman's coronet. And on it was written: "I await you at the masquerade ball on such-and-such a date."

All evening long Sofia Petrovna was horribly agitated. Who was the red domino? It went without saying that it was he, Nikolai Apollonovich. After all, she had called him by that name, so a red buffoon had come. In such a case what was an act like that, directed at a defenseless woman, to be called?

Base, base, base!

If only her husband would come back soon, he would teach that insolent wretch a lesson. She turned red, her eyes crossed, she bit her handkerchief, and was covered with perspiration. If only someone would come!

But no one appeared.

But suppose it was not he? And she felt distinctly put out. It was a pity to give up her conviction that the buffoon was he. In these thoughts there was a sweetly familiar feeling. She must have wanted him to reveal himself as the basest of villains.

No, it was not he: after all he was no villain, no young whipper-snapper. But if he were really the red buffoon? Who was the red buffoon? She could give herself no coherent answer. But, all the same. . . .

Then and there she ordered Mavrushka to say nothing. But she did go to the masquerade ball. And—on the sly.

The fact was that Sergei Sergeyevich Likhutin had categorically forbidden her to attend masquerade balls.

He was meekness itself . . . up to a point: his honor as an officer. He would say only: "I give my word of honor as an officer—such-and-such shall be, but that shall never be." And he would not budge: inflexibility, a kind of cruelty. On such occasions he would push his spectacles up on his forehead, turn dry and unpleasant, and would seem carved from white cypress. He would bang down a cypress fist; Angel Peri would then rush out of her husband's room in a fright; her little nose would wrinkle, and teardrops would fall.

Among Sofia Petrovna's visitors who discoursed on "revolution-evolution" was a respected contributor to a newspaper whose last name was Neintelpfein. Sofia Petrovna had an awful lot of respect for him, so she confided in him. It was he who had taken her to the masquerade ball, where buffoon-harlequins, señoritas, and oriental ladies flashed their eyes from behind velvet masks. She modestly strolled through the rooms on the arm of Neintelpfein, the respected contributor to a newspaper. A red domino kept rushing around, searching for someone, extending his black mask, below which rustled a thick fan of lace.

It was then that Likhutina told the respected Neintelpfein what had happened, while of course keeping all the threads concealed. He was a respected contributor to a newspaper: from then on a day did not go by without a story in the "Daily Chronicle."

The domino was discussed and argued about. Some saw revolutionary terror in it; others said nothing and shrugged their shoulders.

Even in the Likhutins' little hothouse Count Aven, Ommau-Ommergau, and Life Hussar Shporyshev began talking about the appearances of the domino; and they dropped a few "phoophoos" on the topic; and the crafty Ukrainian type gave a crooked little laugh. Yes indeed, Neintelpfein had proved to be an utter swine. But Neintelpfein did not show his face. He kept zealously spinning out lines in the newspaper; and the absurd business spun on and on.

An Utterly Smoke-Sodden Face

Nikolai Apollonovich Ableukhov stood leaning over the balustrade of the staircase in a varicolored dressing gown. He cast an iridescent shimmer in all directions, creating a sharp contrast to the alabaster column and pillar from which a white Niobe raised her alabaster eyes heavenward.

Leaning over the railing, he shouted something or other in the direction of the vestibule. The shout was answered with silence, and then, a protesting falsetto:

"Nikolai Apollonovich, you've taken me for someone else."

Nikolai Apollonovich bared his teeth in an unpleasant smile:

"Is that you, Alexander Ivanovich?"

And he added hypocritically:

"I didn't recognize you without my spectacles."

.   .   .   .

Mastering the unpleasant feeling caused by the stranger's presence, he nodded his head from the balustrade:

"To tell the truth, I'm just up. Still in my dressing gown." (On our part we will add: the past few nights Nikolai Apollonovich had been out Lord knows where.)

The stranger with the small black mustache presented a pathetic spectacle against the rich background of the display of antique weapons. Nonetheless, he went on trying to reassure Ableukhov, half jeering, half playing the perfect simpleton:

"It means absolutely nothing, that you . . . it's a trifle. You're not a young lady, and I'm not a young lady either."

There was nothing to be done. Overcoming the unpleasant feeling within him, Nikolai Apollonovich resolved to move downstairs, but to his annoyance a slipper slipped off his foot, and a bare sole began wagging from beneath the dressing gown. Nikolai Apollonovich stumbled. Assuming that Nikolai Apollonovich, in an access of obsequiousness, was rushing downstairs, the stranger himself rushed upstairs and left wet traces on the steps. Bewildered, he stood between the vestibule and the top of the stairs with an embarrassed smile.

With a desperate show of independence he shrugged off his shabby overcoat and emerged in a gray, motheaten checked suit.

Seeing that the imposing lackey had reached for the soaking wet bundle, my stranger flared up:

"No, I'll take *this* with me."

The stranger cast surprised fleeting glances at the series of rooms, and Nikolai Apollonovich, gathering up the skirts of his dressing gown, preceded the stranger. Their peregrination through the glittering series of rooms seemed irksome to them both. Nikolai Apollonovich was relieved that he could present not his face but his shimmering back. The smile had disappeared from his distended lips. Nikolai Apollonovich was scared out of his wits. Spinning in his brain was: "Some kind of charity fund—for a victimized worker, for weapons. . . ." In his soul an aching: no, no.

In front of the door Nikolai Apollonovich made a sudden and abrupt turn. A flicker of a smile. They looked each other expectantly in the eye.

"After you."

"Don't trouble yourself."

Nikolai Apollonovich's reception room created a sharp contrast to his study, being varicolored like . . . like his Bukhara dressing gown, which was repeated in all the appurtenances of the room: the low divan, which resembled an oriental ottoman, and the dark brown tabouret incrusted with small bands of ivory and mother-of-pearl, and the hanging African shield of thick hide, and the rusty Sudanese spears with massive hafts,† and the spotted leopard skin with gaping jaws. On the tabouret stood a dark blue hookah, and a three-legged censer with a crescent moon. But most astonishing of all was a varicolored cage, where green parakeets were spinning about.

Nikolai Apollonovich drew up the varicolored tabouret. And the stranger lowered himself onto the edge of the tabouret and took out a cigarette case.

"Do you mind?"

"Go right ahead."

"You don't . . ."

"No, I don't."

And he immediately added:

"However, when others wish to . . ."

"Do you want to open the vent?"

"Why no, not at all: I like the smell of smoke."

.   .   .   .

"Don't defend tobacco, Nikolai Apollonovich. I speak from experience. Smoke penetrates the gray matter, the hemispheres get all clogged up."

The stranger suddenly began plucking at his mustache in distress.

"Aren't you going to have a look at my face?"

Nikolai Apollonovich brought blinking eyelids close to his face.

"You see?"

"Yes. . . ."

"An utterly smoke-sodden face," the stranger interrupted, "the face of a smoker!"

Nikolai Apollonovich felt the hemispheres of his own brain clogging up and sluggishness pouring into his organism, but he was now not thinking of the properties of tobacco smoke but of how to get out of a ticklish situation with dignity, if the stranger were to . . .

This heavy leaden feeling had nothing to do with that cheap cigarette but rather with the host's depressed state of mind. Nikolai Apollonovich was expecting his visitor to cut short the chatter that had been set going with one purpose only—to torment him with waiting. Yes, he would cut it short and remind him of how he had once given . . .

In a word, he had given his pledge and was obliged to honor it not by honor alone. He had given his promise out of despair. A failure in his personal life had driven him to it. But the failure had been erased. One would have expected the promise to go away by itself. But the promise remained, if only because it had not been taken back: Nikolai Apollonovich had all but forgotten about it. But it, the promise, lived on. Nikolai Apollonovich himself regarded the promise as a joke.

The appearance of the upstart intellectual filled Nikolai Apollonovich with almost total terror. Nikolai Apollonovich recalled the sad circumstance: all the details of the situation involving the horrible promise. And he found them murderous.

But why? It was not so much that he had given the promise as that he had given it to an unreliable party.

Nikolai Apollonovich was a student of the methodology of social phenomena.

And so he grew pale, turned green. This latter tint came from the atmosphere of the room.

"See here, Nikolai Apollonovich (Nikolai Apollonovich gave a frightened start) . . . actually I haven't come here to talk about tobacco . . . tobacco is quite incidental.

"Tobacco's all very well and good, but actually, I didn't come here about tobacco but on business . . .

"And I'm not even here on business. The crux of the matter is a service you . . ."

Nikolai Apollonovich turned even bluer. He plucked away at a button on the divan, and then began plucking out pieces of horsehair.

"It's a bit awkward, but remembering . . ."

Hearing the shrill falsetto in which "remembering" was pronounced, Nikolai Apollonovich nearly shrieked:

"My proposal?"

But he took himself in hand, and merely remarked:

"I am at your service," and as he said it he thought that his politeness had spelled his doom.

"Pardon me . . . may I have an ashtray?"

.   .   .   .

Arguments in the Streets Became More Frequent

Those were foggy days, strange days. Noxious October marched
on with frozen gait. It hung out dank mists in the south. October
blew off the golden woodland whisper, and that whisper fell to
earth, and there fell the rustling aspen crimson, to wind and chase
at the feet, and whish, plaiting yellow-red scatterings of leaves.
And that sweet chirruping, which in September swims in a leafy
wave, had not swum for a long time. And now the tomtit hopped
forlorn in branches black, which all autumn long send forth their
whistling from woods, gardens, and parks.

Now an icy tree-felling wind was coming upon us in clouds of
tin. But all believed in spring: a popular cabinet minister had indicated that spring was coming.†

Now the ploughmen had ceased to scratch at their lands, and
abandoning their harrows and wooden ploughs, they assembled in
small clusters by their huts. They talked and argued, and then suddenly, all of one mind, moved on the master's colonnaded house.†
Through all the long nights the sky shone bloody with the glow
of conflagrations in the countryside.

Yes! Thus it was in the villages.

Thus it was in the towns as well. In workshops, in print shops,
in hairdressers', in dairies, in squalid little taverns, the same prating
shady type was always hanging around. With a shaggy fur hat
from the fields of bloodstained Manchuria† pulled down over his
eyes, and with a Browning from somewhere or other stuck in his
side pocket, he thrust badly printed leaflets into people's hands.

Everyone feared something, hoped for something, poured into
the streets, gathered in crowds, and again dispersed. In Archan-
gelsk, in Nizhne-Kolymsk, in Saratov, in Petersburg, in Moscow
everyone acted the same way: everyone feared something, hoped
for something, poured into the streets, gathered in crowds and
again dispersed.

Petersburg is surrounded by a ring of many-chimneyed factories.

A many-thousand swarm plods towards them in the morning,
and the suburbs are all aswarm. All the factories were then in a

state of terrible unrest. The workers had turned into prating shady types. Amidst them circulated Brownings. And something else again.

The agitation that ringed Petersburg then began penetrating even to the very centers of Petersburg. It first seized the islands, then crossed the Liteiny† and Nikolaevsky Bridges. On Nevsky Prospect circulated a human myriapod. However, the composition of the myriapod kept changing; and an observer could now note the appearance of a shaggy black fur hat from the fields of bloodstained Manchuria. There was a sharp drop in the percentage of passing top hats. Now were heard the disturbing antigovernment cries of street urchins running at full tilt from the railway station† to the Admiralty waving gutter rags.

Those were foggy days, strange days. Noxious October marched on. Dust whirled through the city in dun brown vortexes, and the rustling crimson fell submissively at the feet to wind and chase at the feet, and whish, plaiting yellow-red scatterings of words from leaves.

Such were the days. Have you ever slipped off at night into the vacant plots of city outskirts to hear the same importunate note "oo?" Oooo-oooo-ooo: such was the sound in that space. But was it a sound? It was the sound of some other world. And it attained a rare strength and clarity. "Oooo-oooo-ooo" sounded softly in the suburban fields of Moscow, Petersburg, Saratov. But no factory whistle blew; there was no wind; and the dogs remained silent.

Have you heard this October song: of the year nineteen hundred and five?

Beloved Delvig Calls for Me

His hand resting on the marble banister, Apollon Apollonovich caught his toe in the carpeting, and—stumbled. His step slowed involuntarily. Quite naturally, his eyes lingered on an enormous portrait of the Minister.

A shiver ran down Apollon Apollonovich's spine: the place was badly heated.

He had a fear of space.

The landscape of the countryside actually frightened him. Beyond the snows, beyond the ice, and beyond the jagged line of the forest the blizzard would come up. Out there, by a stupid accident, he had nearly frozen to death.

That had happened some fifty years ago.

While he had been freezing to death, someone's cold fingers, forcing their way into his breast, had harshly stroked his heart, and an icy hand had led him along. He had climbed the rungs of his career with that same incredible expanse always before his eyes.

There, from there an icy hand beckoned. Measureless immensity flew on: the Empire of Russia.

Apollon Apollonovich Ableukhov ensconced himself behind city walls for many years, hating the orphaned distances of the provinces, the wisps of smoke from tiny villages, and the jackdaw. Only once had he risked transecting these distances by express train: on an official mission from Petersburg to Tokyo.

Apollon Apollonovich did not discuss his stay in Japan with anyone. He used to say to the Minister:

"Russia is an icy plain. It is roamed by wolves!"

And the Minister would look at him, stroking his well-groomed gray mustache with a white hand. And he said nothing, and sighed. On the completion of his official duties he had been intending to . . .

But he died.

And Apollon Apollonovich was utterly alone. Behind him the ages stretched into immeasurable expanses. Ahead of him an icy hand revealed immeasurable expanses.

Immeasurable expanses flew to meet him.

Oh Rus, Rus!

Is it you who have set the winds, storms, and snows howling across the steppe? It seemed to the senator that from a mound a voice was calling him. Only hungry wolves gather in packs out there.

Undoubtedly the senator had been developing a fear of space.

The illness had been aggravated since the time of that tragic death, and the image of his friend visited him night after night, and through all the long nights kept looking at him with a velvety gaze and kept stroking the well-groomed gray mustache with his hand:

> He's gone, and Rus he has deserted,
> The land he raised aloft. . . .†

That fragment of verse arose whenever he, Apollon Apollonovich, traversed that hall.

And still another fragment arose:

> My turn has come, in very truth . . .
> Beloved Delvig calls for me,
> The comrade of my lively youth,
> The comrade of my youth despondent.
> The comrade of my youthful song,
> Of feasts, and purest dedication.
> To where familiar shades now throng
> His spirit's gone for all the ages.†

Recalling these fragments, he ran out, with particular preciseness, to extend his fingers to the petitioners.

Meanwhile, the Conversation Had a Continuation

Nikolai Apollonovich's conversation with the stranger had a continuation.

"I have been entrusted," said the stranger, taking the ashtray from Nikolai Apollonovich, "with handing over this bundle to you for safekeeping."

"And that's all?!" cried Nikolai Apollonovich, still not daring to believe it, and his face showed turbulent signs of life. He sprang to his feet and moved toward the bundle. Then the stranger stood up too. But when Nikolai Apollonovich's hand reached for the bundle, the stranger's hand unceremoniously seized his fingers:

"I ask you in all seriousness to be more careful, Nikolai Apollonovich."

"Ah . . . yes, yes . . ." Nikolai Apollonovich heard nothing. He seized the bundle by the edge of the napkin.†

"Nikolai Apollonovich, I repeat: be more care-ful."

Nikolai Apollonovich looked surprised.

"Leaflets?"

"Not exactly."

.   .   .   .

At that moment there was a sharp metallic sound: something clicked. The thin squeak of a mouse filled the silence. The soft tabouret overturned; the stranger's steps pattered off into the corner:

"Nikolai Apollonovich, Nikolai Apollonovich," his voice was heard, "a mouse, a mouse! Quick, tell a servant . . . to take . . . it, take it . . . away. I can't stand . . ."

"You're afraid of mice?"

Truth to tell, Nikolai Apollonovich presented a ridiculous spectacle: mousetrap in hand, Nikolai Apollonovich was examining the little gray prisoner with the greatest attention.

"A nice little mouse," he raised his eyes as the lackey appeared. The lackey confirmed it:

"The very same, sir."

"It's running round and round."

Now the stranger peeped forth.

"A nice little mouse," said Nikolai Apollonovich. Nikolai Apollonovich had a tender feeling toward mice.†

.   .   .   .

At last Nikolai Apollonovich carried the bundle into his room. The only thing that struck him ever so slightly was the weight of the bundle. As he passed into his study, he stumbled on the vari-colored carpet, catching his foot in a crease. Thereupon something tinkled. The stranger sprang up. Behind Nikolai Apollonovich's back† an arm described that very same zigzag line which had frightened the senator.

Nothing happened. And the stranger began to unbosom himself.

"Solitude is killing me. I've completely forgotten how to carry on a conversation. My words get all tangled up."

Nikolai Apollonovich said through clenched teeth:

"It happens to everyone, you know."

And he covered the bundle with a photograph of cabinet size depicting a pretty brunette. As he was covering the bundle with the pretty brunette, Nikolai Apollonovich grew pensive, and a froglike expression flitted over his lips.

Behind his back he could hear:

"I get all tangled up in every sentence. I want to say a certain word, and instead I say something else. Or suddenly I forget the name of the most common object. I keep repeating: a lamp, a lamp, and then suddenly it seems to me that there is no such word. And sometimes there is no one to ask."

Incidentally, about the bundle: had Nikolai Apollonovich paid somewhat more attention to his visitor's advice to be more careful with the bundle, he probably would have understood that this most harmless bundle was not quite so harmless. But he was, I repeat, preoccupied with the photograph.

"It's hard to live in a Torricellian vacuum."

"Torricellian?" Nikolai Apollonovich had taken nothing in.

"That's right, and I'm doing all this for the good of society. Yet what society do I see? A society of gray sow bugs. Ugh! My room's just swarming with sow bugs."

The stranger had accidentally hit on his favorite topic. Having hit on his favorite topic, he forgot the purpose of his visit, the damp bundle, and the number of cigarettes he was consuming. Like people who are talkative by nature but who are condemned to silence, he sometimes felt the need to communicate something to someone, it didn't matter what or to whom: friend, enemy, porter, policeman, child, or hairdresser's dummy in a window. At night he talked to himself. In the luxurious surroundings of the reception room, the need to talk suddenly awakened:

"They say that I am not I, but some kind of 'we.' But, I ask you, why should that be so? It's that my memory has gone to pieces. Solitude is killing me. Sometimes it's enough to make you angry!"

Here the stranger broke off. Nikolai Apollonovich, closing the drawer, now turned to the stranger and saw that the latter was pacing back and forth in the study, strewing ashes about and contemplating the satin domino that was spread here. Seeing all that,

Nikolai Apollonovich flushed deeply. By doing so, he only helped shift the stranger's field of attention.

"What a beautiful domino, Nikolai Apollonovich."

Nikolai Apollonovich rushed to the domino.

He all but snatched the domino away. Like a thief caught red-handed, he hid it away with great fuss. Having done so, he calmed down. But the stranger, truth to tell, had forgotten the domino and had returned to his favorite topic.

"Ha, ha!" He lit a cigarette as he walked. "So you are surprised how I can act at all. I act according to my own discretion. No matter what you may think, my discretion makes a dent in *their* activity. Strictly speaking, it is not I who am in the Party. The Party is in me. Does that surprise you?"

"To tell the truth, it does surprise me. To tell the truth, I wouldn't think of undertaking a joint action with you."

"And nevertheless you took my bundle. So we are acting to-gether."

"Oh, where do you see an action in that?"

"Of course, of course." And the stranger was silent for a moment, looked at him, and then said quite openly:

"I've long wanted to have a heart-to-heart talk with you. I see few people. You know about the methodology of social phenomena and you know your Marx, but I haven't read him. Don't think I'm not well-read, but I'm not in that, in statistics."

"In what, then? Allow me, there's some cognac in the sideboard."

"I have no objection."

Nikolai Apollonovich reached into the sideboard, and there ap-peared a small cut-glass decanter with small matching glasses.

Nikolai Apollonovich always offered cognac.

As he poured the cognac, Nikolai Apollonovich was thinking that he now had a most convenient opportunity to renounce the proposal he had made. But from cowardice he did not want to display cowardice now. And furthermore, he did not want to bur-den himself with a conversation, when he could renounce it in writing.

"I'm now reading Conan Doyle," chirruped the stranger. "To tell the truth, the range of my reading will strike you as being weird. I'm reading the history of gnosticism,† Gregory of Nyssa, Ephraem Syrus, and the Apocalypse.† That's my privilege, you know. When all's said and done, I'm a colonel in the Movement who's been transferred (for meritorious service) to staff headquar-ters, while you, Nikolai Apollonovich, with all your methodology and your intelligence, are only a noncom. But you're a theoretician. And as far as generals and theory are concerned, well, things are in rather bad shape. They are leaders of the church. A greenhorn

seminarian who's studied Harnack† is nothing but an annoying ecclesiastical appendage as far as a leader of the church is concerned.
And you too are merely an appendage!"

And the stranger fell into thought, poured himself a glass, drank
it off and poured another.

"Weren't you in exile, then?"

"Yes, in the Yakutsk region."

Silence fell.

They downed another glass.

"I made a successful escape from the Yakutsk region.† I was
taken out in a sauerkraut barrel. And now I'm active in the underground. Don't imagine I acted in the name of utopias or in the
name of your strait and narrow way of thinking. After all I was a
Nietzschean.† We are all Nietzscheans, and you are a Nietzschean,
although you wouldn't admit it. For us Nietzscheans, the masses,
who (as you would say) are stirred by social instincts, become an
apparatus of implementation, where all people (and even those like
you) are a keyboard,† on which play the flying fingers of a pianist
(please note my expression), surmounting all difficulties. That's
what we all are like."

"That is, athletes of the revolution?"

Again an awkward silence fell. Nikolai Apollonovich kept plucking horsehair from the ottoman. He did not want to get into a
theoretical argument; he was accustomed to ordered argument.

"Everything is built on contrasts: the public good is what got
me to those icy spaces. And the more I sank into the void out there,
the more I gradually shed Party prejudices. Categories, as you
would say."

Out there, beyond the window panes, in the greenish fog, a
platoon was marching. Soldiers in greatcoats passed by. Bayonets
bristled black in the fog.

Nikolai Apollonovich had a strange sensation of coldness. Suddenly—

"What is it?"

Nikolai Apollonovich raised his head.

"Nothing special, your father has just driven up."

.   .   .   .

Apollon Apollonovich did not like his rooms when the dust-
covers were on. The parquet floors echoed hollow and sharp.

The hall itself was a corridor of vastly wide dimensions. From
the garlanded ceiling, out of a circular molding of fruit hung a
chandelier of tiny glass pendants, draped with a muslin dust-cover.
And its tiny crystals quivered.

And the parquet was like a mirror.

Placed everywhere along the walls—not walls but snow—were long-legged chairs fluted in gold and upholstered in pale yellow velours. Everywhere rose slender white alabaster columns. Mounted atop each slender column was an alabaster Archimedes. Some solicitous hand had hung medallion frames, within which were paintings in pale tones that imitated the frescoes of Pompeii.

The solicitous hand belonged to Anna Petrovna. And Apollon Apollonovich pursed his lips. He moved into the study with something large and round in his hand, in order to lock himself in. The spaces brought on an unaccountable melancholy. Out of them, it seemed, someone strange was coming on the run.

That Person

The stranger began to fidget: the alcohol was having its effect. Conversations with himself and with others always produced a feeling of guilt in him. A loathing for conversation would well up in him. He would transfer the loathing to himself. Outwardly these innocuous conversations enervated him horribly. The more he talked, the more grew the desire to talk, until he felt an astringent sensation in his throat. He could not stop and would exhaust himself. He went on talking to the point where he felt actual attacks of persecution mania, which continued in his dreams—three nightmares per night: Tartars, Japanese, or Orientals would wink at him. But what was most surprising, at such times there would come to memory the meaningless word *enfranshish*, the devil only knows from where. This word helped him struggle. Even when he was awake the fateful face appeared on a piece of dark yellow wallpaper. The fateful phenomena would start with attacks of anguish brought on by his confinement in one place. Alexander Ivanovich would rush out and stop at squalid little taverns. As he sat drinking, a disgraceful attraction for the stocking on the leg of a certain simple-hearted girl student would come over him. Everything would end with the *enfranshish* dream.

"Here you are, Nikolai Apollonovich, listening to my chatter. However, I'm not arguing with you but only with myself. The person I'm talking with means nothing. I talk with walls and posts. I don't listen to other people's ideas. I hear only what concerns me. I struggle: solitude attacks me. For weeks on end I stay home and smoke. And then it seems to me *it's all wrong*. Do you know how it is?"

"I can't picture it clearly. I've heard that this is caused by the heart."

"My soul seems to be universal space.† And it's from there that I look at everything."

Not waiting for an answer, he added:

"I call my habitation on Vasilievsky Island that space: four walls covered with yellow wallpaper. Nobody comes to see me. Morzhov comes, and also a certain *person*."

"How did you happen to get there?"

"*That person . . .*"

"Again?"

"Always him, the guardian of the damp threshold!"

"Now I understand where you cast your shadow from—the shadow of the Elusive One."

"From four yellow walls."

"How much do you pay for your lodgings?"

"Twelve roubles. No, pardon me, twelve and a half."

"And that's where you devote yourself to . . ."

"Yes, there. There I arrived at the conviction that all windows are holes cut into unembraceable infinities."

"And you probably also arrived at the idea that those at the top of the Movement know what is inaccessible to those at the bottom, because the top—but what is the top?"

But Alexander Ivanovich replied:

"It is a void."

"Then what is all the rest for?"

"Why, it's in the name of sickness. . . ."

"What?"

"Yes, the sickness that's wasting me away. The name of this strange sickness is as yet unknown, but I know the symptoms: anguish, hallucinations, vodka, smoking; a frequent and dull ache in the head; a queer feeling in the spinal cord. It comes—in the morning. You think I'm the only one? You're sick too, Nikolai Apollonovich. Almost everyone is sick. Now hold on a minute, I know what you're going to say. Nonetheless, every Party worker suffers from this same sickness. It's just that the signs are more exaggerated in me. Whenever I met a comrade in years gone by, I liked to study him. There were meetings lasting many hours, various business, conversations about noble and lofty things. Then, you know, the comrade goes and invites you to a restaurant."

"Well, what of it?"

"Well, vodka, and so on. Glass after glass. And I would keep watching. If a smirk of a certain kind appeared on his lips (as to which kind, I wouldn't know how to tell you, Nikolai Apollonovich), then I knew: you couldn't rely on the person you were talking with. That person was sick, and nothing would protect him from softening of the brain. Such a person is capable of going back on a promise (Nikolai Apollonovich shuddered). He is capable of theft and betrayal and rape. His presence in the Party is a provocation. And from that time on I have understood the meaning of those little wrinkles around the lips and those little grimaces. Every-

where, everywhere I come across brain disorder, elusive provocation, a little laugh of *this kind*—just which kind, well, that I'm
certainly not about to tell you. But I know how to spot it unerr-
ingly!"

"And you don't have it?"

"I do!"

"So you, therefore, are a provocateur?"

"Me? Yes, a provocateur. But the provocation is in the name of
a great idea; and then again not in the name of an idea, but of something in the air."

"What something?"

"Define it in words? I can call it a general thirsting after death,
and I intoxicate myself with it."

"Have you been drinking for long?"

"Yes, yes, and other erotic feelings have appeared too. I have
never been in love with women, but—how should I put it—only
with separate parts of the female body, and with their wearing
apparel: stockings, for instance."

"Hmm, well. . . ."

Both again fell silent.

"When I have insomnia, my favorite posture, you know, is to
stand pressed flat against the wall with my arms outstretched to the
sides. And while spread-eagled against the wall (I stand that way
for hours, Nikolai Apollonovich) I once came to a very unusual
conclusion. The conclusion was somehow strangely connected with
a phenomenon which is understandable if you take into account the
development of my sickness."

But Alexander Ivanovich considered it best to say nothing about
the phenomenon.

The phenomenon consisted of a hallucination. A face would appear on the wallpaper. The face was swathed in saffron yellow
reflected light. A Semite† or perhaps a Mongol would fix a gaze
full of hatred on Alexander Ivanovich. Alexander Ivanovich would
light a cigarette; through the haze of tobacco smoke the Semite or
Mongol would move his yellow lips, and one word alone would
reverberate within Alexander Ivanovich:

"Helsingfors."†

Alexander Ivanovich had been in Helsingfors after escaping from
his place of exile. There he had met *a certain person.*

But why Helsingfors?

Alexander Ivanovich's agitation communicated itself to Ableukhov. The twelve cigarette butts positively irritated him.

"I have a splitting headache. We can continue our conversation
out there, in the open air. Wait a moment, I just want to change
my clothes."

"A splendid idea."

A sharp knock interrupted the conversation. Nikolai Apollonovich resolved to find out who was knocking. Distractedly, Alexander Ivanovich flung open the door. A skull with ears thrust itself
through the opening of the doorway. The skull and the head of
Alexander Ivanovich nearly banged together. Alexander Ivanovich
recoiled in bewilderment.

And in the open doorway stood Apollon Apollonovich with . . .
a watermelon under his arm.

"I seem to be intruding. Kolenka, I was just bringing you a nice
watermelon—here it is. . . ."

It was the tradition of the house in the autumn season that on his
way home Apollon Apollonovich would sometimes buy an Astrakhan watermelon, of which he was very fond.

For a moment all three were silent. Each was experiencing the
most obvious fear.

"Papa, this is a university friend, Alexander Ivanovich Dudkin."

"My pleasure, sir."

Apollon Apollonovich saw before him only someone timid and
beaten down by poverty.

Alexander Ivanovich saw before him merely a pathetic old man.

Nikolai Apollonovich . . . but he too calmed down.

Apollon Apollonovich entered the conversation. Alexander Ivanovich answered disconnectedly. He kept blushing and his replies
were beside the point. He paid attention only to the last word of
each sentence, and thus caught a string of disjointed exclamations. . . .

"As a Gymnasium student Kolenka knew the names of all the
birds. He read Kaigorodov."†

In this disjointed manner the sixty-eight-year-old man shouted at
Alexander Ivanovich. Something akin to sympathy stirred in him.

"You and . . . so to speak . . . Alexander . . . err . . ."

"Ivanovich . . ."

"And Alexander Ivanovich . . ."

Apollon Apollonovich thought to himself: Oh well, perhaps it's
all for the best. As for the *eyes*—I must have imagined it. Apollon
Apollonovich thought: poverty is no crime. Except: why did they
have to drink?

"Where are the two of you going?"

"We have some business. . . ."

"Perhaps . . . you would care to stay for dinner. . . . Alexander
Ivanovich, would you care to dine . . ."

Alexander Ivanovich looked at his watch.

"However, I don't want to inconvenience you. . . ."

.   .   .   .

"Goodbye, papa. . . ."

"My respects, gentlemen."

.   .   .   .

After they had opened the door and begun to walk along the hollow echoing corridor, the small figure of Apollon Apollonovich appeared behind them, in the half-twilight of the corridor.

And as they walked along in the half-twilight of the corridor, there stood Apollon Apollonovich. Neck outstretched, his eyes followed the pair with curiosity:

"Alexander Ivanovich Dudkin. . . . A student at the university."

.   .   .   .

In the vestibule Nikolai Apollonovich stopped in front of the lackey, trying to catch a thought that had scampered off.

"Ah . . . ah . . . the little mouse!"

Nikolai Apollonovich went on rubbing his forehead, as he tried to remember what he should express with the help of the verbal symbol "little mouse." He often experienced such lapses of memory after reading serious treatises.

"Listen, what did you do with the little mouse?"

"It was let out on the embankment."

Reassured as to the fate of the little mouse, both Nikolai Apollonovich and Alexander Ivanovich set out on their way.

However, they set out because it seemed that someone was looking at them from the balustrade of the staircase: searchingly, and sadly.

.   .   .   .

Strike

Shaggy Manchurian fur hats were pouring onto the streets and melting into the crowd. The crowd kept growing. Shady types and Manchurian fur hats were moving in the direction of a gloomy building† with becrimsoned upper stories. By the gloomy building the crowd consisted of nothing but shady types and Manchurian fur hats.

And they pushed and shoved through the entryway doors—how they pushed, how they shoved! But how could it be otherwise? A worker has no time to bother with manners. A bad smell hung in the air.†

At the intersection near the pavement a small detachment of policemen were sheepishly stamping their feet in the cold. Their commanding officer looked sheepish. Gray himself in a gray coat,† the poor fellow kept shouting and deferentially hitching up his sword, with downcast eyes. And from behind there came at him rude remarks, rebukes, laughter and even, my, my, obscene abuse—from the middle-class type Ivan Ivanovich Ivanov, from his wife and better half, and from Puzanov, a merchant of the first guild (fisheries and a steamship line on the Volga), who had happened to be passing by and had revolted with the rest.† And the officer kept shouting:

"Keep moving, folks, keep moving!"

Shaggy-legged horses snorted more insistently behind a fence. From behind the sawtoothed timber fence a shaggy head would rear now and then. If you had climbed on the fence, you could have seen men rounded up from the steppes, whips in their fists, rifle barrels slung across their shoulders, growing more and more angry as they impatiently pranced in their saddles. The shaggy little horses pranced.

This was a detachment of Orenburg Cossacks.

Inside the building hung a saffron murk, illuminated by candles. Nothing could be seen here but bodies, bodies and more bodies: bent, half-arched, bent hardly at all, and not bent. Bodies were sitting and standing everywhere. They occupied the tiers of seats running around the amphitheater, and the lecture podium could not be seen.†

"Oooo-oooo-ooo." A humming filled the space of the hall and through the "ooo" sometimes was heard:

"Revolution . . . Evolution . . . Proletariat . . . Strike. . . ." Again: "Strike. . . ." Yet again: "Strike. . . ."†

And more humming.

All the talk was about how at such-and-such a place and at such-and-such a place they were already on strike. And at such-and-such a place and at such-and-such a place a strike was in the making. And for that reason they should strike too, strike right here on this spot: don't budge!

Escape

Alexander Ivanovich was returning home along a prospect running parallel to the Neva. A light flew by; the Neva opened up from under the arch of the Winter Canal; on the little arched bridge he again noticed the same shadow.

Alexander Ivanovich was returning to his wretched habitation, to sit in solitude and keep track of the life of the sow bugs. He had left that morning to escape the crawling sow bugs. Alexander Ivanovich's observations had led him to the thought that peace at night depends on how you spend the day. You bring home with you what you have experienced on the streets, in squalid restaurants, in tearooms.

Then what was he returning home with?

His experiences dragged after him, like a tail invisible to the eye; Alexander Ivanovich experienced the experiences in reverse order, as they retreated behind his own back. It seemed to him that his back had opened up. Out of this back, as out of a door, something like the body of a giant reared and prepared to fling itself out of him: the experiences of today's twenty-four hours.

Alexander Ivanovich was thinking that he had but to return home and the events of the last twenty-four hours would come crashing through the door.

He left the glittering bridge† behind him.

Beyond the bridge, against the background of St. Isaac's, a crag rose out of the murk. Extending a heavy patinated hand, the enigmatic Horseman loomed;† the horse flung out two hooves above the shaggy fur hat of a Palace grenadier; and the grenadier's shaggy fur hat swayed beneath the hooves.

A shadow concealed the enormous face of the Horseman. A palm cut into the moonlit air.

From that fecund time when the metallic Horseman had galloped hither, when he had flung his steed upon the Finnish granite,† Russia was divided in two. Divided in two as well were the destinies of the fatherland. Suffering and weeping, Russia was divided in two, until the final hour.

Russia, you are like a steed!† Your two front hooves have leaped far off into the darkness, into the void, while your two rear hooves are firmly implanted in the granite soil.

Do you too want to separate yourself from the rock that holds you, as some of your mad sons have separated themselves from the soil? Do you too want to separate yourself from the rock that holds you, and hang, bridleless, suspended in air, and then plunge down into the chaos of waters? Or, could it be that you want to hurtle through the air, cleaving the mists, to disappear in the clouds along with your sons? Or having reared up, have you, oh Russia, fallen deep into thought for long years in the face of the awesome fate that has cast you here, amidst this gloomy north, where even the sunset itself lasts many hours, where time itself in turn pitches now into frosty night, now into diurnal radiance? Or will you, taking fright at the leap, again set down your hooves and, snorting, now out of control, carry off the great Horseman, out of these illusory lands into the depths of plain-flat spaces?

May this not come to pass!

Once it has soared up on its hind legs, measuring the air with its eyes, the bronze† steed will not set down its hooves. There will be a leap across history. Great shall be the turmoil. The earth shall be cleft. The very mountains shall be thrown down by the cataclysmic earthquake, and because of that earthquake our native plains will everywhere come forth humped. Nizhny, Vladimir, and Uglich will find themselves on humps.†

As for Petersburg, it will sink.

In those days all the peoples of the earth will rush forth from their dwelling places. Great will be the strife, strife the like of which has never been seen in this world. The yellow hordes of Asians† will set forth from their age-old abodes and will encrimson the fields of Europe in oceans of blood. There will be, oh yes, there will—Tsushima! There will be—a new Kalka!†

Kulikovo Field, I await you!†

And on that day the final Sun will rise in radiance over my native land. Oh Sun, if you do not rise, then, oh Sun, the shores of Europe will sink beneath the heavy Mongol heel, and foam will curl over those shores. Earthborn creatures once more will sink to the depths of the oceans, into chaos, primordial and long-forgotten.

Arise, oh Sun!

.   .   .   .

A turquoise gap swept across the sky, while a blot of burning phosphorous flew to meet it through storm clouds and was unexpectedly transformed into a brightly shining crescent moon. Everything flared up: the waters, chimneys, granite, the two goddesses above the arch,† the roof of the four-story house; and for an instant the cupola of St. Isaac's appeared illumined; and the bronze laurel wreath flared; and the lights on the islands went out one by one. In the middle of the Neva an indistinct vessel turned into a fishing schooner; on the captain's bridge there glowed what even could have been the pipe of a blue-nosed bosun, in a fur hat with earflaps, or the small bright lantern of a sailor on watch.

At this point human destinies were distinctly illuminated for Alexander Ivanovich. He could perceive: what would be, what never was to be. Thus all became clear, but he was afraid to glance into his own destiny. He stood shaken.

And the moon cut into a cloud. . . .

Again raggedy arms and misty strands began scudding madly. A blot of phosphorous shone dimly and indistinctly.

A deafening, inhuman roar! Headlights gleaming, an automobile, belching kerosene, hurtled from under the arch toward the river, and yellow, Mongol mugs† cut across the square.

Styopka

A road winds from Kolpino:† there is no gloomier spot! You approach Petersburg on the train, you wake up, and beyond the train windows all is dead. Not a soul, not a village, and the earth itself is a corpse.

Many-chimneyed, smoke-columned Kolpino!

A road winds from Kolpino, and also a line of telegraph poles. There a workman was plodding along. He had worked in a gunpowder plant. He had been kicked out,† and he was hoofing it to Petersburg. Stones lay heavy and dead. Railway barriers flew up, striped mileposts followed one after the other, and the telegraph wire tinkled on the poles.

Squatting behind factories were many-storied heaps. Squatting behind chimneys were factories—here, there and everywhere. In the sky there was no trace of a cloud, and everywhere the horizon was choking with soot.

And noxious cinders dirtied everything. And chimneys bristled against the cinders. Chimneys rose up high; chimneys squatted; over there rose a row of slender chimneys which from a distance became fine hairs. You could count the fine hairs; the arrow of a lightning rod jutted up.

My Styopka paid all this no mind. He sat for a while, with his boots off. He retied his foot-cloths and then began trudging toward the noxious blot of soot.

Toward evening the door of a porter's lodge opened. The door squealed, and the porter, Morzhov,† raised his head. His fat sloppy wife (she always had an earache) had piled up plump pillows and had spent the day exterminating bedbugs.

At this point the door of the porter's lodge opened with a squeal. Styopka stood uncertainly in the doorway (Morzhov and he came from the same village: it stood to reason that Styopka would go to him).

Toward evening a bottle appeared; pickles appeared; and so did the shoemaker Bessmertny,† with a guitar.

"How 'bout that . . . an old buddy from my village!" smirked Morzhov.

"That's all 'cause they don't know what's what," shrugged the shoemaker Bessmertny. He touched a string, and it went plunk, plunk.

"And how's your dad?"

"Drunk as usual."

"How 'bout that . . . an old buddy from my village," said Morzhov, touched to the heart, and taking a pickle in his fingers, he bit off a piece from the same.

"That's all 'cause they don't know what's what," shrugged the shoemaker Bessmertny. He touched a string, and it went plunk, plunk. And Styopka kept talking about just one thing:† how peculiar folk had been turning up in their village and what these peculiar folk had managed to do. In the village they had been proclaiming that a child was to be born, meaning deliverance for all. Soon it would come to pass, they said.

"That's all 'cause they don't know what's what! Nobody knows what's what."

But not another peep out of Styopka. He didn't mention that they'd been getting notations at the Kolpino factory. And likewise about everything else—the whys and the wherefores. Not a word out of Styopka. He sang a ditty:

> Tim-taray, tim-tarah,
> Oh my darling Annie,
> Don't you touch my little bird,
> I'll give you a penny.

The shoemaker Bessmertny merely shrugged his shoulders at the song. Then with all five fingers he began strumming the guitar. And he sang:

> Never shall I see you more,
> Never shall I see you,
> A flask of strong ammonia
> Is in my pocket ready.
> A flask of strong ammonia
> My parched dry throat will swallow!
> I'll writhe and fall down in the street
> And never see you more, my love.

But Styopka was not to be outdone, and he amazed them with:

> An angel stood with trumpet gold,
> Above all sorrow and temptation.
> Oh light, oh light,
> Immortal light!
> Illume us, oh Immortal light,
> Us children in thy sight:
> Thou who art
> Ever in Heaven.

The gentleman had dropped in from his quarters in the garret and was listening. He inquired about those peculiar folk: how they made their proclamations, and when all this was to come to pass. The gentleman was haggard, and he emptied glass after glass. Styopka had some edifying words for him:

"You're a sick man, sir. It won't be long till tobacco and vodka finish you off. I used to be a drinker, sinner that I am, but now I've taken the pledge. Everything started with tobacco and vodka. And I know who's behind it: the Japs!"

"And how do you know?"

"About vodka? Why, Lev Nikolaevich—didn't you read his little booklet, sir? It says so right there."†

"And how do you know about the Japs?"

"That's how it is with the Japs, everybody knows the way the Japs are. Don't you remember the cyclone that passed over Moscow? They said this and that about it. It was the souls of the slain, they said. Must be from the beyond. They must have died unrepentant.† Must mean there's gonna be a revolt."

"And what will happen to Petersburg?"

"The Chinese are putting up some heathen temple or other."†

Then the gentleman took Styopka up to his place in the garret. The gentleman's quarters looked rather disreputable.

He took him there, sat him down opposite, pulled some piece of writing or other† out of a battered suitcase. He read it off:

> "Your political convictions are as plain to me as the nose on your face. It is all the work of the devil, it is all demonic possession.
>
> "A great time draws nigh. A decade remains until the beginning of the end. Write this down and pass it on to posterity. Of all years, the most significant will be 1954. This will concern Russia. Russia is the cradle of the Church of Philadelphia.† I now see why Solovyov spoke of Sophia."†

And Styopka snuffled.

"That's it, that's it! And who was the gent who wrote that?"

"Why, he's abroad, a political exile."

"That's it, that's it!"

.   .   .   .

"And what do you think will happen?"

"First off, killings, then general discontention and then all sorts of sicknesses, pestilence, famine. And then, as people in the know say, there'll be turmoil: the Chinamen will rise up against themselves, the Mussulmen will get all stirred up. Only they won't get away with it."

"And then what?"

"All that's gonna happen toward the end of 1912. But in the year thirteen. . . . But that's not all! There's a certain prophecy: let us hearken, it is said . . . the sword, it is said, is raised against us . . . while to the Japs—the victor's laurel. And then again, the birth of the new child. And further: they say the Prooshan Imperor. . . . There's a prophecy for you, sir! We've gotta build a Noah's Ark!"†

"How should we build it?"

"All right, sir, we'll see! Let's talk about it in a whisper."

"But what will we whisper about?"

"About just one thing: about the Second Coming of Christ."

"What nonsense. . . ."

·   ·   ·   ·   ·   ·   ·   ·

"Even so, come, Lord Jesus!"†

End of the Second Chapter

Chapter the Third
in which is described how Nikolai Apollonovich Ableukhov makes a fool of himself and his venture

No second-class Don Juan he,
No demon, nor a gypsy proud,
He's just an everyday young man,
And simply metropolitan.†

Pushkin

A Holiday†

In a certain important place a certain phenomenon occurred, i.e., it really happened.

And apropos of this, people appeared at the above-mentioned place in embroidered uniforms, and, so to speak, turned out to be in place.

It was a day full of the extraordinary. It was clear. Everything that could sparkle did sparkle: Petersburg roofs and Petersburg spires.

Had you found the time to cast a glance at that important place, you would have seen: glitter on the windows, and glitter beyond the windows, on columns and on parquetry: lacquer, luster, and glitter!

On this extraordinary morning, a little figure, all in dazzling white, sprang out of dazzling white sheets which had suddenly flown up from the bed. This small figure resembled a circus rider. It began, as was its habit, to firm up its body with calisthenics, squatting up to twelve (and more) times. After this it sprinkled its bare skull and arms with eau de cologne (triple strength).

After performing the ablution on his skull, arms, chin, and ears, Apollon Apollonovich Ableukhov, like other little old men, squeezed into starched linen, pushing two ears and a bald spot through the opening of an armorlike shirt. Entering the dressing room, Apollon Apollonovich (like other little old men of exalted rank) took his small red-lacquered boxes out of a small wardrobe. Under their lids, on soft velvet cushions, lay all his rare decorations. He had been brought a small resplendent uniform (smaller than those worn by others), with a glittering gilded chest, white worsted trousers, and a pair of gloves, an odd-shaped hat box, and a scabbard (from its hilt dangled a silver fringe). Under the pressure of his yellow fingernail, all ten lids sprang open; and there were extracted: the White Eagle, and corresponding star; and a blue ribbon. All this went onto his chest. Apollon Apollonovich, all white and gold, stood before the mirror (all aglitter and ashimmer!)† pressing an elegant sword to his hip with his left hand, and with his right pressing a plumed tricorne and a pair of gloves to his chest.

Nikolai Apollonovich had not slept at all that night. Late in the evening, a smart carriage† had flown up to the house. And Nikolai Apollonovich had distractedly jumped out of the carriage and had begun ringing as hard as he could. And when the door was opened, he had run up the staircase without removing his greatcoat, all entangled in its skirts. He had run through a series of rooms. Shadows kept moving back and forth by the yellow house, and Nikolai Apollonovich kept pacing in his room. At two in the morning, steps could still be heard in his room: at two-thirty, at three, at four.

Unwashed and sleepy-eyed, Nikolai Apollonovich was sitting by the fireplace. Apollon Apollonovich stopped despite himself, and was reflected in the parquetry and the mirrors. He stood against a background of pier glasses, surrounded by a family of fat-cheeked cupids who thrust flambeaux through golden garlands. And Apollon Apollonovich drummed his fingers on a small incrusted table. Nikolai Apollonovich came to with a start, leaped up, and squinted: a little old man all white and gold!

Nikolai Apollonovich cursed his mortal self, and insofar as he was the image and likeness of his father he cursed his father. His godlikeness had to hate his father. Nikolai Apollonovich knew his father sensuously, down to the finest nuances and barely perceptible tremors. Sensuously he was absolutely equal to his father. He did not know where he ended and where in him began this senator, this wearer of sparkling decorations on a gold-embroidered chest. He did not so much picture himself as actually experience himself in the sumptuous uniform. And something compelled him to spring up before the little old man all white and gold.

"Good morning, papa!"

The senator, with a show of extravagantly exaggerated naivete, replied in a gay and informal fashion:

"My respects, sir!"

Whenever both came into contact with one another, they gave the appearance of two air vents turned face to face, and the result was a most unpleasant draft.

Love was the last thing this closeness could resemble: Nikolai Apollonovich sensed it as being a most shameful physiological act. At this moment he was capable of regarding the discharge of the familial relationship in the same way he regarded a discharge from the body.

"Why, you're all dressed up today!"

And fingers thrust into fingers; and fingers pulled apart. Apollon Apollonovich evidently wanted to express something, to give a verbal explanation of the reasons for his appearance in uniform. But Apollon Apollonovich only managed to have a coughing fit. The lackey appeared and said: "The carriage is here!" Apollon Apollonovich was pleased and began to make haste.

Nikolai Apollonovich recalled old Ableukhov's most recent official circular, and Nikolai Apollonovich came to the conclusion that his parent, Apollon Apollonovich, was a scoundrel!

Meanwhile, the little old man was already ascending the staircase which was carpeted in red.† As they ascended, his legs formed angles, which soothed his spirit: he loved symmetry.

Little old men came up to him: sidewhiskers, beards, bald spots, chins, and chests adorned with decorations. They guided the movement of our wheel of state. Standing grandly at the balustrade was a small gold-chested cluster who were discussing the fateful rotation of that wheel, until the Master of Ceremonies, staff in hand, requested them to line up.

Immediately after the levee, the little old men once more swarmed together by the columns of the balustrade. One sparkling swarm suddenly took form, and from it came a velvety beelike droning. Someone shorter than the rest was standing there. He was surrounded by little old men; he could not be seen. When Count Witte,† heroically proportioned, a shining blue ribbon across his chest, his hand passing through his gray hair, came up with studied casualness and squinted, he saw that it was Apollon Apollonovich who was droning on. Apollon Apollonovich interrupted his speech and with vague cordiality, but with cordiality all the same, extended his hand to the hand which had just signed the terms of a certain treaty.† Count Witte bent over toward the head which came up to his shoulder, and cracked a joke. But his joke evoked no smile. The little old men did not smile at the joke either. And the small cluster melted away. Apollon Apollonovich descended the staircase with Witte. Above them descended the little old men; below them, a hook-nosed ambassador, a red-lipped little old man, oriental; amidst them, all gold, ramrod straight, descended the senator against the fiery background of the carpet that covered the staircase.

· · · · · · · ·

At that hour the military review was on. A carré of the Imperial Guard was drawn up there.†

Behind the steel bristle† of grenadiers' bayonets one could see ranks of cavalry detachments on white horses. An unbroken, golden, ray-reflecting mirror began slowly advancing toward the designated point. The multicolored standards of the squadrons fluttered in the breeze. Silver bands made melodic entreaty. There—rank upon rank of squadrons—Cuirassiers and Horse Guards. One could also see the ranks of riders in the squadrons—Cuirassiers and Horse Guards, so fair-haired, so enormous, clad in armor, wearing white, smooth, tight-fitting trousers, and breastplates, and helmets topped some with a silver dove, some with a two-headed eagle. Rank upon rank, the squadrons pranced by. Topped with a metal dove, the pale-mustachioed Baron Ommergau danced by on a horse. Topped with a dove of the same kind, Count Aven pranced by too. Cuirassiers and Horse Guards! Out of the dust, in a bloody cloud, plumes lowered, Hussars swept by at a gallop on gray chargers. Their pelisses flashed scarlet. Behind them—the white flash of mantles. The earth thundered and sabers clanged upward in a stream of silver. A red cloud of Hussars flew by and off to the side somewhere. And the parade ground stood empty. And again, there, in that space loomed horsemen, but now sky blue, their armor glistening in a play of silver: a division of Gendarmes of the Guard. A trumpet-flourish made its complaint. But they were suddenly hidden from view by a dun brown cloud of dust. The drums rattled: and infantrymen marched by.

Off to a Mass Meeting†

With the slush gone, the roofs of Petersburg were bathed in warm sunlight.

Angel Peri had been left alone. Her husband was not there: he was in charge of provisions. Uncoiffured, the Angel was fluttering in a kimono between the vases of chrysanthemums and Mount Fuji-yama. The kimono flapped like satiny wings, and its wearer, still obsessed by the same idea, was biting now her handkerchief, now the end of her braid. Nikolai Apollonovich remained the basest of base villains; but the contributor to a newspaper—he too!—was an utter swine!

In order to get a grip on herself somehow, the distraught Angel climbed onto a quilted settee. She opened her book, *Man and His Bodies*. This book had already been opened repeatedly by the Angel, but . . . the book kept falling out of her hands. Angel Peri's little eyes kept closing. From time to time she would wheeze and gently snore.

Baroness R. R. had already made inquiries about the book: "What do you have to say to me about it, ma chère?" But "ma chère" said nothing, and Baroness R. R. shook her finger: after all, there was good reason why the inscription in the book began with the words "My devachanic friend,"† and ended with "Baroness R. R.—a mortal shell, but with a Buddhic spark."

But wait a moment: just what are "devachanic friend" and "shell"? Certainly Besançon would explain that. And Sofia Petrovna would immerse herself in Henri Besançon. She stuck her little nose into Henri Besançon, detecting there the odor of the Baroness herself (opopanax), and the doorbell rang, and in flew Varvara Evgrafovna:

"What's this?" said Varvara Evgrafovna, and she bent over the book.

"What's this? Who gave it to you?"

"The Baroness."

"Of course. But what is it?"

"Besançon. . . ."

"You mean Annie Besant. Isn't it rubbish? Have you read the 'Manifesto'?"

But the little crimson lips pouted.

"The bourgeoisie, sensing its end, has seized upon mysticism."

And through her pince-nez Varvara Evgrafovna threw the Angel a triumphant glance that brooked no opposition. Fortunately, Varvara Evgrafovna was not in the mood for a scene. Crossing her legs, she wiped the pince-nez.

"You of course are going to the Tsukatovs' ball."

"I am," replied the Angel.

"A mutual acquaintance of ours will be at the ball, Ableukhov."

At this the Angel flushed.

"Well then, please give him this letter." She slipped a letter into the Angel's hand.

"Give it to him, and that's all there is to it. You will, won't you?"

"I . . . I will. . . ."

"Very well, then. Time's a-wasting. I'm off to a mass meeting."

"Varvara Evgrafovna, be a darling, take me along too."

"We may get beaten up. . . ."

"No, take me, take me along!"

"All right, let's go. Only you're going to take time getting dressed and powdering yourself, and so on and so forth, so be quick about it."

"Right away! I'll just be a second!"

.   .   .   .

"Oh, heavens, hurry up, hurry! Mavrushka, my corset! The black wool dress, that one, and the shoes that—not those—the ones with the high heels." And the kimono flew across the table onto the bed. Mavrushka got all flustered: Mavrushka knocked over a chair.

"No, not that way, tighter, tighter. Those aren't hands you have but stumps. And the garters, what about them? How many times have I told you?" The corset set up a crackle.

And Sofia Petrovna Likhutina, an ivory hairpin in her teeth, squinted at the letter. On the letter was inscribed: *For Ableukhov*.

An unruly lock of hair popped loose at the back of her head.

A letter! And there on the letter: *For Ableukhov*. But here is what was strange: it was Lippanchenko's handwriting.

And now wearing a black wool dress which fastened at the back, she fluttered out of the bedroom.

"Let's go, let's be off. Oh, by the way, the letter . . . who's it from?"

"?"

"Well, never mind, never mind!"

Why was she in such a hurry? To try, while they were on their way, to worm something out of her, ask questions, get answers?

Ask what?

At the entryway they bumped into Lippanchenko:

"Well, well, well: where are you off to?"

Sofia Petrovna waved her hand in annoyance:

"To a mass meeting, a meeting."

But that crafty Ukrainian type would not let up:

"Fine. I'll come along with you."

Varvara Evgrafovna flared up and stopped; she stared at the Ukrainian:

"I seem to know you. You rent a room at . . . at the widow Manton's, I believe."

At this point the shameless Ukrainian got all disconcerted: he began to huff and puff, raised his hat slightly and fell behind.

"Who's *that*?"

"Lippanchenko."

"But, that's not possible; he's a Greek from Odessa named Mavrokordato. He visits the person in the room right next to mine. I advise you not to receive him."

Sofia Petrovna was not listening. Mavrokordato, Lippanchenko—it was all the same.

·　·　·　·　·　·　·　·

Noble, Trim, and Pale of Mien . . .

They were walking along the Moika.

The last gold and last crimson of the garden had fallen in a quiver of leaves.

"Oooo-oooo-ooo . . ." such was the sound in space.
"Do you hear?"
"What?"

.   .   .   .

"Oooo-ooo. . . ."

.   .   .   .

"I don't hear a thing. . . ."

And yet it sounded softly in forests and fields, in the suburban spaces of Moscow, Petersburg, Saratov. Have you heard this October song of the year nineteen hundred and five?

"That must be a factory whistle: a strike somewhere."

No factory whistle blew; there was no wind; and the dogs remained silent.

The blue of the Moika was right at their feet. That same light-colored three-storied building rested on its columns. Above the third story ran narrow strips of ornamental moulding, ring after ring—rings of moulding.

Up ahead, where the canal curved, a little to the left, above a stone projection, the dazzling cupola of St. Isaac's rose austerely in the glassy turquoise.

There's the Embankment: the depths, the greenish blue. There, far, far off, as though farther off than they should have been, the islands sank and cowered; and the buildings cowered; and the depths, the greenish blue might at any moment wash over them, might well surge over them. And over this greenish blue, a pitiless sunset sent forth its reflections in all directions, and the Troitsky Bridge flushed crimson. The Palace flushed crimson.

Suddenly over these depths and over this greenish blue, against the background of the sunset, appeared a sharp silhouette. The wings of a gray caped greatcoat flapped in the wind; and a waxen face, with pouting lips, was thrown back nonchalantly. The eyes seemed to be searching for something in the bluish expanses beyond the Neva, could not find it, and looked right over a modest little fur hat. They saw neither her nor Varvara Evgrafovna. They saw only the depths, the greenish blue. They were raised and lowered—looking there, beyond the Neva, where the banks cowered and the buildings of the islands were bathed in crimson. And up ahead ran a snorting striped bulldog, carrying a small silver whip in its teeth.

Coming alongside them, he squinted slightly, and lightly touched his cap-band. He said nothing and walked on. And the buildings merely flushed crimson.

Her eyes a bit crossed, Sofia Petrovna quickly buried her little face in her muff, and nodded her little head sideways: not at him, but at the bulldog. Varvara Evgrafovna was positively gawking.

"Ableukhov?"

"Yes, seems to be."

And on hearing the reply (she was so nearsighted), Varvara Evgrafovna began whispering to herself:

> Noble, trim, and pale of mien,
> Flaxen hair for all to see;
> In ideas rich, in feelings poor,
> N. A. A.—who can he be?

Is it he?

> Known as revolutionary,
> Though aristocratic, bold,
> Better than his wretched family,
> Better by a hundredfold.

There he was, he who would transform the rotten order, and to whom she intended to propose—marriage: on the completion of his preordained mission, after which a universal explosion would follow. Here she choked (Varvara Evgrafovna had the habit of swallowing her saliva).

But Sofia Petrovna was not listening. She turned and saw: there, standing on the landing by the Palace in the bright, crimson thrust of the last rays, was Nikolai Apollonovich, turned toward her in a strange manner, hunched, his entire face buried in his collar, which pushed his cap up. It seemed to her that he was smiling in a highly unpleasant manner and, in any event, he cut a rather comic figure. Wrapped up in a greatcoat, he seemed stooped, somehow armless, with the wing of the greatcoat flapping preposterously in the wind.

He kept standing there for a long time, stooped, and he smiled to himself in a highly unpleasant manner, cutting the rather comic figure of an armless man with a greatcoat flapping so preposterously in the wind, against a crimson blotch of slanting rays. He was not looking at her: how could he have made her out with his nearsightedness? He looked far off, as though farther off than he should have—where the buildings of the islands sank, where they shimmered in the ever-encrimsoning haze.

And she? She wanted her husband, Sergei Sergeyevich Likhutin, to go up to that villain and suddenly strike him in the face with his cypress fist and say what needed to be said.

The pitiless sunset sent forth ray after ray from the very rim of the horizon; and rosy tinctures played and rippled; and still higher, small white clouds, like fine indentations of broken mother-of-pearl, were immersed in all that turquoise blue. All that turquoise blue poured evenly amidst the fragments of rosy mother-of-pearl. Yes, soon now the dark blue, the bluish green depths will surge: onto the houses, the granite, the water.

There will be no sunset.

Comte, Comte, Comte!

Apollon Apollonovich appeared out of the doorway. The lackey had already removed the lid from the steaming soup tureen.

Through the left-hand door in sprang Nikolai Apollonovich, wearing a student uniform with a very high collar.

Apollon Apollonovich shifted his gaze from one object to another. Nikolai Apollonovich felt disconcerted. Two unnecessary arms dangled from his shoulders. In an access of sterile obsequiousness he ran up to his father and began wringing his hands.

Apollon Apollonovich precipitously stood up before his son (anyone else would have said—sprang up).

Nikolai Apollonovich stumbled against the table leg.

Apollon Apollonovich proffered his lips. Nikolai Apollonovich applied his lips to the other lips.

And Apollon Apollonovich sat down. Apollon Apollonovich seized the pepper pot. Apollon Apollonovich always overpeppered his soup.

"Back from the University?"

A froglike expression flitted across the grinning face of the respectful, loving son. Not a trace of the Greek mask remained. A cascade of smiles, grimaces, and civilities began to gush forth before the darting gaze of the dear distrait papa. The hand raising the spoon trembled.

"Back from the office, papa?"

"No, from the Minister. . . ."

.   .   .   .

We have seen that while sitting in his office, the senator had arrived at the conviction that his son was a scoundrel. Thus the sixty-eight-year-old papa was committing a mentally graspable act of terrorism against his own flesh and blood.

But those had been merely office conclusions, which were unsuitable for the dining room.

"Would you like some pepper, Kolenka?"

"I'd like some salt. . . ."

Apollon Apollonovich, eyes flitting and darting, assiduously avoided thinking of the office, according to the established tradition of this hour.

"And I like pepper: it's tastier. . . .

"I see!

"I see!

"Fine."

He was engaging his loving son (or better said, himself) in conversation.

The silence grew heavier.

The senator was not troubled by the silence. Nikolai Apollonovich, in his search for a topic of conversation, experienced real torment.

And he burst forth unexpectedly:

"Well . . . I . . ."

"Yes, what is it . . ."

"Well . . . nothing. . . ."

Nikolai Apollonovich, without himself expecting it, again burst forth:

"Well . . . I . . ."

"What do you mean 'Well, I'?"

He could think of no continuation to the words that had popped out.

But Apollon Apollonovich, disturbed by his son's verbal perturbation, suddenly looked up whimsically:

"Excuse me, but what's on your mind?"

And in his loving son's head senseless associations began whirling about.

And out whirled:

"Well . . . I've . . . read in Cohen's *Theorie der Erfahrung* . . ."†

Again he stumbled to a halt.

"And what's that book about, my dear boy?"

Apollon Apollonovich in addressing his son now observed all the traditions of the past: in dealing with *this arrant rogue* he called him "Kolenka," "loving son," and "my dear boy."

"Cohen is a representative of serious neo-Kantianism."

"You mean Comtianism?"†

"No, Kantianism, papa."

"But didn't Comte refute Kant?"

"But Comte is unscientific. . . ."

.   .   .   .

"I don't know, I don't know, dear friend: in my time we didn't consider that to be so."

.   .   .   .

Apollon Apollonovich slowly rubbed his eyes with his tiny fists, repeating distractedly:

"Comte . . ."

Apollon Apollonovich decided that his brain was again suffering unpleasantly from affluxes brought on by his hemorrhoidal indisposition of all last week. His dark blue eyes suddenly fixed in a stare:

"And what is that book about, Kolenka?"

.   .   .   .

Nikolai Apollonovich cultivated this talk about philosophy with instinctive cunning. A conversation about Cohen was a perfectly neutral conversation. It did away with the possibility of *other conversations*. A certain serious talk kept being put off (month after month). And besides, Apollon Apollonovich encouraged conversations of just this kind in his son. In the past, Nikolai Apollonovich, on coming home from the Gymnasium, would explain all the details about Roman cohorts and Apollon Apollonovich encouraged his interest in cohorts. In later years Apollon Apollonovich would lay his hand on Kolenka's shoulder:

"Kolenka, you really should read Mill's *Logic*:† it's a useful book . . . in two volumes. In my time I read it from cover to cover."

Nikolai Apollonovich, having devoured Sigwart,† now began appearing with a volume of Mill. Apollon Apollonovich, in a seemingly casual manner, would ask him:

"What are you reading?"

"Mill, papa."

"I see, I see. Very fine!"

. . . .

And now, completely split apart, they were unconsciously returning to old memories.

At one time Apollon Apollonovich had been a professor of the philosophy of law.† At that time he had read a great deal from beginning to end. But all that was gone without a trace. When faced with the elegant pirouettes of familial logic, Apollon Apollonovich felt an indeterminable weight, and he did not know how to express his objections.

He thought: "Yes, one must give Kolenka his due. His mental equipment, so to speak, functions."

Nikolai Apollonovich sensed with pleasure that his parent was an alert listener.

And a semblance of friendship would develop by dessert, and sometimes they regretted having to break off the conversation, as if both feared that when alone, each would, one toward the other . . .

Now both rose, and began strolling through the enfilade of rooms. The enfilade grew dark; and from afar, from the drawing room, came reddish flashes: a fire was crackling.

Thus they had once wandered through the empty enfilade—a very small boy and . . . his father. He was patting the fair-haired boy on the shoulder, and pointing out the stars:

"The stars are far away, Kolenka. From the nearest one it takes the light two years and then some to reach the earth. That's the way it is, my boy!" And furthermore, the tender loving papa had written a verse for his son.

> Noodle-doodle, dummy-wummy,
> Little Kolya's dancing,
> On his head a dunce-cap wears,
> On his horse he's prancing.

The outlines of small tables were taking shape. A ray of light was flashing from the windowpane; the incrustations were beginning to glitter. Had the father really come to the conclusion that the blood of his blood was that of a scoundrel? And had his son really mocked him too?

> Noodle-doodle, dummy-wummy,
> Little Kolya's dancing,
> On his head a dunce-cap wears,
> On his horse he's prancing.

Had that ever been? Perhaps that had never really been . . . anywhere, any time?

Both were sitting in the satin drawing room, for the sake of aimlessly prolonging another such encounter. They were peering into each other's eyes. The flame in the fireplace gave off warmth. Shaven and gray, Apollon Apollonovich was now silhouetted against the twinkling flame, shaven and old, ears and skull. He had been portrayed with just such a face on the cover of some trashy rag.

"My dear friend, are you often visited by . . . hmmm . . ."

"Who?"

"Oh, what's his name . . . the young man . . ."

"The young man?"

"With a small mustache."

Nikolai Apollonovich gave a broad grin:

"Alexander Ivanovich Dudkin! No."

After a moment's thought, he added:

"Well, yes, he drops by now and then."

. . . .

"If . . . if . . . this is an indiscreet question, then. . ."

"What?"

"Does he come on university matters?"

. . . .

"However . . . if my question is, so to speak, out of place. . ."

. . . .

"Is he a student?"

"He is."

"Not at the Technological Institute?"

"No."

Apollon Apollonovich knew that his son was lying. He looked at his watch. He rose indecisively. Nikolai Apollonovich was tormentingly aware of his arms, and his eyes began to roam.

"Well, yes . . . there are many branches of knowledge in the world. Each specialty is profound, you're right. You know, Kolenka, I feel tired."

He kept standing, looking . . . he did not ask about it but looked down. Nikolai Apollonovich felt ashamed.

A hand trembled . . . two fingers.

"Good night, papa!"

"My respects, sir!"

A bustle, a rustle, a squeak: a mouse.

.   .   .   .

The door of the senator's study opened. Candle in hand, Apollon Apollonovich ran into the room that was comparable to no other, in order to devote himself to . . . to reading the newspaper.

.   .   .   .

Nikolai Apollonovich stood at the window.

A phosphorescent blot raced across the sky, misty and mad. The far stretch of the Neva gradually misted over, and the soundlessly flying surfaces began glimmering green. A tiny red light flashed on and off, blinked and moved on into the spread of murk. Beyond the Neva rose the immense buildings of the islands, darkening, and they cast shining eyes into the mists—soundlessly, tormentingly. And they seemed to be weeping. Higher up, raggedy arms madly stretched vague outlines; swarm upon swarm, they rose above the Neva's waves.

.   .   .   .

The embankment was empty. The shadow of a policeman would pass, emerge black and distinct from the fog and once more melt away. The buildings beyond the Neva would disappear in the fog; the spire of Peter and Paul cast a glint.

The shadow of a woman. It did not move off into the fog but stood looking up at the window. Nikolai Apollonovich smiled a highly unpleasant smile: applying his pince-nez, he scrutinized the shadow.

No, no, it was not she!

The black shadow melted away in the fog.

.   .   .   .

A metal bolt rattled in the depths of the corridor. A light flickered in the depths: Apollon Apollonovich, candle in hand, was returning from the place that was comparable to no other. From a distance his mouse-colored dressing gown and the enormous outlines of his dead ears stood out sharply in the dancing candlelight. Apollon Apollonovich Ableukhov moved by out of utter darkness and once more sank into utter darkness.

.   .   .   .

Nikolai Apollonovich thought: "It's time."

Nikolai Apollonovich knew that the mass meeting would last until late at night, that *she* was going to the meeting. Nikolai Apollonovich thought: "*It's time.*"

Tu-Tum: Tum, Tum!

Sofia Petrovna modestly buried her little nose in her downy muff. Behind her, the Troitsky Bridge stretched away into those mute places, and on the iron bridge, above the damp, damp railing, above the greenish waters teeming with germs, behind her passed, in the gusts of Neva wind—bowler, cane, coat, ears, nose.

Suddenly her eyes stopped moving, dilated, blinked, crossed: under the damp railing sat a bowlegged striped bulldog. It was slavering a small silver whip in its teeth. She cast a glance and saw: above the damp railing a waxen face was thrust out of a greatcoat. His lips were pouting, and it seemed to her that he was thinking a thought which had echoed within her these past few days, because these past few days the words of a certain romance had been so tormentingly singing themselves:

> Gazing at the rays of purple sunset,
> You stood upon the banks of the Neva.†

He stood upon the banks of the Neva, staring dully into the green, but no—letting his gaze soar there, where the banks cowered, where the buildings of the islands squatted, and from where, above the white fortress walls, the pitiless spire of Peter and Paul, tormentingly sharp, reached up so coldly to the sky.

Her entire being reached out to him. What need now for words, for reflections! But he had not noticed her. Eyes dilated and glassy, he looked like an ugly armless monster.

She moved away. Nikolai Apollonovich slowly turned in her direction. He began tripping off, stumbling and entangling himself in the long skirts of his greatcoat. A smart carriage was waiting on the corner. And the carriage flew off. It overtook her. Nikolai Apollonovich, leaning out and holding the bulldog by the collar, turned toward the small figure. He looked, he smiled, and the carriage flew past.

Suddenly the first snow began to fall, and it danced and sparkled in lively little diamonds. A bright circle of light from a street lamp illuminated a side of the palace, and a small canal and a little stone bridge. The Winter Canal stretched away into the depths. A smart carriage was awaiting someone there, at the corner. A greatcoat lay casually in the carriage.

For a long time Sofia Petrovna stood on the arch of the little bridge and kept dreamily looking at the vapor rising from the splashing canal. She had stopped at this spot before. She would sigh over the fate of Liza, and would reflect in all seriousness on the horrors of *The Queen of Spades*,† on its divine, enchanting, marvellous harmonies. And she would softly hum:

"Tu–tum: tum, tum! . . . Tu–tu–tum: tum, tum!"

She caught the sound of running steps. She looked, and did not even let out a shriek: suddenly, from around the side of the palace, burst a red domino. It seemed somehow bewildered, and thrashed about here and there as though in search of something. And catching sight of the shadow of a woman on the arch of the little bridge, it rushed in that direction. It kept stumbling on the cobblestones, its mask with spiteful-looking eye-slits pitching forward; and beneath the mask a thick swarm of lace played in an icy stream. As the mask ran in the direction of the little bridge, Sofia Petrovna had no time to grasp that the domino belonged to a buffoon, and that some prankster with no taste (we know who) had felt like playing a joke, that behind the velvet mask and the lace beard was a human face. The oblong slits were fixed upon her in a stare. Sofia Petrovna thought (with her tiny little brow) that a fissure had opened up in the world, and that from this fissure—not from the world—the buffoon had come rushing upon her. Just who this buffoon was, she could not have said.

The domino stumbled and flew onto the little bridge. The broad satiny folds of the domino flew up with a rustle, and fell over the railing in a red stream. Bright green trouser straps were suddenly exposed and the buffoon became a pathetic buffoon. An overshoe slipped on a bulge in the pavement. The buffoon crashed headlong to the ground. Above him a loud guffaw rang out:

"You monster, you red buffoon!"

Now some sort of bearded people came running, and there was a whistle. And the buffoon dashed to the smart carriage, and in the carriage something red could be seen floundering helplessly, as it kept struggling to throw a greatcoat over its shoulders.

From behind the bend of the Winter Canal a bulldog started racing after the carriage, barking. Stumpy little legs flashed by. Two agents of the secret police sped in pursuit on rubber tires.

Shadows

Said one shadow to another:
"You didn't say a word about the red domino."
"Oh, you know?"
"I followed him right up to his apartment."
"And?"
"The incident hasn't come to a head."

.   .   .   .

"Do you have any evidence?"
"What's gotten into you? Getting evidence is no problem at all.
Be my guest!"

.   .   .   .

"Evidence? You need evidence? And what about the Petersburg
'Daily Chronicle'? Have you been reading the 'Chronicle'?"
"I admit I haven't."
"But look, it's our duty to know what Petersburg is talking about.
You would have understood that the news about the domino pre-
ceded his appearance at the Winter Canal."
"Hmmm."
"Ask me who wrote all this for the 'Chronicle'."
"Well, who?"
"Neintelpfein, my collaborator."

.   .   .   .

"I admit I didn't expect you to pull off something like that."
"And yet you jump on me and make nasty cracks. The undertaking has been set like a clock mechanism. You are in blissful
ignorance, and all along my Neintelpfein has been creating a real
sensation."

.   .   .   .

"I hope you will order your agents to leave Nikolai Apollonovich
in peace for the time being."

A Mad Dog Yelped

She could not reconcile herself to this incident, which had disgraced her forever. It would have been better had Nikolai Apollonovich insulted her in some other way. It would have been better
had he slapped her, it would have been even better had he thrown
himself off the little bridge in his domino. All the rest of her life she
would have remembered him with an awful trembling, she would

have remembered until the day she died. Sofia Petrovna Likhutina did not regard the Winter Canal as any prosaic spot where one could permit oneself to do what he had permitted himself. Not for nothing had she sighed, again and again, at the strains of *The Queen of Spades*. Yes, yes: her situation had something in common with Liza's (what it had in common, she could not have said). And it went without saying that she had dreamed of seeing Nikolai Apollonovich there as Hermann.† Hermann? Hermann had acted like, like . . . in the first place, he had thrust his mask at her in a cowardly manner from around the side of the palace. In the second place, he had frenetically flapped his domino in front of her and then had sprawled on the little bridge, with a prosaic show of trouser straps (it was these trouser straps that had utterly infuriated her). Crowning all the outrages, all so uncharacteristic of Hermann, was the fact that Hermann had fled from some sort of policemen, and he had not torn the mask from his face in a heroic, tragic gesture. He had not said, in a hollow, sinking voice: "I love you." And he had not shot himself. No, Hermann's disgraceful conduct had extinguished the dawn of those days! No, Hermann's disgraceful conduct had transformed the domino itself into a harlequinade. She had been debased by his disgraceful conduct. After all, what kind of Liza could she be if there were no Hermann! Vengeance on him, vengeance!

She whirled into her apartment like a thunderstorm. In the vestibule hung a coat and a cap: her husband was now at home, and Sofia Petrovna Likhutina flew in to see him without removing her coat, flinging the door wide open—with her streaming boa, her soft little muff, her little face inflamed and swollen unattractively.

Sergei Sergeyevich was getting ready for bed. His tunic hung in a modest manner on a clothes hook, and he himself, in a dazzling white shirt crossed by suspenders, was kneeling, forehead on the ground, as if broken in two. The icon gleamed; the icon lamp sputtered. Outlined in the half-light of the icon lamp was a face, with a sharply pointed goatee and a hand of the same color. And the hand, and the face, and the goatee, and the white chest had been carved from hard wood of some kind. Lips barely moving, Sergei Sergeyevich was bowing almost into the small pale blue flame. His bluish fingers, squeezed together tightly, scarcely moved as they pressed against his forehead in order to make the sign of the cross.

Second Lieutenant Likhutin first placed his bluish fingers on his chest and on both shoulders. He bowed, and only then did he turn around, somewhat reluctantly. Now he got to his feet and began brushing the specks of dust from his knees, and he asked:

"What's wrong, my dear Sonya?"

Her husband's cool composure irritated and somehow even offended her, just as that bluish flame—there in the corner—offended her. And she fell onto a chair, covering her little face with her muff. She filled the entire room with sobs.

Sergei Sergeyevich's face grew kinder and softened, and a wrinkle furrowed his brow. A compassionate expression appeared. But Sergei Sergeyevich had only a vague picture of how he should act: whether to let the tears flow and then endure a scene and accusations of coldness, or whether to go cautiously down on his knees before Sofia Petrovna, lift her little head from the muff with a gentle hand, embrace her, and cover her with kisses. He was afraid of seeing a hint of contempt and boredom on her face, so he chose the middle way: he simply tapped her trembling shoulder:

"Come, come, Sonya . . . please stop . . . my dear little girl."

"Oh, leave me alone, leave me alone!"

"What's wrong? Let's talk about it!"

"Leave me alone, leave me alone! You're . . . cold-blooded."

Sergei Sergeyevich stepped back from his wife, stood there a moment, and sank into an armchair beside her.

"Ahhh! To abandon your wife this way! . . . Always in charge of provisions out there! Always away! And to know nothing! . . ."

"Sonya, my dear, you're mistaken if you think I don't know. But . . . don't you see!"

"Oh, please leave me alone!"

.   .   .   .

"Don't you see, my dear: since the time that . . . I moved out of our room into this one. . . . In a word, I have my pride, and I don't wish to place restraints on your freedom. . . . I understand you. I know very well it's not easy for you. . . . I have my hopes that sometime again. . . . But I won't insist, I won't insist! Now do try to understand me. My distance, my cool composure, so to speak, aren't the result of coldness at all. . . . But I won't insist, I won't insist!"

.   .   .   .

"Perhaps, my dear, you would like to see Nikolai Apollonovich Ableukhov? It would seem something has happened between you two? Tell me everything, tell me. We'll talk about the situation together."

"Don't you dare mention him to me! He's a cad, a cad! Anyone else would have shot him down long ago. But you? No, leave me alone."

And she told him everything, everything, in an incoherent and agitated fashion.

Sergei Sergeyevich Likhutin was a simple soul. And simple folk are much more strongly struck by the inexplicable weirdness of an action than by baseness or murder. It is easy to understand human treachery. And to understand something is almost to find justification for it. But how can it be explained when an honorable man from good society suddenly takes it into his head to get down on all fours and flap the tail of his frock coat? Something that has no purpose can have no justification. No, better if a completely honorable man squanders official funds and goes unpunished. But let him never get down on all fours.

Sergei Sergeyevich Likhutin clearly pictured the domino straddle-legged in the unlighted entryway, and . . . he began to blush, he blushed carrot red. The blood rushed to his head. He and Nikolai Apollonovich had been childhood playmates, and he had been surprised at his talent for philosophy. Sergei Sergeyevich had nobly permitted him to come between himself and his wife, and Sergei Sergeyevich Likhutin angrily, vividly, distinctly pictured the buffoonish grimaces in the unlighted entryway. In agitation he began to pace the tiny little room, his fingers clenched in a fist, raising his fist each time he made a sharp turn. Whenever he lost control of himself, this gesture appeared. And Sofia Petrovna plainly sensed what the gesture meant, and she grew a little frightened at the silence which accompanied the gesture.

"Why are you . . . ?"

"Nothing . . . in particular . . ."

And Sergei Sergeyevich Likhutin kept pacing the little room, his fingers clenched in a fist.

How vile, vile, vile! He had been standing behind the front door . . . ah?!

Nikolai Apollonovich's conduct had astonished the second lieutenant in the extreme. He experienced a combination of loathing and horror. He experienced the feeling that comes over people at the sight of idiots performing their bodily functions all over themselves or at the sight of a furry-legged insect. Bewilderment, outrage, and fear turned into fury. To have ignored his letter, to have insulted the honor of an officer with such a clownish stunt!! Sergei Sergeyevich Likhutin vowed to crush the horrible spider, crush it. And once he had made that decision, he went on pacing, red as a lobster, his fingers clenched in a fist, raising his muscular arm whenever he made a turn. And he unwittingly filled even Sofia Petrovna with fear. With half-parted swollen little lips, with tears not yet daubed from her glistening little cheeks, she was attentively observing him right from there, from that very chair.

"What's wrong with you?"

But Sergei Sergeyevich replied in a rough voice. Menace, severity, and repressed fury could be heard in this voice.

"Nothing . . . in particular."

At this moment Sergei Sergeyevich experienced something like loathing for his beloved wife, as if she herself had shared in the disgrace of the red mask.

"Go to your room, go to sleep . . . leave this to me."

And Sofia Petrovna Likhutina, weeping no longer, left without protest.

Sergei Sergeyevich Likhutin kept pacing and giving a cough now and then, most unpleasantly and distinctly: kh–kh–kh–kh. Sometimes his wooden fist, which seemed to be carved from fragrant hard wood, raised above the little table, and it seemed that any moment the little table would fly into pieces.

The fist unclenched.

Sergei Sergeyevich Likhutin undressed, pulled up the blanket, and—the blanket slid off. Sergei Sergeyevich Likhutin was staring at some point with unseeing eyes, and to his own surprise, he said in a loud whisper:

"I'll shoot him down like a dog."

Then from the other side of the wall came an injured voice:

"What is it?"

.   .   .   .

"Nothing . . . in particular."

Sergei Sergeyevich dove under the blanket: pulled it up—to sigh, beseech, and threaten. . . .

.   .   .   .

Sofia Petrovna impetuously threw off her dress, and emerging from a cascade of things that she contrived to scatter about in three or four minutes, she threw herself, all in white, onto the bed, letting fall into her hands her black-haired little face with pouting lips, above which the outline of a little mustache was clearly visible. A fountain of objects had fallen all around her. Mavrushka did nothing but pick up after her mistress. Whenever Sofia Petrovna thought of some article of apparel, the article was never there, and then flew: blouses, handkerchiefs, dresses, and pins of various kinds.

Sofia Petrovna listened closely to the tireless pacing of Sergei Sergeyevich, and she listened to the sounds of the piano upstairs. Up there someone was playing, over and over again, the same tune from times of old: a polka-mazurka to which they had danced with her, laughing, when she was but a two-year-old tot. And to the accompaniment of these innocent sounds, Sofia Petrovna's rage gave way to weariness and apathy toward her husband, in whom she herself, in her opinion, had aroused jealousy toward that other one. Her feeling of discomfort made her husband positively disagreeable to her, just as if some alien hand had reached for the secret little casket containing letters, which was locked up in the drawer over there. In Nikolai Apollonovich's disgraceful conduct she discovered a source of sweet. . . . She regretted that he had fallen in front of her there in the guise of a pathetic buffoon, and yet she felt like torturing him. As for her husband, she did not feel like either tormenting or kissing him. And she discovered that her husband was neither here nor there in all this. But now she had told her husband everything. She found it offensive that her husband could now touch not only her, but Nikolai Apollonovich as well. The second lieutenant would of course draw false conclusions from the incident. He would of course be incapable of understanding anything. And Sofia Petrovna listened closely to the sounds of the polka-mazurka and to the pacing on the other side of the partition. Out of the luxuriance of black-braided hair protruded her pearly little face with its dark blue eyes, now somehow dulled, as she clumsily clasped her trembling knees.

Her gaze fell on the fold-down mirror of her dressing table. And beneath the mirror she spied the letter she was supposed to deliver at the ball (she had forgotten about the letter). Her first impulse was to send the letter back. How dared they force letters on her! And she would have sent it back if her husband had not interfered in everything just before (would he never go to bed!). Now, influenced by her feeling of protest against "interferences," she took a very simple view of the matter. Of course, she should tear the envelope open and read the secrets in it. After all, she had the right (how dared he have secrets!). In an instant Sofia Petrovna was at her dressing table. She had just touched her hand to the letter meant for someone else, when again a whispering was heard on the other side of the wall.

"Well, what is it?"

"Nothing . . . in particular."

The bed set up a plaintive squealing. All grew quiet. And with a trembling hand Sofia Petrovna unsealed . . . and as she read, her swollen little eyes grew big. Their dullness gave way to a dazzling glitter, and her little face flushed in a play of colors: at first it turned rosy pink, and when she had finished, her face was crimson.

Nikolai Apollonovich was totally at her mercy. She had discovered a way to avenge her sufferings by dealing him an irreparable blow, and he would receive that blow from these very hands. He had wanted to frighten her with his buffoonish masquerade, but he had not known how to carry off the buffoonish masquerade properly. Now let him utterly erase that self in her memory, and let him be Hermann! Yes, yes, yes: she would deal him a wicked blow by delivering the letter. For a moment she felt dizzy at the prospect of the course to which she had committed herself. But it was too late to shrink back, to stray from the course. A blood red domino? Since he had evoked the image of a domino before her, then let all the rest come to pass: let him really be a blood red domino!

The door gave a squeak. Sofia Petrovna just managed to crumple the letter in her hand. Standing in the doorway of her bedroom was her husband all in white—in his drawers. The appearance of an outsider in such an indecent state drove her into a fury:

"You could have dressed."

Sergei Sergeyevich got completely flustered, quickly went out, and reappeared in a dressing gown (she had managed to conceal the letter). With an unpleasant firmness, which was unusual for him, he addressed her simply:

"*Sophie*. . . . Give me your promise: you won't go to the soirée tomorrow.

"I hope you will give it. Common sense should tell you as much."

Silence.

"I would like to think that after everything that has just happened, you . . .

"I have given my word of honor as an officer, on your behalf, that you will not be at the ball."†

Silence.

"Otherwise I will be compelled, quite simply, to forbid it."

"All the same, I'm going."

"No, you are not going!!"

She was stunned by the menacing tone with which Sergei Sergeyevich uttered this sentence.

"No, I am going."

A silence ensued, during which the only thing that could be heard was a kind of gurgling from Sergei Sergeyevich, which made him clutch at his throat and shake his head twice, as if attempting to ward off the inevitable. With an incredible effort at suppressing the explosion inside him, he sat down quietly.

"See here, I didn't press you for any details. You were the one to call me to witness."

The thought of what had just occurred forced him to experience something like those depths of depravity into which his wife had begun to slide on an inclined plane. What was depraved about it except for the preposterousness of what had occurred? He sensed that this was no ordinary love affair, no betrayal, and no mere fall. No, no: over all this hung the aroma of excesses, poisoning the soul forever, like prussic acid. He had smelled the odor of bitter almonds when he came in, and he felt a strong choking sensation. He knew

for certain that if Sofia Petrovna, his wife, should turn up tomorrow at the Tsukatovs, if she should meet the domino, everything
would collapse into ruins.

"See here. After what has. . . . Don't you understand that this is
vile, vile. That, when all is said and done, I have given my word
that you will not be there. Have pity on yourself, and on me, and
also on . . . him, because otherwise . . . I . . ."

Sofia Petrovna grew even more indignant at the interference of
this officer, who had dared to appear in her bedroom and interfere
so preposterously. Picking a dress up off the floor (she had noticed
that she was deshabille), and covering herself, she moved off into
the corner. From the shadowy corner she shook her head:

"Perhaps I wouldn't have gone, but *now* I will go, I will go, I
will go!"†

What was that? In the room there was a deafening shot, an inhuman howl, a falsetto cry. And the man of cypress wood leaped
up. The armchair fell over with a crash. The blow of a fist smashed
the dressing table in two.† The door slammed. And everything became deathly quiet.

The strains of the polka-mazurka broke off. There was a stamping up above, a babble of voices. The indignant tenant began
banging on the floor upstairs with a scrub brush.

And Likhutina cringed and broke into offended sobs. For the
first time in her life, she had occasion to meet with sheer fury.
Standing here just now had been not even . . . a man, not even . . .
a beast, but—a mad dog.

The Senator's Second Space

Apollon Apollonovich's bedroom: four perpendicular walls and
the single gash of a window with a lace curtain. The sheets, towels,
and pillowcases were distinguished by their whiteness. The valet
sprayed the sheets with an atomizer.

Instead of perfume, Apollon Apollonovich recognized only triple-
strength eau de cologne.

Apollon Apollonovich always undressed without help.

He would throw off his dressing gown briskly. In a most precise
manner he would fold and place on a chair his little jacket and his
miniature trousers. And in his underwear, just before going to bed,
he would firm up his body with calisthenics.

He would fling his arms and legs apart, and twist his torso, squatting up to twelve and more times. Lying on his back, Apollon
Apollonovich would set about working his legs.

He resorted to exercises especially on the days when he suffered
from hemorrhoids.

Afterwards he would pull up the blanket in order to embark upon a journey, for sleep is a journey.

Apollon Apollonovich did the same today.

Completely covered up (except for the tip of his nose), he hung suspended over a timeless void.

"What do you mean a void? What about the walls, the floor? And so forth?"

Apollon Apollonovich always saw *two* spaces: one, material (the walls of the rooms, of the carriage), the other, not exactly spiritual (it was also material). Now, how should I put it: over Ableukhov's head, Ableukhov's eyes saw bright patches and dots of light, and iridescent dancing spots with spinning centers. They obscured the boundaries of the spaces. Thus one space swarmed in the other space; you know, the kind that seems to be made of Christmas tree tinsel, of little stars and of little sparks.

He would close his eyes and open them. And the misty spots and stars, like foam on bubbling blackness, would unexpectedly and suddenly form into a distinct picture: of a cross, a polyhedron, a swan, a light-filled pyramid. And all would fly apart.

Apollon Apollonovich had his very own secret: a world of contours, tremors, sensations—a *universe* of strange phenomena just before sleep. Apollon Apollonovich, while falling asleep, would remember all the inapprehensibilities of the past, rustlings, little crystallographic figures, stars racing through the gloom (one such star kept drenching the senator with golden boiling water, and shivers ran over his skull). He would remember everything he had seen the day before so as not to remember it again.

Just before the last instant of diurnal consciousness Apollon Apollonovich, while falling asleep, would notice that the bubbling vortex suddenly formed into a corridor stretching off into an immeasurable expanse. What was most surprising was that the corridor began from his head, i.e., it was an endless continuation of his head, the sinciput of which suddenly opened up into an immeasurable expanse. Thus the old senator, just before falling asleep, would get the impression that he was looking not with his eyes but with the center of his very head, i.e., he, Apollon Apollonovich, was not Apollon Apollonovich, but *something* lodged in the brain, looking out from there, from the brain. With the opening up of the sinciput, something could run along the corridor *until it plunged into the abyss.*

That is what the senator's *second space* was.

His head under the blanket, he now hung suspended from the bed. Now the lacquered floor fell away from the legs of the bed into the unknown, but a distant clatter reached the senator's ears, like the clatter of small pounding hooves.

And the clatter was drawing near.

A strange, very strange, extremely strange circumstance: he cocked an ear at the moon, and yes: very likely someone was knocking.

He stuck out his head.

A star moved toward the sinciput and promptly disappeared. The panels of the parquet floor instantly rose up from the abyss to meet the legs of the iron bed. And Apollon Apollonovich, tiny and white, resembling a plucked chicken, suddenly rested his yellow heel on the rug.

And he ran out into the corridor.

The moon illuminated the rooms.

In his undershirt, a lighted candle in his hands, he journeyed forth into the rooms. Trailing after his troubled master was the bulldog with his little docked tail, jangling his collar and breathing heavily through his pug nose.

Like a flat lid, the hairy chest heaved in deep wheezes. And a pale green ear hearkened. And a pier glass gave back a strange reflection of the senator: his arms and chest were swathed in blue satin. The satin gave off a metallic glint. Apollon Apollonovich found himself in armor, like a little knight. From his hands protruded not a candle but a luminous phenomenon.

Apollon Apollonovich plucked up his courage and rushed into the hall. The clatter came from there.

"Tk–tk . . . tk–tk–tk. . . ."

"According to just what article of the Code of Laws?"

As he shouted this out, he saw that the phlegmatic bulldog was breathing heavily and peaceably beside him; but—what effrontery! —from the hall came a shout:

"According to an emergency regulation!"

Indignant at this reply, he rushed into the hall.

The luminous phenomenon was melting away in his little fist. It flowed between his fingers like air; it came to rest at his feet in a little ray. The clatter was the clicking of the tongue of some worthless Mongol with a face he had already seen during his stay in Tokyo. Nonetheless, it was Nikolai Apollonovich: seen in Tokyo. Apollon Apollonovich did not want to understand this. He rubbed his eyes with his little fists (two points rubbed one against the other —the space of the hand and the space of the face). And the Mongol (Nikolai Apollonovich) was approaching with a mercenary motive.

The senator shouted a second time:

"According to just what regulation?

"And what paragraph?"

Space replied:

"There are neither paragraphs nor regulations!"

. . . .

And unknowing, unfeeling, suddenly bereft of weight, of the very sensation of his body, he lifted the space of his pupils upward (tactile sensation could not tell him definitely that his eyes had been lifted upward by him, for the sense of corporeality had been thrown off by him)—in the direction of where the sinciput was located. And he saw there was no sinciput. There, where heavy bones compress the brain, where sight no longer exists, there Apollon Apollonovich saw in Apollon Apollonovich only a gaping circular breach (in place of the sinciput). The breach was a blue circle. At the fateful moment when according to his calculations the Mongol (imprinted on his consciousness but no longer visible) was stealing toward him, something, with a roar like the wind in a chimney, began rapidly pulling his consciousness out through the blue sincipital breach: into that which lies beyond.

Something scandalous had taken place (and his consciousness noted that there had already been something similar but he could not recollect when). Something scandalous had taken place: a wind had blown Apollon Apollonovich out of Apollon Apollonovich.

Apollon Apollonovich flew out through the circular breach, into darkness, above his own head (which looked like the planet *earth*), and—he flew apart into sparks.

There was pretemporal gloom; and consciousness swarmed—not, for example, a universal consciousness, but consciousness, pure and simple.

Putting forth two sensations, consciousness now turned back. They descended like arms, and sensed: a form of some kind (reminiscent of the bottom of a bathtub), filled with stinking abomination. The sensations began splashing about in the bathtub with the dungy water. The sensations now stuck to the vessel. Consciousness struggled to break away, but the sensations were pulling a heavy something.

And consciousness saw that very thing it inhabited: a little old yellow man. He was resting his yellow heels on a rug.

Consciousness proved to be the little old man himself. From his bed the little old man was listening closely to the distant clatter.

And Apollon Apollonovich understood: his journey through the corridor, through the hall, through his head had been only a dream.

And hardly had this thought occurred to him when he woke up: a double dream!

And he was not sitting but lying down, his head under the blanket. The clatter turned out to be a slamming door.

Nikolai Apollonovich had returned home.

"I see . . .

"I see . . .

"Fine."

Except something was wrong with his back: a fear of being touched on the spine. Was this the beginning of:

tabes dorsalis?

End of the Third Chapter

Chapter the Fourth
in which the line of the narrative is broken

God grant I may not lose my mind . . .†
Pushkin

The Summer Garden†

From time to time the sullen pedestrian quickened his step, and was finally lost from view: the Field of Mars cannot be worsted in five minutes.

The Summer Garden lay somber.

The statues each stood hidden beneath boards.† The boards looked like coffins standing on end. The coffins lined the paths. Both nymphs and satyrs had taken shelter in them, so that the tooth of time might not gnaw them away with frost. Time sharpens its teeth for everything—it devours body and soul and stone.

From times of old that garden had grown emptier, grayer, and smaller.† The grotto had fallen into ruin, the fountains splashed no longer, the summer gallery had collapsed, and the waterfall had dried up. The garden had shrunk and now cowered behind the bars.

Peter himself had planted this garden, watering the balsamine and mint with his own hand.† From Solikamsk he had ordered cedars, from Danzig barberries, and from Sweden apple trees. He built fountains all over; and through the shattered, shivered mirrors showed the red camisoles of the well-born, their curling ringlets, and the faces of blackamoors, and ladies' crinolines. Leaning on the faceted knob of a black and gold walking stick, a gray-bewigged cavalier was escorting his lady to the basin; and the snout of a seal protruded from the foaming green waters; and the lady oh'ed and ah'ed. The gray-bewigged cavalier smiled and pointed his walking stick toward the black monster.

The Summer Garden extended further then, encroaching on the expanse of the Field of Mars in allées planted on both sides with greenery and meadowsweet. Enormous shells from Indic seas raised pinkish horns from porous stones, and a well-born person, removing a plumed hat, applied his ear to the opening: a chaotic roar was heard. Fruit drinks were sipped in front of the grotto.

And in later times, beneath the elaborate pose of an Irelli statue, which extended fingers into the darkling day, there was the sound of whispers, sighs, the flash of large pearls from strolling ladies-in-waiting. That was in the spring, on Whit Monday. The evening atmosphere thickened. It trembled under a mighty organlike voice, which flew from sweetly dozing elms, and from there suddenly spread light: festal, green. There, illuminated all in green, horns raised, musicians in bright red huntsmen's garb filled everything around with melody, making the zephyrs tremble: the languid lament of those upraised horns—have you not heard it?†

All that had been; now it is no longer. Paths ran in every direction, and above the roof of Peter's small house† wheeled a frenzied flock. Suddenly it swooped down onto the branches.

Nikolai Apollonovich, clean-shaven, was making his way along a frozen path. There was a strange light in his eyes. Scarcely had he decided to immerse himself in work today when he suddenly received a note. He was being called to a rendezvous in the Summer Garden. And it was signed "S." Who could "S" be? It was Sofia (she must have disguised her handwriting).

Nikolai Apollonovich had an agitated appearance. For about a week now dust had been settling freely onto a page of commentaries on Kant. He felt a sweet current flowing within him—somehow vaguely, remotely. Nameless tremors stirred within him. Perhaps this was love? But he denied love.

He was now looking about uneasily, searching the paths for a familiar outline wearing a black fur coat and carrying a little black fur muff. But there was no one. Not too far off some frumpy female was slumped on a bench. The frumpy female raised herself up, shuffled her feet, and began advancing on him.

"You didn't recognize me?"

"Oh!"

"It seems you still don't recognize me? Why, I'm Solovyova."†

"Varvara Evgrafovna!"

"Well then, let's sit down here."

Nikolai Apollonovich sank down in torment. The rendezvous had been fixed for just this place. What an unfortunate circumstance! Nikolai Apollonovich began trying to think of a way to get rid of this frumpy female as quickly as possible. He looked to the right, to the left, but there was still no sign of the familiar outline.

There, a darkish network of intersecting branches rose and stretched, somewhat dull, against the steely horizon. At times the darkish network set up a murmur, at times the darkish network began to sway.

"Did you receive the note?"

"Which one?"

"Why, the one signed 'S'."

"You mean that's *you*?"

"Why, of course."

"What does 'S' have to do with it?"

"What do you mean? After all, my last name is Solovyova."

Everything collapsed.

"I wanted to . . . I thought . . . did you receive a short poem signed *A Flaming Soul?*"

"No, I didn't."

"How can that be? Is it possible the police are tampering with my letters? Ah! I would like to ask you something about the meaning of life."

.   .   .   .

"Excuse me, Varvara Evgrafovna, I have no time."

"What do you mean?"

"Goodbye! Please excuse me. We'll set a more convenient time for a talk."

Varvara Evgrafovna tugged at his overcoat. He stood up resolutely. He resolutely held out his scented fingers to her. Before she had time to think of something to do, he was already fleeing from her in annoyance, haughtily wrapping himself in the furs of his caped greatcoat. The leaves stirred up from the spot.† They eddied in dry circles about the skirts of the greatcoat. The circles narrowed and curled in ever more restless spirals. The golden spiral whispered something and danced more briskly. A vortex of leaves swirled, wound round and round, and moved off to the side somewhere, off to the side somewhere, without spinning. One red webbed leaf flew up and dipped to the ground. A darkish network of intersecting branches stretched into the steely horizon. He moved into the network, and as he passed, a frenzied flock of crows took wing and began wheeling above the roof of Peter's small house. And the network began to sway and murmur, and timid and doleful sounds winged down. They merged in an organlike swell. The evening atmosphere thickened. The heart felt as if there were no present, as if out of those very trees the somberness would be illuminated by a quivering bright green light. The bright red huntsmen with horns upraised would elicit melodic organ swells from the zephyrs.

Madame Farnois

And my, was it ever late when Angel Peri deigned to open her innocent little eyes from the depths of the pillows! But the little eyes kept closing. She deigned to remain in a state of drowsiness for quite a while longer. Beneath her curls swarmed things inapprehensible and restless, half-hints. And her first thought was the thought of the soirée that evening: what *ever* is going to happen there! But when she tried to develop this thought, her little eyes shut; the restless feelings, the half-hints started up again. One thing alone emerged: Pompadour, Pompadour, Pompadour! And why Pompadour?† But her soul illumined the word: the Pompadour costume—Valenciennes lace, silvery slippers, pompons! In the last few days she had been having long arguments with her dressmaker. Madame Farnois had not wanted to yield on the matter of blonde lace: "Why do you want blonde lace?" But how could she do without blonde lace? Madame Farnois at first had said: "With your taste and mine, how can it not be in the style of Madame Pompadour!" But Sofia Petrovna had not wanted to yield, and Madame Farnois proposed that she take the fabric back. "Take it to Maison Tricotons. There, Madame, they wouldn't think of contradicting you." But to give it to Tricotons—fie, fie, fie! And the blonde lace was abandoned, as was the chapeau Bergère. But without a pannier for the long skirt—impossible.

On this they reached an understanding.

As she became absorbed in her reflections on Madame Farnois, Angel Peri had the tormenting feeling that once again everything was all wrong and that something really had happened. But using her drowsiness as an excuse, she did not want to try to catch at the elusive impression of the events that had actually occurred yesterday. At last she recalled: the *domino and the letter*. And she sprang out of bed, and recalled: there had been a third word of some kind, which had been in her mind as she fell asleep. The third word was: husband, officer!

Now she had to confront an unattractive word, for no sooner had she rushed to the closed door of her husband's room—assuming that her husband, Second Lieutenant Likhutin, had gone off as usual to be in charge of provisions—when suddenly, to her amazement, she found the room locked against her. Second Lieutenant Likhutin had ensconced himself there.

Only now did she recall yesterday's outrageous scene. And she slammed her bedroom door. (He had locked himself in? So would she!) But after locking herself in, she noticed the broken dressing table.

"Would you like your coffee in your room, madam?"

"I don't want any."

.   .   .   .

"Someone's here, madam!"

"From Madame Farnois?"

"No, from the laundry!"

.   .   .   .

Silence.

At midday a cuirassier called with a two-pound bonbonniere of chocolates, from Krafft's. The bonbonniere was received. He was not.

Around two o'clock a life-uhlan called with a bonbonniere from Ballet's:† not received.

A life-hussar was also not received.

At close to ten a girl from Madame Farnois appeared armed with a box and was promptly received. There was tittering, the bedroom door gave a click and a curious tear-stained little face poked out in curiosity. An irritated shout rang out:

"Why, bring it in at once!"

But at the same time a head poked out of the study, took a good look, and withdrew.

Petersburg Vanished into the Night

An enormous crimson sun raced above the Neva, and the buildings of Petersburg seemed to be melting away, turning into the lightest of smoky amethyst lace. The windowpanes sent off cutting flame-gold reflections, and from the tall spires flashed rubies. And indentations and projections stretched away into the burning conflagration: caryatids, cornices of brick balconies.

The rust red Palace bled. It had been built by Rastrelli.† At that time the old palace had been an azure wall amidst a white flock of columns; the late Empress Elizaveta Petrovna would open her window onto the distances of the Neva. Under Alexander Pavlovich the palace had been repainted yellow. Under Emperor Alexander the Second the palace had been repainted a second time: it became rust red.

The row of lines and walls was slowly darkening against the waning lilac sky, and sparking torches flamed here and there, and here and there blazed the tiniest of flames.

And there the past was having its sunset.

A short plump lady, all in black, was walking about beneath the windows of a yellow house. A little reticule, not in the fashion of Petersburg, trembled slightly in her hand. She suffered from shortness of breath. Again and again her fingers plucked at her chin, which was dotted with little gray hairs. She was trying to open the little reticule with trembling fingers, but the little reticule would not obey. Finally the little reticule opened and the lady took out a small handkerchief. And she turned toward the Neva, and she began to weep.

Finally, she hurried to the entryway, and rang.

The door flew open. The little old man with gold braid who had opened the door thrust a bald patch out of the opening and screwed up eyes made teary by the unbearable glare from beyond the Neva.

The lady grew agitated: perhaps because she was deeply moved, perhaps because she was trying to hide her timidity.

"Don't you recognize me?"

At this the lackey's bald patch began to tremble and it fell onto the tiny reticule (onto her hand):

"Oh, our dear lady, our dear mistress! Anna Petrovna!"

"Yes, here I am, Semyonych . . ."

"How did you get here? Where from?"

"From Spain . . . I just want to see how you're getting along here without me."

"Our dear mistress, our own. . . . Do come in, please!"

The entire staircase was still covered by that same velvety carpet. The same display of weapons glittered. Under the watchful eye of the mistress a Lithuanian helmet had once been hung here, and there—a sword completely rusted through. Still glittering were the Lithuanian helmet from here, the cross-hilted sword from there.

"But there's no one home, ma'm, not the young master, not . . ."

Above the balustrade still stood the same pedestal of white alabaster as before.

"How have you been getting along without me?"

"Not at all, ma'm . . . otherwise, no particular consequences: everything like before, ma'm. Have you heard about the master, Apollon Apollonovich?"

"I have."

"Yes, ma'm, every kind of honor. By the Tsar's grace and favor! . . ."

"And what about Kolenka?"

"Kolenka, ma'm, Nikolai Apollonovich, that is, what a smart young lad if I may say so! He's gotten so good looking."

Placed along the walls were long-legged chairs. From everywhere between the chairs reared slender cold columns. Cold male alabaster figures gazed from atop the slender white columns. And over there were paintings in pale tones: frescoes of Pompeii. Lacquer and luster enveloped her, the same oppressive feeling as before, the old hostility. Oh, yes: in the lacquered house the storms of life were flowing—noiselessly and destructively.

"Will you be staying with us, madam?"

"I? . . . I'm staying in a hotel."

· · · · · · ·

In this melting gray, dots appeared in windows and stared in amazement: lights, little lights, tiny lights. They swelled in intensity. They stood out in rust-colored blots. And from on high fell the blue, dark violet, black of the night!

Their Dancing Slippers Tapped

The doorbell kept ringing.

Beings in blue, white, and pink gowns, in a swirl of gossamer, fans, silks, exuded an atmosphere of violet, lily-of-the-valley and tuberose. Their delicate shoulders, shoulders dusted with powder, were soon to be covered with perspiration. Just before the dancing began, faces, shoulders and bare arms seemed paler and thinner than on ordinary days. Their white fans fluttered. Their dancing slippers tapped.

The doorbell kept ringing.

What looked like broad-chested genii in tight-fitting tailcoats, in uniforms and in pelisses entered: students of the law, hussars and just others—without beards. They exuded an unfailing joyfulness and reserve. They penetrated the glittering gossamer circle. And lo and behold—a light downy fan was now beating like a butterfly wing upon the chest of a student of the law. A broad-chested hussar was exchanging suggestive and frivolous remarks. And against the red background of hussar attire a slightly pink profile stood out.

The Tsukatovs, strictly speaking, were not giving a ball: it was merely a children's party, in which the grownups wanted to take part. It was rumored that there would even be maskers. The possibility of their appearance was surprising, if truth be told. The host, the possessor of two silver sidewhiskers, was called Coco. In this dancing household he was known as Nikolai Petrovich, the head of the household, the father of two girls: of eighteen and fifteen.

These sweet beings were wearing gossamer gowns and silver dancing slippers. They waved their downy fans at the housekeeper, the maid, and the mastodonically proportioned zemstvo official[†] (a relative of Coco) who was visiting them. Finally came the long-awaited ring. The door of the brilliantly lighted ballroom flew open, and a hired pianist, poured into a tight-fitting tailcoat and resembling a long-legged black bird, bumped into a passing waiter, and made him rattle a pasteboard tray all covered with party favors. The diffident hired pianist spread out a row of sheet music. He gently dusted the piano keys. From time to time and without visible purpose he would depress the pedal, which made him resemble a conscientious locomotive engineer testing his boilers. Reassured that the instrument was in good working order, the hired pianist tucked up the tails of his coat, set himself down on the low stool, flung back his torso, and let his fingers fall on the keys. And he froze, and then a thunderous chord shook the walls.

With his fingers Nikolai Petrovich Tsukatov parted the silvery lace of his sidewhiskers. His bald spot and smoothly shaven chin glistened. He scurried from couple to couple, here dropping an innocent little joke to a youth in pale blue, there jabbing his fingers into the broad chest of a mustachioed man.

The air was alive with flashes and quivers. There was a deafening "Rre–cul–ez! . . .

"Balancez vos dames!"

And again:

"Rrre–cul–ez. . . ."

Nikolai Petrovich Tsukatov had spent his whole life dancing, and now Nikolai Petrovich was dancing that life to a close. He was dancing it out inoffensively, without vulgarity. No cloud darkened his soul, which always shone, as did his bald spot, which glowed like the sun, or as did his shaven chin between sidewhiskers, which looked like the crescent moon between clouds.

Everything in his life had always gone dancingly.

He had begun to dance while still a boy. He danced better than anyone else. Toward the end of his Gymnasium days new acquaintances had danced into his life. Toward the end of his university days he had danced himself out of the circle of acquaintances into a circle of protectors. Nikolai Petrovich launched into dancing out a career. He danced an estate down the drain, and he launched into balls. With remarkable ease he brought into his house his helpmeet Lyubov Alexeyevna. The helpmeet proved to have a dowry, and Nikolai Petrovich now danced in his own house. He had succeeded in dancing out the birth of two daughters and their education.

So that now he was dancing himself out.

The Ball

During a merry waltz the drawing room is an appendage: a refuge for mamas. But Lyubov Alexeyevna, taking advantage of her husband's good nature and the fact that their household was profoundly indifferent to everything and was a neutral place, taking advantage of this, she left it to her husband to preside over the dances. She presided over meetings between persons of all kinds. Here met: a zemstvo official and a government official; journalists and the director of a Department; a demagogue and an anti-Semite. This household had been visited, even lunched in by Apollon Apollonovich.

And while her husband wove the patterns of the contredanse, more than one conjuncture of circumstances was being woven in this indifferently cordial drawing room.

Here too people were dancing: in their own way.

This evening visitors to the drawing room were threading their way through the ballroom. A man of truly antediluvian mien and distracted visage was threading his way through, one of his coattails hitched up, causing his half-belt to stick out between the skirts of his coat. He was a professor of statistics.† A ragged beard hung from his chin, and onto his shoulders drooped his feltlike mane.

In view of developing events, something on the order of a rapprochement was in the making between one of the groups of partisans of moderate, humanitarian reforms, and those with patriotic hearts—a conditional rapprochement brought about by the avalanche of mass meetings. The partisans of gradual, humanitarian reforms, shaken by the roar of the avalanche, had in their fright begun snuggling up to the partisans of the existing norms. But as yet they had not taken the first step. The liberal professor, however, had undertaken to step across (so to speak) this fateful threshold. Let us not forget that the latest protest petition had been signed by him, and at the latest banquet† his glass had been raised to greet the coming spring.

Entering the ballroom, the professor felt discomfited. His lower lip dropped away from his mouth. He was at a loss for words, and he fished a handkerchief out of his pocket to wipe the damp from his mustache. He blinked at the couples flying in the patterns of the quadrille.

He moved toward the drawing room, into the tremulous light of an azure chandelier.

A voice stopped him on the threshold:

"Don't you understand, madam, the connection between the war with Japan, the kikes, and the Mongol invasion? The antics of our Russian kikes and the emergence of the Boxers in China are closely connected."

"I understand, I understand!"

But the professor came to a stop. He was a liberal, a partisan of truly humanitarian reforms. He had come to this house for the first time, hoping to meet Senator Ableukhov here. But apparently he was not here. The editor of a conservative newspaper was. And the professor of statistics began huffing and puffing, blinking angrily, and snorting into his raggedy beard.

But the hostess's double chin had already turned to the professor, and it had turned to the editor of a conservative newspaper. With her lorgnette she presented each to the other. Both were taken aback, and then each slipped his fingers into the other's.

The professor was embarrassed, made a slight bow and gave a snort, sat down in an armchair and began to fidget, while the editor acted as if nothing had happened. Ableukhov could have rescued him, but Ableukhov was not there.

Meanwhile was heard:

"Do you understand, madam, the activity of Jew-Masonry?"

The professor could bear it no longer. Turning to the hostess, he observed:

"Allow me, madam, to interject a modest scientific remark. The source of such 'information' is clear: the pogrom mentality!"

Meanwhile, over there, over there . . .

Elegantly striking a thundering bass chord, the hired pianist ended the dance tune. With his other hand he turned the music expertly. His hand suspended in air between the keyboard and the music, his fingers spread, he turned his torso expectantly toward the host, flashing the enamel of his dazzling white teeth.

In response to the pianist's gesture, Tsukatov unexpectedly thrust his chin from between his sidewhiskers, giving his special signal to the pianist. And then, head lowered, butting at empty space, he rushed about in front of the couples, twisting the end of a graying sidewhisker with two fingers. Running after him, an angelic being helplessly trailed her heliotrope scarf. But Tsukatov flew at the pianist, roaring like a lion for all the ballroom to hear:

"Pas-de-quatre, s'il vous plaît!"

And after him flew the helpless being, her heliotrope scarf unfurling. Servants appeared running smartly into the corridor. From somewhere small tables, stools and chairs were carried out and carried in. A mountain of freshly made sandwiches was carried in on a platter. A stack of delicate china plates was carried in.

Couple after couple poured through the corridor. Chairs were moved about.

Curls of cigarette smoke rose in the corridor and in the smoking room. They rose in the vestibule. Pulling off a glove and thrusting his hand into his pocket, a young cadet fanned his cheeks with a glove darkened by perspiration. Two young girls were hugging and telling each other secrets of the heart which perhaps were just a few minutes old.

Visible from the corridor was a corner of the buzzing dining room, to which open-faced sandwiches, bottles of wine, and bottles of sparkling drinks were being carried.

And now no one remained in the ballroom but the hired pianist, wiping his burning fingers and passing a cloth over the keys. In his presence the servants opened the vents in all the windows one after the other. Now, resembling a long-legged black bird, he hesitantly set out along the lacquered corridor. He was looking forward with pleasure to tea and sandwiches.

Through the doors floated a forty-five-year-old lady, her chin falling onto her bosom. She was looking through her lorgnette.

A little way off, the professor of statistics stumbled upon the zemstvo official, who was standing, bored, by the passageway. He recognized him, smiled affably, and plucked at a button of his frock coat with two fingers as if grasping at his last means of salvation. And now was heard:

"According to statistical data . . . the annual rate of consumption of salt by the average Dutchman . . ."

As If Someone Were Lamenting

They were waiting for the maskers. And there were no maskers. Apparently it had only been a rumor.

The tinkle of the doorbell was heard. Someone uninvited was giving a reminder of his existence. He was seeking admission out of the fog, out of the slush of the street. But no one answered. Again came a ring.

A ten-year-old-girl ran out into the glittering depopulated ball-room. A door banged out there. A faceted knob began to turn. When a void had formed between the wall and the edge of the door, a black half-mask thrust its nose in.

A black beard of curling lace materialized. After the beard, satin appeared in the door, and the child gave a joyful smile, clapped her hands and with a shriek—"The maskers are here!"—rushed back into the depths of the house, where a befogged professor standing on fat legs could scarcely be made out in the hanging clumps of bluish tobacco smoke.

The domino, stepping over the threshold, trailed its bloody satin across the parquetry. It was barely mirrored in the panels which shimmered in a crimson ripple of its own reflections, as if a little pool of blood were flowing from panel to panel. Heavy footsteps started stamping toward it.

And the zemstvo official stopped in perplexity, clutching at a tuft of his beard. The lonely domino begged not to be driven out into the Petersburg slush, begged not to be driven out into the malignant fog. The zemstvo official apparently wanted to make a little joke, and grunted:

"Mm . . . yes, yes. . . ."

The domino was advancing on him, a bright red arm outstretched.

"Tell me, please . . ."

The masker kept entreating. He rushed past, torso thrust forward.

"Well, how do you like that. . . ."

Suddenly with a wave of the hand he turned and began to make his way back to the place where in azure electric light the professor of statistics was standing motionless, foggily visible in the clumps of tobacco smoke. He was almost knocked over by a swarm of young ladies, who came running, waving their ribbons and party favors.

The swarm ran out to have a look at the masker who had strayed in. They stopped by the door. Gay exclamations were followed by a confused rustling. The rustling ceased. There was silence. Behind the young ladies, someone unexpectedly recited:

> Who are you, stern, awesome guest,
> Fateful domino?
> Look: in crimson he's come dressed,
> Draped in cape aflow.†

And someone stammered:

"Tell us, domino, aren't you the one who's been running about on the prospects?"

"My friends, have you read today's 'Daily Chronicle'?"

"What about it?"

"Why—the domino again. . . ."

"My friends, that's nonsense."

Suddenly one of the young ladies, the one who had fixed a stern gaze on the unexpected guest, began whispering to her girlfriend quite distinctly:

"Oh, it's all nonsense!"

"Not at all, not at all!"

"Has the cat got the nice domino's tongue?"

"Nothing can be done with him."

"And he calls himself a domino!"

"And what do you say to this?"

This was shouted by a young cadet, and he sent a rustling stream of confetti at the domino over the motley heads of the young ladies. For an instant the arc of a paper streamer uncoiled in the air. As the paper arc coiled, it lost momentum and fell to the floor. The domino did not react. It merely stretched out its arms. Suddenly someone said:

"Friends, let's go back."

And the swarm ran off.

Only she who was closest of all to the domino lingered for a moment. She measured the domino with her gaze, for some reason gave a sigh, and walked away, and again turned around.

A Wizened Little Figure

Nikolai Apollonovich, as if in a fog, caught sight of the estimable zemstvo official, while somewhere in the distance, in a labyrinth of mirrors, figures of laughing young ladies swam past before him. And when he was assaulted by remote echoes of questions from this labyrinth, and by the thin paper serpent of confetti, he marveled, as one marvels in a dream: at the emergence of a reflection into the real world. He himself looked at everything that existed as wavering reflections; as for the reflections, they took him merely for a ghost who had emerged from the other world. He had scared them away.

Now once again distant echoes of events reached him. And he turned, and somewhere there, somewhere there—indistinct, phantasmal—a little figure, without hair, without mustache, without eyebrows, cut quickly across the ballroom. From the strain of peering through the slits Nikolai Apollonovich felt a sharp pain in his eyes (moreover, he suffered from nearsightedness). Greenish ears were distinctly outlined somewhere there, somewhere there. Something about it was familiar, intimate, and alive, and Nikolai Apollonovich rushed toward the little figure to get a close look. The little figure reeled back, even seemed to clutch at its heart, and was now looking at him. Before him was a kindred face, all covered with tiny wrinkles which had eaten away at his cheeks, forehead and chin. From a distance it could have been taken for the face of a eunuch (and a young one rather than old). But close up it was actually a decrepit old man with prominent sidewhiskers. In a word, under his very nose, Nikolai Apollonovich saw his father. Apollon Apollonovich, fingering the links of his watch chain, had fastened frightened eyes on the advancing satin domino. Something like a surmise flashed through his mind. Nikolai Apollonovich felt an unpleasant shuddering: despite everything, it was terrifying to look from behind the mask at that gaze, before which he always lowered his eyes otherwise. Despite everything, it was terrifying to read the fright and helplessness in that gaze. And the surmise was read as a certainty, and Nikolai Apollonovich thought that he had been recognized. That was not so. Apollon Apollonovich was thinking that some prankster with no sense of tact was trying to terrorize him with the symbolic color red.

And he began taking his pulse. Nikolai Apollonovich had more than once noticed this gesture which was made on the sly (apparently, the senator's heart was getting tired of functioning). And seeing the gesture now, he felt something akin to pity. But Apollon Apollonovich hurried off, his heart racing.†

Suddenly the doorbell rang: the room filled with maskers. Black Capuchins formed a chain around their red confrere and broke into a dance of sorts. The hems of their cassocks swirled. The points of their cowls flew up and down: embroidered on each was a skull and crossbones.

At this, the red domino, trying to shake loose, fled from the ballroom. The Capuchins raced after him in pursuit. Thus they flew
along the corridor and flew into the dining room. All those sitting
at the tables began banging their plates in welcome:

"Capuchins, maskers, clowns."

Flocks of young ladies jumped up from their places. Up jumped
hussars and students of the law. Holding a goblet of Rhine wine,
Tsukatov bellowed his "vivat."

And someone remarked:

"Friends, this is too much."

He was dragged off to dance.

In the ballroom the hired pianist, arching his spine, set his shock
of hair dancing over his flying fingers which were pouring out
roulades: the treble started up and the bass slowly got under way.

After taking a good look at a black Capuchin with satins all
awhirl, a being in a violet skirt suddenly leaned toward the opening
in the Capuchin's cowl (a mask stared her in the face). She grasped
the hump of a striped clown, one of whose legs (blue) flew up,
while the other (red) bent. But the being was undaunted: she raised
her hem slightly, and a silvery dancing slipper peeped forth.

And off they danced—one, two, three . . .

And all the señoritas, monks, and devils set off after them, fans,
bare backs, and scarves.

Pompadour

Everything stretched away there, and—there, there was the murky
blur of walls and floor. Out of a fountain of things, out of a muslin-
lace foam—there, there—was emerging a beautiful woman with lux-
uriantly fluffed hair and a beauty spot on her cheek. It was Madame
Pompadour!

The hair, curled in ringlets, was gray. The powderpuff was
poised in tiny slender fingers above the powderbox. Tightly cor-
seted, she bent forward from her pale azure waist, a black mask in
her hand. From the decolletage heaving breasts showed in shadowy
outline, from narrow short sleeves frothed Valenciennes lace. This
lace frothed around the decolletage, below the decolletage. The
pannier skirt, which seemed puffed out by the breath of zephyrs,
sparkled with a garland of silver vines shaped in delicate festoons.
On a dancing slipper gleamed a silver pompon. But this attire did
not improve her appearance. Her heavy lips pouted too much, her
eyes were slightly crossed, and there was something witchlike
about her.

Mavrushka handed her a light-colored staff with a gold handle
from which fluttered ribbons. When Pompadour reached for the

staff, she found a note: "If you go out, you will never again return to my house. Likhutin."

Madame Pompadour smiled and stared into the mirror, into its greenish murk. Out of the murky depths thrust a waxen face: and she turned around.

Her husband, the officer, was standing behind her. She burst into laughter, and, raising her pannier skirt slightly by the festoons, she sailed away from him in graceful curtsies. Her crinoline rustled and swayed. And when she was in the doorway she smilingly thumbed her nose at the officer with the hand from which a satiny mask dangled. She broke into peals of laughter.

"Mavrushka, my coat!"

Then Second Lieutenant Likhutin, calm, and smiling at the mask, jangled his spurs, and deferentially stood with her fur coat in his hand. With even greater deference he draped the coat over her shoulders, opened the door wide and politely showed her the way out, out into the darkling dark. While she passed, all a-rustle, out into the darkness, her humble servant clicked his spurs. Darkness surged from everywhere, and the outer door slammed. Sergei Sergeyevich Likhutin, with those same abrupt gestures, began pacing about everywhere and everywhere extinguishing the electric lights.

The Fateful

Elegantly striking a thundering bass chord with one hand, the hired pianist expertly turned the music with the other. Nikolai Petrovich Tsukatov unexpectedly thrust his smooth-shaven chin from between his sidewhiskers and exclaimed:

"Pas-de-quatre, s'il vous plaît!"

Without recognizing Madame Pompadour, Nikolai Apollonovich offered her his hand. And glancing at the red cavalier with a gesture of her upturned mask, Madame Pompadour extended a submissive hand. With her other kid-gloved hand (holding a fluttering fan), Madame Pompadour raised her azure hem slightly, and a dancing slipper peeped forth.

And off they danced, off they danced.

One, two, three, and—the gesture of a little foot!

"Do you recognize me?"

"No."

One, two, three, and—a plié, and a dancing slipper peeped forth.

"I have a letter."

Behind the first pair—the domino and the marquise—there set out: harlequins, señoritas, prim young beings, fans, silvery backs, and scarves.

One arm of the red domino encircled the azure waist, while the other, taking her hand, felt a letter in its hand. The dark green, black, and worsted arms of the gentlemen in each couple, along with red hussar arms, grasped all the slender waists of the heliotrope, gris-de-perle, rustling ladies.

.   .   .   .

Apollon Apollonovich tried to hide the signs of his heart trouble. Today's bout had been brought on by the appearance of the red domino. The color red was emblematic of the chaos that was leading Russia to its doom.

Apollon Apollonovich was ashamed that he had been frightened.

Recovering from this bout, he cast glances about the ballroom. The images that flitted there left such a repulsive aftertaste: he saw a monster with a double-eagled head. Cutting across the ballroom was the wizened little figure of a knight whose bright sword blade had the image and likeness of a luminous phenomenon. It hurried off, indistinct and bleary. It was without hair, without mustache, greenish ears distinctly outlined and a diamond-studded decoration dangling from the chest. From among the maskers and Capuchins a one-horned being hurled itself upon the little knight and broke off the knight's luminous phenomenon. From a distance something clanked and fell in the likeness of a beam of light. This picture awakened in his consciousness the memory of some incident in the past. And he became aware of his spine, thinking that he had tabes dorsalis. He turned away from the ballroom; he passed into the drawing room.

At his appearance everyone rose, and the professor of statistics drawled:

"We have had occasion to meet! I am happy to see you. I have a matter to discuss with you, Apollon Apollonovich."

To which Apollon Apollonovich replied drily:

"But my dear sir, I receive from one to two in the Office."

With this reply he cut off all possibility of a meeting between the government and. . . . The conjuncture of circumstances disjunctured. The professor had no alternative but to leave that household and in the future to raise his glass at banquets without inhibition.

The editor of the conservative newspaper orated on:

"You think that the ruin of Russia is being planned in hopes of achieving social equality. Fat chance! They want to sacrifice us to the devil."

"What?" asked the hostess in surprise.

"You are surprised because you've read nothing."

"Excuse me, please," interjected the professor, "you are relying on the fabrications of Taxil."†

"Taxi?" interrupted the hostess, who fished out her notebook and began writing it down:

"Taxi?"

"They are preparing to sacrifice us. The higher degrees of Masonry have been converted to Palladism. This cult . . ."

"Palladism?" interrupted the hostess. Once again she began writing it down in her notebook.

"Pa-lla-. . . . How do you spell it?"

A tray with cooling fruit punch had already been brought in. It was set down in the room between the drawing room and the ballroom. Now one, now another young girl, ablaze with light, face flushed, broke out of the ripple of dancing couples, broke out and ran in white silk dancing slippers into the adjoining room, delicate heels tapping. She hastily poured the tart moisture from a pitcher, and swallowed it.

And fluttering out behind her came a student of the law, and rolling his "r's" like a Frenchman, in a newly acquired bass voice, kept snatching the fruit punch from the young girl and taking a sip.

And the happy couple rushed back into the seething ballroom. And the student of the law embraced the young girl's waist with a snowy glove. The young girl flung herself back against the snow white glove. Both suddenly began to fly about and sway in rapture, their feet flashing and shattering the patterns of the gowns and fans that flew all around them. They themselves became what seemed like radiant splashes of light.

. . . .

"Taxil fabricated a scurrilous fiction about the Masons and people believed it. But later Taxil admitted that his statement to the Pope had only been a way of mocking the obscurantism of the Vatican, and for this he was excommunicated."

In came a fussy little fellow with an enormous wart by his nose. He began smiling at the senator and rubbing his fingers together. He led him off into a corner:

"You see, Apollon Apollonovich . . . the Director of Department X has proposed . . . to ask you a ticklish question."

The little fellow could be heard whispering into the pale ear, and Apollon Apollonovich said in a kind of fright:

"Speak to the point."

"That's precisely it, that's just the question."

"So my son? . . ."

"It's a pity the joke has already assumed such an inappropriate character, that the press . . .

"And you know, we have turned the matter over to the city police . . .

"Naturally, it's only for his own good. . . ."

The senator asked:

"The domino, you say?"

"That one over there."

The fussy little fellow indicated the adjoining room, where the stoop-shouldered domino, moving about in fits and starts, trailed his satin over the panels of parquetry.

A Scandalous Uproar†

The domino went out of the ballroom and into a corner. He tore open the envelope. The note crackled in his rustling hands. In an attempt to see better, the domino pushed the half-mask up on his forehead; the lace beard fell in two luxuriant folds on either side of his face like two wings on a woman's hat. And his hand trembled, and the note trembled. Sweat appeared on his brow.

Now the domino did not see Madame Pompadour, who was observing him from a corner. He was engrossed in reading. He had thrown open the satin flaps of the domino, revealing his ordinary suit, a dark green frock coat. Nikolai Apollonovich pulled out a gold pince-nez, and applying it to his eyes, he bent over to read the note.

Suddenly his entire body reeled back. He stared ahead in horror. But he did not see her, and Sofia Petrovna now wanted to rush from the corner, for she could not endure a gaze like that. People came in. The domino nervously concealed the note in his hand. But the red domino forgot to lower his mask and stood, mask raised, his mouth half open, his eyes unseeing.

A young girl ran up and stopped before a pier glass. Resting a foot on the chair, she was tying her white dancing slipper.

Suddenly she caught sight of the domino with raised mask and she exclaimed:

"So that's who you are! Hello, Nikolai Apollonovich, hello there! Who would have recognized you?"

Nikolai Apollonovich gave a strange sort of jerk and broke into a run: into the ballroom.

There were two rows of dancers in a shimmering play of pink, gris-de-perle, heliotrope, light blue, and white silks: shoulders were draped with shawls, scarves, veils, and bugle-beads; backs glittered like scales.

There were two rows of dancers in black, green, and red hussar worsteds, gold collars, and padded shoulders.

But Nikolai Apollonovich flew headlong past the maskers, and the bloody satin trailed behind him on the small lacquered panels.

The flight of the red domino, mask upraised, face thrust forward, created a really scandalous uproar. People rushed from their places. There were hysterics. In fright, maskers revealed their dumfounded faces. Recognizing the fleeing Ableukhov, Shporyshev grabbed him by the sleeve: "Nikolai Apollonovich, for heaven's sake, what's wrong with you?" But Nikolai Apollonovich bared his teeth in a pitiful-looking attempt to laugh. He could not manage a smile. He disappeared through the doorway.

Young ladies exchanged impressions with one another. The maskers—all the little knights, harlequins, señoritas—who only minutes ago were mysteriously gliding about, now lost all meaning. From behind the mask of the two-headed monster, who ran up to Shporyshev, a voice was heard:

"What does all this mean?"

And Shporyshev recognized the voice: it was Verhefden!

The commotion in the ballroom was transmitted to the drawing room. There the guests stood in the tremulous azure light, foggily visible in the clumps of bluish tobacco smoke, and they looked in alarm. And the wizened little figure of the senator stood out—lips pursed, two sidewhiskers and the outline of ears. Thus had he been portrayed on the cover of some trashy rag.

But in the ballroom an epidemic of surmises ran riot with respect to the strange behavior of the senator's loving son. It was said, in the first place, that this behavior was the result of some drama in his personal life, and the rumor was launched that Nikolai Apollonovich was the very same domino who was creating a sensation in the press.

But What If . . .

Sofia Petrovna Likhutina stopped in the middle of the ballroom.

Before her rose a picture of her terrible vengeance. The little envelope had now passed into his hands. She scarcely understood what she had done. She had not understood what she had read yesterday. But now she clearly pictured the contents of the note: the letter invited him to throw some sort of bomb, which, it seemed, was located in his desk. It was proposed, so it seemed, that he throw the bomb at . . .

And Sofia Petrovna stood among the maskers, barely bending forward from her azure waist, wondering what all this meant. Of course, it was a vicious and base joke. She had wanted to use the joke to frighten him: he was a coward. But what if . . . what was in the letter was true? What if . . . Nikolai Apollonovich was keeping a bomb in his desk? And if people found out about it? Would he now be arrested?

Then she began twisting and turning uneasily. Her Valenciennes lace fluttered, and the garland of delicate festoons sparkled on her skirt. A small cluster of gray-browed matrons was making ready to leave a ball that offered *this* kind of merriment. One of them, stretching out her neck, called to her daughter, a shepherdess. And another, raising a miniature lorgnette, grew uneasy. The disquieting atmosphere of something scandalous hung in the air.

And plaints and whispers could be heard.

"No, but did you see? Do you understand?"

"Don't speak of it, it's horrible."

"I have always said, *ma chère*, that he had raised a scoundrel. *Tante Lise* said so, and *Nicolas* said so."

"Poor Anna Petrovna. I can understand her!"

"There he is!"

"He has horrible ears."

"He's to be made a minister."

"He will lead the country to its doom."

"He has to be told."

"And how the Tsukatovs are fawning on him! It's simply disgusting to watch."

"They won't dare tell him why we are leaving. *Madame* Tsukatov comes from a line of priests."

.   .   .   .

But what if . . . Nikolai Apollonovich was really keeping in his desk . . . ? He might bump against the desk (he was so absentminded). In the evening he perhaps pursued his studies at this desk, a book open in front of him. Sofia Petrovna clearly imagined the sclerotic Ableukhov forehead with small bluish veins, bent over the desk (and in the desk—a bomb). A bomb was something that must not be touched. And a shudder went through Sofia Petrovna.

An obese man (a Spaniard from Granada) suddenly glued himself to Sofia Petrovna.† She stepped to the side, and the Spaniard from Granada also stepped to the side:

"You're no high-born lady, you're just a sweetie-pie."

"Lippanchenko!" And she struck him with her fan.

"Lippanchenko! Kindly explain to me . . ."

But Lippanchenko interrupted:

"Don't play naive."

"Lippanchenko!"

"I saw how you delivered . . ."

He said with a greasy laugh:

"Come away with me into this wondrous night. . . ."

She tore away from Lippanchenko.

He clicked his castanets in pursuit.

But what if this wasn't a joke, and what if. . . . No, no! Such horrors do not exist in this world. No one could be so monstrous as to force a lunatic son to. . . . All this must be just a joke on the part of his friends. She had been foolish enough to let this friendly joke frighten her. And look at him, look at him: he too had been frightened by this friendly joke. Why, he was simply a little coward. He had run away there too (at the Winter Canal). She did not regard the Canal as any prosaic spot from which one could run away.

He had not conducted himself like Hermann. He had slipped, fallen, and exposed his trouser straps. Now he had not had the sense to laugh at the naive joke of his friends, the revolutionaries. He had not recognized her as the bearer of the letter. He had run through the ballroom, the laughingstock of the cavaliers and their ladies. No, let Sergei Sergeyevich teach this insolent coward a lesson! He would challenge him to a duel.

Sergei Sergeyevich Likhutin! Since last night he had been conducting himself in a most unseemly manner: snorting into his mustache and clenching his fist, entering her bedroom in nothing but his drawers, having the gall to pace about in the very next room until the wee hours.

She dimly pictured yesterday's insane shouts, the bloodshot eyes and the falling fist. Could it be that he had lost his mind? He had been acting suspiciously for a long time: his silence of three whole months. His running off to work all the time was suspicious too. She was all alone, poor thing. She wanted her husband to embrace her like a child, to lift and carry her in his arms. . . .

Instead up jumped the Spaniard.

"How about it? Aren't you coming?"

Where was Sergei Sergeyevich? She was fearful of returning to the small apartment on the Moika where he would be lying in wait, like a beast.

She stamped her little heels.

"I'll show him!"

And again:

"I'll teach him a lesson!"

Sofia Petrovna Likhutina gave a shudder as she remembered the grimace with which Sergei Sergeyevich had handed her the cloak. The way he had stood there! The way she had burst out laughing, raising her pannier skirt slightly by the festoons, and had sailed away from him in curtsies (why hadn't she curtsied when she delivered the letter—curtsies were becoming to her)! She was fearful of returning home.

But it was even more terrible here. Almost everyone had gone their separate ways, the young people and the maskers. The host was walking about telling a story. He cast a forlorn glance at the emptying ballroom and the crowd of harlequins.

But the harlequins had swarmed together and were comporting themselves in a strange way. One of them began dancing and singing:

> The von Sulitzes withdrew,
> Gone Ableukhov too . . .
> The prospects, streets, the harbor
> Are filled with fateful rumor! . . .
> And you, perfidious perjurer,
> You praised the wicked senator . . .
> But there's no law in Russia more,
> The criminal code all now ignore!
> Just look, the patriotic dog
> Wears medals like a pompous frog;
> But behavior terroristic
> Is the time's characteristic.

In the twinkling of an eye Nikolai Petrovich grasped how utterly tasteless the ditty was. He flushed deeply. He gave the carrot-colored harlequin a most genial look. He walked away from the door.

· · · · · · · ·

Now almost all the guests had gone their separate ways, and a solitary Sofia Petrovna was wandering from room to room.† In the deserted enfilade she suddenly saw a white domino, which at that very moment seemed to rise up out of nowhere, and—

—someone sad and tall, whom she seemed to have seen a great many times, all swathed in white satin, moved toward her through the emptying rooms; through the slits of his mask came the bright light of his eyes; it streamed from his forehead, from his stiffening fingers . . .

Sofia Petrovna trustingly called out to the dear figure wearing the domino:

"Sergei Sergeyevich!"

No, there was no doubt: he had repented of his scandalous conduct of the day before. He had come to fetch her, to take her away.

Sofia Petrovna called out to the sad and tall one:

"Is it really you?"

But the sad and tall one slowly shook his head, and bade her be silent.

She trustingly reached out her hand to the white domino. How cool the satin! And her tiny hand rustled as it touched the white arm. And now she hung on it powerlessly (the arm of the figure wearing the domino proved to be hard as wood). From under the white lace protruded a tuft of beard, like a sheaf of grain.

"Have you forgiven me?"

From under the mask came a sigh in reply.

"Why are you silent?"

The sad and tall one remained silent.

Now they were passing into the vestibule. The inexpressible surrounded them. Here the inexpressible was everywhere around. Removing her black half-mask, she buried her face in her furs. The sad and tall one put on his coat but did not remove his mask. Sofia Petrovna looked at the tall one in amazement. She was astonished that he had not been handed an officer's coat, but only a thin shabby overcoat, from which his fingers protruded, strangely reminiscent of lilies. She flung herself toward him, away from the lackeys who were observing the spectacle. The inexpressible surrounded them. Here the inexpressible was everywhere around.

But the sad and tall one on the lighted threshold slowly shook his head and bade her be silent.

The sky had become a solid mass of dirty slush. The fog had come down to the ground, and was now gloom through which glowed the rusty blots of street lamps. Above one rusty blot hung the hunched caryatid of the entryway. And how it protruded! A piece of the little house next door—bay windows and carved wooden sculptures—protruded. The outline of her unknown companion loomed before her.

The wave of a hand in the fog:

"Cab!"

And she understood everything. The sad outline had a caressing voice—

—which she had heard a great many times: so very recently, last night, in a dream; and yet she had forgotten!—

A beautiful and caressing voice, but, there was no doubt: it was not the voice of Sergei Sergeyevich. And yet she had wished that this beautiful stranger was her husband. But her husband had not come.

Who could this be?

The unknown outline was raising his voice. It grew stronger and stronger. And it seemed that behind the mask was Someone, Enormous beyond Measure. Silence attacked the voice. A dog replied. The street stretched away off there.

"Who *are* you?"

"You, all of you deny me. I look after all of you. You deny me, and then you call unto me to . . ."

Now, for an instant, Sofia Petrovna Likhutina understood who was before her. Her throat was contracted by sobs, and she wanted to fall at these slender feet and wind her arms around the knees of the unknown one, but at this moment a carriage rumbled up. And the cabbie moved into the bright light from a street lamp. The outline helped her into the carriage. When she stretched her trembling hands out of the carriage in supplication, the outline bade her be silent.

But the carriage had started up. If only it had stopped and, oh, if only it had turned back, to that bright spot where He had been standing a moment ago, and where He was no longer.

She Had Forgotten What Had Been

Sofia Petrovna Likhutina had forgotten what had been. What was to come had sunk into the blackish night. The irremediable was creeping over her. The irremediable was embracing her, and into it receded: house, apartment, and husband. And she did not know toward what she was moving. Behind her fell away a piece of what had just been: masquerade ball, harlequins, and even, even the sad and tall one. She did not know whence she had come.

After that which had recently been, all of the day just past was falling away: the bickering with Madame Farnois about "Maison Tricotons." She moved back still further, in search of some buttress for consciousness in the impressions of the day before that, but that day too had fallen away, like the cobblestones on a paved road; and it was dashed against some dark bottom. And a cobblestone-shattering crash resounded.

The love of that fateful unhappy summer flashed by, and fell away from her memory. And a cobblestone-shattering crash resounded. There flashed by and fell away: her conversations in the spring with *Nicolas* Ableukhov, the years of marriage, the wedding. Thus a kind of void was tearing off and swallowing piece after piece. There echoed metallic crash after crash, shattering the cobblestones. Her whole life flashed by, her whole life fell away, and her life had not yet existed, ever, and it was as if she had not been born into life. The void began immediately behind her back (everything had collapsed there), and the void continued on into the ages. In the ages only crash upon crash could be heard: pieces of lives were falling. There was the pounding of a metallic steed, with a ringing clatter against stone. Behind her he was trampling everything that had flown off. There, behind her back, the metallic Horseman had started up in pursuit.†

She turned around and saw an extraordinary sight: a Mighty Horseman. Two flaming nostrils pierced the fog there like a white hot pillar.

And Sofia Petrovna came to with a start: a rider overtook the carriage and flew into the fog, brandishing a torch. A heavy bronze helmet flashed past, and behind it, rumbling and spewing sparks, flew a fire brigade.

"What's going on there, a fire?" she asked the driver.

"They say the islands are on fire."†

The driver announced this to her out of the fog. The carriage came to a stop on the Moika.

Everything surfaced in her mind and seemed horribly prosaic. It was as if there had never been dancing maskers or the Horseman. The maskers now seemed only pranksters and they probably were acquaintances who visited her house. And the sad and tall one was just one of the *comrades* (and how nice of him to have escorted her to a carriage). Sofia Petrovna now bit her plump lip in annoyance. How could she have confused him with her husband and whispered in his ears nonsensical admissions of some guilt or other? And now gossip would start making the rounds.

Indignantly she gave the entryway door a violent push. Indignantly the door banged. Darkness enveloped her, the inexpressible enclosed her for an instant. But Sofia Petrovna Likhutina was thinking how she would have Mavrushka prepare the samovar. While the samovar was being prepared, she would give her husband a good talking to. Mavrushka would bring in the samovar, and she and her husband would make up.

Sofia Petrovna Likhutina rang. The doorbell gave notice to the apartment at this late hour. In a moment she would hear Mavrushka's bustling step. No step was heard. Sofia Petrovna took offense and rang again.

You had only to leave the house and that fool of a girl. . . . Her husband's a fine one too! Here he's been waiting for her impatiently, he must have heard the bell and, of course, he understands that the servant has fallen asleep. But he doesn't budge! Who does he think he is to still be offended!

Sofia Petrovna kept on ringing, and the doorbell kept on tinkling. No one! And she put her ear to the keyhole, and on the other side, just inches away, she could clearly hear an irregular heavy breathing. Lord in Heaven, who could it be breathing so heavily there?

Mavrushka? No, not Mavrushka. Sergei Sergeyevich Likhutin? Yes, him. Then why didn't he say something, why didn't he open up, why was he breathing so irregularly?

With a premonition that something was wrong, Sofia Petrovna began pounding desperately:

"Open up!"

And behind the door someone continued to breathe heavily, with horrible irregularity.

"Sergei Sergeyevich! Enough of this!"

Silence.

"What's happened to you? Well?"

There was a tap–tap–tapping——away.

"What's going on? Oh Lord, I'm afraid, I'm afraid."

Something gave a loud wail and ran away from the door. There was a shuffling and a moving of chairs. The lamp gave a loud tinkle, and there was the rumble of a table being pushed away. All fell quiet.

And then—a horrifying din, as if the ceiling were collapsing and as if the plaster were raining down. In this din, Sofia Petrovna Likhutina was struck by one sound only: the falling from somewhere above of a heavy human body.

Alarm

Apollon Apollonovich Ableukhov, to speak in banalities, could not stomach having to leave his house unnecessarily. Leaving the house with a report for the minister was meaningful, as the Minister of Justice once remarked to him.

Apollon Apollonovich could not stomach face-to-face conversations, which, naturally, entailed looking each other in the eye. From his desk ran telephone wires: to all departments. Apollon Apollonovich listened with pleasure to the hum of the telephone.

But once, in reply to his asking from what department they were calling, someone slapped the palm of a hand over the mouthpiece of the telephone with all his might. Apollon Apollonovich had the impression that he had received a slap in the face.

Every verbal exchange had to have a goal, plain and straight as a line. He relegated everything else to teadrinking and smoking what he called "butts." He supposed that the Russians were drinkers and nicotine addicts (he proposed to raise the tax on products of the latter sort). The Russians' red noses were a dead giveaway. Apollon Apollonovich charged like a bull at everything red.

He was the possessor of a little gray nose and the slender waist of a sixteen-year-old girl. And he was proud of it.

Apollon Apollonovich had gone to the Tsukatovs with a single purpose: to strike a blow against a department which for some reason had started flirting with a moderate party that was suspect not for rejecting the established order, but for wanting to change the established order ever so slightly. Apollon Apollonovich detested compromises.

Apollon Apollonovich considered it his unpleasant duty to spend an evening at the Tsukatovs, where the object of his observation was: the convulsive twitchings of dancing legs and the blood red folds of clownish getups. He had once seen rags like that: on the square in front of the Kazan Cathedral.† There the rags were called banners.

Red rags at a soirée in the presence of the head of a Government Institution struck him as an inappropriate joke. The convulsive twitchings of dancing legs made him think of a regrettable measure necessary for preventing crimes.†

Apollon Apollonovich grew disagreeable.

He thought that if these apparently innocent dances were permitted, dances of a different sort would be continued in the streets.

Apollon Apollonovich himself had danced in his youth: the polkamazurka, the lanciers.

One circumstance had aggravated his melancholy mood: that stupid domino had brought on an attack of angina (whether or not it had been an attack of angina, he was still uncertain). Well then: he had encountered a domino, that ridiculous buffoon, in the ballroom. It had run up to him simpering.

Apollon Apollonovich tried to recall where he had seen simpering of this sort. But he could not recall.

Apollon Apollonovich had sat imperious, ramrod-straight, and with a dainty porcelain cup in his hand. His little legs with their sinewy calves rested perpendicularly on the rug, so that the lower and upper parts formed ninety-degree right angles. Apollon Apollonovich looked like an Egyptian depicted on a rug.

Apollon Apollonovich was expounding his prohibitionist system to the professor of statistics, the leader of a moderate party, and to the editor of the conservative newspaper, once the liberal son of a priest.†

He had nothing in common with either one of them. Both had fat bellies and both, of course, had red noses (from alcoholic beverages). One was the son of a priest. Apollon Apollonovich had an understandable weakness: he could not abide the sons of priests. When Apollon Apollonovich's duties made it necessary for him to converse with priests, he was always aware of how bad their feet smelled.

Suddenly Apollon Apollonovich began twisting and turning between the frock coats belonging to the priest's son and the moderate traitor. His agitation stemmed from a shock to his aural membrane. The hired pianist had once again let his fingers fall on the piano, and to him the musical harmonies sounded like the squeaking of fingertips over glass.

Apollon Apollonovich saw the convulsive twitchings of legs that belonged to the criminals—oops, sorry—to the young people who were dancing. His attention was again struck by the domino.

Apollon Apollonovich vainly tried to recall where he had seen him. And he could not recall.

And when a mangy little fellow flew up deferentially, Apollon Apollonovich became animated in the extreme.

The fact of the matter was that the mangy little fellow was an essential figure in a time of transition. Apollon Apollonovich in principle disapproved of his existence, but . . . what could you do? Once the figure existed, you had to reconcile yourself to it. The one good thing about the mangy little fellow was that he knew his own worth, did not deck himself out in bombastic phrases, like the professor, and did not bang his fist in a most unseemly manner, like the editor. He unobtrusively served various departments in his own way, while attached to just one of them. Apollon Apollonovich valued the little fellow, for he did not try to stand on an equal footing—in a word, he was an unabashed lackey. With lackeys Apollon Apollonovich was eminently courteous.

And Apollon Apollonovich absorbed himself in conversation with the little figure.

What he found out struck him like a thunderbolt: the blood red domino, of which he had just been thinking, proved, according to the account of the little fellow, to be. . . . No (Apollon Apollonovich winced as if he had seen someone slicing a lemon): the domino proved to be—his son!

Was his son really of *his own blood*? The son, after all, could prove to be the son of Anna Petrovna because of the accidental predominance of maternal blood. And in the maternal blood, as certain inquiries had shown, ran the blood of priests! (Apollon Apollonovich had made those inquiries after his spouse had run off.) The blood of priests had *defiled* the Ableukhov stock, and had presented him with simply a *vile* son. Only a *mongrel* could embark on *undertakings of this sort* (there had as yet been nothing of the sort in the Ableukhov stock).

What struck the senator above all was that the kike press was already writing about these vile doings of his loving son. Apollon Apollonovich regretted that he had not found time to glance through the "Daily Chronicle."

Apollon Apollonovich stood up and wanted to rush off into the adjoining room, but a Gymnasium student poured into a tight-fitting suit flew up to him out of that very room. Apollon Apollonovich was about to offer him his hand, but on closer examination he proved to be. . . . Apollon Apollonovich, confusing the layout of the rooms, had almost crashed into a mirror.†

An unusually jumpy Apollon Apollonovich went up to the card tables, making a sudden display of courtesy and curiosity about subjects of every kind. Of the professor of statistics, he inquired, quite out of the blue, about the province of Ploshchegorsk.† Of the zemstvo official, he inquired about the consumption of pepper on the island of Newfoundland.

Suddenly whisperings and wry chucklings reached him. The convulsive twitchings of dancing legs abruptly ceased. For a moment his spirit grew calm. But then his mind began to function with horrifying clarity. His fateful premonition had been borne out: his son was a scoundrel of the very worst sort. For several days on end to have donned a domino, to have put on a mask, to have stirred up the kike press!

Nikolai Apollonovich had really gotten himself into . . . (and Apollon Apollonovich could not form a clear and distinct idea of *into what exactly*).

At any rate, Apollon Apollonovich would lose his new position: he could not accept it until he had washed away the disgraceful spots which had been made by his unworthy son and which had besmirched his honor.

Apollon Apollonovich offered a finger to one and all and rushed headlong out of the drawing room, accompanied by his hosts. While he was flying through the ballroom, he looked around in the direction of the walls and saw a small cluster of gray-browed matrons whispering up a storm.

His ear caught:

"A plucked chicken."

Apollon Apollonovich could not abide the sight of headless plucked chickens for sale in shops.

The Letter

Nikolai Apollonovich had left the Tsukatov house a quarter of an hour before the senator. He came to, in a state of utter prostration, in front of their entryway. Standing in dark slush, in an utterly dark and dreamlike state, he mechanically counted the number of waiting carriages and followed the movements of someone sad and tall who was there to keep order.

Suddenly the sad and tall one strolled past under his very nose. It was a police officer, who was incensed by the presence of a student in a greatcoat and shook his little flaxen white beard.

Through the utterly dreamlike state, through the dark slush peered the rusty blot of a street lamp. A piece of the little house next door protruded. The house was black, one-storied, with carved wooden sculptures.

Scarcely had Nikolai Apollonovich set off when he noticed that soft parts of some kind were sloshing in a puddle. He tried to control them, but the soft parts would not obey him. They had every appearance of the outline of feet, but he did not feel any feet (there were no feet). In this state he sank down by the ledge of the little black house.

This was natural in his situation. It was natural for him to fling open his greatcoat, exposing the red blur of the domino. He rummaged in his pockets and drew out a crumpled little envelope. He read through the contents again, in an attempt to detect some trace of a joke, or some trace of mockery.

"Remembering your proposal of last summer, we hasten to inform you, comrade, that you are instructed to proceed to the completion of the deed . . ." Nikolai Apollonovich could read no further, because the name of his father was there. And then: "The material you require, in the form of a bomb, has been duly delivered in a bundle. It is desirable that the deed be done in the next few days." Then followed a slogan. Both the slogan and the handwriting were familiar: it had been written by The Unknown One.

There was no doubt.

Nikolai Apollonovich's arms and legs drooped, his jaw sagged.

Nikolai Apollonovich kept trying to catch at idle thoughts: thoughts of the number of books that would fit on the shelf of a bookcase, and of the patterns made by the flounces on the skirt of a person he had formerly loved (that this person was Sofia Petrovna he did not remember).

He tried not to think, not to understand: could there be any understanding of *this*? *This had come, had crushed, and was roaring.* If you thought about it—you would throw yourself through a hole in the ice.

In his soul something bellowed piteously like a bullock under the knife in a slaughterhouse.

He tried to clutch at externals: that caryatid—it was just a caryatid. . . . But no! He had never seen anything like it: it was hanging over a flame. And over there the little black house.

No!

There was more than met the eye to this little house, more than met the eye to everything. Everything within him was dislocated, torn loose. He had torn loose from himself.

Here were his feet. No, no! Not feet but soft parts uselessly dangling here.

The door of the entryway, in which he had just been acting like a madman, began opening and closing. People poured out, carriages set off, lantern lights set off. With an effort, Nikolai Apollonovich set off from the ledge of the little house into an alleyway.

And the alleyway was empty, as empty as his soul. For a minute he tried to remember that events of the mortal world do not infringe in the least on thought, and that the thinking brain is merely a phenomenon of consciousness. His *true* contemplative spirit was capable of illuminating the way for him, even with *this*; capable of illuminating even . . . *this*. . . . All around—*this* rose. It rose as fences. At his feet he noticed a gateway and a puddle.

And nothing gave illumination.

Consciousness struggled in vain to give illumination. It gave no illumination. Horrible darkness! Looking around, he crept up to a blot of light from a street lamp. Under the blot a stream of water babbled in the gutter, an orange peel swept past.

Nikolai Apollonovich again addressed himself to the note:

"Remembering your proposal of last summer"—Nikolai Apollonovich read it again and tried to find something he could take exception to. He could find nothing.

"Remembering your proposal of last summer . . . ." A proposal had indeed been made. He had forgotten about it. Only once had he remembered it, but then the domino had swept everything away. He cast an eye over the recent past. There had been a lady. Nothing special, just a lady.

And there was no center of consciousness. There was a gateway instead. In his soul was an empty hole. And over this hole Nikolai Apollonovich fell to thinking. When and where had he stood in the same way before? He remembered: he had stood in exactly the same way in the gusts of Neva wind, leaning over the railing of a bridge, and looking into germ-infested water (all that had happened before, and had happened a great many times).

"We hasten to inform you that . . ." Nikolai Apollonovich read. And he turned around. Steps sounded at his back. Some kind of mysterious shadow loomed in the gusts of the alleyway. Behind him Nikolai Apollonovich spied: bowler, cane, coat, goatee, and nose.

All that moved on, paying no attention (only a step was heard, and the beating of the heart). Nikolai Apollonovich turned around and looked into the dingy fog—where all that had swiftly moved on. He stood for a long time, stooped (all that had happened before), and, with open mouth, he cut the rather comic figure of an armless man (for he was wearing a caped greatcoat), with the wing of the greatcoat flapping so preposterously in the wind.

"The material you require, in the form of a bomb, has been duly delivered in a bundle. . . ." Nikolai Apollonovich took exception to this phrase: it had not been delivered! All this was a joke. He had no bomb!?

.   .   .   .

In a bundle!?

.   .   .   .

At this point he recalled: the bundle, the suspicious visitor, the miserable September day, and all the rest. He had taken the bundle, and the bundle had been wet.

Unutterable fright gripped him. He felt a stabbing pain. Darkness enveloped him. And the "I" proved to be merely a black receptacle, if not a small cramped storeroom. And at this instant, in the darkness, in the place where his heart was located, a spark flared. With frenzied speed it turned into a swollen crimson sphere. The sphere expanded, expanded, expanded, and the sphere burst. Everything burst. A mangy little fellow with a wart by his nose had stopped only two paces from him, in front of an old fence—to take care of a natural need. He turned his face to Ableukhov:

"Coming from the ball?"

"Yes, I am. And what's wrong with that? Attending a ball isn't a crime yet."

"I know that."

"You do?"

"A piece of a domino is showing beneath your greatcoat."

"So what!"

"And yesterday it also showed . . ."

"What do you mean?"

"By the Winter Canal. . . ."

"I beg your pardon, sir."

"Come now, are *you* the domino?"

"Which one do you mean?"

"Why, *the* domino."

"I don't understand you. To come up to a stranger . . ."

"You're by no means a stranger. You're Nikolai Apollonovich. And you are also the *Red Domino* they're writing about in the papers."

The little gentleman did not let up:

"I know your father. I've just had a chat with him."

"Oh, believe me," Nikolai Apollonovich got all agitated. "These are just foul rumors of some sort."

But, having attended to his natural need, the little fellow buttoned up his shabby overcoat and gave a knowing wink:

"Where are you off to?"

"To Vasilievsky Island." Nikolai Apollonovich blurted out a lie.

"And I'm going to Vasilievsky too."

"I meant, to the Embankment."

.   .   .   .

"You yourself don't seem to know where you're headed, and therefore, let's drop into a nice little restaurant."

A Companion

Apollon Apollonovich Ableukhov, in a gray coat and a tall black top hat, leaped through the open entryway door in fright.

Someone shouted out his name. The black outline of a carriage promptly moved into the circle of light from a street lamp, and presented its coat of arms (a unicorn goring a knight). Apollon Apollonovich was just about to spring into the carriage and fly off in it into the fog when the entryway door was flung open. The mangy little fellow who had revealed the honest truth appeared in the street and scuttled off to the left.

Apollon Apollonovich then lowered his foot and touched a glove to the brim of his top hat. He ordered the driver to return home without him. And then he did something unknown in the history of his life for some fifteen years: blinking in bewilderment, his hand pressed to his heart, he set off at a run after the retreating back of the little fellow. He began waving his little hand.

I am communicating this minor detail about the behavior of a person recently deceased solely for the benefit of those who are gathering materials for his future biography of which mention has recently been made in the newspapers.

The wind blew off his black top hat. Apollon Apollonovich got down on all fours over a puddle to extract the top hat. He began to shout at the retreating back:

"Mm . . . listen here!"

The back paid no heed.

"But stop!"

It turned its head, and, recognizing the senator, ran to meet him (it was not the back running to meet him, but rather, the back's possessor, the fellow with the wart). In astonishment he set about fishing the top hat out of the puddle.

"Your Excellency! Apollon Apollonovich! Fancy meeting you here. Allow me, sir, here you are, sir." (With these words the mangy little fellow handed the dignitary his top hat, which he had wiped with the sleeve of his own coat.)

"But your carriage . . . ?"

Apollon Apollonovich interrupted:

"The night air is good for me."

Both set out in the same direction.

Apollon Apollonovich raised his eyes and looked at his companion, blinked, and said—said in confusion:

"I . . . my friend, er . . . dear sir (Apollon Apollonovich mixed up the informal and formal modes of address) . . .

"Actually . . . I wanted to have your address, Pavel Pavlovich. . . ."

"Yakovlevich!"

"Pavel Yakovlevich . . . I have a poor memory for names."

Apollon Apollonovich unbuttoned his coat and took out a small leatherbound notebook. They stopped under a street lamp.

"My address is subject to change. Most frequently it is Vasilievsky Island, Eighteenth Line, house number 17. Care of master shoemaker Bessmertny. To Precinct Clerk Voronkov."

Apollon Apollonovich arched his eyebrows. His features expressed amazement.

"But why," he began, "why . . ."

"Why is my name Voronkov, when I am Morkovin? My real residence is on the Nevsky."

Apollon Apollonovich thought: What can you do? The existence of such figures in a time of transition, within the bounds of legality, is a necessity, a sad one, and yet a necessity.

"At the present, Your Excellency, as you see, I am devoting all my time to investigative work. These are critical times."†

"Yes, you are right."

"A crime of nationwide significance is being plotted. Watch out: a puddle. A crime . . ."

"I see . . ."

"Very soon it will be brought to light that— Here's a dry spot, sir, allow me to take your arm."

Apollon Apollonovich was crossing a square. His fear of space awakened, and he now drew closer to the little fellow.

He tried to pluck up his courage. An icy hand touched him. It took him by the arm and led him past the puddles. And he walked and walked and walked, led on by an icy hand. Spaces flew to meet him. Apollon Apollonovich cast a respectful glance at the guardian of the existing order.

"An act of terrorism is being plotted?"

"A certain high official is to fall. . . ."

Apollon Apollonovich had received a threatening letter. The letter had informed him that in the event he should accept the new position, a bomb would be thrown at him. Apollon Apollonovich had nothing but contempt for anonymous letters. He had torn up the letter, and had accepted the new position.

"Excuse me, please, but who is their target now?"

Something strange occurred. All the objects around suddenly cowered, dampened, and looked nearer than they should have, while Mr. Morkovin seemed ancient, yet somehow familiar. A wry little smile flitted over his lips.

"What do you mean who? It's you, Your Excellency, you!"

Apollon Apollonovich could not realistically imagine that this tightly gloved hand of his, these legs, this tired (believe me!) heart would, under the effect of the expansion of the gases from some bomb or other . . .

"What do you mean?"

"Just what I say, sir, it's very simple."

Simple? Apollon Apollonovich could not believe it. He gave a vehement snort into his two sidewhiskers (the sidewhiskers too!) and pursed his lips (there would be no lips left either). Then he shrank, lowered his head, and looked at the dirty rivulet that gushed at his feet. Everything around was babbling and whispering: autumn's old-womanish whisper.

Mr. Morkovin felt sorry for this aged outline sagging into the mud, and he added:

"Don't you be alarmed, Your Excellency. The strictest measures have been taken. We will not permit it. There is no danger either today or tomorrow. Just be patient."

Morkovin could not help thinking: How he has aged. Why, he's simply a ruin. Apollon Apollonovich turned his beardless countenance toward him and smiled sadly.

A moment later Apollon Apollonovich rallied, looked younger, and set off, ramrod straight, into the dingy murk, his profile resembling the mummy of a pharaoh.

The night was black, dark blue, and lilac, shading off into the reddish blots of the street lamps. There loomed gateways, walls, fences, yards. And from them issued a babbling of some kind.

Ooo! How damp, how brain-chilling!

Demented

We left Sergei Sergeyevich at the moment when, deathly pale and with an ironic smile, he rushed into the vestibule after his disobedient wife. With a click of his spurs, he took his stand in front of the door. After Sofia Petrovna Likhutina had rustled provocatively by, right under the angry second lieutenant's nose, Sergei Sergeyevich began pacing about everywhere with vigorous gestures and everywhere extinguishing the electric lights.

Why then did he reveal his state of mind in precisely this way? What in the world was the connection between all *this disgusting business* and the electric lights? There was just as little sense in it as in the connection between the angular, sad figure of the second lieutenant in a dark green uniform, and the goatee provocatively adorning a face that seemed carved from fragrant wood. There was no connection at all. Except in the mirrors: an angular reflection, stepping up to the surface of a mirror, grasped itself by its slender neck. Oh, oh! There was no connection at all.

"Click" went the switches, plunging the man and his gestures into darkness. Perhaps this was not Second Lieutenant Likhutin?

Put yourself in his horrible position: of having such a disgusting reflection in the mirrors, all because a domino had besmirched the honor of his home, and because he was now obliged, according to the word he had given, never again to allow his wife to cross his threshold. Yes, go ahead and put yourself in his horrible position. All the same, it was Second Lieutenant Likhutin: none other than he.

"Click-click" went the switch in the adjoining room. It clicked in a third as well. Mavrushka grew alarmed, and she shuffled out of the kitchen and into all the rooms.

She grumbled:

"What's going on now?"

Then the lieutenant coughed out of the darkness:

"Get out of here."

"What do you mean, sir?"

"Leave these rooms."

.   .   .   .

"The beds aren't even made."

.   .   .   .

"Out, out!"

.   .   .   .

Scarcely had she left the room when a shout reached the kitchen:

"Pack up and get out!"

"How can I do that, sir?"

"Get out at once!"

"Where will I go?"

"I don't want to see your face!"

"Sir!"

"Out, out!"

Mavrushka grabbed her coat and out she went. And she started crying. Goodness, how scared she was! The master wasn't himself. She ought to have gone to the porter and to the police station, but stupidly all she could think of was going to a girlfriend's.

.   .   .   .

The horrible lot of an ordinary, normal man whose life is determined by dictionaries of easily understandable words and acts. The acts draw him on, like a fragile vessel rigged out with words and gestures. If the fragile vessel runs aground on the submerged rock of inapprehensibility, it is wrecked, and the sailor drowns. At life's slightest jolt, ordinary people are deprived of reason. No, madmen know no such dangers. Their brains are more subtle. The ingenuous brain finds impenetrable that which such brains penetrate. There is nothing for it but to be wrecked, and—it is wrecked.

Since the evening before, Second Lieutenant Likhutin had felt an unexpected and unbearable pain in his head, as if his forehead had banged loudly against an iron wall. While he stood before the wall he saw that the wall was not a wall: it was penetrable. There, beyond the wall, was invisible light of some kind, and the laws of nonsense. . . . Likhutin moaned and shook his head, feeling his brain working very keenly, while reflections crept over the walls: a small steamboat was going by on the Moika, leaving bright bands of light on the waters.

And Likhutin moaned. He gave his head a shake. His thoughts were all tangled up, everything was all tangled up. In his thoughts he began with an analysis of his wife's acts; and he ended by catching himself thinking all sorts of nonsensical rubbish: perhaps the hard surface was impenetrable for him alone, and the mirrored reflections of the rooms were really the rooms themselves. In the real rooms lived the family of a transient officer. The mirrors should be closed up: it was embarrassing to watch and study how the married officer behaved—with his wife. You could find rubbish there, and Likhutin was catching himself thinking rubbish of this sort. And he found that he himself was involved with this rubbish. Likhutin turned off the electric lights: the mirrors would have distracted him horribly. And he required an effort of the will to seek and find something in himself.

Second Lieutenant Likhutin began pacing about everywhere and extinguishing the electric lights.

What was he to do now? The evening before—*it had begun.* What was it and why *had it begun?* Except for the fact of Ableukhov's disguise, there was nothing to grab hold of here. In this delicate matter his head refused to serve him. Blood gushed into his head: a towel on the temples would be nice now. Likhutin placed a towel on his temples, and tore it off again: such a knocking, such a thumping, such a beating, such a twitching of the veins!

He struck a match again: rust red flames lit up the face of a madman. It pressed right up against the clock: two hours had passed, or one hundred twenty minutes. Should he count the seconds as well?

"Two times sixty are one hundred twenty!"

He clutched his head.

"Carry one. The mind has smashed against the mirror. . . . The mirrors ought to be removed! Twelve, carry one, yes: a sliver of glass. . . . No, one second of life. . . ." His thoughts got all tangled up. Likhutin was pacing in the darkness: tap-tap-tap went his step.

"Two times six are twelve. Carry one. One times six are six. Plus one. Add two zeroes. That makes seven thousand two hundred big fat seconds."

Having triumphed over this complicated brainwork, Sergei Sergeyevich was now displaying an ecstasy that was altogether incongruous. Suddenly he remembered, and his face darkened.

"Seven thousand two hundred seconds since she ran off. Two hundred thousand seconds—no, it's all over!"

On the expiration of the two hundred seconds, the two hundred and first one marked the beginning of the time when his word of honor as an officer was to be fulfilled. The seven thousand two hundred seconds had seemed to him like seven thousand years. It seemed to Sergei Sergeyevich that ever since the creation of the world he had been imprisoned in this gloom with an unbearable headache and with thought which had come to life spontaneously. Likhutin bustled about in the corner. He began crossing himself. He hastily threw a rope out of a box, uncoiled it, and made a noose with it. It refused to tighten. In despair he ran into the study. The rope trailed after him.

What on earth was he doing—keeping his word? Good grief, no. He simply took a piece of soap out of a soap dish, squatted, and soaped the rope over a basin. His actions took on fantastic dimensions.

Just judge for yourselves!

He climbed up on a table (he had removed the tablecloth from the table), and he placed a chair on the table. Clambering up on the chair, he carefully took down the lamp, and cautiously lowered it to his feet. In place of the lamp he attached to the hook the rope, which was very slippery from the soap. He crossed himself and froze. And he slowly raised the noose.

A brilliant thought dawned on Sergei Sergeyevich: he had to shave and, what's more, he had to calculate the number of thirds and fourths.

With this thought in mind, Likhutin proceeded into the study. By the light of a candle-end he began shaving his hairy neck. (But the skin on his neck was tender, and the skin now had a pimply look.) He shaved his chin and neck, but the razor accidentally lopped off half his mustache. He had to finish the job. (They would break down the door, come in and see him with half a mustache, and . . . in such a position.)

And Sergei Sergeyevich shaved himself clean. And now he looked like a perfect idiot.

Well, then, no point in lingering. Of course, his face was now perfectly clean-shaven. Precisely at that moment the doorbell rang in the vestibule. He threw the razor down in annoyance, his fingers all covered with hairs. What to do, what to do? For only a minute did he think that his undertaking should be put off. There was no time to lose—the doorbell. Then and there he leaped up onto the table, and removed the noose from the hook. The rope would not obey his soapy fingers. He climbed down, crept into the vestibule, and noticed that the blue-black gloom in the rooms was slowly beginning to melt away. It had turned gray. In the graying gloom, objects were becoming clearly defined: the chair standing on the table, and the lamp lying there. And the wet noose.

In the vestibule he pressed against the door and froze. His agitation had induced such a degree of forgetfulness that no action at all was conceivable. He did not notice how heavily he was breathing. On the other side of the door he heard his wife's outcries. He shouted for all he was worth, and upon shouting, realized that all was lost. He rushed to put his plan into execution. He leaped up onto the table and stuck out his neck. He hastily tightened the rope around his neck, which had a pimply look to it, and slipped two fingers between the rope and his neck.

Then for some reason he gave a yell.

And he pushed the table away with his foot, and the table rolled away on brass casters. (This was the sound Sofia Petrovna had heard.)

What Next Then?

A moment—

Sergei Sergeyevich's legs jerked convulsively. He distinctly saw the reflections of the street lamps on the air vent of the stove, and he distinctly heard a knocking and scratching at the door. Something pressed two fingers forcibly against his chin. He could not tear them loose. He felt that he was choking. He heard a cracking (the veins had probably burst in his head), and the plaster was falling. Sergei Sergeyevich crashed down (into death). And Sergei Sergeyevich arose from death, after receiving a swift kick. He came to with a start, and understood that he had not arisen but had instead sat down on something solid (the floor). He felt a very sharp pain in his spine, and felt his fingers jammed between the rope and his throat. Likhutin began tearing at them, and the noose widened.

He understood that he had nearly hanged himself. He had fallen short of hanging himself. And he sighed with relief.

The inky gloom had turned gray, and had become a gray gloom. Likhutin saw that he was sitting in an absurd position. The gray walls with their gray Japanese landscapes were merging imperceptibly with the night, and the ceiling was losing the lacy pattern cast by the street lamp.

An instinctive sigh broke from Sergei Sergeyevich, as instinctive as the movements of drowning people before they go under. Likhutin (don't smile!) had seriously been intending to settle all accounts with this world. He would have realized his intention had the ceiling not been rotten (blame the builder of the house for that). So the sigh of relief had nothing to do with him as an individual personality but rather with his fleshly integument. It, this integument, was sitting on its haunches and taking everything in. Sergei Sergeyevich's spirit displayed cool composure.

His thoughts had cleared, and a dilemma arose: what was he to do? His revolvers were hidden away, and it would take a long time to find them. And to use a razor—ooo! To begin experimenting with a razor? No: better to stretch out here on the floor, leaving everything else to fate. In that case Sofia Petrovna would immediately rush to the porter. They would telephone the police, a crowd would gather, the doors would be forced open, they would burst in, and would see him, Second Lieutenant Likhutin, a rope around his neck, squatting amidst the plaster.

No, no! It would never come to that: the honor of the uniform was dearer to him than his word of honor. And only one thing remained: to make up with his wife as quickly as possible and provide an explanation for the plaster.

He threw the rope under the sofa and in a most ignominious manner ran to the door of the apartment.

Breathing heavily he opened it and stood indecisively on the threshold with a feeling of shame (*he had fallen short of hanging himself*), as if in tearing loose from the hook he had broken off what was storming within him: the rage at his wife, the rage at Nikolai Apollonovich's conduct. After all, he himself had perpetrated an unheard-of outrage: he had thought to hang himself, but instead, he had torn a hook out of the ceiling.

No one had rushed into the room. Nevertheless, someone was standing there (he could see). Likhutina had flown in, and had burst into sobs:

"What does this mean? And why the darkness?"

But Sergei Sergeyevich stood with downcast eyes.

"Why all the racket?"

But Sergei Sergeyevich pressed her cold little fingers in the darkness.

"Why are your hands all soapy? Sergei Sergeyevich, what *is* this?"

"You see, Sonyushka . . ."

"Why are you hoarse?"

"I . . . I . . . stood too long in front of an open window (that was careless of me, of course) . . . and so I got hoarse."

He stammered to a halt.

"Don't, don't," he almost shouted, pulling at his wife's hand because she was about to turn on the light, "not here, not now, let's go into this room."

He pulled her into the study.

In the study objects stood out distinctly, and the dawn sky shone through the window. And Sofia Petrovna saw before her . . . something indescribable: she saw the blue face of an idiot she did not know.

"What have you done? You've shaved yourself clean? You're nothing but a fool!"

"You see, Sonyushka," came his hoarse whisper, "circumstances are involved that . . ."

But she was not listening. Instinctively alarmed, she rushed to inspect the rooms.

"You'll find things in a mess there. . . . The ceiling's cracked in there."

Sofia Petrovna was not listening. She stood before a pile of plaster, in the midst of which showed the black hook that had crashed to the floor. The table had been violently pushed aside, and from under the soft couch protruded a noose. Likhutina bent down.

Suddenly everything was illuminated.† A rosy pink ripple of tiny clouds, like a mother-of-pearl web, floated by, a touch of light blue here and there. All was suffused with the timid, astonished question: "But how can this be? How?" A tremor of light was barely perceptible on the windows and on the spires; on the spires was a ruby red shimmer. Voices whispered in her soul. Everything was illuminated. From the window fell a pale pink, pale red wedge of light.†

She reached her hand toward the rope. She kissed the rope, and began quietly weeping. The image of her far-off and newly returned childhood was rising, rose above her, and stood at her back. She turned around and saw: there stood her husband, gangling, sad, and clean-shaven:

"Forgive me, Sonyushka!"

And she fell at his feet, weeping:

"My poor dear, my beloved!"

What they whispered between themselves, only God can say. It remained between them.

"Now, now, God will forgive."

A pinkish, raggedy little cloud from the stack of a small passing steamboat stretched along the Moika. From the stern ran a gleaming green band, which struck the bank and rippled amber. It surged away from the bank, broke against a band which was racing to meet it, and the bands began gleaming like a swarm of annulated serpents. Into the swarm passed a dinghy. All the serpents were cut up into tiny strands of diamonds. They entwined into silver tinsel, to rock like stars on the watery surface. The agitated waters grew calm, and the stars were all extinguished. From the bank rose a green, white-columned building: a piece of the Renaissance.

A "Solid Citizen"

Out of the darkness protruded the lofty side of a house made of heavy masses. Two Egyptians held up the balcony on their hands. Past the house and the million-tonned bulks walked Apollon Apollonovich, overcoming all the heavy masses. Before him was the outline of a miserable little rotting fence.

At that point a door flew open. White steam billowed forth. Curses, the twanging of a balalaika, and a voice were heard. He paid attention to the voice.

The voice was singing:

> In spirit fly we to Thee, Lord,
> We soar aloft to Heaven;
> We thank Thee truly from our hearts
> For food that Thou has given.

The door slammed shut. Apollon Apollonovich had always suspected that a "solid citizen" was something petty that went speeding past the windows of his carriage. Now all spaces had been displaced, and the life of the "solid citizen" was around him on all sides as gateways. The "solid citizen" himself was before him as only a voice.

So that's what the "solid citizen" is like! Apollon Apollonovich conceived an interest in the solid citizen, and there was an instant when he wanted to knock on the first door to find a solid citizen. He remembered what the solid citizen was planning to do to him . . . and his top hat slipped to the side, his worn-out shoulders sagged—

—Yes, yes: they had blown him to bits, no, not him but another, sent by fate. Apollon Apollonovich remembered the gray mustache, the greenish depths of the staring eyes. The two of them had once been bending over a map of the Empire (that had been exactly on the day before . . .). *They* had blown to bits the *first among equals*. People say *it* lasts but a second. After that there is absolutely nothing. Well, what of it? Every statesman is a hero, but—brr, brr . . .—

Apollon Apollonovich Ableukhov adjusted his top hat as he passed into the rotting life of the solid citizen, into the networks of walls, gateways, fences, all filled with slime, into this public

latrine, continuous, squalid, rotten, empty. It now seemed to him
that he was hated by even this miserable little rotting fence. *They*
hated him. Who were they? An insignificant little band? At this
point cerebral play rapidly erected misty planes before him. All the
planes were blown to bits. The gigantic map of Russia rose before
him, who was so small. Was it possible that *these* were enemies: the
gigantic totality of tribes that inhabited these expanses?   What?
One hundred million? Or more?†

"From the cold cliffs of Finland to fiery Colchis. . . ."†

What? They hated him? No, Russia was a vast expanse. Him?
They were planning to . . . planning to. . . . No, brr, brr. . . . Idle
cerebral play.

> It's time, my friend, it's time! . . . My heart begs
>   for some peace.
> The days chase on the days, each serving to
>   decrease
> The sum of our own being. Together you and I
> Propose to live some more. But lo! We too
>   shall die.†

With whom then was he proposing to live? With his son? His
son was a scoundrel. With the "solid citizen"? The solid citizen
was planning to. . . . Once he had proposed to spend his entire life
with Anna Petrovna, and on retiring from government service to
settle at his dacha in Finland, but then, Anna Petrovna:

"She's left, you know: it can't be helped. . . ."

Apollon Apollonovich understood that he had no helpmeet in life
(until this minute he for some reason had found no time to remember this), and that death in the line of duty would after all be the
crowning glory of his life. And he now had a somewhat childlike
feeling—sad, quiet, and comfortable. And he heard the murmur of
the little puddle, like someone's entreaty: about what had not been,
but what might have been.

The gloom that had been suffocating the night slowly began
melting away. It turned gray and became gray gloom, and then the
gray was barely perceptible. The rust red street lamps which had
been casting light all around were gradually drained of light. They
became dull dots, peering in surprise into the grayish fog. It seemed
that a gray procession of lines and walls, with their planes of faint
shadows and their gaping window-apertures, were airy lace, made
in patterns of the most delicate workmanship.

Toward him ran a shabbily dressed adolescent: a girl of about
fifteen.† Behind her in the fog moved the dark outline of a man. He
accosted her. But Apollon Apollonovich regarded himself as her
knight. He removed his top hat:

"My dear young lady, may I be so bold as to offer you my arm and see you home? It is not entirely safe for young persons to be on the street."

The girl saw a little black figure respectfully raising its top hat.

They walked on in silence. Everything seemed wet and old, as if it had receded into the ages. Apollon Apollonovich had seen all this before from afar. And now here it was: gateways, little houses, walls, the girl fearfully pressed against him; for her he was not a senator, but just a kindly old man.

They walked as far as a little green house with a rotted gateway. The senator tipped his top hat, and his senile mouth twisted ruefully. The dead lips began chewing. From somewhere afar came a sound—something like the singing of a violin bow: the crowing of a Petersburg chanticleer.

In the sky, somewhere off to the side, there was a spurt of flame. Everything was illuminated: a rosy pink ripple of tiny clouds, like a mother-of-pearl web, floated into the flames. The procession of lines and walls grew more massive and distinct. Heavy masses of some sort emerged—indentations and projections, entryways, caryatids, cornices of brick balconies.

The lace metamorphosed into morning Petersburg. There stood the five-storied houses, the color of sand. The rust red palace was bedawned.

End of the Fourth Chapter

Chapter the Fifth

*in which an account is given of the little fellow
with the wart by his nose and of the sardine tin
with horrible contents*

*Tomorrow morn the day will dawn
And dazzle us with all its light,
And I by then may well be gone
Down to the secret realms of night.*†

Pushkin

The Little Fellow

Nikolai Apollonovich turned around and fixed the little fellow's face with a stare.

"With whom have I the honor . . ."

"Pavel Yakovlevich Morkovin. . . ."

The face told him nothing: bowler, cane, coat, goatee, and nose.

"It pleases you to affect this tone of indifference. . . ."

A bright apple of light flared, then a second and a third, and a line of electric apples now marked out the Nevsky Prospect, where all night long cheap restaurants display their blood red signs, beneath which feathered ladies dart, amidst top hats, cap-bands, bowlers.

Nikolai Apollonovich knew that the circumstances of his encounter with the enigmatic Pavel Yakovlevich did not permit him to cut the encounter short in any dignified way. He had to worm out what had been said between him and his father. And he delayed taking leave of him.

The Neva opened out. Here was the stone curve of the Winter Canal; here the wind made its onslaughts. And beyond the Neva rose the outlines of islands and houses; and they cast their amber eyes into the mists; and they seemed to be weeping.

Here was the square. In the square loomed a crag; the steed flung out its hooves. A shadow covered the Horseman: there was no Horseman. And on the Neva was a fishing schooner of some kind.

They walked along the bridge.

Ahead of them walked a couple: a forty-five-year-old sailor in a fur cap with ear-flaps and with a gray-streaked rusty red beard. His neighbor was some kind of giant,† with a dark green felt hat, black hair and a tiny nose, a tiny mustache.

"This way, Nikolai Apollonovich, that's it, this way, here!"

"Oh, but really. . . ."

"What's the matter, you bored?"

"It's just that I'm sleepy."

Nikolai Apollonovich gave his shoulders a barely perceptible shrug. He squeamishly opened the door to the restaurant.

A thick white steamy pancake smell was mingled with dampness. The coat check fell burning into the palm of his hand.

"You see, everybody knows me: Alexander Ivanovich, Butishchenko, Shishiganov, Pepp . . ."

Nikolai Apollonovich's curiosity was aroused by three circumstances. In the first place, the stranger had emphasized that he was acquainted with his father (that surely meant something). In the second place, the stranger had let drop the name of Alexander Ivanovich. Finally, the stranger had mentioned several names (Butishchenko, Pepp) which had such a familiar ring.

"My, there's a nice one," Pavel Yakovlevich gave him a nudge, calling attention to a prostitute with a Turkish cigarette between her teeth.

"How do you feel about women?"

"?"

"Forget it, forget it!"

Around them was heard:

"Who?"

"Ivan!"

"Ivan Ivanych!"

"Ivan Ivanych Ivanov."

"That's a lot of claptrap."

"Ivan!"

"Ivan Ivanych!"

"Iv–van Iv–vanych Iv–vanov is a pig!"

Over there a musical contraption suddenly yowled. Ivan Ivanych Ivanov stood up beneath the contraption, waving a bottle.

How had he, Nikolai Apollonovich, gotten himself into such a vile place, at a time when . . .?

Embittered and anguished within the ferocious contraption, erupting and banging in tambourines, our immemorial times of old, like a volcanic eruption flowing down upon us from out of the depths, grew in volume and wept into the room:

"A–baaate, agi-taaa–tions of paaa–sions . . .
"Fall siii–lent, heart hooope–less and weaaa–ry . . ."†

·   ·   ·   ·   ·   ·   ·   ·

"Ha–ha–ha–ha–ha! . . ."

Hey, a Glass of Vodka!

"Come on, admit it—Hey, two glasses of vodka!—admit it." Pavel Yakovlevich was shouting. He had become bloated and gross. His yellowish face was distended: here, pouch-shaped, there, nipple-shaped.

"I'll just bet I'm a riddle to you."

Over there was a table. Sitting at it was the forty-five-year-old sailor (apparently a Dutchman).

"A little picon in it?"

And a hulk—of stone†—sank down next to the Dutchman at the table.

"Well now, young man?"

"What is it?"

"What do you have to say about my conduct outside?"

"Oh, why are you going on about that?"

"Have a second one?"

"All right."

Pavel Yakovlevich was poking about, intent on trying to pierce a slippery mushroom with a trembling fork.

"Isn't it true it was all a bit odd *there*?"

"Where do you mean?"

"Why, *there*, by the fence. No, waiter, no sardines."

At the tables a mongrel breed was swilling away: not quite people, not quite shadows. All were inhabitants of the islands, and the inhabitants of the islands are a strange, mongrel breed: not quite people, not quite shadows.

Pavel Yakovlevich was becoming bloated and gross: here, pouch-shaped, there, nipple-shaped. And over there—a small white wart.

"Have a third?"

"All right."

.   .   .   .

"Well, what do you have to say about our conversation by the gateway?"

"About the domino?"

"What else!"

"I'll still say what I said."

Nikolai Apollonovich wanted to turn away from the smelly lips, but he controlled himself. He got a wet kiss on the lips, and his lips stretched in a forced smile, twitching nervously. They began trembling (thus twitch the legs of dissected frogs when they are touched by the ends of electric wires).

"Well now, that's better. Put it out of your mind. Let's forget about the domino. I just brought up the domino to strike up an acquaintance."

"Pardon me, you've spilled some sardine oil on yourself," Nikolai Apollonovich interrupted.

"You'll have to agree it's a crazy idea that you're the domino. I says to myself: aha, Pavlusha, yes, old buddy—I says to myself—it came to me in a flash—by the fence, while I was, so to speak, answering the call of nature . . . just a pretext to get acquainted, pure and simple!"

They moved away from the counter to the tables.

"Waiter, a clean tablecloth.

"And some vodka."

They sat down and placed their elbows on the table. Nikolai Apollonovich felt himself beginning to get drunk (because of fatigue). Colors and sounds assaulted his brain.

"Yes, indeed, here's a curious little point. . . . Fine, I'll have kidneys in Madeira. And you? Kidneys too?"

"What point do you mean?"

"Two orders of kidneys. . . . What point? Well, now, I'll own up. The ties, the ties that bind us . . ."

"?"

"Ties of kinship."

"?"

"Blood ties."

The kidneys were served.

"Don't imagine that those ties— Some salt, pepper, and mustard! —have to do with the shedding of blood. But why are you trembling? Oh, how you're flushing and blushing, just like a young lady! That pepper's really something!"

Nikolai Apollonovich, like Apollon Apollonovich, overpeppered everything.

"What did you say?"

"That pepper's . . ."

"About blood . . ."

"About ties? By blood ties I mean ties of kinship."

Pavel Yakovlevich tied on a napkin and poked around in the napkin like a maggot in a corpse.

"Excuse me, I must have failed to understand: tell me, what do you mean by blood kinship?"

"As it turns out, Nikolai Apollonovich, I happen to be your brother."

Nikolai Apollonovich half rose, his nostrils quivering nervously, his thatch of hair bristling: his hair was of a nebulous color.

"Illegitimate, naturally. I am the fruit of your father's affair . . . with a seamstress."

The Ableukhovs had always treasured the purity of their blood, and he treasured it too.

"Therefore, your papa had an interesting little affair in his youth . . ."

Nikolai Apollonovich thought that Morkovin would continue with the words: "which ended in my appearance . . ."

"Which ended in my appearance in the world."

All this seemed to have happened before.

"Let's drink to it."

Embittered and anguished within the ferocious contraption, erupting and banging in tambourines, our immemorial times of old grew in volume and surged, and wept into the room.

   .   .   .   .   .   .

"My father . . ."

"Our *mutual* father."

"If you like, *our mutual* father."

"And why that shrug of the shoulder? My, my!" Pavel Yakovlevich interrupted. "You shrugged, why?"

"Why?"

"Because, Nikolai Apollonovich, you find such kinship offensive. Well, well, how brave you've become."

"Why should I be cowardly?"

"Ha, ha!—You've become brave because in your opinion . . . some kidneys? . . ."

"Much obliged."

"Some sauce? . . . You will forgive me for applying the psychological method to you.† I'm feeling you out, my dear fellow."

Nikolai Apollonovich squinted. His fingers drummed on the table.

"The same thing goes for our kinship. That too was probing, to see how you would react. I must both vindicate you and cause you pain. All that's left to point out is that we are brothers . . . but by different fathers."

"?"

"I was having my little joke about Apollon Apollonovich: there was never any such affair. There have never—heh, heh, heh—been any affairs! He is an exceptionally moral person!!"

"Then why are we brothers?"

"Because of our convictions."

"How can you know my convictions?"

"You are a thoroughly convinced terrorist, Nikolai Apollonovich."

"A terrorist?"

"A terrorist, out and out. You see, I let those names drop for a very good reason. Butishchenko, Shishiganov, Pepp. This was a subtle hint. You may understand it any way you like. Alexander Ivanovich Dudkin, the Elusive One. . . . Eh? Eh? . . . Get it? Get it? Now don't get all flustered. Our theoretician is quite the rascal. Ooo—I could just kiss you!"

"Ha, ha"—Nikolai Apollonovich reeled back in the chair—"ha, ha."

"Ee—hee—hee," echoed Pavel Yakovlevich.

"Ha, ha," continued Nikolai Apollonovich.

"Ee—hee—hee," giggled Pavel Yakovlevich.

The hulk at the next table turned toward them angrily and stared intently.

"I'm going to tell you something," said Nikolai Apollonovich, in all seriousness, mastering his outburst of laughter (his laughter had been forced), "you are quite wrong: I take a negative view of terror."

"Come now, Nikolai Apollonovich! After all, I know everything: about the bundle, about Alexander Ivanovich, about Sofia Petrovna. . . ."

.   .   .   .

"I know it—in my official capacity."

"Are you in government service?"

"Yes, in the secret police."

I Doom Irrevocably

For a moment both froze. Reaching around the table, Pavel Yakovlevich grabbed hold of Nikolai Apollonovich's button. With a guilty smile Nikolai Apollonovich took out a small leatherbound book, which proved to be a notebook.

"Be so kind as to hand me that book for inspection!" Nikolai Apollonovich did not resist: his torture had passed all limits.

Pavel Yakovlevich was bending over the notebook with his head thrust forward, making it seem attached not to his neck, but to his two fists. For a moment he became a monstrous creature. Its little eyes blinking, hair like matted dog fur, and snarling with laughter, the head began scurrying over the table on ten fingers. Leafing through the notebook, it looked like a ten-legged spider.

Obviously Pavel Yakovlevich was trying to frighten him with a mock investigation (oh, what a charming little joke!). Snarling with loud laughter, he threw the notebook back.

"For heaven's sake, why such submissiveness? After all, I'm not about to interrogate you. Don't be afraid. I have been assigned to the secret police by the Party. And there was no need for you to get so alarmed."

"Are you making fun of me?"

"Not a bit. If I were a policeman, you would have been arrested, because you made a movement worthy of attention. You clutched at your chest. You have a document there? So that gesture gave you away. Agreed?"

"Perhaps."

"Allow me to remark: you've slipped up. You took out a perfectly innocent notebook when nobody asked to see this notebook. You took it out merely to distract attention from something else. You didn't achieve your purpose. You didn't distract, you attracted. You made me think that you must have some other document in your pocket. Oh, you're so scatterbrained. Just take a look at this page here: you've revealed a little love secret. Here, look, feast your eyes."

. . . .

"Why this torture? If you really are who you claim to be—hey, waiter, the check!—then your conduct, your affectations are unworthy!"

Nikolai Apollonovich stood in clouds of billowing steam, his mouth agape but not laughing, in a halo of fair hair. His teeth bared like an animal, he turned around disdainfully and threw a half-rouble onto the table.

The adjoining tables had been emptying. Suddenly the electric lights went out too. The rust red light of a candle glowed gently, and the walls melted away. One section of paint-daubed wall swam into view. From there, from afar, under full sail, winging his way toward Petersburg was the Flying Dutchman. (Nikolai Apollonovich's head was spinning from the seven glasses he had forced down.) From the table rose the forty-five-year-old sailor. He disappeared in the gloom.

Morkovin, straightening his shabby frock coat, looked at Nikolai Apollonovich tenderly and pensively. For a minute or so they did not utter a word.

Finally Pavel Yakovlevich said:

"Now, now, it's just as hard on me as it is on you. . . .

"What's the point of holding back, comrade? . . ."

. . . .

"?"

. . . .

"Yes, we certainly have to settle on which day you'll keep your promise. . . . Nikolai Apollonovich, you're a rare bird. Could you really imagine for a moment that I was wandering through the streets after you just for the fun of it?"

Then he added in a dignified tone: "The Party, Nikolai Apollonovich, is awaiting an answer."

Nikolai Apollonovich was descending the stairs, which receded into darkness. While below, by the door, *they* stood. Who *they* were he could not have said exactly: a black outline and a green murk, green as green could be, dully glowing phosphorescent. And *they* were awaiting him.

And as he passed, he felt, on both sides, the gaze of someone observing him; and one was the giant. He was standing by the door in the light of a street lamp, like a bronze hulk. Staring at Ableukhov was a metallic face, glowing phosphorescent. A green, many-tonned arm pointed menacingly.

"Who is this?"

"He who dooms us all—irrevocably."

The restaurant door banged shut.

And again the bowler trotted along beside him, along the wall.

"And what if I refuse?"

"I will arrest you."

"Me? Arrest me?"

"Don't forget that I am . . ."

"A conspirator?"

"An official of the secret police!"

"But what would the Party say to you?"

"The Party would vindicate me. Using my position in the secret police, I would take vengeance on you on behalf of the Party."

Then, from the most ragged of the clouds streaks of bustling rain began to fall, chirring, whispering, curling cold patterings on bubbling puddles.

"Nikolai Apollonovich, all joking aside: I am very serious. I must remark that your doubts and your indecisiveness are killing me. You should have weighed all the odds beforehand. You could have refused (it's been two months). You didn't bother to do that. You have three alternatives. Choose: arrest, suicide, or murder. Do you understand me now?"

Petersburg, Petersburg!

Precipitating out as fog, you have pursued me with cerebral play. Cruel-hearted tormentor! Restless specter! For years you have attacked me. I have run along the horrible Prospects, to land with a flying leap on this very same gleaming bridge. . . .

Oh, green waters, teeming with germs! I remember that fateful moment: on a September night I too leaned over the damp railing. . . .†

Nikolai Apollonovich turned around. Behind him he saw nothing, no one. Above the damp, damp railing, above the greenish water teeming with germs, he was gripped by nothing but wailing gusts of wind. Here, on this very spot, two and a half months earlier, Nikolai Apollonovich had given the horrible promise.

The square was empty,† and the Senate and the Synod raised their three stories. Nikolai Apollonovich raised curious eyes toward the immense outline of the Horseman. Not long before it had seemed that there was no Horseman (a shadow had covered him); but now the metal lips were parted in an enigmatic smile.

The storm clouds were rent asunder and, in the moonlight, clouds swirled like the green vapor from melted bronze. For a moment, everything flared: waters, roofs, granite. The face of the Horseman and the bronze laurel wreath flared. And a many-tonned arm extended imperiously. It seemed that the arm was about to move, and that metallic hooves at any moment would come crashing down upon the crag, and through all of Petersburg would resound:

"Yes, yes, yes . . .

"It is—I . . .

"I doom: irrevocably!"

For a moment everything was suddenly flooded with light for Nikolai Apollonovich. Yes, he understood: he must.

Roaring with laughter he fled from the Bronze Horseman.

"I know. . . .

"I am doomed irrevocably."

In the distance a shaft of light: it was a black court carriage carrying bright red lanterns. The spectral outline of a footman's tricorne and the outline of the wings of his greatcoat flew, with the light, out of the fog and into the mist.

The Griffins

. . . Not a minute to lose! Steps must be taken. But what steps? After all, wasn't he the one who had sown the seed of the theory of the insanity of showing pity? He had expressed his opinions to that silent band regarding his repressed feeling of disgust for those withered aristocratic ears, for everything up to and including . . . the neck . . . with its subcutaneous vein.

He hired a late-passing cab.

The Admiralty presented one eight-columned facade. It glowed pink and disappeared. On the other side of the Neva the walls of an old building cast their bright carrot color. A black and white striped sentry booth stood as always on the left. A grenadier guard of the Pavlovsk Regiment paced back and forth in a greatcoat, a sparkling bayonet thrown over his shoulder.

The clear morning was ablaze with shimmering sparkles on the Neva, and transformed the whole expanse of water into an abyss of pure gold into which plunged the stack of a small steamer. Suddenly he spied a wizened little figure quickening its steps along the pavement, that very figure which . . . in which . . . which he recognized: Apollon Apollonovich! Nikolai Apollonovich wanted to slow the driver down to give the little figure time to move far enough away so that. . . . But it was already too late. The head turned toward the driver. Nikolai Apollonovich, not wanting to be recognized, buried his nose in his beaver collar. A collar and a student cap were all that could be seen.

Apollon Apollonovich Ableukhov heard the rumble of a carriage at his back, and when the driver had drawn abreast of the senator, the senator saw, sitting inside, a misshapen young man, hunched up, his greatcoat wrapped around him in a most unpleasant manner. And when the young man, his nose buried in his greatcoat, looked at the senator (eyes and a student cap were all that could be seen), the senator's head snapped away toward the wall.

When they caught sight of him, the eyes of the unpleasant young man dilated, dilated, dilated: in that look full of horror, which had been pursuing him more and more often. Yes, they looked with *that same* look, and they flashed in *that same way* as they dilated. And the carriage passed him, bouncing on the cobblestones. And he glimpsed the number plate: 1905.

Nikolai Apollonovich sprang out of the carriage and, clumsily getting all entangled in the skirts of his greatcoat, looking aged and somehow evil tempered, he made a quick dash for the entryway, waddling like a duck. And the wings of his greatcoat flapped in the air against the backdrop of the crimson dawn.

Nikolai Apollonovich tugged at the door bell. Oh, if only Semyonych would open the door right away! Otherwise that wizened little figure (why wasn't he in his carriage?) would appear out of the fog. And on either side of the massive porch of the house he now saw a griffin, jaws agape, tinged pink by the dawn, holding rings for flagstaffs in its claws. And over the griffins the Ableukhov coat of arms was sculpted in stone. The coat of arms depicted a long-plumed knight, surrounded with rococo curlicues, being gored by a unicorn. A thought passed through Nikolai Apollonovich's head like a fish skimming the surface of the water: Apollon Apollonovich, who lived beyond the threshold of this door, himself was the knight being gored. After this thought another glided dimly by, without rising to the surface: the old family coat of arms applied to all the Ableukhovs, and he, Nikolai Apollonovich, was also being gored. But by whom?

This mental twiddle-twaddle lasted but a fraction of a second, and there, on the pavement—in the fog—he already spied a little figure hurrying toward the house. It was bearing down on him rapidly! Apollon Apollonovich Ableukhov looked like death in a

top hat. Nikolai Apollonovich—the crazy thoughts people have!—
pictured Apollon Apollonovich at the moment when he was performing his conjugal duties, and he experienced a familiar feeling
of nausea with renewed intensity (that was how he had been conceived).

The little figure was drawing nearer. Nikolai Apollonovich, to
his disgrace, perceived that he was overcome by the familiar feeling
of confusion, and. . . .

Nikolai Apollonovich leaped off the steps of the porch. Waddling like a duck, he ran—now it was inescapable—to meet his father,
and avoiding his eye, he said:

"Good morning, papa!"

Apollon Apollonovich was thinking that this young man, so shy
in appearance, was a scoundrel. But in his son's presence Apollon
Apollonovich was disconcerted by this thought:

"I see, I see, good morning. . . . Well, fancy meeting you here."

On the porch the griffins gaped their beak-shaped jaws. And the
long-plumed knight of stone, all in rococo curlicues, was being
gored by a unicorn. The more the precursors of day diffused in
blinding brightness, the more massively and distinctly did all the
projections of the buildings stand out, and the more purple was
the familiar blood red griffin with gaping jaws.

The doors burst open. The odor of the familiar premises enveloped the Ableukhovs.

The Ableukhovs rushed side by side through the doorway, each
embarrassed.

Red as Fire

Both knew that they were faced with a conversation, that a conversation was imminent. Apollon Apollonovich handed his top hat
to the lackey and dawdled over his galoshes. Nikolai Apollonovich
could not tell whether he knew the story of the red domino or not.
His luxuriant beaver fell onto the lackey's arm in a flash of silver.
And now Nikolai Apollonovich stood in his domino before the very
eyes of his father, in whose mind these lines began spinning:

> Fiery pigments, ever bright,
> I shall cast upon my hand;
> Red as fire may he stand
> In vast chasms of the light.†

He plucked at his sidewhiskers with his veiny hand.

"Ah . . . ah . . . a domino? . . . Well, fancy that!"

"I was at a masquerade. . . ."

"I see . . . Kolenka . . . I see. . . ."

Apollon Apollonovich stood chewing his lips ironically. His skin gathered in tiny wrinkles. It stretched taut on his skull. A serious talk was in the air: the fruit had ripened; it would fall; it fell and —suddenly:

> Apollon Apollonovich dropped a pencil (by the staircase). From ingrained habit, Nikolai Apollonovich rushed to pick it up. Apollon Apollonovich rushed to forestall him, but he stumbled and fell, his hands touching the bottom steps. His head fell forward and down and unexpectedly landed under the fingers of his son's hand. Nikolai Apollonovich caught sight of his father's neck (an artery was throbbing on one side). The neck's warm pulsation frightened him. He snatched his hand away, but he snatched it too late: at the touch of the cold hand the senator's head convulsed in a spasm. His ears twitched slightly. Like a jumpy Japanese ju-jitsu teacher, he threw himself to the side and straightened up on cracking knees.

All this lasted but a moment. Nikolai Apollonovich handed his father the tiny little pencil.

"Here!"

A trifle had knocked them one against the other, and had produced in both an explosion of thoughts and feelings. Apollon Apollonovich got completely flustered by the fear he felt in response to politeness (this male in red was the flesh of his flesh, and to be frightened by one's own flesh was disgraceful). He had been sitting *under* his son, on his haunches. Apollon Apollonovich felt annoyance as well. He assumed a dignified manner, bowed from the waist, and compressed his lips primly:

"Thank you. I wish you pleasant dreams."

Nikolai Apollonovich felt a rush of blood to his cheeks, and when he thought he was beginning to blush, he had actually turned crimson. Apollon Apollonovich, seeing that his son was turning crimson, himself began to blush. In order to hide the blush, he flew up the staircase, with coquettish grace.

Nikolai Apollonovich found himself alone, plunged deep into thought. But the voice of the lackey wrenched him out of it:

"How could I have been so dim! I seem to be losing my memory completely. Master, dear master, if you only knew what's happened!"

"What's happened?"

"Something that—ohhh! . . . I hardly dare say. . . ."

Nikolai Apollonovich lingered on the steps of the gray velvet-carpeted staircase. A fine network of deep purple patches was now falling from the window onto the spot where his father had just stumbled. It looked like blood (on an ancient weapon).

"What's happened is really something! Why, the mistress! . . .

"Our mistress, Anna Petrovna . . .

"Has come back!!"

. . . .

A feeling of nausea made Nikolai Apollonovich begin yawning, openmouthed, at the dawn. He stood there red as a torch.

"Has come back!"

"Who has come back?"

"Why, Anna Petrovna."

"Who's Anna Petrovna?"

"Your mother. . . . What's the matter, master, dear boy: you're acting like a stranger. It's your mother who's come back."

"?"

"Yes, sir, from Spain, she's returned to Petersburg."

. . . .

"She sent a letter by messenger. She's staying at a hotel because . . . you yourself know why. . . ."

"?"

"His Excellency, Apollon Apollonovich, had just gone out when there was a messenger with a letter. . . . Well, I put the letter on the table, and slipped the messenger twenty copecks. . . .†

"I reckon not an hour had gone by when, merciful heaven, she herself suddenly turned up in person . . . really and truly she must have been sure, I swear to God, she must have known nobody was home."

. . . .

The battle mace glittered. A patch of fallen daylight glowed blood red: a column extended from the wall to the window. Dust specks danced in it. Nikolai Apollonovich thought this was how the blood danced in him. Man was a column of steaming blood.

. . . .

"So I goes and I opens the door . . . there stands a strange lady, dressed real simple, and all in black. I says to her: 'What can I do for you, madam?' And she answers me: 'Mitry Semyonych, don't you really recognize me?' And I rushes and kisses her hand: 'Anna Petrovna, our dear lady,' I says. . . ."

. . . .

You have only to touch the first person you meet with a razor blade and the white hairless skin will be slit open (this is how a suckling pig in aspic with horseradish sauce is sliced).

.   .   .   .

"And Anna Petrovna—may God grant her health—kept looking, and so she kept looking. She looked at me and burst into tears: 'I want to see how you've been getting along without me. . . .' And from a little reticule—not in our fashion—she took out a small handkerchief. . . .

"I have the strictest orders not to admit. . . . Except I let our mistress in. . . . And she. . . ."

Instead of showing any surprise, compassion, or joy, Nikolai Apollonovich flew up the staircase, the blood red satin trailing in the air like a tail.

The reason why Nikolai Apollonovich interrupted Semyonych and flew up the staircase was that he had a clear picture of a scoundrel committing an act. He pictured the scoundrel, the snip-snip of gleaming scissors in the scoundrel's fingers as he clumsily flung himself on a little old man to clip through an artery. The little old man had a neck with a throbbing pulse—it was crayfishlike, somehow. And the scoundrel went snip-snip with the scissors through the artery. And stinking, sticky blood poured over his scissors. And the little old man—beardless, wrinkled, bald—broke into sobs, and stared him straight in the eyes, squatting on his haunches, trying to squeeze shut the opening in his neck, from which blood was spurting in a barely audible whistle.

This image rose before him (for, when the old man had sprawled on all fours, he could have torn the battle mace off the wall, given a swing and . . .). He was frightened.

That was why he had fled through the rooms, heels clattering.

A Bad Omen

The rooms were now radiant with sunlight. The small incrusted tables shot arrows through the air. All the mirrors burst into laughter, because the mirror that looked from the drawing room into the hall now reflected a Petrushka. He was running, and mirror threw reflection at mirror. Reflected in the mirrors was a Petrushka, who had flown headlong into the drawing room, and now stood rooted to the spot, his eyes darting from mirror to mirror, because he saw that the first mirror had reflected a skeleton in a buttoned-up frock coat, protruding from which, right and left, were a naked ear and a small sidewhisker.

Apollon Apollonovich, seeing a marionette in the mirrors instead of his son, waited for it to come closer.

Apollon Apollonovich pulled the hallway door shut, and retreat was cut off: he had to finish what he had started. He regarded the conversation as a surgical operation. Like a surgeon briskly walking up to an operating table on which scalpels, saws, and drills were laid out, Apollon Apollonovich, rubbing his fingers, walked toward *Nicolas*, stopped, took out his eyeglass case, twirled it between his fingers, put it away, and gave a cough:

"Very well then, the domino. . . ."

"What about it! . . . People were masked. . . . So I did the same . . . got myself a costume. . . ."

Nikolai Apollonovich thought that his father's tiny fifty-six-inch-long body (twenty-one inches in diameter), was the periphery of an immortal center. Entrenched there was the "I." But any old board that broke loose at the wrong time could crush the center. Under the influence of this thought which he had perceived Nikolai Apollonovich thinking about him, Apollon Apollonovich ran off to a small table standing at a remove, and drummed his fingers on it. Nikolai Apollonovich advanced on him, laughing:

"It was a lot of fun, actually. . . . Actually, we danced. . . ." He thought: skin and bones, and blood, without a single muscle. This anatomical obstacle should be blown to bits. If all that were to be evaded today, it would come upon him in a rush tomorrow evening.

Apollon Apollonovich instinctively glanced in the gleaming mirror and caught the look. He turned on his little heels and caught the end of the sentence:

"Then we played petits-jeux."

Apollon Apollonovich made no reply. That sullen look was fixed on the parquetry. Apollon Apollonovich remembered: once upon a time this "Petrushka" had been a tiny body which he had carried in his arms with paternal tenderness, a little boy with fair curls, who would put on a little paper dunce-cap and clamber up on his neck. And Apollon Apollonovich, his voice out of tune and cracking, would hoarsely croon:

> Noodle-doodle, dummy-wummy,
> Little Kolya's dancing:
> On his head a dunce-cap wears,
> On his horse he's prancing.

He would carry this little child's body up to this very same mirror. Age and youth would be reflected there. He would point out the reflections to the boy:

"Just look, son: there are strangers there."

Kolenka would cry and scream at night. And now? Apollon
Apollonovich saw another body, strange, large. . . .

And Apollon Apollonovich began circulating about the room.

"You see, Kolenka . . ."

He sank into a deep armchair.

"Kolenka, I must. . . . That is, not I, but, I hope, *we* must . . .
have a little talk. Do you have time to spare just now? The question, and a disturbing one at that, is that . . ." He stumbled in mid-
sentence and again ran up to the mirror (at that moment chimes
rang out). Death in a frock coat looked out of the mirror into the
drawing room. And the mirror cracked: a jagged needle-thin line
cut through it like a flash of lightning, with a faint crackling sound,
and it froze there for all time in a zig-zag.

A superstitious person would have said:

"A bad omen!"

Nikolai Apollonovich evidently was again attempting to put off
the little talk. A little talk was now superfluous: everything would
explain itself anyway. Nikolai Apollonovich regretted that he had
not made his getaway from the drawing room in time.

"Papa, I must confess that I have been expecting our little talk."

"Are you free?"

"I am."

He could not tear himself away from his father. He stood before
him. . . . Here I must say:

Oh, worthy reader: we have presented the exterior of the wearer
of diamond-studded decorations without any humor, just as it would
appear to any ordinary observer, and not as it revealed itself to us.
We, after all, have had frequent occasion to observe it at close
quarters. We have penetrated into a soul shaken to its very founda-
tions and into the whirlwinds of consciousness. It would be advisable to remind the reader of the way that exterior looks in its
general outlines, for as is the appearance, so too is the essence. Were
this essence to appear before us, were the whirlwinds of consciousness to sweep by, tearing the frontal bones apart, then . . . but not
another word! But an outsider looking on would see: the skeleton
of a gorilla.

"Kolenka, go to your room. Collect your thoughts before we talk.
If you find inside yourself something that would be advisable for
us to discuss, come to my study."

"Very well, papa."

"Oh, by the way, take off that sideshow getup. I don't like this
whole business at all."

"?"

"No, I don't like it! I don't like it in the least!!!"

Two yellow little bones drummed sharply on the card table.

By the Card Table

Nikolai Apollonovich remained standing by the card table. His glance kept shifting back and forth over the little boxes and the little shelves that stood out from the walls. Yes, here was where he had played. Here he had sat for hours on end, in this very same armchair, where tiny garlands curled their way over the pale azure satin of the seat. And here, as before, hung David's "Distribution des aigles par Napoléon Premier," which represented the Emperor in laurel wreath and royal mantle.

What would he say to his father? More lies? When lies were useless? Lies in his situation? Nikolai Apollonovich remembered how he had told lies while still a child.

The grand piano, a yellow period piece on casters, rested on the parquetry. Here his mother used to sit. Here the olden sounds of Beethoven had shaken the walls.

Now the sun glanced in. It cast its sword-beams. The thousand-armed age-old titan illuminated spires, roofs and the sclerotic forehead pressed against the pane. The thousand-armed titan mutely lamented its solitude out there: "Come ye, come unto the age-old sun!"

But the sun seemed to him a colossal thousand-legged tarantula, flinging itself on the earth with insane passion.

He squinted because everything had flared up: the lampshade scattered amethysts, and sparks flashed on the wing of a golden cupid, and the surface of the mirrors burst into flames. One of them had a crack in it.

"And what are we going . . . to . . .?"

Nikolai Apollonovich raised his countenance. . . .

"To do about . . . the mistress?"

He saw Semyonych.

"I . . . really don't know . . ."

Semyonych chewed his lips:

"Should I report this to the master?"

"Do you mean papa doesn't know?"

"Why, I didn't dare . . ."

"Why then, go ahead and tell him."

"Very well, I'll tell him."

And he went into the corridor.

Everything, everything, everything: this sunlit glitter, the walls, the body, the soul—everything would crash into ruins. Everything was already collapsing, collapsing, and there would be: delirium, abyss, bomb.

A bomb is a rapid expansion of gases. The sphericality of the expansion evoked in him a primordial terror, long forgotten.

In childhood he had been subject to delirium. In the night, a little elastic blob would sometimes materialize before him and bounce about†—made perhaps of rubber, perhaps of the matter of very strange worlds. It would produce a quiet lacquered sound on the floor: pèpp—peppèp; and again: pèpp—peppèp. Bloating horribly, it would often assume the form of a spherical fat fellow. This fat fellow, having become a harassing sphere, kept on expanding, expanding, and expanding and threatened to come crashing down upon him.

"Pèpp. . . .

"Pèppovich. . . .

"Pèpp. . . ."

And it would burst into pieces.

Nikolenka would start shrieking nonsensical things: that he too was becoming spherical, that he was a zero, that everything in him was zeroing—zeroing—zero-o-o. . . .

And the governess, Karolina Karlovna Lessing,† in a white bed-jacket, her hair in curl papers, would look at him angrily out of a yellow circle of candlelight, and the circle expanded and expanded. Karolina Karlovna kept repeating:

"Now, mein dear kleiner Kolenka, you calm yourself: dass is just growing. . . ."

She was not looking at him, but—Lessinging, lessening, lessss. . . .

Pèpp Pèppovich Pèpp.

"Am I delirious, or what?"

Nikolai Apollonovich pressed his fingers to his forehead: delirium, abyss, bomb.

And in the window, out the window—from far, far away, where the banks quietly cowered, where the buildings of the islands squatted submissively, the penetrating spire of Peter and Paul, tormentingly sharp, pitilessly gleaming, thrust up into the lofty sky.

Semyonych's step was heard receding down the corridor. No use in delaying: Apollon Apollonovich was waiting.

Packets of Pencils

The senator's study. A desk loomed, but it was not the main thing. Bookcases lined the walls. To the right, Nos. 1, 3, and 5, and to the left, the even numbers. The shelves sagged beneath the books arranged according to plan. In the middle of the desk was a textbook entitled *Planimetry*.

Before going to bed, Apollon Apollonovich very often used to leaf through this little volume, so as to quiet the restless life inside his head with the most blissful outlines of parallelepipeds, parallelograms, cones, and cubes.

The leather-covered back of the armchair tempted him to lean back on such a trying morning. Apollon Apollonovich was stiffly formal. He sat absolutely erect behind the desk, awaiting the appearance of his good-for-nothing son. He pulled open a small drawer. There, under the letter "r," he retrieved a small diary, entitled "Observations," and there, in the "Observations," he began to jot down thoughts that had stood the test of experience.

He was interrupted by a frightened sigh. At this, Apollon Apollonovich pressed down hard and turned. The quill broke.

"Master, Your Excellency . . . I make bold to report to you (I just now remembered) . . ."

Apollon Apollonovich stood out sharply in a composition of lines, both gray and black. He looked like an etching.

"Well, our mistress, you see, sir—I make bold to report to you . . ."

Apollon Apollonovich cocked an immense ear.

"Wha–a–at–eh? . . . Speak up, I can't hear you."

The trembling Semyonych bent toward the pale green ear, which was looking at him expectantly:

"The mistress, sir . . . Anna Petrovna . . . has returned. . . ."

"?"

"From Spain—to Petersburg. . . ."

.   .   .   .

"Wh–a–at?!?"

.   .   .   .

"She is staying at a hotel . . .

"Your Excellency had just gone out when a messenger, with a letter . . .

"Well, I put the letter on the table, and slipped the messenger twenty copecks . . . .

"Hardly an hour had gone by, when suddenly I hear—uhh—someone ringing. . . ."

.   .   .   .

Apollon Apollonovich, one hand placed on the other, sat rooted in the chair, calmly impassive, motionless, and without a thought. His glance fell on the spines of the books: *Code of the Laws of Russia*. Volume One. Volume Two. On the desk, in front of some packets, were a gold inkstand, pens and quills, and a heavy paperweight, on which a little silver peasant (definitely a loyal subject) was raising a convivial bowl.†

.   .   .   .

"So I goes and I opens the door, Your Excellency. The mistress . . .

"I says to her: 'What can I do for you?' The mistress looks at me: 'Mitry Semyonych . . .'

"I rushes and kisses her hand: 'Anna Petrovna, our dear lady,' I says . . .

"She says: 'I just want to see how you've been getting along without me. . . .' "

. . . .

Apollon Apollonovich pulled open a drawer and extracted a dozen little pencils (very, very cheap ones), took two in his fingers, and the little sticks snapped in his fingers. Apollon Apollonovich was wont to express his agony by breaking packets of pencils which were kept for just such an occasion in the drawer under the letter "b."

. . . .

But, all the time he was snapping the packets of pencils, he nonetheless managed to preserve his impassive air, and nobody would ever have said that this stiffly formal aristocrat . . . that the convexity of this forehead concealed a desire to gird the earth with a prospect, as with a chain.

Semyonych withdrew. Apollon Apollonovich, discarding the fragments of the pencils, looked rejuvenated, quickly began adjusting his cravat, quickly jumped up and began scurrying about, all afidget. All of a sudden he looked like his son: a photograph of Nikolai Apollonovich taken in the year nineteen hundred and four.

At that moment, crash after crash resounded from a remote part of the house. And Apollon Apollonovich came to a halt, wanted to lock the study, but hesitated, because the crash proved to be merely the sound of a slamming door (the sound came from the drawing room). There was an agonized coughing, a shuffling of slippers: times of old were gathering strength in his memory in the sounds of the tune to which Apollon Apollonovich had first fallen in love:

"A–baaate, agi–taaa-tions of paaa–sions . . .
"Fall siii–lent, heart hooope–less and weaaa–ry . . ."

"But why? And what of it?"

The door opened. On the threshold stood Nikolai Apollonovich in uniform, even down to the sword (this is how he had been dressed at the ball, except now he had taken off the domino), but wearing slippers and a varicolored Tartar skullcap.

"Well, papa, here I am. . . ."

Apollon Apollonovich, instead of starting in on the domino (now was hardly the time for the domino), began to speak of another matter.

"You see, Kolenka . . . your mother, Anna Petrovna, has returned."

Nikolai Apollonovich thought: "So that's what it's all about." He pretended to be agitated:

"But certainly, I know. . . ."

Actually, for the first time he realized fully that his mother, Anna Petrovna, had returned. But he reverted to his old habit: contemplation of the neck and ears of the old man. The thoroughly flustered mien and the maidenly bashfulness with which the old man . . .

"Anna Petrovna, my friend, committed an action which, so to speak, it is difficult . . . it is difficult for me, Kolenka, to char–ac–ter–ize with sufficient composure."

The squeak of a mouse.

"In a word, the action is well known to you. You will have noticed that I have refrained from discussing this action in your presence, out of deference to your natural feelings."

They were unnatural.

"Yes, papa, I understand you."

"But of course"—Apollon Apollonovich slipped two fingers into his vest pocket and again began scurrying back and forth on a diagonal (from one corner to another)—

"But of course, her return to Petersburg is an unexpected event."

(Apollon Apollonovich let his gaze come to rest on his son, and raised himself slightly on tiptoes.)

"A completely unexpected event for all of us."

"Who would have thought it?"

"That's exactly what I say, who would have thought"—Apollon Apollonovich spread his hands in perplexity and shrugged his shoulders; he exchanged a bow with the floor—"that Anna Petrovna would return." Again he began scurrying back and forth. "This completely unexpected event may end, as you have every reason to suppose, in a change (Apollon Apollonovich raised a finger, his voice rumbling through the entire room) in our domestic status quo. Or else (he turned), everything will remain as before."

"I would have thought . . ."

"In the first instance, she is welcome. . . ."

Apollon Apollonovich bowed to the door.

"In the second instance," Apollon Apollonovich began to blink.

Apollon Apollonovich raised his eyes, and the eyes were full of sorrow:

"Kolenka, I really don't know, but I think. . . . It is difficult to explain to you, out of deference to your natural feelings, which. . . ."

Nikolai Apollonovich felt a surge—can you imagine of what? Of love! For the old despot who was condemned to be blown to bits.

He made a sudden start toward his father. Another instant and he would have fallen on his knees before him to confess and beg for mercy. But the old man pursed his lips, and waved his little hands squeamishly:

"No! Leave me alone, please! I know what you're after! You have heard what I have to say, sir. Now kindly leave me in peace."

Two fingers rapped on the desk. A hand indicated the door:

"You, my dear sir, have been pleased to lead me around by the nose. You, my dear sir, are no son of mine. You are the most horrible of scoundrels!"

All this Apollon Apollonovich did not say but shrieked. Nikolai Apollonovich leaped out into the corridor: those two protruding ears would become—just you wait!†—slush.

Pèpp Pèppovich Pèpp

Nikolai Apollonovich crashed into the door. He ran up to the desk, upsetting a chair in the process.

"Damn it all. . . . Where can it be?

"?

"!

"Ah!

"Here it is. . . .

"Good. . . ."

Nikolai Apollonovich had the habit of talking to himself.

And yes, he was in a hurry. But the drawer would not obey. Out of the drawer he flung small tied packets of letters, and a photograph of cabinet size: a comely little lady looked back at him. The photograph flew off to the side, and right under the photograph was the bundle. He weighed it in his palm: something rather heavy about it. He quickly set it down.

He began undoing the knots of the napkin. Slight, fidgety, he resembled the senator, and even more, a photograph of the senator taken in 1860.

His trembling fingers could not undo the knot. There was really no point in undoing it: everything was clear. Nonetheless, he undid the bundle. His astonishment knew no bounds.

"A bonbonniere . . .

"Wha-a-a . . .?

"A ribbon!"

And when he had torn the ribbon loose, his hopes were shattered (he had been hoping for something). Beneath the pink ribbon, the bonbonniere contained—not sweet candies from Ballet's, but a small tin.

Then, he happened to notice a clock mechanism attached to the side. There was a little metal key which had to be turned so that the small sharp black hand would point to the hour. Nikolai Apollonovich felt that he would not be able to turn the key. After all, there was no way at all of stopping the movement of the mechanism once it had started; and in order to cut off all possibility of retreat, Nikolai Apollonovich grasped the little metal key with his fingers. Whether because his fingers trembled or whether because he felt his head spinning, he tumbled headlong into that abyss which he had wanted to escape. The little key slowly turned to one o'clock, then to two o'clock, and Nikolai Apollonovich jumped off to the side. He glanced at the desk out of the corner of his eye. There lay a small tin containing oily sardines (on one occasion he had made himself sick on sardines, and ever since then he had not touched them). A sardine tin, an ordinary sardine tin: with rounded corners. . . .

"No!"

A sardine tin with horrible contents!

And a life incomprehensible to the mind had already erupted, and the hour hand, the minute hand now crawled, and the nervous fine hair that indicated the seconds began skipping around the circle —until the instant when—

> —the horrible contents of the sardine tin would expand in a rush, uncontrollably; then: the sardine tin would fly apart. . . .
>
> —the gases would briskly spread in circles, tearing the desk to bits with a thunderous roar, and something would burst with a boom inside him; and his body would be blown to bits; mixed with the splinters, mixed with the gases, it would splatter in slush;
>
> —in a hundredth of a second the walls would collapse, and the contents, expanding, would whirl off into the wan sky in splinters, stones, and blood.

Shaggy dense smoke would billow and unfurl and tail onto the Neva.

Once he had turned the key, he had to find a place for the little box (for instance, in the small white bedroom). Or else: crush it beneath his heel.

Crush it beneath his heel?

His ears twitched. He felt nauseated, as if he had swallowed the bomb like a pill. There was a bloating sensation in the pit of his stomach.

He would never crush it, never!

The only thing left was to throw it into the Neva, but there was still time for that. He had only to turn the little key twenty times more and everything would be postponed. But he dawdled, and sank into an armchair with no strength left. He was overcome by drowsiness. His power of thought was weakened, and as it broke away from his body, it sketched meaningless, idle arabesques of some kind. . . .

.   .   .   .

Nikolai Apollonovich had devoted the best years of his life to philosophy, and not without reason: he was hostile to any form of divination. Divination beclouded and obscured the idea of the source of perfection. For a philosopher, perfection is Thought: God, so to speak. Nikolai Apollonovich respected, so to speak, the founders of the great religions.

But why talk about religion? Was there time to think about. . . . Nikolai Apollonovich's final effort to rouse himself from drowsiness was not crowned with success, and he did not manage to recall anything. Everything seemed peaceful . . . prosaically so. His power of thought was weakened, and as it broke away from his body, it sketched meaningless feeble arabesques.

Nikolai Apollonovich Ableukhov had particular respect for the Buddha, assuming that Buddhism had surpassed all religions in two respects: in the psychological—it taught love for all living creatures; in the theoretical—its logic had been developed by Tibetan lamas. Nikolai Apollonovich remembered that he had read the logic of Dharmakirti with commentaries by Dharmottara.†

That was in the first place.

And in the second place: from time to time, while passing from the outer door to the inner door of the entryway, a certain strange, very strange state came over him, as if everything that was beyond the door was not what it was, but something else. Beyond the door there was nothing. If the door were to be flung open it would be flung open onto the measureless immensity of the cosmos, and the only thing left was to . . . plunge into it headfirst and fly past stars and planetary spheres, in an atmosphere of two hundred and seventy-three degrees below zero.

The Last Judgment[†]

This was the state in which he was sitting in front of the sardine tin: he saw, yet did not see; and he heard, yet did not hear. And his body crashed from the parquet floor into absolute zero degrees. His head silently came to rest on the table (on the sardine tin), and looking back at him through the door that opened onto the corridor was—the bottomless, which Nikolai Apollonovich had attempted to push away, while setting off on a distant astral journey,[†] or sleep (which, let us note, is the same thing). The open door opened onto the measureless immensity of the cosmos.

And from the door, from measureless immensity, something was looking at him: some kind of head of some kind of god there (it peered and disappeared). His Kirghiz-Kaisak ancestors had maintained relations with the Tibetan lamas. They swarmed in the Ab-Lai-Ukhov blood in goodly number. Was that not the reason why he had a tender feeling for Buddhism? Heredity told. In the sclerotic veins heredity throbbed in millions of corpuscles.

The dream was interrupted. Anguished and mute, someone was approaching. From there, from there the times of old, like the wail of taxis hurtling upon us, gathered strength in the age-old strains of the tune:

"A—baate, agi—taaa—tions of paaa—sions . . .
"Fall siii—lent, heart . . ."

"Aaah"—came a roar from the doorway. The horn of a taxi? No: it was an age-old head.

Nikolai Apollonovich leaped to his feet.

Was it the head of Confucius or of Buddha? In the doorway, the swish of an iridescent silken dressing gown; and he recalled his own Bukhara dressing gown, with the same iridescent feathers—the dressing gown, over whose smoky-sapphire fabric crawled sharp-beaked, golden, winged miniature dragons. The five-tiered headdress with flaps looked like a miter. Above the head shone a multi-rayed nimbus. In its center was a wrinkled countenance, its lips gaping *Chronically*. Thus a hallowed Mongol entered the room: millennian breezes wafted.

Nikolai Apollonovich was thinking: Chronos[†] had favored him with a visit in the guise of a Mongol ancestor. In the hands of the Stranger he sought the blade of the traditional scythe, but there was no scythe. In the yellowish hand, fragrant as the first lily, was an oriental saucer with a small sweet-smelling heap of rosy paradise apples.[†]

He denied paradise: paradise, or the garden, was incompatible with his idea of the higher good (he was a Kantian). He was nirvanic man.

And by Nirvana he understood Nothingness.

Nikolai Apollonovich remembered: he was an old Turanian† who had been incarnated in the blood, in the flesh of the hereditary nobility, in order to carry out a secret mission: to shake everything to its very foundation. The Ancient Dragon was to feed on tainted blood, and to consume everything in flame. The ancient Orient had rained a hail of bombs on our age. And Nikolai Apollonovich was an old Turanian bomb. Now, having seen his ancestral home, he was exploding, and on his face appeared a Mongol expression. Now he seemed a mandarin of the Middle Kingdom, invested in a frock coat for his passage to the West (for he was on a most secret mission).

Thus the age-old Turanian, dressed for the time being in an Aryan domino, rushed rapidly over to the stack of notebooks, in which he had outlined the theses of a well-reasoned metaphysics. And all the notebooks together formed the immense cause to which his entire life was devoted: the Mongol cause came through everywhere in these notes under the headings, under all the paragraphs: the mission that had been entrusted to him before he was born.

The guest, the hallowed Turanian, stood there. His arms rose rhythmically ever upward, and his garments fluttered up like the winnowing of passing wings. The smoky background of the fabric cleared, deepened, and suddenly became sky, which looked into the rent air of an ordinary study. The dark sapphire crevice proved to be in a room lined with bookshelves (thus the dressing gown had become an enormous crevice opening onto the sky). The tiny dragons twinkled there like tiny stars. . . . Indigo air, with an infusion of stars, was gushing in from there.

And Nikolai Apollonovich rushed to the guest (one Turanian to another), a notebook in his hand:

"Kant (Kant too was a Turanian).

"Value as a metaphysical nothing!

"Social relations based on values.

"The destruction of the Aryan world by means of a system of values.

"Conclusion: the Mongol cause."

The Turanian replied:

"The task has not been understood. Paragraph one—the Prospect.

"Instead of value, numeration: by houses, floors and rooms for time everlasting.

"Instead of a new order, the record of the circulation of the citizens of the Prospect.

"Not the destruction of Europe but its immutability. . . .

"The Mongol cause. . . ."

. . . .

He was condemned, and the wrinkled countenance bent until it nearly touched his. He glanced at the ear, and understood that the old Turanian who was instructing him in all the ways of wisdom was Apollon Apollonovich. That was the one against whom he had raised his hand.

And that was the Last Judgment.

.   .   .   .

"How then can this be? Who can this possibly be?"

"Your father."

"Who?"

"Saturn."†

.   .   .   .

The Last Judgment was at hand.

There was no Earth, no Venus, no Mars, merely three revolving rings.† A fourth one had just blown up, and an enormous Sun was still preparing to become a world. Nebulae whirled past. Nikolai Apollonovich had been cast into measureless immensity, and distances flowed.

Afterwards he found himself on Earth. The sword of Saturn hung suspended, and the continent of Atlantis collapsed. Nikolai Apollonovich was a depraved monster. Then he was in China, and there Apollon Apollonovich, the Emperor of China, ordered him to slaughter many thousands (which was done). In more recent times thousands of Tamerlane's horsemen had poured down on Rus. Nikolai Apollonovich had galloped into this Rus on a charger of the steppes. He was then incarnated in the blood of a Russian nobleman. And he reverted to his old ways: he slaughtered thousands *there*. Now he wanted to throw a bomb at his father. But his father was Saturn. The circle of time had come full turn. The kingdom of Saturn had returned.

The flow of time had ceased to be. All was being destroyed.

"Father!"

"You wished to blow me to bits, and therefore, all is being destroyed . . ."

"Not you, but . . ."

"All is crumbling into ruins, toppling onto Saturn. . . ."

The atmosphere was darkening outside the windows. All had reached a burning hot state, expanding uncontrollably. It was whirling horribly.

"Cela . . . tourne . . ." howled Nikolai Apollonovich, who had been deprived of his body but had not noticed it.

"No, sa . . . tourne. . . ."

.   .   .   .

Having been deprived of his body, he nonetheless felt his body: the invisible center, which had formerly been consciousness, seemed to have a semblance of what it had been. Logic had turned into bones, and syllogisms were wrapped all around like sinews. The contents of logic were now covered with flesh. Thus the "I" again presented its corporeal image, although it was not body. And in that which had exploded was revealed an alien "I": it had come running from Saturn. It had returned to Saturn.

He sat as he used to sit previously—without body but in a body. (How very peculiar!) Outside the windows, in the darkness, re-sounded: *tourne–tourne.*

The chronology was running backwards.

"What then is our chronology?"

But Saturn, Apollon Apollonovich, roaring with laughter, replied:

"None, Kolenka, none at all: the chronology, my dear boy, is—zero."

"Oh! Oh! What then is 'I am'?"

"A zero."

"And zero?"

"A bomb."

Nikolai Apollonovich understood that he himself was a bomb. And he burst with a boom.

.   .   .   .

He awoke from his dream. He understood: his head was lying on the sardine tin.

A dreadful dream. But what was it? He could not recollect. His childhood nightmares had returned: Pèpp Pèppovich Pèpp, swelling from the little blob, was in the sardine tin—

—Pèpp Pèppovich Pèpp is
a Party bomb, chirring inaudibly;
Pèpp Pèppovich Pèpp will expand and
expand. And Pèpp Pèppovich Pèpp:
will burst!

"Am I delirious, or what?"

Again in his head began whirling: what to do? Only a quarter of an hour left. Should he turn the key?

He turned the little key twenty times. Twenty times something wheezed. The ravings had passed, so that morning could remain morning, day could remain day, evening could remain evening. But as the coming night waned, no movement of the little key would postpone anything: the walls would collapse.

End of the Fifth Chapter

Chapter the Sixth

in which are related the events of a gray little day

> *Behind him e'er the Horseman Bronze*
> *With heavy tread came riding on.*†
>
> Pushkin

The Thread of His Being Once Again Has Been Found

Alexander Ivanovich half opened his eyes which kept wanting to close. The night had been an event of gigantic proportions.

The transitional state between wakefulness and sleep was as if he were jumping out of a narrow window from the fourth floor. Sensations were opening a breach: he was flying into this breach.

The awakening flung him down headlong from there. His body hurt and ached all over.

He noticed: he was being shaken by violent chills. All night long he had tossed and turned. Something had happened, most likely. . . .

His delirious flight went on and on. Along something like misty prospects, or the steps of a mysterious staircase. Or rather, fever was running through his veins. Memory was telling him something, but what it was kept slipping away. There was some connection he could not make.

Good and frightened (when he was alone he was afraid of illness), he thought: it wouldn't hurt to sit it out at home.

"I could use a bit of quinine.

"And some strong tea . . .

"With some dried raspberries . . ."†

A sigh escaped him.

"I should strictly abstain. . . . Not read Revelation. . . . Not go down to visit the porter. . . . Not have chats with Styopka. . . ."

Thoughts of tea, vodka, Styopka, and Revelation calmed him.

But after washing his face with cold water from the faucet, he once more felt an onrush of nonsense.

He ran his eyes over the twelve-rouble room (garret lodgings).

What a wretched habitation!

The bed consisted of cracked boards laid on wooden trestles. Dried spots, probably from bedbugs, stood out on them.

The trestles were covered with a skimpy mattress stuffed with bast. The thin knitted blanket could hardly be called striped: the suggestions of blue and red stripes were covered with deposits due less to dirt than to many years of active usage (it too had made the journey to the Yakutsk region and back).

Hanging on the wall was a small icon depicting Serafim of Sarov at prayer† (Alexander Ivanovich wore a cross under his shirt).

In addition to the bed there was a small smoothly planed table. Tables of just this kind are used as washbasin stands in summer cottages. Tables of just this kind are sold in outdoor markets. It served both as a writing table and as a night stand. A washbasin was lacking: Alexander Ivanovich availed himself of the services of a water faucet and of a sardine tin containing a sliver of Kazan soap. There were also some clothes hooks. The tip of a worn slipper protruded from under the bed (once, in a dream, this slipper had been a living creature, like a dog or a cat; it had shuffled about on its own, crawling around the room and rustling in the corners; when he had tried to feed it a soft piece of chewed white bread the shuffling creature bit his finger with the jagged hole at its tip; he woke up).

There stood a swelling brown suitcase which had altered its original shape.

All the furnishings of this habitation paled before the color of the wallpaper, unpleasant and insolent—somewhere between dark yellow and darkish brown, with damp spots. In the evenings a sow bug crawled across one of the spots.

Alexander Ivanovich Dudkin looked over his habitation. He had an urge to get out of the room—into the dingy fog, there to merge with shoulders, backs, greenish faces on a Petersburg prospect.

Swarms of October mists stuck to the window. He felt the desire to be permeated by the fog and to drown in it the nonsense that was chirring in his brain, to extinguish the flashes of raving by exercising his legs. He had to pace from prospect to prospect, from street to street, until the brain was numbed, and then collapse on the table of some eatery and let the vodka burn his gullet.

Putting on his shabby overcoat he once more thought:

"Now would be the time for a bit of quinine!"

Who's he kidding—quinine!

"Now would be the time for some strong tea with dried raspberries!"

The Staircase

The staircase!

Menacing, shadowy, damp, it had pitilessly echoed the sound of his shuffling step. That had been last night. He had come this way: it had not happened in a dream.

Annihilating silence was spreading everywhere. It formed rustlings. And thick lips of some sort—uncontrollably, untiringly—smacked and gulped saliva in long, distinct swallows. There were sounds woven from the moaning of the ages. From above, from the windows, gloom was swept up now and then into ragged outlines; and a tarnished turquoise spread beneath his feet, without a single sound.

The moon looked down.

But the swarms—shaggy, smoky—rushed over the moon: the turquoise gradually darkened.

Alexander Ivanovich recalled: yesterday he had run up the staircase, summoning his last ounce of strength, without the slightest hope of overcoming—but what exactly? And some kind of outline was running after him.

And was dooming him irrevocably.

.   .   .   .

The staircase!

On a gray day it is prosaic. Here dull thumps and thuds: that's someone chopping cabbage. Over the railing is draped a tattered rug, smelling of cats—from apartment number four. A floor polisher is hitting it with a carpetbeater. Some pale blond hussy sneezes into her apron from the dust.

.   .   .   .

Oilcloth-covered doors!

That one, that one, and that one. . . . On that one the oilcloth has torn loose, and shaggy tufts of horsehair stick out of holes here and there. And to this one a small card is attached with a pin; and on it is written: "Zakatalkin." Who he may be, what his first name is, what his patronymic is, what his profession is—I leave it to you to judge. "Zakatalkin"—and that's it.

A violin bow industriously saws out a familiar tune. A voice is heard:

"To the fa–a–atherland belo–o–oved. . . ."

I suppose Zakatalkin is a fiddler in some miserable little restaurant orchestra.

And, Tearing Loose, He Broke into a Run

Away from here! Out onto the street!

He had to start pacing once again, to pace on and on until the brain was completely numbed, so that he would dream no more of phantoms dark. To pace all over Petersburg, to lose himself in the

damp reeds, in the hanging vapors of the seashore, and to put everything out of his mind in his stupor and then come to his senses
amidst the cozy lights of the Petersburg suburbs.

He started down the staircase at a trot, but he came to an abrupt
halt. He noticed some shady type wearing an Italian cloak and a
fantastically turned-down hat hurrying along, frantically twirling
a heavy cane in his hand.

This strange shady type flew at him slap-bang. He very nearly
poked him in the chest. His head jerked back. Under his very nose
Alexander Ivanovich Dudkin saw a forehead covered with perspiration and with a throbbing vein. By this twitching vein he recognized Ableukhov.

Nikolai Apollonovich cut him off with a menacing whisper:

"You, of course, understand: *I cannot and furthermore I do not
want to*. In a word—*I won't do it*."

"!"

"My refusal is irreversible. You can pass that on. And I ask you
to leave me in peace."

Nikolai Apollonovich turned. Twirling his heavy cane, he rushed
back down the stairs.

"But stop!" Alexander Ivanovich hurried after him and felt the
steps tremble as he flew down the staircase.

"Nikolai Apollonovich?"

He caught Ableukhov by the sleeve, but he tore loose.

He quickened his pace across the small courtyard.

Alexander Ivanovich made a grab for the door, intensely alarmed,
and in two leaps overtook him.

He clamped a hand on the retreating edge of the Italian cloak.
For a moment they began grappling among the stacks of firewood.
Nikolai Apollonovich, gasping with rage, shrieked some insulting
nonsense:

"Do you call *this* public action? Party work? Surrounding me
with agents. Having me followed everywhere, while you've lost
faith in everything yourself. . . . You, my dear sir, you . . . you
are . . ."

Finally, tearing loose once more, Nikolai Apollonovich broke into
a run.

The Street

They were now flying along the street.

"Nikolai Apollonovich," the agitated Dudkin would not let up,
"you must agree: we can't part without some explanation."

"There's nothing more to talk about," Nikolai Apollonovich flung
at him as he ran.

"Explain yourself more clearly," Alexander Ivanovich insisted.

Hurt and astonishment were written all over his features. Nikolai Apollonovich could not help but notice that the astonishment was genuine.

And he turned around, in less of a temper now, and said in a whining and vicious tone:

"What more is there to explain? I have the right to demand. . . . After all I'm the one who's suffering, not you, not your comrade. . . ."

"What?"

"To have given me the bundle . . ."

"So?"

"Without warning, without explanation . . ."

Alexander Ivanovich blushed.

"And then vanishing into thin air. . . . And then threatening me with the police through some middleman or other. . . ."

Alexander Ivanovich gave a nervous start:

"Wait, what police? What disgusting filth is this? What are these insinuations? Which one of us is out of control?"

But Nikolai Apollonovich rasped:

"Oh, you, I'd like to" . . . came his rasp (his mouth seemed about to bite his ear) ". . . I'd gladly . . . right now, on this very spot . . ."

There, over there . . .

On a summer evening, in the window of that gleaming little house, a little old woman was chewing her lips.

Alexander Ivanovich knew that that very same missile had been brought first to his garret, from that very same little house.

He could not help but shudder.

He understood only one thing from the raving of the senator's loving son about the police, about a decisive, irreversible refusal.

"Listen here, it all comes down to the bundle."

"Precisely: you handed *it* over to me for safekeeping."

They were talking by that same little house in which the bomb had come into being. The bomb, having become a mental bomb, had come full circle.

"Nikolai Apollonovich, you are insulting me. What do you find reprehensible about my conduct?"

"What do you mean?"

"The Party?"—he uttered the word in a whisper—"asked you to look after the bundle temporarily. You agreed, didn't you? And that was that. If you find it unpleasant to keep the bundle, I can stop by and pick it up."

"Oh, please, wipe that innocent expression off your face. If it were just a matter of the bundle . . ."

"Shh! Quiet: we might be overheard."

"Then . . . I would have understood you . . . don't feign ignorance."

"But what are you so upset about?"

"About the use of coercion."

"There was no coercion."

"About the agents."

"But there was *no* coercion, I repeat. You agreed."

"Yes, last summer."

"What do you mean, last summer?"

"Yes, in principle I gave my consent or rather, I offered, and . . . perhaps . . . I gave a promise, on the assumption that there could not possibly be any compulsion, since there is no compulsion in the Party. If you resort to compulsion, then you are nothing but a pack of petty intriguers. Well, what if I did give a promise? Don't you suppose I thought the promise could be taken back?"

"Now wait a minute. . . ."

"And do you suppose I knew they would twist my offer into *this* . . . that they would propose that I . . ."

"Now wait a minute, I really must interrupt. What promise are you talking about? . . . But you can't mean *that* promise?"

He seemed to remember that on one occasion, in a squalid little tavern, Nikolai Stepanych Lippanchenko had informed him that Nikolai Apollonovich had. . . . He did not want to remember! . . . And he quickly added:

"But I'm not talking about *that*, *that's* not the point."

"What do you mean it's not? The whole point is the promise, the promise which has been interpreted as irreversible and in a base manner."

"Not so loud, Nikolai Apollonovich, what's base about it? Where's there any baseness?"

"What do you mean, where?"

"Where? The Party asked you to look after it temporarily, and that's all."

"That's all?"

"All."

"If it had been just a question of the bundle, then I would have understood you. Excuse me. . . ."

He gave a wave of the hand:

"But can't you see that the conversation is going round in circles, it's the same old story, over and over again, and nothing more. . . ."

"You've got a one-track mind, you've been harping about coercion, or something of the sort. I just recalled: rumors have reached me . . ."

"Well?"

"About an act of violence which you proposed to us. So the intention originated with you!"

Alexander Ivanovich remembered (*that person* had told him about it in the squalid tavern). Through some middleman, Nikolai Apollonovich had proposed to do away with his father. It was his recollection that *the person* had added: there was only one thing for the Party to do—decline. The unnatural choice of victim, the suggestion of cynicism verging on something utterly vile—his sensitive heart had reacted to all this with a paroxysm of loathing (Alexander Ivanovich had been drunk at the time; later, the entire conversation with Lippanchenko had struck him as merely the play of his besotted brain, not as sober reality). This he remembered.

"I should say . . ."

"To demand from me," interrupted Ableukhov "that I . . . with my own hand . . ."

"Yes, exactly."

"That's vile!"

"Yes, vile. And, Nikolai Apollonovich, I didn't believe it. If I had believed it, you would have gone down . . . in the Party's opinion."

"So you regard it as vile?"

"Yes, I'm sorry to say. . . ."

"There, you see! You yourself call it vile. Still, didn't you have a hand in it too?"

At this point something suddenly upset Dudkin:

"Just a minute . . ."

And clutching at the buttons of the Italian cloak, he fixed his eyes on some point beyond:

"Don't get carried away. We're accusing each other, yet we're both agreed . . . on what this act is to be called. . . . Didn't we say base?"

Nikolai Apollonovich shuddered:

"Of course it's base!"

They fell silent.

Nikolai Apollonovich, taking a handkerchief out of his pocket, stopped, and began wiping his face.

"This surprises . . . me. . . ."

"Me too. . . ."

In bewilderment they looked each other in the eye. Alexander Ivanovich again touched the edge of the cloak:

"To disentangle the whole knot, answer me this: the promise to . . . with your own hand (and so on). . . . It didn't originate with you?"

"No! Definitely not!"

"Consequently, you were not a party to a murder of this kind, even in thought. I'm asking you because a thought sometimes expresses itself accidentally, through gestures, intonation, glances—even through a trembling of the lips. . . ."

"No, no . . . that is"—here he caught himself remembering that he had once caught himself giving voice to a suspicious train of thought. And catching himself, he blushed:

"I did not love my father. . . . And more than once I expressed myself. . . . But that I should. . . . Never!"

"I believe you."

Nikolai Apollonovich, at the worst possible moment, suddenly blushed to the tips of his ears. Because he had blushed, he wanted to explain himself, but Alexander Ivanovich shook his head, not wishing to get anywhere near the unutterable thought that had come to them both in a flash.

"There's no need . . . I believe you . . . I have something else in mind. Here's what I want you to tell me now frankly: am I supposed to be a party to it?"

Nikolai Apollonovich looked at his naive companion in surprise —looked, blushed, and with an excess of passion, which he now required to conceal a certain thought, loudly shouted:

"In my opinion, yes. . . . You helped *him*. . . ."

"Who?"

"The Unknown One."

"?"

"It was the *Unknown One* who demanded . . ."

"!"

"That a vile act be committed."

"Where?"

"In a disgusting note."

"I know of no such person."

"The Unknown One," a baffled Nikolai Apollonovich insisted, "is your Party comrade. Why are you so surprised? What surprises you?"

.   .   .   .

"But I assure you there is no *Unknown One* in the Party."

.   .   .   .

"What? There is no *Unknown One* in the Party?"

"Not so loud. . . . No."

"For three months I've been receiving notes . . ."

"From whom?"

"From him."

Each fixed goggling eyes on the other; and one let his drop in horror, while a shadow of faint hope flickered in the eyes of the other.

.   .   .   .

"Nikolai Apollonovich"—his fear overcome, crimson blotches of boundless indignation suffused Alexander Ivanovich's cheeks—"Nikolai Apollonovich!"

"Well?"

But Alexander Ivanovich still could not catch his breath.

"Well, don't keep me in suspense!"

But Alexander Ivanovich shook his head and said nothing. An inexpressible something streamed from his forehead, from his stiffening fingers.

He said with an effort:

"I assure you, on my word of honor: I had no part in this business."

Nikolai Apollonovich did not believe him.

"Well, then, what docs all this mean?"

And he looked with unseeing eyes off into the recesses of the street. How the street had changed!

"That doesn't make it any easier. I didn't sleep at all last night."

The top of a carriage hurtled off into the recesses of the street. How the street had changed, and how these grim days had changed it!

A wind from the seashore swept in, tearing off the last leaves, and Alexander Ivanovich knew it all by heart:

There will be, oh yes, there will be bloody days full of horror. And then—all will crash into ruins. Oh, whirl, oh swirl, last days!

Oh whirl, oh swirl through the air, you last leaves!

A Helping Hand

"So *he* was at the ball?"

"Yes, *he* was."

"He was having a talk with your father."

"Precisely, he mentioned you too."

"Afterwards you met in an alleyway?"

"He took me to some restaurant or other."

"His name?"

"Morkovin."

.   .   .   .

Nikolai Apollonovich began gabbling away, his profile, teeth bared, bent low, resembling an ancient tragic mask, which was incompatible with his lizardlike restlessness.

He went on with his effusions about the ball, about the mask, about his flight through the ballroom, his sitting on the steps of a little house, about the gateway, the note, and finally about the tavern.

Abracadabra! They had lost their minds: *that which dooms irrevocably*—was real.

. . . .

Rolling toward them down the street were many-thousand swarms of bowlers. Rolling toward them were top hats, and the froth of ostrich feathers.

Noses sprang out from everywhere.

Beaklike noses: eagles' and roosters'; ducks' and chickens'; and—so on and on—greenish, green, and red. Rolling toward them senselessly, hastily, profusely.

"Consequently, you suppose that error has crept into everything?"

Having made this tentative overture, Nikolai Apollonovich felt clumps of goosebumps breaking out all over his body. (But what if he were only pretending?)

Alexander Ivanovich tore himself away from his contemplation of noses.

"Not error, but charlatanism of the vilest kind is at work here. This absurdity has been deliberately maintained in order to stifle the Party's public action."

"Then help me. . . ."

"An impermissible mockery"—Dudkin interrupted him—"made up of gossip and phantoms."

Alexander Ivanovich extended his hand to Ableukhov. Here, incidentally, he noticed that Nikolai Apollonovich was shorter than he (he was not distinguished by his height).

"Come now, keep cool."

"It's easy for you to say keep cool. I didn't sleep at all last night."

He reassured him:

"I'm confident that I can disentangle the knots of these vile machinations. I will immediately initiate inquiries, and . . ."

He hesitated: he could make inquiries of Lippanchenko; but was he in Petersburg?

"And . . . ?"

"I'll give you an answer tomorrow."

Alexander Ivanovich was struck by one small fact.

Nevsky Prospect

All the shoulders formed a viscous and slowly flowing sediment. The shoulder of Alexander Ivanovich stuck to the sediment, and was, so to speak, sucked in. In keeping with the laws of the organic wholeness of the body, he followed the shoulder and thus was cast out onto the Nevsky.

What is a grain of caviar?

There the body of each individual that streams onto the pavement becomes the organ of a general body,† an individual grain of caviar, and the sidewalks of the Nevsky are the surface of an open-faced sandwich. Individual thought was sucked into the cerebration of the myriapod being that moved along the Nevsky.

And wordlessly they stared at the myriad legs; and the sediment crawled. It crawled by and shuffled on flowing feet; the sticky sediment was composed of individual segments; and each individual segment was a torso.

There were no people on the Nevsky, but there was a crawling, howling myriapod there. The damp space poured together a myria-distinction of voices into a myria-distinction of words. All the words jumbled and again wove into a sentence; and the sentence seemed meaningless. It hung above the Nevsky, a black haze of phantasmata.

And swelled by those phantasmata, the Neva roared and thrashed between its massive granite banks.

The crawling myriapod is horrible. It has been moving along the Nevsky for centuries. Higher, above the Nevsky, the seasons run their course. The cycle there is mutable, but here it is immutable. The times of year have their limit. The human myriapod has no limit; all the links are interchangeable; it is always the same; beyond the railway terminal it turns its head;† its tail thrusts into the Morskaya; along the Nevsky shuffle the individual arthropodic links.

Exactly like a scolopendra!

Dionysus

"Do you understand? Do you understand me, Alexander Ivanovich?" repeated Nikolai Apollonovich.

"Yes, I understand you."

"Life has been stirring . . ." Nikolai Apollonovich said, "in the tin. The mechanism has been ticking in a strange manner."

At this Alexander Ivanovich thought:

"What is this tin business?"

But listening more attentively, he understood: he was talking about the bomb.

"I set it in motion. It was, how shall I put it? dead. I turned the little key—and you know, it even began sobbing, I assure you, like a body being awakened."

"So you started it going?"

"Yes, for twenty-four hours."

"What have you done?! Throw it in the river at once!?" Alexander Ivanovich flung up his hands in horror.

"It made a face at me."

"The tin?"

"Generally speaking, a tremendous number of constantly changing sensations took possession of me when I was standing over it.
A tremendous number . . . the devil only knows what. . . . I was
bursting with disgust. . . . All sorts of rubbish came to mind, and—a
feeling of disgust for *it*, an unaccountable feeling of disgust for the
shape of the tin, for the idea that, maybe, before this, sardines . . .
(I can't stand the sight of them). A feeling of disgust welled up in
me such as you feel toward a hard-shelled insect chirring and chat-
tering in your ears. It dared to chitter something at me."

"Hm!"

"You know, the taste you get when the tin plating's beginning
to wear off dishes. . . . I was bursting, nauseated! Oh, as if I . . . had
swallowed it. . . ."

"Swallowed it? Ugh, how vile!"

"I became the bomb, with a ticking in my belly."

"Quiet! Someone might hear!"

"They wouldn't understand anything, it's impossible. . . ."

"But you know," Alexander Ivanovich said with interest, "when
something is ticking . . . if you just listen closely to the sound, you
will hear something that's there and something that isn't. . . . Once
I tried to scare a neurasthenic. I began tapping my finger in rhythm
with our conversation. Well then, he looked at me, turned pale, and
fell silent, and then he went and asked: 'What is this?' I answered:
'Nothing,' and went on tapping. Would you believe it—he had a
seizure. He got so offended that he stopped recognizing me after
that."

"No, no, it's impossible to understand what it's all about. . . .
Nightmares came back to mind. . . ."

"Could it be your childhood?"

"As if a bandage had fallen off all sensations. You know, something began stirring above my head. I understood what's meant by
one's hair standing on end. It's not the hair—that I understood last
night. My body was like the hair standing on end. It bristled. My
legs and arms and chest were made out of invisible fur. Or here's
another way of putting it: it's as if you were lowering yourself into
a mineral-water bath, and there are little bubbles of carbon dioxide
all over your skin—tickling, pulsating, running faster and faster. And
it develops into a powerful feeling, as if you were being torn to
pieces, pulled in opposite directions: in the front your heart is being
ripped out, and your own spine is being ripped out of your back
like a stick from a wattle fence."

"And you were like Dionysus being torn to pieces, Nikolai Apollonovich. But, all joking aside, now you're speaking in another
language, not that of Kant."

"But I've just told you: the bandage fell off all sensations. . . . Yes, that's right, not that of Kant, you're absolutely right . . . Kant has nothing to do with it!"

"He does, Nikolai Apollonovich, in that here we have logic entering into the blood itself; in other words, there is utter stagnation. Life gave you a terrible shock. The blood rushed to your brain. The pounding of blood can be heard in your words."

"And all of me is swelling up, I've been swelling up for a long time, perhaps for hundreds of years. And I'm walking around like a swollen monster . . . it's horrible."

"It's nothing but sensations."

"You mean . . . I'm not? . . ."

"On the contrary, you've gotten thinner."

"I was standing there, over *it*. . . . Yes, but it wasn't *I* standing there, not I at all, but a giant with the head of an idiot whose sinciput hadn't properly knitted together. My body was prickling all over, and I could distinctly feel the prickling—at a distance of about seven inches from my body! Just think! I was turned inside out."

"It's simply that you were beside yourself."

"It's all very well to say 'beside yourself.' The expression is allegorical, without any basis in the fact of bodily sensations. *Beside yourself* is completely bodily, physiological, if you will. And the sensations of the organs flowed everywhere, suddenly expanded, and spread into space like a bom—"

"Shh!"

"Into pieces!"

"Not long ago when I was at your place with the bundle I asked you why *I* am *I*. You didn't understand."

"But now I understand *everything*. It's horrible, isn't it horrible. . . ."

"It's not horrible—it's a truly Dionysian† experience, not a verbal one, it goes without saying."

"The devil only knows what it was!"

"Calm yourself, Nikolai Apollonovich, you're terribly tired. No wonder; you've gone through so much! It would lay anybody low." Alexander Ivanovich felt the need to get away from all this chatter so as to give himself a calm account of what had happened.

Revelation

To pace, once more to pace, to collapse on the table of some eatery, think things out and drink vodka.

He was supposed to have delivered the letter himself, on the instructions of *a certain person*. And deliver it to Ableukhov.

He had taken the letter with him when he set out for Ableukhov's with the bundle. And he had forgotten to deliver the letter. He had handed it to Varvara Evgrafovna, who said that she would be seeing Ableukhov. This letter might have been . . . the fateful one.

But no!

It was not that one. According to Ableukhov, the letter had been handed to him at the ball by a masker.

Alexander Ivanovich calmed down. The letter he had received from Lippanchenko was definitely not *the* one.

He had just grasped all this and was about to cut through the flow of carriages when:

"Alexander Ivanovich!"

Nikolai Apollonovich, all out of breath, was running through the crowd, sweaty and trembling all over:

"Just a minute . . ."

Oh Lord!

"Alexander Ivanovich, it's difficult to part from you. . . . I have something else to tell you. . . ." He led him over to the nearest shop window.

"Something else has been revealed to me . . ."

"Nikolai Apollonovich, I must be off, and on a matter involving you."

"Just a second, half a second . . ."

Nikolai Apollonovich's whole aspect betrayed—well, all right—a kind of inspiration.

"I was growing, you see, into an immeasurable expanse, all objects were growing along with me, the room and the spire of Peter and Paul. There was simply no place left to grow. And at the end, at the termination—there seemed to be another beginning there, which was most preposterous and weird, perhaps because I lack an organ to grasp its meaning. In place of the sense organs there was a 'zero.' I was aware of something that wasn't even a zero, but a *zero minus something*, say five, for example."

"Listen," interrupted Alexander Ivanovich, "tell me this: did you receive the letter through Varvara Evgrafovna?"

"The letter . . ."

"Not *that* one, not the *note*, the letter sent through Evgrafovna."

"Oh, you're talking about the verses signed *A Flaming Soul*?"

"Well, I don't know about that."

"Yes, yes, I certainly received it. Uh, what was I saying? That 'a *zero minus something*' . . ."

"Oh Lord, that again! Why don't you go and read the Apocalypse."†

"I've heard that from you before. I'll be sure to read it, when you've reassured me concerning . . . *all this*. I feel that I'm starting to get interested. I'll stay put at home, take a bromide, and read the Apocalypse. There's something still left from last night: everything's real, yet not quite real. . . . Look: this shop window—there are reflections in the window, there's a gentleman going by—look: there we are, you see? Yet it's somehow strange. . . ."

"Yes, it's strange," Alexander Ivanovich nodded his head in affirmation. Lord knows, he was certainly a specialist in the "how strange" area.

"Or consider this: objects . . . the devil only knows *what* they are. Real yet not quite real. For instance, the tin is just a tin; but no, it's not just a tin but . . ."

"Shh!"

"A tin with horrible contents!"

"You'd better throw the tin into the Neva at once, and everything will go back to where it was. Everything will return to its proper place."

"It will not, it won't. . . ."

Alexander Ivanovich, truth to tell, did not know how to deal with this babbling: whether to try calming him down or to break off the conversation.

"Nikolai Apollonovich, you've been sitting over your Kant in a shut-up airless room. You've been hit by a squall. You've listened to it carefully, and what you've heard in it is yourself. Anyway, your states of mind have been described, and they're the subject of observations."

"Where, where?"

"In fiction, in poetry, in psychiatry, in research into the occult."†

Alexander Ivanovich smiled at how illiterate this mentally developed scholastic was, and he continued:

"A psychiatrist . . ."

"?"

"Would call . . ."

"Yes–yes–yes . . ."

"Well, your 'real yet not real'—try calling it a pseudohallucination."

"?"

"That is, symbolic sensations of a kind that do not correspond to the sensation produced by a stimulus."

"Well, so what? To say that is to say nothing at all!"

"Yes, you're right."

"No, it won't do."

"Of course, a modernist would call it the sensation of the abyss, and he would search for the image that corresponds to the symbolic sensation."

"But that is allegory."

"Don't confuse allegory with symbol.† Allegory is a symbol that has become common currency. For example, the usual understanding of your 'beside yourself.' A symbol is your act of appealing to what you experienced there, over the tin. A more appropriate term would be the term: pulsation of the elemental body. That's precisely the way you experienced yourself; as the result of a shock, the elemental body in you went into a very real spasm. For an instant it separated from the physical body, and so you experienced everything that you experienced there. According to the teaching of certain schools, the experiences of the elemental body transform verbal meanings and allegories into real meanings, into symbols. The writings of the mystics abound in symbols. After what you have experienced I advise you to read these mystics."

"I told you I will and I will."

"And with regard to what happened to you I can merely add: sensations of that kind will certainly be your first experience in the afterlife, as Plato describes it,† citing the assurances given by the Bacchantes. There are schools of experience where such sensations are deliberately produced and where nightmares are transformed, by hard work, into harmonious regularity, as one studies rhythms, movements, pulsations, and as one introduces the sobriety of consciousness into the sensation of expansion, for example. But why are we standing here? We've gone on and on. You need to go home and . . . throw the tin into the river. Sit tight, and don't set foot outside the house (you're probably being watched). Keep taking bromides. You're horribly worn out. No, better not take bromides. People who abuse bromides become incapable of doing anything. Well, it's time for me to dash—on a matter involving you."

Alexander Ivanovich darted into the flow of bowlers, turned, and shouted out of the flow:

"And throw the tin into the river!"

His shoulder was sucked into the shoulders. He was rapidly borne off by the headless myriapod.

Nikolai Apollonovich shuddered. He would return, slip *it* into his side pocket, and—into the Neva with it!

Nikolai Apollonovich felt that he was expanding. At the same time he felt: it had begun to drizzle.

The Caryatid

Opposite the black of an intersection a caryatid hung suspended above the street.

From there loomed the Institution where Apollon Apollonovich held sway.

The bearded caryatid at the entryway had crushed an impetuous hoof into the wall. And it seemed that he would break loose and spill into the street!

What he sees is mutable, inexplicable, inapprehensible: clouds sailing by.

And beneath his feet he sees the flow of the myriapod along the pavement, where deathlike is the rustling of moving feet and where green are the faces. They give no sign that somewhere momentous events are rumbling.

From observing the procession of bowlers, you would never say that momentous events were rumbling† in the town of Ak-Tyuk, in the theater in Kutais. In Tiflis a local policeman had discovered that they were manufacturing bombs. The library in Odessa had been closed. The universities of Russia were one big mass meeting. The citizens of Perm had started acting ornery. The Reval iron works had already begun running up red flags.

From observing the procession of bowlers, no one would have said that a strike had already begun on the Moscow–Kazan railway line.† Here and there windows had been smashed in the stations, warehouses broken into, and work was being stopped on the Kursk, Windau, Nizhny–Novgorod and Murom railway lines. And railway cars stood idle. And no one would have said that momentous events were rumbling in Petersburg. Typesetters from all the printing shops had elected delegates and had held meetings. Factories were on strike: the shipyards, the Alexandrovsky Factory.

The circulation was not disrupted: the bowlers continued their deathlike flow.

. . . .

The gray caryatid bent over and looked at that same crowd. There was no limit to his contempt, and no limit to his despair.

Oh, had he the strength!†

His muscular arms would unbend and straighten. His chiselled sinciput would jerk loose. His mouth would tear open in a thunderous roar. The street would be drenched in steam. The cornice of the balcony would break apart into heavy stones. The venerable statue would break off into the street in a hail of stone, describing an arc.

. . . .

On that gray day a heavy door flew open. A clean-shaven gold-braided lackey in gray beckoned the coachman. The horses tore up to the entryway and the lackey gave a stupid look and snapped to attention. Apollon Apollonovich Ableukhov, slightly stooped, bent, unshaven, with swollen face and drooping lip, touched raven black gloves to his raven black top hat.

Apollon Apollonovich cast a glance full of indifference at the lackey, the carriage, the coachman, the great black bridge, the expanses of the Neva, where the foggy, many-chimneyed distances were so wanly etched and where rose the Island, ashy and indistinct.

The carriage door with the unicorn coat of arms was slammed shut. The carriage flew headlong into the fog, past the dull-blackish cathedral and the monument to the Emperor Nicholas, onto the Nevsky, where the tatters of a red calico banner fluttered. The contours of the carriage and the outline of the footman's tricorne and the wings of his greatcoat now cut into the shaggy sediment. Manchurian hats, cap-bands and visored caps broke into song as one.

The carriage came to a halt.

Get Away, Tom!

"Mais j'espère que oui," jangled the voice of a foreigner.

Alexander Ivanovich did not like to eavesdrop.

It was growing dark, dark blue.

His steps were not heard. Alexander Ivanovich crossed the threshold.

A heavy fragrance, a mixture of perfumery and medicines.

Zoya Zakharovna was endeavoring to get some foreigner to sit down.

"I hope you have formed a fine impression of Russia. What unprecedented enthusiasm, isn't it?"

"Mais j'espère . . ."

Zoya Fleisch turned her somewhat distracted gaze on the Frenchman, and then on Alexander Ivanovich. Her bulging eyes were protruding. She looked like a large-headed brunette of about forty. Her powder was flaking.

"Do you need to see *him?*" she asked unexpectedly. Hostility lurked in that quick question, and perhaps hatred. But the hatred was hidden with a smile: dirt is concealed in sticky sweet candies set out for display.

"All the same I'll wait for *him*."

Alexander Ivanovich reached for a pear. Zoya Zakharovna moved the fruit bowl away.

Pears were all very well and good, but they weren't what mattered.

What mattered was the voice which had begun singing from somewhere back there, horribly cracked and with an impossible accent. That was no way to sing and no one sings like that. You could imagine that the singer was a man with dark hair. He had a chest like so: sunken. And the eyes of a cockroach. Very likely a consumptive, from Odessa, or even a Bulgarian† from Varna, propagandizing something, and full of hatred.

Meanwhile Zoya Fleisch:

"Yes, yes, yes, we are living through events of historic significance . . . vigor and youth . . . a historian will write . . ."

"Pardon, madame, monsieur viendra-t-il bientôt?"

Alexander Ivanovich almost tripped over a Saint Bernard gnawing on a bone.

The cottage windows looked out on the sea: dark blue.

And the eye of a lighthouse began blinking, "one–two–three," and went out. The dark cloak of a passerby. The waves curled in crests. Lights on the shore were scattered in tiny grains. The many-eyed seashore bristled with reeds. A siren wailed.

"Here's an ashtray."

But Alexander Ivanovich was easily offended, so he ground out his cigarette butt in a flower vase.

"Who's that singing there?"

"What? You don't know? You might as well know, it's Shishnarfiev. That's what comes from being a lone wolf. He's wonderfully artistic."

He merely asked:

"A Bulgarian?"

"Oh, no, not at all."

"A Persian?"

"From Shemakha. He was almost killed in the massacre at Isfahan."†

"Ah. . . ."

And Zoya Zakharovna turned to the Frenchman.

Alexander Ivanovich was thinking that the features of Fleisch's face had been taken from several beautiful women: the nose from one, the mouth from another, the ears from a third beauty.

But brought all together they were irritating.

The Frenchman put her in her place.

"Excusez, dans certains cas je préfère parler personnellement. . . ."

The waves could be seen foaming. A vessel was rocking, crepuscular, dark blue. It cut through the gloom with sharp-winged sails. Bluish night was slowly thickening on the sails.

A cab drew up to the little garden, and the body of a fat bulky man, suffering from shortness of breath, leisurely tumbled out, burdened with half a dozen parcels. One hand seemed to be fiddling with a leather purse. From under an arm a bag fell toward a mud puddle; the paper tore and Antonov apples rolled in the mud.

A sinister head covered by a cap with ear-flaps was settled on the chest. The deep-set little eyes did not dart, but wearily fixed on the window panes.

And Alexander Ivanovich managed to detect (just imagine!) joy, the animal joy of having supper after travails endured. Thus a beast, upon returning to its lair, seems meek, and displays the benignity of which it is capable. It amiably sniffs at its mate and licks its cubs.

And this is *the person?*

Yes, this is *the person.*

.   .   .   .

"Lippanchenko!"

"Hello."

The dog jumped up, its paws falling on *the person's* chest.

"Get away, Tom!"

The person put up a desperate defense of his purchases. A mixture of humor and helpless malice left an imprint on his square face.

"He's slobbered over everything again!"

But the dog's tongue gave the tip of the nose a lick. *The person* gave a helpless shout:

"For heaven's sake, Tommy!"

He stopped laughing and snapped, without the slightest courtesy:

"I'll be with you in a minute. I just have to . . ."

His drooping lip quivered, and written all over the lip was:

"They won't let me alone even here."

The person was stamping about in the corner: his overshoes would not come off. He stood in the corner, taking his time about removing his shabby overcoat and rummaging in his pocket. His hand slid out of his pocket with a toy, a tumble-up doll.

"Here's something for Akulina's little Manka."

He turned to the Frenchman:

"This way . . . please. . . ."

And he flung at Dudkin:

"You'll have to wait."

Frontal Bones

"Zoya Zakharovna . . ."

"Huh?"

"Shishnarfiev is an active representative of Young Persia,† he has an artistic nature. But what's the Frenchman doing here?"

"If you know too much you'll get old before your time," she replied, mangling the Russian proverb, and her inordinately large breasts began to stir under her bodice.

There was a mixed smell of perfumery and a tooth being prepared for treatment (anyone who has sat in dentists' offices is familiar with it; the smell is not among the most pleasant).

"And you're still . . . the recluse. . . ."

"If I weren't a recluse, so what? Somebody else would be."

Alexander Ivanovich amended himself:

"You're right: living such a distracted life doesn't suit me."

"Is that why you've strewed ashes all over the tablecloth?"

But Alexander Ivanovich reached for a pear and said to himself: "What a tightwad she is."

He liked Duchess pears, but the fruit bowl with the pears was no longer on the table.

"Here's an ashtray."

"I was reaching for a pear."

But Zoya Zakharovna did not offer any pears.

He looked through the half open door: silhouettes could be seen. Frenchie was gabbling away, and *the person* was booming on and seizing writing implements, now one, now another. He was scratching the back of his head. Alexander Ivanovich detected a gesture of out-and-out self-defense.

Tom had slowly lowered his muzzle onto the checked knee of *the person. The person* was absentmindedly stroking his fur. Alexander Ivanovich's observations were interrupted:

"Why have you stopped coming to see us?"

"No particular reason. You said yourself I'm a recluse."

But the gold of her filling gleamed.

"Are you offended with him?"

"How could you think that?" But it came out unconvincingly.

"They're all offended. Oh this Lippanchenko business! It's ruining— Try to understand: this Lippanchenko is a role he has assumed. Without this Lippanchenko he would have been arrested. He protects all of us with this Lippanchenko."

A bad smell from her mouth—Alexander Ivanovich moved away.

"You just tell me." She grabbed the atomizer. "Where would you ever find such an active worker? Tell me, who would agree, as he did, to reject all sentimentality and become simply Lippanchenko?"

Alexander Ivanovich thought: *the person* is too much of a *Lippanchenko*.

"I assure you . . ."

But she interrupted:

"Aren't you ashamed to abandon him like *this*, to be *so* secretive, to drop out of sight. Why, Kolechka . . . to break off intimate ties. . . ."

Here Alexander Ivanovich recalled: *the person* was Kolechka.

"Well, what if he does take a drink, and have his little flings? After all, better men have been known to take to drink and debauchery."

Alexander Ivanovich smirked.

"What?"

"No . . . I . . . nothing. . . ."

"Remember Helsingfors and our boating excursions . . ." Sorrow could be heard in Zoya Zakharovna's voice. "And now, this gossip . . ."

"What gossip?"

He gave a shudder.

"Gossip about Kolechka! You think he isn't tormented, that he doesn't cry out at night? (Alexander Ivanovich made a mental note: *he cries out at night.*) How they talk about him! They have no conception of what that man has sacrificed. He keeps silent, he grieves, he's gloomy. He looks unpleasant"—and tears could be heard in Zoya's voice—"because of his . . . his . . . unfortunate outward appearance. Believe me, he's just a child."

"A child?"

"A child! Just look: the doll, the tumble-up doll," she pointed at the doll, her bracelet flashing. "You'll leave, after telling him a lot of unpleasant things, while he, he . . . !"

"?"

"He'll sit the cook's little daughter on his lap, play dolls with her. . . . He's accused of treachery. . . . Heavens, he plays with toy soldiers!"

"Well, what do you know!"

"Tin soldiers! He orders them by the box from Nürnberg. That's the kind of man he is!"

Alexander Ivanovich was coming to the conclusion that *the person* was compromised. And, truth be told, he hadn't known that. He now took that into consideration as he let his gaze wander back to where they were sitting.

The low, narrow forehead was hanging at a sharp angle. The deep-set piercing little eyes inquisitively flitted from object to object. The lip quivered slightly and sucked at the air. The face composed itself with insurmountable disgust into *a strange whole*, which Alexander Ivanovich then carried in his memory back to the garret where he would pace at night, begin booming, suck the air, let his eyes flit about and squeeze out of himself inexpressible meanings which nowhere exist.

He peered attentively at the oppressive, heavy-set features.

That frontal bone . . .

It protruded outward in a stubborn effort to understand, come what may, at whatever price, to understand or . . . fly to pieces. This small forehead betrayed neither rage nor treachery, but an effort to understand, without thought. And it was unable to understand. Low and narrow, creased with wrinkles, it seemed to be weeping.

The inquisitively piercing little eyes . . .

Had one raised their lids,† they would have become . . . just . . . little eyes. . . .

And they were full of sorrow.

And the lip that was sucking the air resembled—honestly!—the lip of a nursing infant of a year and a half. Were a nipple to be inserted between his lips, it would not have been surprising if he had begun sucking. In the absence of a nipple the movement gave the face a nasty cast.

Just imagine! Playing with toy soldiers!

Such an analysis of the monstrous head revealed only one thing: the head was the head of a premature child whose puny brain had been covered before its time by enormous bony growths. And while the frontal bone was protruding outward in arcs above the eyes (cf. the skull of a gorilla), beneath the bone, perhaps, an unpleasant process called, in common parlance, softening of the brain was already in progress.

The combination of sickliness and rhinocerouslike stubbornness had added up to a chimera. The chimera grew night after night—on a piece of dark yellow wallpaper—into a real Mongol.

Not Good . . .

A strange business!

Heretofore, from way back, the conduct of *a certain person* with regard to Alexander Ivanovich had had the nature of creating endless obligations. And irksome obligations. For months on end *that person* had been fashioning an ornamental design of flattery.

And that flattery was readily believed.

Alexander Ivanovich felt a physical revulsion. He had been avoiding *the person* these past few days, while he was undergoing an agonizing crisis of loss of faith in everything. But *the person* was everywhere present. Alexander Ivanovich had flung mockingly open challenges at him. *The person* had taken up the challenges with cynical laughter.

He knew that *the person* was laughing at their common cause.

He kept reiterating to *the person* that their Party's program was without foundation, and *the person* agreed. He knew that *the person* had a hand in the working out of the program.

He tried to shock *him* with his credo and with his assertion that the Revolution was a hypostasis. *The person* had nothing against mysticism: he listened attentively, and tried to understand.

But he was unable to understand.

He accepted all his protests and all his extreme conclusions in submissive silence. He would pat him on the shoulder and would drag him off to some tavern. They would sip cognac. *The person* would say:

"I am a rowboat, but you are a battleship."

Nevertheless, he had packed him off to the garret. He had hidden him there. The battleship lay in drydock without a crew. All its sailings had been limited to sailings from tavern to tavern.

One impression remained with him: if serious help were ever suddenly needed, *the person* had to provide that help.

And today an opportunity had presented itself.

The person, he believed, would be able to disentangle it all.

But *the person's* tone had changed. The tone had become unpleasant, offensive, and forced (heads of institutions receive petitioners in just such a tone).

Like it or lump it!

After the conversation with the Frenchman (the Frenchman had withdrawn), *the person* did not emerge from the study, but continued sitting there, at his small writing table, as if Alexander Ivanovich were not there at all and as if he were not an acquaintance but the devil only knows what.

And it was growing dark.

And in the darkening half-twilight of the small study *the person's* yellow jacket stood out. His square head was slightly inclined (all that could be seen above his back was a sweep of dyed hair). He presented a broad back and an unwashed neck. The back rather bulged and presented itself all wrong—indecently, mockingly. The shoulder and the back positively burst with mocking insolence out of the half-twilight. He felt disgusted. He spat.

The deep fold of his neck bulged between the back and the back of the head in a faceless smile. The neck had the appearance of a face, as if a monster with a completely noseless and eyeless mug had sat down in the armchair. The fold of the neck looked like a toothless mouth rent wide.

There, on splayed feet, slumped a clumsy monster.

Alexander Ivanovich jerked his shoulder around and presented his own back to that back. He fell to plucking at his little mustache with an air of independence. He would have liked to look offended. All he managed was to look independent. He plucked at his little mustache with an air of nonchalance. Oh, he should have left, slamming the door. To leave was impossible: Nikolai Apollonovich's peace of mind depended on this conversation, and therefore, he depended on *the person*.

Alexander Ivanovich presented his own back to that back. But the back with the neckfold was nonetheless a magnetic back. He turned toward it, and *the person*, in his own turn, turned around, and his low narrow inclined forehead stared fixedly, resembling a wild boar about to sink in a tusk. This turning gesture cried out with the very obvious desire to deliver an insult. And the expression of the little eyes said caustically:

"So that's how it is, old chum. . . ."

Alexander Ivanovich clenched a fist in his pocket and turned away.

He grunted twice, so that his impatience would register on *the person's* hearing (he had to stand up for himself but not offend *the person* too much). But the grunting came out like a timid spasm in the throat of a schoolboy standing before his teacher. What was wrong with him? Why such timidity? He wasn't afraid of *the person*. He was afraid of the hallucinations on the wallpaper.

He grunted again. *The person* reacted:

"You'll have to wait."

What kind of tone was that?

At last *the person* raised himself up slightly. His palm described a gesture of invitation in the air.

Alexander Ivanovich was at a loss. His rage expressed itself in his fidgety forgetting of the most ordinary words:

"You see . . . I've . . . come . . ."

But *the person* leaned back in the armchair and began drumming a gnawed finger on the table, and he gave a hollow boom:

"I would ask you, my dear friend, to be as brief as possible."

And thrusting his chin into his Adam's apple, *the person* stared out the windows:

"Well, sir?"

And he squinted his little eyes.

Alexander Ivanovich Dudkin blushed and felt that he could not squeeze out another sentence.

The person remained silent.

And the red leaves beyond the windowpanes exchanged whispers as they fell off the trees; and the branches formed a misty network. The blackish network began to sway, and the blackish network began to murmur. Disconnectedly, helplessly, getting all tangled up in his words, Alexander Ivanovich set forth the Ableukhov incident. And *the person* grew more stern. At the point in the story where the provocateur Morkovin made his appearance, *the person* twitched his nose with a self-important air, as if up to this point he had been trying to appeal to the narrator's sense of ethics, and from this point on the narrator had become utterly unethical; and here *the person's* patience snapped:

"There, you see? And you maintained . . ."

And Alexander Ivanovich shrieked:

"But I've told you everything!"

The person said in a barely audible whisper:

"Not good, not good at all. . . . Aren't you ashamed!"

Shishnarfiev appeared in the adjoining room. The oppressive accent of a Young Persian. Shishnarfiev was hidden from view by a potted palm.

As for Alexander Ivanovich, he felt a sense of horror. Menace lurked in the words of the dreadful person he was talking with. He began squirming on the chair.

And frontal bones approached his forehead:

"I must cool you down. The letter to Ableukhov was written by me."

This tirade was delivered with a dignity which had overcome everything, even itself, and which condescended to . . . indulgence.

"What?"

"And it was sent through you. Or have you forgotten?"

The person pronounced the words "have you forgotten" with an air suggesting that Alexander Ivanovich knew all about this, but was pretending not to know.

"I delivered it, I assure you, not to Ableukhov, but to Varvara Evgrafovna."

"Enough, Alexander Ivanovich, old chum. The letter found its addressee. And the rest is just evasion."

"And you are the author of the letter?"

"What surprises you about that?"

"What surprises me?"

"Excuse me, I would say that your astonishment borders on dissembling."

And Alexander Ivanovich flung himself at *the person*, exclaiming:

"Either I've lost my mind or you . . ."

The person gave him a wink:

"Come now, old chum, I saw you spying on us. Do you think you can get away with that?"

Giving the appearance of suppressing a guffaw, *the person* laid a heavy arm on his shoulders, in an imposing manner, and added:

"Not good. . . . Not good at all. . . ."

And he was gripped by just that same strange, oppressive and familiar sense of doom that he experienced in front of the piece of dark yellow wallpaper on which something fateful would appear. He felt that he was guilty.

And *the person* fixed him with his low, narrow forehead.

"Not good. . . ."

Silence ensued.

"The accusation is a serious one. The accusation, I'll tell you bluntly, is so serious that . . ." *the person* gave a sigh.

"But what facts do you have?"

"They are being gathered . . . about you. . . ."

That was all he needed!

Getting up, *the person* cut off the tip of a Havana cigar, made a series of ambiguous "hm, hm, hm's," and strode into the dining room.

He shouted in the direction of the kitchen:

"I'm dying of hunger."

He strode back.

· · · · · · ·

"Your visits to the porter's quarters, your friendship with the police, with the porter, with the precinct clerk Voronkov . . ."

A questioning glance full of horror. *The person* went on whispering:

"You don't know who Voronkov is?"

"Who is he? What about it?"

But Lippanchenko guffawed:

"You find it appropriate to visit with a police agent, you find it appropriate to share a bottle with a police agent."

"I beg your pardon!"

"The fact of your participation in a provocation has not yet been established. I warn you in advance, as a friend: my dear fellow, you're up to something pretty fishy."

"?"

"Pull out of it!"

He realized clearly that the words "pull out of it" were the condition imposed by *a certain person.* He was not to insist on a full explanation of the incident. And it seemed that *the person himself* had been compromised by something.

But scarcely had Alexander Ivanovich taken slight heart when that same ominous expression—as in the hallucination—flitted over the face of *the person*. And the frontal bones strained in a strong and obstinate effort to break down his will, or . . . fly to pieces.

And the frontal bones broke it down.

Alexander Ivanovich slumped as if drowsy, and *the person* again took the offensive. The square head bent forward.

And the little eyes wanted to say:

"Eh, eh, eh. . . . So that's what you're up to."

And spit sprayed from his mouth:

"All Petersburg knows it."

"Knows what?"

"About the exposure of T. T."

"What?!"

"Yes. . . ."

Had *the person* deliberately wanted to divert Alexander Ivanovich's mind from anything that would allow him to make discov-

eries about *the person*'s conduct, he succeeded completely: the news
of the exposure of T. T. struck him like a clap of thunder:

"Good Lord!"

"Good Lord!" jeered *the person*. "You certainly knew that. Until
the experts present their evidence, let us assume that. . . . Only, not
another word about Ableukhov."

Alexander Ivanovich had an idiotic look about him. And the
gaping grinning mouth of *the person* taunted him:

"Don't pretend that Ableukhov's role and the reasons compelling
me to use this assignment as a means of punishing him are unknown
to you. That rotten little swine has managed to play out his role,
and our little calculation was correct—our calculation that he would
be spineless, like you." *The person* had relented. By stating that
Alexander Ivanovich suffered from spinelessness, he was magnani-
mously withdrawing the accusation he had just made a moment
before, and with the word "spineless" something fell from Alexander Ivanovich's soul. He tried to persuade himself that he had been
mistaken.

"Our little calculation was correct. This allegedly noble son hates
his father, and is allegedly preparing to do him in. At the same time
he scurries around among us with his little reports, collecting scraps
of paper, and presenting the collection to his dear father."

"Nikolai Stepanovich, he wept."

"What a strange bird you are. Tears are the usual condition of an
educated police agent. You also weep. I don't mean to say that you
too are guilty."

(Not so: *the person* had already mentioned guilt repeatedly, and
this "not so" horrified Alexander Ivanovich for an instant. And one
thing flashed through his subconscious: "A bargain is being struck;
he's proposing that I believe the slander he's spreading, or, if not
believe it, then at least go along with it. That's the price for withdrawing his slander of me." All that had already flashed beyond
the threshold of consciousness. The truth had been locked up beyond that threshold, and he was already thinking that he believed
this slander.)

"Alexander Ivanovich, you're clean, but as for Ableukhov, I have
put a dossier, right here, in this very drawer, for safekeeping. I
will submit it to the judgment of the Party." Genuine distress could
be detected in the tone of his voice (the bargain had been success-
fully struck).

"Later on, believe me, I will be understood. But now the situation
demands that the contagion be torn out by the roots, as quickly as
possible. I am acting on my initiative alone. Believe me, I regretted
having to sign the sentence, but dozens are perishing on account of
that senator's loving son of yours. Both Peppovich and Pepp have

been arrested. Remember, you yourself almost perished. Remember the Yakutsk region. You're standing up for him? Weep then, weep. For do-zens are perishing!!!"

.   .   .   .

And darkness was falling. Bookcases, armchairs, tables—everything had receded into darkness. Alexander Ivanovich kept on sitting here alone: darkness had entered his soul. He was weeping. *The person* had gone out.

And Alexander Ivanovich recalled the nuances of what *the person* had said. *The person* probably was not lying. Alexander Ivanovich's suspicions might have been explained by his pathological condition: the nightmare prompted by chance might by chance have been connected with some ambiguous expression on *the person's* face. Alcoholism had laid the ground for mental illness; the food to nourish this illness had been at hand; and the hallucination involving the Mongol and "Enfranshish" had done the rest. Well, what after all was the Mongol on the wall? Delirium.

"Enfranshish, enfranshish. . . ." What was that? Abracadabra, an association of sounds—nothing more.†

True enough, he harbored unpleasant feelings toward *the person*. But it was also true that he was obligated to *the person*. And his disgust and horror had no justification.

He was sick.

And darkness was falling. It had fallen, it surrounded him. And desk, armchair, bookcase stood out. Darkness had entered his soul. He was weeping.

Here he remembered: Nikolai Apollonovich delivering a paper in which all values were debunked. The resulting impression was not among the most pleasant, and moreover, Nikolai Apollonovich, truth to tell, had manifested curiosity about Party secrets. With the abstracted look of a clumsy meddling degenerate, he stuck his nose into everything. His abstracted air could have been put on. After all, a provocateur of a higher type could, of course, possess all the outward appearance of Ableukhov—the sorrowfully pensive look, the froglike expression of the lips. Alexander Ivanovich was becoming convinced. Yes, yes, Nikolai Apollonovich did act strangely.

The more he persuaded himself of Ableukhov's close involvement with the exposure of T. T., the more his turbulent, oppressive feeling passed. And something almost carefree entered his soul. He especially hated the senator, but at times he had been fond of Nikolai Apollonovich. But now the senator's son too was joined with the senator in a paroxysm of disgust and in a desire to exterminate the whole tarantula breed:

"Dregs, dregs! Oh! Dozens are perishing."

And better the sow bugs, better the piece of dark yellow wallpaper. Better even *the person: the person* possessed the grandeur of hatred. He could merge with *the person* in the desire to extirpate.

Soon *the person* again burst into the room and laid the palm of his hand on his shoulders.

.   .   .   .

"Come, let's have something to eat. Have a bite with us. Only not a word about all this at supper. It's depressing. And there's no reason for Zoya Zakharovna to know. She's really tired. So am I. We're all exhausted. We're all nerves. We're nervous people. Well, let's have supper, let's have supper."

At supper they drank.

Once More Sad and Melancholy

Alexander Ivanovich kept ringing, but the porter did not open up. Only a dog behind the gates replied to the bell. A midnight rooster raised a voice to midnight and fell silent. And the Line stretched away off there—into the void.

Alexander Ivanovich felt something akin to satisfaction. His arrival was being delayed. Rustlings, cracklings, and squeakings could be heard in these mournful walls.

And he would have to master twelve cold steps in the gloom. And after making a turn, count them off again.

This he would do four times.

Ninety-six hollow-echoing steps. Then stand before the felt-covered door, and fearfully insert his half-rusty key. To light a match was very risky. God knows what sheer nastiness (such as a mouse) might be revealed by the flame.

For that reason he kept lingering by the gates.

And lo—

> —someone, whom Alexander Ivanovich had seen many a time, again appeared in the depths of the Eighteenth Line; he quietly stepped into the bright circle of light from the street lamp, but it seemed that the light had begun streaming from his head, from his stiffening fingers—

And Alexander Ivanovich remembered: once a little old woman wearing a straw hat had hailed this nice inhabitant of the Eighteenth Line. And had called him Misha.

Alexander Ivanovich always trembled whenever the sad and tall one directed his all-seeing gaze, his sunken cheeks, at him when passing by.

"Oh, if only! . . .

"If only he would hear me out! . . ."

But the sad and tall one passed by, without looking, without stopping.

Alexander Ivanovich turned and wanted to call quietly to the unknown one.

But the place into which he had disappeared irrevocably—was empty.

From there winked the yellow light of a street lamp.

.   .   .   .

He kept ringing, and the wind moaned in the gateway. Across the way it hit an iron sign full blast. And the iron reverberated distinctly and loudly into the darkness.

Matvei Morzhov

The gates creaked.

The porter, Morzhov, admitted him across the threshold. Retreat was cut off.

"How come so late?"

"Business."

"Still trying to find a job?"

"Yes, I am."

"It figures. Ain't no jobs nowadays. Maybe in the local police."

"They wouldn't have me in the local police."

"Figures."

Morzhov now and then would send his old lady, who suffered from earaches, to Alexander Ivanovich with a slice of meat pie, or with an invitation. They used to have drinks on holidays in the porter's lodge.

Alexander Ivanovich hated his garret. He used to stay there for weeks on end without going out, when going out seemed risky.

The company would be joined by the precinct clerk Voronkov and the shoemaker Bessmertny. And of late Styopka had been hanging around in the porter's lodge too.

In the courtyard he clearly heard singing coming from the porter's lodge:

> There're some gals
> Don't want a clerk.
> Me, I'd like one
> Just O.K. . . .
> They're real edjucated
> People,
> And they know
> Just what to say. . . .

.   .   .   .

"Company again?"

Morzhov scratched the back of his head:

"We're having ourselves a little fun."

Alexander Ivanovich remembered that the name of the precinct clerk Voronkov had been pointedly mentioned—there. For some reason *the person* knew the precinct clerk Voronkov quite well.

> Buy me, mamma,
> For a dress
> Lots of silk
> That's purty gray!
> And there's no one
> That I'll love
> But that dear boy
> Alex-ei!

.   .   .   .

Morzhov snapped in a sullen tone:

"How about it? You joining us?"

And he would have dropped in. It was warm and tipsy there; in the garret, lonely and cold. No, the precinct clerk Voronkov was there, and the devil only knows what he was all about!

And how they were singing away:

> Buy me, mamma,
> For a dress
> Lots of silk
> That's purty green!
> And there's no one
> That I'll love
> But the son
> Of old Moskveen!

"How's about a drink?"

"No."

Then Morzhov walked away and flung open the door of the porter's lodge: steam bathed in light, din and smells. And—bang: the door slammed shut.

The moon now illuminated the sharp outlines of the courtyard and the stacks of firewood, between which Alexander Ivanovich scampered as he made his way toward the entryway.

From the porter's lodge came the words:

> The tracks of the railway rush onward! . . .
> Signals and switches! Embankment!
> The soil all weakened by flooding,
> The train crashing down from the ties.

The sight of the carriages broken! . . .
The sight of unfortunate people! . . .†

The rest could not be heard.

. . . .

They had kept watch for Alexander Ivanych. This is how it had started: once, while on his way home, he had spotted coming down the stairway a man he did not know, who had said:

"You are connected with Him. . . ."

Who was *He?* Connected with Whom? Alexander Ivanovich had fled headlong from the unknown man. The latter had not followed.

And it had happened a second time: on the street he had met a man with a horrible face (inexpressibly so). Some lady he did not know, thoroughly frightened, had grabbed him by the sleeve:

"It's horrible. Did you see? What is it?"

But the man had passed by.

Soon thereafter, one evening on the landing he was seized by hands of some kind. They pushed him toward the banister, trying to shove him off. Alexander Ivanovich broke loose. The staircase was empty.

Of late he had been hearing inhuman cries . . . from the staircase. There would be a sudden cry . . . there would be a cry, and then it would cry no longer.

But the other tenants did not hear those sudden cries.

One time he had heard the cry—there, by the Horseman. It was the same cry. It was an automobile. One time Stepan, who often whiled away the nights with him, heard it cry out; but to Alexander Ivanovich's importuning questions he only replied gloomily:

"It's you *they*'re looking for."

And not another word. Styopka began avoiding Alexander Ivanovich. And as for spending the night—not a chance. And Styopka said not a word either to the porter or the shoemaker. And neither did Alexander Ivanovich.

Who were *they* and why were *they* looking?

. . . .

Alexander Ivanovich cast a glance at the window on the garret-story. Through the window he could see some angular shadow or other restlessly moving about. He felt for his key. He had it. But who was there, in his locked room?

A search? . . . Oh, if only it were! He would have welcomed a search. He would have been thrown into the Fortress† by real people.

"It's you *they*'re looking for. . . ."

Alexander Ivanovich promised himself ahead of time that he would not be frightened. Anything that might happen was only cerebral play.

A Dead Ray Was Falling through the Window

Yes, exactly: *they* were standing there. Just as *they* had been standing there the last time he had returned at night. And *they* were waiting for him. Who? Two outlines. A ray was falling from the fourth floor.

Palish patches lay there, horrible, calm.

And the banister ran into one patch. And by the banister were two outlines. Standing to his right and left, they let him pass. They did not stir, they did not quiver. He felt an unblinking eye fixed on him from the darkness.

Should he not go up to *them*, should he not whisper the exorcism:

"Enfranshish, enfranshish!"

How would you feel if you had to step into this palish patch and be illuminated, and sense the piercing gaze of observers on both sides, feel observers behind your back, yet not quicken your step.

All Alexander Ivanovich had to do was rush upstairs and they would rush up after him.

The palish patches began to melt (a black cloud covered the moon). And—

Alexander Ivanovich could bear it no longer.

He flew onto the landing. Oh, what poor judgment!

Throwing down a lighted match, he leaned over the banister and cast a frightened glance. The balusters of the banister flared up. In the flickering light he could clearly discern silhouettes.

One proved to be that Makhmoud fellow, the denizen of the basement. In the light cast by the falling match Makhmoud was whispering to an ordinary looking little fellow, who was wearing the expected bowler: he had an Oriental face with a hook nose.

The match went out.

Yet: it had betrayed Alexander Ivanovich's presence. Feet began shuffling up the stairs. A boisterous voice resounded in his ear:

"Andrei Andreich Gorelsky?"

"No, I'm Alexander Ivanovich Dudkin."

"Yes, but according to your passport . . ."

Alexander Ivanovich shuddered. He was living with a false passport.[†] His real name was Alexei Alexeich Pogorelsky, not Andrei Andreich.

"What can I do for you?"

"Your apartment, hmm, turned out to be locked. And there is someone in there. I preferred to wait for you at the entrance, but this back staircase . . ."†

"But who's in there?"

"It was the voice of someone from the lower classes, I think, who answered me from in there."

Thank heavens! Styopka was in there.

"What can I do for you?"

"We have a mutual friend, Nikolai Stepanych Lippanchenko, who treats me like I was his own son. I've taken the liberty of. . . . Actually, I live in Helsingfors. I come here just on visits. My home is in the south."

Alexander Ivanovich realized that his visitor was lying. This same situation had been repeated once before (perhaps the whole business had happened in a dream).

He thought: Something doesn't add up here, but I mustn't let on.

"With whom do I have the honor?" he said.

"Shishnarfne. We've met."

"Shishnarfiev?"

"No, Shishnarfne. They added the "v" ending to make it Russian. Actually, we were both there at the same time today—oh yes, yes, at Lippanchenko's. I sat there for two hours waiting for you to finish your conversation about business matters. But I couldn't wait for you any longer. So Zoya Zakharovna gave me your address. I've been wanting to see you. *I've been looking for you a long time.*"

"Have we met before?"

"Yes. Don't you remember? In Helsingfors."

Alexander Ivanovich recalled that he had seen him in a Helsingfors coffeehouse. The face did not take its suspicious eyes off Alexander Ivanych.

"Oh yes, yes, don't you remember?"

Precisely: it was in Helsingfors that all the symptoms of impending illness had begun: the cerebral play insinuated by someone.

At that time he had had occasion to develop his highly paradoxical theory about the necessity of destroying culture.† The period of humanism had outlived its time and was over. History was wind-eroded marl. A period of healthy barbarism was at hand, pushing up out of the lower strata of the people, out of the upper strata (the revolt of the arts against form, the interest in the exotic), out of the bourgeoisie too (ladies' fashions). Oh, yes, yes: Alexander Ivanovich had preached burning the libraries, universities, museums, and summoning the Mongols. (Later on he took fright.)

He had preached all that in a Helsingfors coffeehouse at one time. And someone had asked what his attitude might be toward Satanism.

Shishnarfne had sat at the table next to him.

His preaching of barbarism had come to an unexpected end (right there in Helsingfors). Alexander Ivanovich had seen himself (while in a somnolent state) being whirled through what might most simply be called interplanetary space, for the purpose of performing a certain vile act. That had been in a dream, but a hideous dream which had decided him to stop preaching. Alexander Ivanych did not remember whether he had committed *the act* or not. The dream had been the beginning of his illness. He did not like to remember the dream.

He took to reading Revelation.

The reminder of Helsingfors had its effect now. Despite himself he thought:

So that's why these past few weeks "Hel–sing–fors, Hel–sing–fors" has been drumming away at me, without any sense.

"Shishnarfne . . . I know it from somewhere. . . ."

And Shishnarfne continued:

"Won't you allow me to come in? I must admit I've gotten tired waiting."

Gripped by uncontrollable fear, Alexander Ivanovich now shrieked:

"Please do!"

But he thought:

Styopka's there to come to my rescue.

. . . .

"How could he have gotten in? Why, I have the key."

But feeling around in his pocket he realized the right key wasn't there. Instead of the key for the door he had the key for the suitcase.

Petersburg

On the trestle bed, over a candle stub, Stepan lay sprawled before a book with Church Slavic letters.

Alexander Ivanovich now remembered Styopka's promise to bring him the Prayer Book (he was interested in St. Basil the Great's admonitory prayer to demons).†

"Stepan! I'm glad to see you!"

"Here, sir, I've brought what you—" but glancing at the visitor who had just come in, Styopka added "what you asked for."

"Don't leave, stay a while. . . . This gentleman here is Mr. Shishnarfne."

At this point the candle stub burned out. The wrapping paper on which it stood flared up, and the walls danced in the light.

.   .   .   .

"No, sir, excuse me, I've got to be on my way," Stepan said, fidgeting, averting his eyes and not looking at the guest.

He took the Prayer Book with him.

What was he going to do about Stepan now? Stepan would not forgive him, and now Stepan must be thinking:

Well, if *this* sort has taken to dropping in, a Prayer Book's of no earthly use. *This* sort doesn't drop in on just anybody.

And so, and so if even Stepan has his suspicions? How would he get along without Stepan?

"Stepan, stay a while."

"Why, it's *you* the gentleman's come to see, not me. It's you *they're* looking for."†

And the door slammed behind Stepan. Alexander Ivanovich wanted to shout after him to at least leave the Prayer Book, but he was too ashamed. And the flames did a dying dance on the walls. The paper burned away, and everything turned green.

.   .   .   .

He invited his visitor to take a seat at the table. He himself stood in the doorway, so that if need be he could get out onto the staircase and lock the visitor in.

But the visitor was leaning on the window sill, smoking a cigarette, and his contour was outlined against the transparent green spaces beyond the window (there the moon raced on).

"I seem to be disturbing you."

"Not at all, I'm very glad you're here." Alexander Ivanovich said reassuringly as his hand tried the door handle.

"But I've so wanted to see you. . . . All the more since I'm leaving at first light."

"Leaving?"

"Yes, for Finland, Sweden. . . . However, I come from Shemakha. The climate here is especially bad for me."

"Yes," Alexander Ivanovich replied, "Petersburg is built on a swamp."†

What a sudden start the contour gave:

"For the Russian Empire Petersburg is just a dot. Just look at the map. Our capital city, adorned with monuments . . ."

"You say 'our capital city,' but it's not yours. *Your* capital city, I believe, is Teheran. For you, an Oriental . . ."

"Why no, I've been to Paris and London. As I was saying," the black contour hurried on, "it's not customary to mention the fact that *our* capital city belongs to the land of spirits when reference books are compiled. Karl Baedeker keeps mum about it. A man from the provinces who hasn't been informed of this takes only the visible administrative apparatus into account; he has no shadow passport."

"What do you mean?"

"It's very simple. I know what to expect in the land of the Papuans: a Papuan! Karl Baedeker gives fair warning. But what if on the way to Kirsanov I were to come across the encampment of a Papuan horde? Incidentally, France is arming them on the quiet and plans to bring them to Europe. You'll see. That should be of use for your theory of the overthrow of culture. Remember? I was a sympathetic listener in the Helsingfors coffeehouse!"

Hearing the reference to this theory produced a vile feeling in Alexander Ivanovich. After his horrible dream he had realized the connection between his theory and Satanism.

The contour was growing thinner and thinner against the window. It seemed merely a small piece of black paper pasted on the window frame. But the voice kept resounding in the middle of the clearly defined square of the room, and it moved very perceptibly away from the window in the direction of Alexander Ivanovich. An independent, invisible center!

"A Papuan is an earthborn being. You can come to terms with a Papuan with the help of hard liquor, to which you've been rendering tribute these past few days, and which has brought about our meeting. And besides, certain institutions exist in Papua which have been approved by the Papuan parliament. . . ."

The visitor had become merely a layer of soot on the moon-illuminated pane. Whereas his voice grew stronger and stronger, assuming the quality of a rasping gramophone screech:

"The biology of the shadow has not yet been studied. You can't understand its needs. It enters through the germs that you swallow in tap water."

"And in vodka,"† Alexander Ivanovich interjected on his own part, and involuntarily thought: What's happening to me? Have I swallowed the bait of delirium? Have I been echoing myself, answering myself? But in his thoughts he decided he had to cut himself off from this nonsense. If he didn't immediately break this nonsense down with his conscious mind, his conscious mind would break down into nonsense.

"No, my dear sir: it's me you're taking into yourself with vodka. But with water you swallow germs, and I'm no germ.† Look here: from the very first day of your stay in Petersburg your stomach hasn't been digesting properly. Cholerine's been a constant menace, and the consequences are symptoms which you can't rid yourself of by lodging complaints with the local police. Your anguish, hallucinations and depression are all the consequences of cholerine. Off to the Farce Theater with you!"†

He's mocking me! Alexander Ivanovich thought.

"In a word, complaints addressed to the visible world are never acted on, like all complaints. The tragedy is that we are in an invisible world: the world of shadows."

"Is there such a thing?" shrieked Alexander Ivanovich, as he made ready to leap out of his cubbyhole and lock in the visitor who was growing ever more subtle. A man of all three dimensions had entered the room. He had leaned against the window and had become a contour (or, two-dimensional), had become a thin layer of soot of the sort you knock out of a lamp. Now this black soot had suddenly smoldered away into an ash that gleamed in the moonlight, and the ash was flying away. And there was no contour. The whole material substance had turned into a phonic substance that was jabbering away. But where? It seemed to Alexander Ivanovich that the jabbering had now started up inside him.

"Mr. Shishnarfne," said Alexander Ivanovich to space (for there was now no Shishnarfne).

And he chirruped as he answered himself:

"Petersburg is the fourth dimension which is not indicated on maps, which is indicated merely by a dot. And this dot is the place where the plane of being is tangential to the surface of the sphere and the immense astral cosmos. A dot which in the twinkling of an eye can produce for us an inhabitant of the fourth dimension, from whom not even a wall can protect us. A moment ago I was one of the dots by the window sill, but now I have appeared . . ."

"Where?" Alexander Ivanovich wanted to exclaim, but he could not exclaim, because his throat exclaimed:

"I have appeared from your larynx."

Alexander Ivanovich looked around him in bewilderment while his throat kept ejaculating:

"You need a passport here. However, you are also registered there.† The passport has been made out inside you. You yourself will put your signature on it inside you by performing an extravagant little action. It will come, it will come."

Had he at that moment been able to stand aside and take a look at himself he would no doubt have been horrified: he would have seen himself clutching at his stomach and straining his throat as he bellowed into the void in front of him.

"But when was I registered with you there?"

"Then, after the act," his mouth answered him.

And suddenly the curtain was rent. And he remembered . . . that dream, in Helsingfors, when *they* whirled him through some sort of . . . still and all . . . spaces.

And he had committed it.

He had joined himself to them. Lippanchenko was merely the image that hinted at it. Their strength had entered him. Racing from organ to organ, looking for his soul in the body, it was gradually taking possession of the whole of him.

And all the while *it* was happening, he had thought that *they* were looking for him. But *they* were within him.

"Yes, our spaces are not yours. Everything there flows in reverse order. Ivanov becomes some sort of Japanese: Vonavi."

And he understood: "Shishnarfne—Shish–nar–fne. . . ."

From his vocal apparatus came the reply:

"You summoned me. . . . Here I am. . . ."

Enfranshish had come for his soul.†

.   .   .   .

Alexander Ivanovich leaped out of his own room, and the key gave a click.

"Yes, yes. . . . It is I . . . I destroy irrevocably."

.   .   .   .

The moon replied. And in the utter darkness grayish, gray, palish, pale patches glowing phosphorescent appeared faintly, in dim outline.

The Garret

The garret was not locked. Dudkin rushed into it.

Late at night the garret is strange. The floor is thickly strewn with earth.† It's soft underfoot. Suddenly a beam trips you up and sends you down on all fours; and transverse strips of moon reach out like white crossbeams: you pass through them.

Suddenly . . .

A beam confers a blow on your nose.

Motionless white patches—drawers, towels, and sheets. The flutter of a breeze—and the patches stretch out noiselessly: drawers, towels, and sheets.

Alexander Ivanovich had concealed himself. He sighed in relief.

Through the broken window a song was heard:

> Buy me, mamma,
> For a dress
> Lots of silk
> That's purty green. . . .

Alexander Ivanovich listened attentively. What could he hear? You know already: the distinct sound of a cracking crossbeam, a thick silence, or a web woven only from rustlings. In the corner "shushes" and "hushes" and—the tension-charged atmosphere of steps unheard, and—the gulping of saliva by thick lips.

In a word, just normal sounds. No reason to fear them.

He had no desire to leave the garret. He walked amidst drawers, towels, and sheets. He thrust his head between the pieces of glass in the broken window: the waft of calm, of peaceable melancholy.

Clear, distinct, blindingly simple were the whole well-defined square of the courtyard, which seemed small and toylike, and the silvery stacks of firewood. In the porter's lodge they were still carousing. From the lodge came a raspy song:

> I see, oh Lord, my iniquity:
> Unrighteousness deceived my eyes,
> Unrighteousness blinded my eyes.
> I was sorry to lose my white body,
> I was sorry to lose my many-colored raiment,
> My savory food,
> My foaming brew.
> I, Pontius, trembled at the archpriests,
> I, Pilate, took fright at the Pharisees.
> I washed my hands—and washed away my conscience,
> An innocent man I gave over to be crucified.

It was being sung by the precinct clerk Voronkov and the shoemaker Bessmertny who lived in the cellar. Alexander Ivanovich thought: "Should I go down and join them?"

The sky was clearing. A blinding silver stream washed the roof of the Island building beneath him.

And the Neva seethed.

And it cried out there mournfully in the whistle of a small late-passing steamboat, on which could be seen the receding eye of a lantern. The Embankment stretched on. Above the boxes of yellow, gray, brownish red houses, above the columns of gray, brownish red palaces—rococo and barocco—rose the dark walls of an enormous temple, its gold cupola, its colonnade thrust sharply up into the world of the moon: St. Isaac's.

And the Admiralty raced up into the sky like an arrow.

· · · · · · · ·

The entire square was empty.

Metallic hooves fell and clanged on the crag. The horse snorted through its nostrils into the white-hot fog. The outline of the Horseman detached itself from the horse's croup. A jangling spur scratched the horse's flank.

The horse flew down off the crag.

A weightily sonorous* clatter swept across the bridge to the Islands. The Bronze Horseman flew on. The muscles of his metallic arms flexed. The horse's hooves fell on the cobblestones. The horse's laughter rang out, reminiscent of the whistling of a locomotive. The steam from its nostrils scalded the street with luminous boiling water. Horses snorted, bucked and reared, and passersby shut their eyes.

Line after Line flew by, a piece of the left bank, in wharves and smokestacks, in heaps of hemp-stuffed bags; vacant plots, barges, fences, tarpaulins, and numerous small houses flew by; out of the fog gleamed a side of that restless tavern.

Here the oldest Dutchman of all leaned forward, away from the threshold, into cold pandemonium. A lantern quietly quivered beneath the bluish face in a black leather hood. The Dutchman's ear could catch the horse's clatter, because the Dutchman had abandoned the company of his fellow seamen, whose glasses clanked from one morning to the next.

He knew very well that the feasting would drag on to the small wan hours. He knew very well that when midnight finished ringing out, the sturdy Guest would fly again to meet the sound of the glasses, would down a glass of fiery Allasch, would shake the two-hundred-year-old hand which from the captain's bridge would turn the ship's wheel away from the deadly forts of Kronstadt.† The muzzle of a cannon would send out a roar in pursuit of the stern that had not replied to its signal.

The vessel would not be overtaken. It would pass into the low cloud that clung to the sea.

The Dutchman knew all this. He could make out the shape of the flying Horseman. The clatter could be heard. Flaming nostrils snorted and pierced the fog like a luminous white-hot pillar.

.   .   .   .

Alexander Ivanovich moved away from the window, calmed, subdued, and shivering from the cold. The white patches of drawers, towels, and sheets began swaying.

He had now made up his mind to return.

Why It Had Happened . . .

He was sitting on the bed, and resting from his nightmare. The visitor had been here, and here had crawled the sow bug. There was no visitor now. The hallucination had been followed by an interval of clarity.

*Pushkin.†

Consciousness shone like the moon—forwards and backwards.

Amidst his four walls he seemed to himself merely a captive prisoner, that is, if a captive prisoner does not have a sense of freedom greater than others, and if this narrow little interval between the walls was not equal to universal space.

Universal space is as vacant as his room! Universal space is the ultimate to which wealth can attain. A beggar's habitation would seem luxurious compared to the wretched furnishings of universal space.

.   .   .   .

While resting from the attacks of delirium, Alexander Ivanovich thought of how he had risen above the mirage of sensuality.

But a voice objected:

"The vodka?"

"The smoking?"

"The lustful feelings?"

His head drooped. The reasons for the illnesses, the fears, and the feelings of persecution were insomnia, cigarettes, and excessive drinking.

His attack of acute madness was illuminated in a new way. He knew the truth of acute madness. Madness was the report delivered to his self-knowing "I" by his diseased sense organs. Shishnarfne was the symbol of its anagram.† It was not he who was trying to overtake and pursue him, but his own organs which were trying to overtake his "I." Alcohol and insomnia were gnawing away at the structure of his body. He was linked with the spaces. He had begun to disintegrate, and the spaces had cracked. Germs had crawled into the cracks of sensation. Specters had begun to hover in the spaces. Who is Shishnarfne? The reverse of abracadabra or— Enfranshish. A dream induced by vodka. Thus, Enfranshish and Shishnarfne were but stages of alcohol.

"I shouldn't smoke or drink."

Suddenly he shuddered.

He had betrayed. He had given Nikolai Apollonovich up to Lippanchenko out of fear. He remembered the disgraceful buying and selling. Without believing, he had believed, and in this lay his betrayal. Lippanchenko was more of a traitor. That he was betraying them, Alexander Ivanovich knew, but he hid this knowledge from himself (Lippanchenko had power over his soul). This was the root of his illness: the recognition that Lippanchenko was a traitor. Alcohol and dissipation were merely the consequences; the hallucinations were merely the final links in the chain that was being forged by Lippanchenko. Why? Because Lippanchenko knew that he *knew*; and by virtue of this knowledge Lippanchenko would not let loose.

Lippanchenko had enslaved his will. The enslavement of his will had occurred because he kept wanting to dispel the horrible suspicion, and he kept driving away suspicion by keeping company with Lippanchenko. Suspecting his suspicion, Lippanchenko kept him within arm's reach. Thus they had become tied one to the other. He was pouring mysticism into Lippanchenko, and Lippanchenko alcohol into him.

Alexander Ivanovich distinctly recalled the scene with Lippanchenko. That cynic, that base villain had outmaneuvered him. And he remembered Lippanchenko's neck, with its repulsive fold; and the neck laughed insolently until Lippanchenko caught him staring at the neck. Having caught him staring at the neck, he understood everything.

He set about trying to frighten him. He stunned him with his attack; and he jumbled all the cards. Then he offered him a way out: believing in Ableukhov's treachery.

He had believed, and the act had been committed. The deed had been done.

This is what the nightmare was about.

. . . .

Alexander Ivanovich translated that nightmare into the language of his feelings. The staircase, the wretched little room, and the garret were the body. The frenzied inhabitant of the spaces, whom they were attacking, who was fleeing from *them*, was the self-knowing "I" which was lugging the organs that had fallen away. Enfranshish was a foreign substance which had entered his habitation in vodka. Developing like a germ, it raced from organ to organ. It caused sensations of persecution, so that having struck at the brain, it could cause irritation there.

. . . .

The first meeting with Lippanchenko came to mind. The impression had not been among the most pleasant. Lippanchenko displayed curiosity about all the weaknesses of the people who kept company with him. A provocateur, of course, could very well possess a clumsy outward appearance, a pair of mindlessly blinking little eyes.

As he slowly became engrossed in Lippanchenko, in the contemplation of the parts of his body, his quirks, his little mannerisms, his little jokes, before him arose a real tarantula.

And something steely entered his soul:

"I know what I shall do."

Everything would come to an end. Why had he not thought of this before? And his mission took shape.

Suddenly—

A Guest

Alexander Ivanovich heard a noise thundering below. And it was repeated on the staircase. Crash after crash resounded, the crash of metal, shattering stone—higher and higher, closer and closer. A burglar was breaking and entering below on the staircase. He strained to hear whether someone would open a door and put an end to the racket.

Someone made of metal was moving up toward the landing. Now many tons were falling with an earth-shattering din. The steps were splintering, and now the landing at the door flew away with a crash.

And there was a sudden cracking as the door flew off its hinges. And the wan semidarkness out there billowed in smoking, bright green clouds. The spaces of the moon now began right at the shattered door, at the landing. And the black room opened up—into ineffabilities. In the middle of the threshold, from walls which admitted vitriol-hued spaces, stood an immense body, glowing phosphorescent, its crowned, patinated head inclined and heavy patinated arm stretched forth.

The Bronze Horseman stood there.

The lusterless mantle hung heavily from the fitfully gleaming shoulders and from the scaly armor. At the instant when the walls of the building fell apart in vitriol spaces, the destinies of Evgeny were repeated.† Exactly: the past was dismantled, and Alexander Ivanovich exclaimed:

"I have remembered, I have been waiting."

The bronze-headed giant had been galloping through periods of time right up to this very instant, coming full circle. The ages had flowed on, and Nicholas had ascended the throne, and the Alexanders had ascended the throne, and Alexander Ivanovich, a shadow, had been tirelessly overcoming the periods of time, racing through the days, through the years, through the damp Petersburg prospects, in his dreams and when awake. And in pursuit of him, in pursuit of all thundered the crash of metal, shattering lives.

I have heard that thundering roar. Have you heard it?

Apollon Apollonovich was a crashing blow on stone; and Petersburg was a crashing blow on stone; the caryatid which shall break loose was a crashing blow. Pursuits are inevitable, and inevitable too are the crashing blows. You can find no shelter in a garret. The whole garret was Lippanchenko's doing, and the garret was a snare. Break out, break out of it! By crashing blows on Lippanchenko!

Lippanchenko would fly to pieces under the blows. The garret would crash down. Petersburg would collapse in ruins. The caryatid would collapse too. And the bare head of Ableukhov would crack in two.

The Bronze Horseman said to him:

"Greetings, my son!"

And—three steps: the sound of three cracking beams; and the cast-bronze emperor brought his metallic rear down on a chair with a hollow crash; and the gleaming green elbow fell with all the weight of bronze onto the table, clanging like church bells. The emperor slowly removed his bronze wreath from his head. The laurels tore loose in a thundering roar.

And his hand, clanking and clattering, took out a glowing red hot pipe, and he indicated the pipe with his eyes, and winked at the pipe:

"Petro Primo Catharina Secunda."†

His hand stuck the pipe between his lips. A green wisp of molten copper smoke began curling distinctly in the moonlight.

Alexander Ivanych—Evgeny—now understood for the first time that he had been running in vain for a century, from December to October, and in his wake came a rumbling without the slightest wrath—through villages, towns, entryways, stairways. He was forgiven. Everything that had happened along with everything that was coming was merely spectral transiences of ordeals to be endured until the last trumpet sounded.

In the bronze recesses of the Horseman a bronze thought flashed. His stone-shattering hand, glowing red hot, fell and broke his collar bone:

"Die, endure yet a little while."

The Metallic Guest† sat before him, glowing red hot in the moonlight, singeing, crimson red. Now he turned white hot, and flowed over Alexander Ivanovich, who was kneeling before him, in a stream that could reduce all to ashes. He poured into his veins in metals.

Scissors

"What's this?"

And a red spot crawled by over the pillow. Ugh! There flashed through his consciousness:

"A bedbug."

He raised up slightly on his elbow:

"Is it you, Styopka?"

He saw a teapot and a cup.

"How nice: a bit of tea."

"What's nice about it? You're burning up."

He noticed with surprise that he was not undressed; not even his thin overcoat had been removed.

"How do you happen to be here?"

"I dropped by. You were lying down and groaning. You were tossing and turning, you're burning up with fever."

"What do you mean, Styopka, I'm perfectly all right."

"Some all right! I've made you some tea."

Last night boiling water had flowed through his veins (that much he remembered).

"Yes, friend, I really had quite a fever last night."

"You'll boil away from all that alcohol."

"There were little devils, indeed there were."

"You'll drink yourself silly until you start seeing a Green Dragon . . ."†

"And so will all Russia, my friend. . . ."

"What?"

"From the Green Dragon . . ."

"Russia is Christ's. . . ."

"You're crazy. . . ."

"You'll drink until you see the white . . . woman. . . ."†

Delirium tremens was stalking him. No doubt about it.

"You might go to the pharmacy. You might buy me some quinine, the bitter-salty kind."

"Guess I could."

"And Styopushka, while you're about it, get some dried raspberries. I'd like some raspberry jam with my tea."

To himself he was thinking:

"Raspberries are good for making you sweat."

No sooner had he finished washing up when *it* again flared inside him, jumbling reality and delirium.

While he was talking with Styopka, something had seemed to be lying in wait for him behind the door, something primordially familiar. There—behind the door? He leaped out there. The landing opened out behind the door, and the banisters hung suspended over the abyss. And Alexander Ivanovich clicked his dry tongue over the abyss, shivering from a chill. He felt a coppery sensation in his mouth.

"No, *it's* lying in wait in the courtyard."

But in the courtyard: no one, nothing.

He ran about searching every nook, every passage (between the cords of stacked firewood). The asphalt gleamed silver. The aspen wood gleamed silver and: no one, nothing.

"But where is *it*?

"In a metallic place."

It would appear again.

The memory of a memory remained, and of a business which brooks no postponement.

With steps taut as springs he began running toward the foggy intersection of two streets. Gleams of light splashed from windows.

And objects glittered.

And indeed, on a corner of the intersection stood a cheap little shop, selling knives, forks, and scissors.

He went in.

From behind a high dirty desk a sleepy mug (must be the owner of the drills and saws) dragged itself toward the counter that glittered with steel. The low narrow forehead was hanging at a sharp angle.

"I could use a, I could use a . . . ."

And, not knowing what to take, Alexander Ivanovich brushed his hand against the teeth of a small saw: it gave a squeal. The proprietor was looking him over askance. No wonder: Alexander Ivanovich had rushed out in the same overcoat he had been wearing in bed. The overcoat was rumpled and smudged with dirt, and he had not put on a cap, and his tousled head would have frightened anyone.

And the proprietor, trying to control himself, boomed out:

"A saw?"

"No, you know, a saw . . . it would be awkward with a saw. . . . Perhaps, you know, a Finnish . . ."†

But the person cut him off:

"No knives."

His little eyes seemed to say:

"If I let you have a knife . . . heaven knows what a mess you'll get into."

He was struck by a certain resemblance. At this point the figure of the proprietor turned its back, and cast a glance that would have felled an ox.

"Well, what's the difference: scissors. . . ."

What he was intending, in essence, was—snip!

As he stood over the scissors he began to tremble.

"Don't wrap them up—no, no . . . I live right around here. . . . They're all right this way. I'll get them there all right. . . ."

Saying this, he slipped into his pocket miniature scissors of the kind used by dandies to trim their nails. And he rushed out.

Surprised and frightened, the low square forehead looked out (from behind the gleaming counter) in a stubborn effort to understand, come what may, at whatever price, to understand, or . . .

The frontal bone was simply unable to understand. The forehead, creased with wrinkles, was very low and narrow. It seemed to be weeping.

     ·   ·   ·   ·   ·   ·   ·

End of the Sixth Chapter

Chapter the Seventh

or, the events of a gray little day go on and on

I'm tired, friend, so tired. My heart begs for some peace.
The days chase on the days. . . .[†]

Pushkin

Measureless Immensities

We left Nikolai Apollonovich at the moment when Dudkin shook his hand and rapidly darted into the black flow of bowlers, while Nikolai Apollonovich felt that he was expanding.

Right up to that instant massifs of deliriums had been towering in his soul. Within twenty-four hours monstrous Gaurisankars[†] of events had collapsed on him: the Summer Garden, the red silk, the ball (harlequins and jesters both), the yellow hunchbacked Pierrot, a certain pale blue masker, the note, the escape to the latrine, the mangy little fellow, and Pepp Peppovich Pepp, or, the sardine tin, which . . . still went on . . . ticking.

The sardine tin, which was capable of turning everything nearby into . . . in a word, into slush.

We left Nikolai Apollonovich standing by a shop window, but we abandoned him. Droplets of drizzling rain had begun falling between the senator's son and ourselves.

Umbrellas were being opened all around.

Nikolai Apollonovich was standing by the shop window and thinking that there was no name for this hideous, oppressive thing. This hideous thing had been going on for twenty-four hours, or eighty thousand seconds, points in time. Each moment was advancing. And advancing on him was a moment which was somehow briskly spreading in circles, which was slowly turning into a swelling sphere. This sphere was bursting, and his heel was slipping into voids. Thus a wanderer in time was collapsing into the unknown and until . . . a new instant.

No, there was no name for this hideous, oppressive thing!

Thoughts of some kind began pounding; they arose not in the brain but in the heart.

A most clever, well worked out plan was arising; and comparatively speaking, a safe plan, but . . . a base one, yes, base!

But was Nikolai Apollonovich capable of thinking up this plan on his own?

All these past few hours, fragments of thoughts had been floating before his eyes, in a play of starlike sparks, like the gay tinsel on a Christmas tree. They fell ceaselessly into a place illuminated by consciousness—out of darkness into darkness. Now the tiny figure of a buffoon made faces, now a lemon yellow Petrushka galloped by—out of darkness into darkness—through the place illuminated by consciousness. But consciousness cast a dispassionate light on the swarming images; and when they had been welded one into the other, consciousness traced on them a staggering, inhuman meaning. Nikolai Apollonovich spat in disgust:

"I am an out-and-out scoundrel."

But his papa had come to the very same conclusion.

·   ·   ·   ·   ·   ·   ·   ·

No, no!

And there were swarms of thoughts thinking themselves; and it was not he thinking, but thoughts thinking themselves—something was being thought, was being sketched, was arising. And it leaped in the heart, bored inside the brain. It was rising above the sardine tin, it had crawled out of the sardine tin into him. He had hidden the sardine tin, it seems, in his desk, and had leaped out of the accursed house. He was wandering about the streets.

But in the streets it still continued to arise, forming, sketching, tracing; if his head was thinking, then it too had turned into the sardine tin which . . . was ticking with thoughts.

Thus the well thought out plan appeared on the field of his consciousness at the inopportune moment when Nikolai Apollonovich, who had dashed into the vestibule of the University (where the chapel was located), was nonchalantly leaning against one of the pillars and chatting with a lecturer who had happened by. Something burst in his soul (in the way a doll inflated with hydrogen bursts into flabby pieces of celluloid). He shuddered, reeled back, tore himself away, and began running, not knowing where himself, because he realized that:

the author of the plan was—he himself.

He rushed out onto Vasilievsky Island in the direction of the Eighteenth Line. The cabbie could hear disjointed whispering behind him:

"Who would have thought it! . . . Eh? . . . A hypocrite . . . a cheat . . . a murderer . . . to save his own skin. . . ."

He jumped out of the carriage, cut across the asphalt of the courtyard and through the stacks of firewood, and flew up the staircase. And he did not know why. Probably out of curiosity: to look the one who had brought him the bundle—Dudkin—right in the eye, because his "refusal" was, of course, a mere pretext.

And at that point he ran into Dudkin. The rest we have seen.

.   .   .   .

Yes, but his heart, warmed by everything that had happened to him, began slowly melting. Feelings throbbed within him. They shook his entire soul and turned it inside out.

As he ran across the pavement, he could have touched the colossus of the house, which towered in piles above the street, with his hand. As soon as it began to drizzle, the side of the house began to swim in the fog.

And the stone colossus had now broken loose, and it was lifting out of the drizzle a lace of contours and faintly defined lines—some kind of rococo. The rococo was receding into nothing.

A wet gleam now appeared on shop windows, on other windows, and on chimneys, and the first trickle gushed from the drainpipe. The sidewalks became speckled with tiny dots and turned dun brown. And a speeding tire snorted mud.

And more, and more, and more. . . .

Nikolai Apollonovich stood in the wet, sheltered by the umbrellas of the passersby. His head began to spin. He leaned against a shop window, and a fragment of his childhood rose before him.

.   .   .   .

He saw his head resting on his governess. The old lady was reading:

> Wer reitet so spät durch Nacht und Wind?
> Es ist der Vater mit seinem Kind. . . .†

Beyond the windows the storm rages in gusts; there the gloom is in riot; there—the pursuit.

And again. . . .

Apollon Apollonovich—small, gray, old—is teaching Kolenka a French contredanse, counting out the steps, beating time with his hands; and instead of music there is Apollon Apollonovich calling out in a rapid patter:

> Who dashes, who gallops through night and wind wild?
> It is a brave horseman and with him his child. . . .

The pursuit ended:

> He held his dear son who lay dead in his arms.

.   .   .   .

Cranes†

Nikolai Apollonovich yearned to return to his real home: the nursery. Everything, everything had to be shaken off. Everything, everything had to be learned, as it is learned in childhood. The sound of childhood rang out. High above fly the cranes. City-dwellers cannot hear them in all the din; but they are flying over the city. Somewhere, on the Prospect, in speeding carriages and in the cries of newsboys, where automobiles raise throaty hoots—here, on the pavement, the inhabitant of the fields will stop as if rooted to the spot and incline his bearded head to one side:

"Shhh!"

"What is it?"

"Listen."

"What?"

"There . . . the cranes are calling."

And at first you hear nothing, then you hear a familiar, forgotten sound, a strange sound.

The cranes are calling.

You both raise your heads—then a third person, a fifth, a tenth.

Amidst all the azure, something familiar appears. The cranes are flying north!

And a circle of gawking people forms, and the sidewalk is blocked. A policeman pushes his way through, unable to contain his curiosity. He stops and throws his head back:

"The cranes!"

Thus the call of the cranes may now and then be heard above the heavy roofs. Thus too the voice of childhood.

And it seemed as if someone sad, whom Nikolai Apollonovich had never seen before, had entered his soul, and that the bright light of his eyes had begun to pierce him. Nikolai Apollonovich shuddered.

"You all pursue and persecute me!"

"What?" He tried to catch the voice:

"I look after all of you. . . ."

Nikolai Apollonovich ran his eyes over space, as if expecting to catch sight of the voice.

There was no possessor of the voice.

.   .   .   .

Who is that there? Over there, on that side of the street? By the colossus of the house? Beneath the pile of balconies?

Yes, standing there.

Just like him, by a shop window, with an open umbrella, looking at him, so it seemed. But his face could not be made out. What was so special? On this particular side of the street stood Nikolai Apollonovich. As for that one, over there—nothing out of the ordinary, the same thing: just a casual passerby looking around self-confidently. As for me, he says, why I can beard any old lion. . . . No, he's clean-shaven.

The outline of his thin overcoat is reminiscent of . . . but of what?

And wearing some kind of cap with a visor.

Shouldn't he go up to him, the owner of the cap?

Just go and have a look at the objects, there . . . behind the glass in the shop window.

And take the opportunity to cast a fleeting glance at him, a glance seemingly absentminded but actually attentive!

And fall down prostrate on the pavement!

"I am sick, I am deaf . . . give me rest!"†

And hear in reply:

"Arise. . . .

"Go. . . .

"Sin no more. . . ."

. . . .

No, of course, there would be no answer.

And the sad one would give no answer, there could be no answers. There would be answers later on—in an hour, in a year, in five, and perhaps even longer—in a hundred, in a thousand years. There will be an answer!

. . . .

All this will change in the twinkling of an eye. And all the passing strangers—those who had passed one before the other (somewhere in a dark alley) in a moment of mortal danger—all will meet!

No one will take away the joy of this meeting.

I'm Going My Own Way . . . I'm Not in Anyone's Way

"What's wrong with me?" thought Nikolai Apollonovich. "This is no time for daydreaming."

Time was passing, and the sardine tin was ticking. He should go straight to his desk, carefully wrap it all up in paper, put it in his pocket, and into the Neva with it.†

And already he was shifting his eyes away from the colossus of the house where the stranger with the open umbrella was standing.

And again he took a look.

The stranger had not moved from the spot. He was waiting—for the drizzle to end. Suddenly he moved into the human flow, into those couples, those foursomes.

"Oh, the hell with him, he's just a stranger!"

Scarcely had he thought this, when the curious cap with the visor once more appeared before him. And at the risk of being run down by a cab, he dashed across the roadway, his umbrella battered by the wind.

How could he turn away now? How could he get away?

"So that's what he looks like?"

From a distance the stranger had shown to better advantage, had seemed more melancholy, more deliberate in his movements.

"Oh, but honestly now! What an idiotic appearance! Oh, that cap! He's running, his overcoat's flapping, his umbrella's ripped, and his overshoes don't fit."

Nikolai Apollonovich felt hostile and he was already preparing to step aside when the stranger (their noses virtually touching) raised his hand to his cap:

"Ah? Ni–ko–lai A–pol–lo–no–vich!"

Nikolai Apollonovich perceived a shady type (perhaps of the petty bourgeoisie) with his neck wrapped up. No doubt he had a boil on his neck.

"It seems you don't recognize me?"

"With whom do I have the honor," Nikolai Apollonovich was about to begin, but looking more closely, he reeled back, tore off his hat, and exclaimed, his face all contorted:

"Fancy greeting you here. . . ."

He had probably wanted to exclaim: "Fancy meeting you here."

It was nonetheless difficult to recognize Sergei Sergeyevich in this chance passerby, who looked like a panhandler. Likhutin was invested in civilian garb, and Likhutin was clean-shaven. Protruding was a pimply-looking void which converted a familiar physiognomy into an unfamiliar one.

"Either my eyes are deceiving me, but . . . Sergei Sergeye-vich. . . ."

"Quite right. I'm in civilian clothes."

"It's not that . . . I don't mean. . . . Still, it's astonishing. . . ."

"What?"

"You've been transfigured somehow. I'll hope you'll excuse. . . ."

"Think nothing of it."

"I mean . . . I wanted to say, you're clean-shaven. . . ."

"Oh, what of it? Why not? So I shaved, so what?" Likhutin went on with increasing irritation. "I'm leaving the service."

"What? Why?"

"For personal reasons."

At this point Likhutin began to draw nearer.

Nikolai Apollonovich began a perceptible retreat.

"Do you have some business with me, Sergei Sergeyevich?"

"Yes, my dear sir, business which . . ."

Nikolai Apollonovich detected a perceptibly menacing note in the hoarse voice of the second lieutenant. It seemed to Ableukhov that Likhutin was trying to grab his arms.

And he leaped off the pavement.

Sergei Sergeyevich went after him, in order to . . . to . . . to. . . . Some of the passersby were looking.

"I haven't been chasing after you so that we could chat about shaving. . . ."†

A third, then a fifth, then a tenth person stopped, thinking that a petty thief had been caught.

"What's it all about?"

What had happened to his memory?

Nikolai Apollonovich had completely forgotten about the domino.

But without a doubt, Sofia Petrovna Likhutina had babbled everything about the incident at the Winter Canal.

"That's all I needed! How ill timed this is."

And avoiding Likhutin's gaze, Nikolai Apollonovich fixed his eyes on a shop window.

Meanwhile, Sergei Sergeyevich Likhutin, Ableukhov's arm firmly in his grip, relentlessly spat out:

"I . . . I . . . I . . . have the honor to inform you that since this morning . . . I . . . I . . . I . . ."

"?"

"I've been on your trail. And incidentally, I've been at your place. They let me into your room. I sat there and waited . . . and I left a note. . . ."

"What a pity that . . ."

"Nonetheless," the second lieutenant interrupted, "I must have an urgent conversation with you."

"Here we go," flashed through Ableukhov's brain. He was reflected in a large shop window.

Meanwhile, pandemonium had broken loose and was whistling along the Nevsky, to attack, rattle, and rustle umbrellas with tiny, steady drops, and drench the sinewy hands of petty bourgeois and workers. Pandemonium whistled along the Nevsky to chase the swarms of cloud there out of Petersburg, through the wastes of Samara, Tambov, and Saratov, into gullies, into sands, into thistles, into wormwood, tearing away high-topped hayricks and spreading its sticky rot across threshing-floors.

The Conversation Had a Continuation

"I have some business with you. I've been asking around everywhere as to how we could meet, and I was at our mutual acquaintance, Varvara Evgrafovna's. Varvara Evgrafovna and I had a painful conversation concerning you. Do you understand what I'm saying? Solovyova gave me a certain address, your friend's—Dudkin, is it? Oh, it doesn't matter. Of course, I went to that address. I ran across you in the courtyard. You were running away from there. Besides, you weren't alone. You looked upset, unwell. I didn't presume to interrupt your conversation."

"Sergei Sergeyevich . . ."

"I didn't presume to interrupt your conversation. I followed you, keeping a certain distance, so as not to be witness to the conversation. I don't like to stick my nose into . . ."

At this point Likhutin grew pensive and gazed into the remoteness of the Nevsky.

"Listen . . ."

"What is it?"

"A note of some kind—an 'oo.' There, there . . . a humming. . . ."

Nikolai Apollonovich turned his head. A strange thing: carriages were speeding by, all in the same direction; the pedestrians quickened their step; some were looking over their shoulders.

"Nikolai Apollonovich, you kept staring at me, but you pretended you didn't notice me."

"I didn't recognize you."

"I nodded to you."

What was going on?

The passersby had stopped. The great broad prospect was free of carriages. Neither hooves nor the swish of tires could be heard.

"Look at that!"

Out of the remoteness of the prospect came a thousand-voiced rumble that grew in intensity. From there hurtled a carriage. In it, a tattered gentleman without a cap was bent over in a crouch, a massive staff clutched in his hand; and the streaming banner made for a strange sight. When the carriage had flown past, all the bowlers, tricornes, top hats, cap-bands, plumes, visored caps, and shaggy fur caps began shuffling, elbowing, and streaming from the sidewalk into the middle of the prospect. And from a rent in the storm clouds the pale disc of the sun poured forth for a moment in a dull yellow reflection.

Separated by a pair of elbows, they began running in the same direction as everyone else. At this point, taking advantage of the crush, Nikolai Apollonovich got the idea of slipping away from this ill timed little talk and rushing home: for the bomb was ticking away in the desk!

But Second Lieutenant Likhutin did not let him out of his sight, and tried as hard as he could to break through the crowd.

"Don't try to lose me, Nikolai Apollonovich; it doesn't matter anyway, you can't get rid of me."

"Just as I thought," Ableukhov now concluded, "he's pursuing me, he won't let me go. . . ."

He felt himself seized again by the second lieutenant's hand. At this point he stopped as if rooted to the spot and simulated indifference.

"A demonstration!"

"No matter: I have business with you."

From somewhere in the distance came the crackle of scattered shots. The red maelstrom of banners grew agitated, and quickly dispersed.

"Sergei Sergeyevich, let's have our talk in a coffee house. Why don't we go to a coffee house?"

"What do you mean a coffee house?"

"But where then?"

"Well, I've been giving it some thought too. . . . Let's take a carriage and go to my apartment."

"But Sergei Sergeyevich, I believe that in view of certain circumstances, which you understand, it would be a bit awkward at your place."

"Oh, come now."

"As an enlightened, humane man, you'll understand. . . . In a word, in a word . . . with respect to Sofia Petrovna . . ."

He got all tangled up and broke off.

They got into a carriage. High time: where the banners had been tossing and the scattered shots had crackled, there was no longer a single banner. There was such a torrent of people that the carriages which had swarmed and clustered there now flew off into the recesses of the Nevsky—in the opposite direction.

Now all had vanished. They turned off the prospect. Toward them rushed a raggedy cloud streaming a band of rain. The bluish band came over them, and once more droplets began to chirr and whisper, curling their bubbles on the surface of the puddles. Nikolai Apollonovich sat wrapped up in his cloak. He had forgotten where he was going. And there remained only the feeling that he was going under duress.

He again felt the weight of the oppressive confluence of circumstances.

The oppressive confluence of circumstances, or: the pyramid of events.

It, the pyramid, is the delirium of geometry, a delirium which nothing can measure. It is a satellite of the planet, yellow and dead like the moon.

Or—delirium that can be measured in digits.

Thirty zeroes—now that's a horror. Yes, but cross out the numeral one and the thirty zeroes will collapse.

There will be zero.

There is no horror in the numeral one. The numeral one is a nonentity, a one and nothing more! But one plus thirty zeroes will make the hideous monstrosity of a quintillion. A quintillion—oh, oh, oh!—dangles from a frail little stick. The one of a quintillion repeats itself more than a billion billion times, themselves repeated more than a billion times.

Yes—

Nikolai Apollonovich lived as a human numeral one, that is, as an emaciated little stick, running his course through time—

> In his birthday suit Nikolai Apollonovich was a little stick; he was ashamed of his thinness and had never yet been to a steambath with anyone.

—for time eternal!

And all the hideous monstrosity of a quintillion (more than a billion billion times, themselves repeated more than a billion times) had fallen right on this little stick. An indecent something had taken a nothing into itself; and this had been swelling from time eternal—

> Thus swells the stomach because of the expansion of gases from which all the Ableukhovs suffered.

—for time eternal.

Veritable Gaurisankars had distended.

In the twinkling of an eye everything that had raced by since morning again raced by: his plan flashed through his head.

The Plan

To sneak in the sardine tin, place it under the pillow; or, no—under the mattress. And—

"Good night, papa!"

In reply:

"Good night, Kolenka!"

To go to his room.

To undress impatiently, turn the key in the door with a click, and pull the blanket over his head.

To shake in his featherbed from the jolts of his beating heart. To long for and strain to hear the bang that would come there, the crash which, naturally, would shatter the silence as it shattered the bed, the table, and the walls; and having shattered perhaps . . . having shattered perhaps. . . .

And to hear the familiar shuffling of slippers toward . . . the place that was comparable to no other.

To turn from his French reading to—a piece of cotton to stop up his ears. To cover his head with a pillow, and realize that nothing would help. And to stick his head out, in an abyss of fear.

Waiting, waiting.

Half an hour left. The greenish first light of dawn; then blue, then gray; and the light of the candle dims. Only fifteen minutes left. And now the candle goes out. And slowly flowing by are eternities, not minutes. The striking of a match. But only five minutes have passed. To reassure himself that it would not be soon, that it would come in ten slow revolutions of time, to be deceived because:

> —an unrepeatable, unique, alluring sound would, all the same—

crash!!

. . . .

Then—

Thrusting his bare legs into his drawers (what do you mean, drawers!), or even in his undershirt, his face white and contorted—

—yes, yes, yes!—

> to spring out of his warm bed, patter barefoot into the black corridor and fly like an arrow: toward the sound unlike any other, breathing in a peculiar smell of burning mixed with gases and . . . something else, more horrible than burning and gases, and. . . .

However, there would very likely be no smell.

To run in, choking with loud coughing, to push himself part way through the black hole in the wall that had formed after that sound.

And there, beyond the hole—

where the demolished bedroom had been, a grim flame would illuminate . . . a mere trifle: belching clouds of smoke.

And yet. . . .

To push himself part way under this curtain of smoke: the remaining red half of a wall; and something flowing. The walls would be wet, and therefore, sticky, sticky. This would be his first impression of the room, and his last. Impressed in his memory would be plaster, fragments of broken parquetry, and torn shreds of scorched rugs. They would be smoldering. A shinbone?

Why had it remained intact, but not the other parts?

And behind him, in the depths of the corridor, an idiotic rumble of voices, an irregular stamping of feet, and the wailing of the kitchen maid, and the crackle of the telephone (they've made haste to call the police).

Then to drop the candelabra, squat, pull his nightshirt down around him, until a compassionate servant—

—on whom it would be eas-
ier to cast the blame—until he would
drag him into the next room and
force cold water down his throat—

Getting up off the floor and seeing: the stickiness that had splashed here after the loud noise, out of the hole, along with scraps of skin that had been torn off (but from which part of the body?) sticking to the wall.

Suddenly to faint.

.   .   .   .

To play out his role to the end.

Twenty-four hours later—a prayer service.† To bow his head, candle in hand.

Only two days later, his godlike countenance thrust into the fur of his caped greatcoat, to walk behind the coffin, out into the street, with an angelic look. And to grip his cap in his white kid-gloved fingers, as he accompanied that exalted retinue. That heap would be borne down the staircase with difficulty by gold-chested, white-trousered little old men.

Eight bald-pated little old men!

.   .   .   .

And yes, yes!

To give testimony at the inquest but of the kind that would cast a shadow (of course, not intentionally) on whoever it might be.

.   .   .   .

Noodle-doodle, dummy-wummy,
Little Kolya's dancing:
On his head a dunce-cap wears,
On his horse he's prancing.

.   .   .   .

The instant when Nikolai Apollonovich was dooming himself to be the executor of the death penalty—in the name of an Idea—that instant, not the gray prospect where he had been rushing about all morning, was the creator of the plan. Yes, action in the name of an

Idea had merged with dissimulation and perhaps with the framing of totally innocent people (the valet).

A lie had been added to parricide; and, most important of all, so had baseness.

· · · · · · ·

> Noble, trim, and pale of mien,
> Flaxen hair for all to see;
> In ideas rich, in feelings poor,
> N. A. A.—who can he be?

· · · · · · ·

He was a base villain.

· · · · · · ·

Everything that had happened was a fact. A fact was a monster: a pack of monsters! Yes, before this Nikolai Apollonovich had been sleeping, reading, eating; he had even been lusting: after Sofia Petrovna.

But, but!

He had been eating not like everyone else, and had been loving not like everyone else. The dreams he had been having were opaque. And his food had seemed tasteless. There had been something that dragged itself behind him and threw a special light on the workings of all his bodily functions.

What did it consist of?

His promise to the Party? He had not taken his promise back, but then, the others were thinking (we know what Lippanchenko was thinking). . . .†

And thus it consisted of the promise that had come into being at the Bridge—there, there—in a gust of Neva wind, when over his shoulder he had caught sight of bowler, cane, mustache (the inhabitants of Petersburg are distinguished by—hmm, hmm, certain qualities!).

Yes, standing at the bridge was only a consequence: lust had driven him there. There was something wrong with the way he experienced feelings of passion.

When Kolenka was called his father's spawn, he felt ashamed. The meaning of "spawn" was later revealed to him by his observations of the peculiarities of animal life. And Kolenka wept. He transferred the shame of his conception to his father.

And he understood that everything that exists is "spawn." People as such do not exist: they are all "things conceived." Apollon Apollonovich is a "thing conceived," an unpleasant sum of blood, skin, and meat—and meat sweats and goes bad at warm temperatures.

The soul did not exist.

He hated his own flesh; he lusted for that of others. Thus from childhood he had been carrying within him the larvae of monstrosities. And when the time was ripe, out they crawled—within twenty-four hours!

This decrepit earthen vessel† had to blow apart, and it was blowing apart.

The Government Institution

The Government Institution. . . .

The torso of a capripede caryatid. A carriage drawn by a pair of steeds flew up to the carriage porch, and a lackey, tricorne on his head, gave the handle a click, and the door flew open, flinging back a coat of arms adorned with tiny crowns (a unicorn goring a knight). Responding to greetings, a hand invested in leather touched the brim of a top hat.

Section-markers arose.

I find the shape of a section-marker† striking: two hooks descending and coupling. Yes, a section-marker is the natural devourer of papers, a phylloxera! There is something mystical about a section-marker. It is the thirteenth sign of the zodiac.

The section-marker was multiplying over Russia. The circulation of the section-marker (directed by Apollon Apollonovich) had begun spreading and multiplying all over halls and steps covered in red fabric.

Apollon Apollonovich was the most popular civil servant in Russia, with the exception of Konshin (whose signature is on the bank notes† in your pocket).

Apollon Apollonovich is in the Government Institution. Rather, "he was," because he is dead—

> —recently I was at his grave. A cross rises over a black marble slab; under the cross is an haut-relief, a carving of a head that bores into you. A demonic, Mephistophelian mouth! And beneath it: "Apollon Apollonovich Ableukhov —Senator," and the year of birth, and the year of demise. Mute grave!—

There are offices in the Government Institution.

And there are simply rooms. In each room are tables. There are copy clerks. Before each of them are quill and ink and a respectable pile of papers. Each scratches away, turns over the leaves of paper, creaks his pen (and I think the sinister plant the "creeper" takes its name from "creaker").†

—There was that very same rustling
above the grave—from birches;
their catkins were falling onto the
black marble cross; and—may he
rest in peace!—

.   .   .   .

Ableukhov sits in his office daily, vein tense, legs crossed, and a
veiny hand on his lapel. The sixty-eight-year-old man lives and
breathes by the sharply defined coupling of the hooks; and his
breathing wafts over the space of Russia. Yes, yes: Apollon Apollonovich, struck by a happy thought, legs crossed, puffs out his
cheeks in a taut balloon, and blows (a habit). And chill breezes
now waft through the unheated rooms and a wind sets up, and in
the outlying areas a hurricane breaks out.

Apollon Apollonovich is blowing!

Yes, yes: Apollon Apollonovich is a city person, a well-brought-
up gentleman. He sits in his office, while his shadow penetrates
walls . . . and pounces on passersby; and whistling, it carouses in
the spaces of Samara, of Saratov, in gullies, in sands, in thistles, in
wormwood, in burrs, it bares sandy patches, fans the flames in the
barn.

Wags would have said: not Apollon Apollonovich, but Aquilon
Apollonovich.

He Ceased Steering

Apollon Apollonovich is lonely.

He is not on top of things. The arrow of his circulars does not
pierce the provinces; it gets broken. Only here and there does an
Ivanchevsky fall, and Kozlorodovs do too. From Saint Petersburg
Apollon Apollonovich now and then bursts out in a paper barrage,
and (of late)—misses.

A hurler of arrowed thunderbolts, he has sent down lightning in
vain. History has changed. The ancient myths are not believed, and
Apollon Apollonovich is not the god Apollo. He is a civil servant.

The circulation of paper was getting smaller, and malicious papers, smelling of printer's ink, were already beginning to undermine
his Institution, in the form of petitions and charges, threats and
complaints.

Now just what sort of vile conduct vis-à-vis the higher authorities was circulating among "solid citizens"? A proclamatory tone
had appeared.

What did this mean?

A great deal: an unreachable Kozlorodov, an assessor, grew insolent, and he set out from his province against the Ivanchi-Ivanchevskys.†

Projects, counsels, and orders proceeded from Apollon Apollonovich. He sat in his office with the swollen vein in his temple, and order after order promptly sped off into the darkness of the provinces.

In Petersburg this darkness had already appeared on the Nevsky in the form of a Manchurian fur hat. The ring of many-chimneyed factories had already stopped spewing smoke.

Apollon Apollonovich was rotating the wheel of the mechanism. He had been turning the wheel a mere five years.

And he felt himself a skeleton from which Russia had fallen away.

Yes, Phlegethontic waves† of paper beat, in dozens and dozens of catastrophes, against the wheel of the immense machine which the senator rotated. A breach opened up in the Institution.

And something scandalous occurred: the Genius winged its way out of the mortal body of the wearer of diamond-studded decorations (he went off his skull), he tumbled down the rungs of the career-ladder.

He fell in the opinion of many.

He arrived at the Tsukatovs' soirée a statesman of national prominence; but when it was revealed that the person who had fled was his son, the senator's shortcomings were revealed: no doubt about it.

Apollon Apollonovich Ableukhov was struck from the list of candidates for an exceptionally high post.

At this point the twilight of Ableukhov began.

Charcoal Tablets

The greenish first light of morning. In his cubbyhole Semyonych was wheezing, tossing and turning, fidgeting; and he was assailed by yawning, scratching, and sneezing.

And yawning got the best of him.

The Tetyurin chimney (of the Tetyurin factory) spoke its piece. Little steamboats gave a whistle. The electric lights on the bridge—snap!—went out. Semyonych raised up slightly.

He began whispering to himself.

"I says to him:

"Your Excellency, I says, sir, I says, here's how it is . . .

"Nobody pays me no mind . . .

"And the young master is a whatcha-may-call-it. Oh Lord, forgive me for saying so . . . they're not masters but a bunch of Hamlits. . . .†

"Not masters but scalawags. . . ."

A door banged there in the corridor. Robbers? Avgiev the merchant had been robbed. Agniev the merchant had been robbed.†

And they had tried to cut Khakhu the Moldavian's throat.

He stuck his head out, thrust his legs into his drawers, and, jaw champing, he jumped out of the warm bed. He shuffled out barefoot: into the black corridor.

The bolt clicked . . . on the water closet: His Excellency, Apollon Apollonovich, the master!

Avgiev the merchant had been robbed! Agniev the merchant had been robbed! They had tried to cut the throat of Khakhu the druggist!

     .   .   .   .

As he was donning his quilted, well worn, mouse-colored dressing gown, Apollon Apollonovich clumsily got all entangled in its raspberry-colored tasseled belt. And out of its raspberry-colored lapels he thrust his rough, unshaven chin (smooth yesterday), studded with needles of white stubble which had appeared during the night like hoarfrost.

He sat, mouth open, chest hairy, drawing the piercing air into his lungs and taking his pulse.

He was much tormented by ceaseless hiccuping.

He was not thinking about the series of telegrams, or about the fact that the responsible position was slipping away forever, or—even!—about Anna Petrovna, but about what one felt like thinking about when facing a little box of blackish tablets.

He was thinking: the hiccuping, the jolts of his heart, the palpitations, which always brought on the sensation of pins and needles in the palms of his hands, were not caused by the heart but by the expansion of gases.

"Yes, it's just my stomach!"

On one occasion, Sapozhkov, the chamberlain who had died from angina pectoris, tried to explain it to him:

"Gases, you know, distend the stomach. The diaphragm contracts, and that causes the jolting and the hiccuping. It's the expansion of gases. . . ."

Recently, in the Senate, while discussing a report, Apollon Apollonovich grew agitated, turned blue, began to wheeze, and had to be helped out of the room.

"It's from gases, you know. . . ."

A tablet sometimes helped him, by naturally absorbing the gases.

     .   .   .   .

"Yes, gases"—and he had set out for . . . for. . . . It was 8:30.

That was the sound Semyonych had heard.

Removing his lap robe, Apollon Apollonovich had moved from
where he was, had opened the door, and at the very door had come
upon:

"You?"

"Me, sir."

"Ah, yes, yes."

"You have to keep your eye out everywhere."

"?"

"There was a sound. . . ."

"What of it?"

"Something banged. . . ."

.   .   .   .

The fact of the matter was that ten minutes earlier Semyonych
had been surprised to notice a tow head protruding from the doorway to the young master's room. It had looked around and withdrawn.

And then the young master had scampered by, all afidget.

He stood there a moment, took several deep breaths, shook his
head, turned around, and did not notice Semyonych† flattened
against the wall in a shadowy corner of the corridor.

Why, look how he's glued to the master's door, can't take his
eyes off it! That's no way for young masters to act!

A snoop?

After all, he's no lackey. He's the son of a general, educated in
the French manner.

"Oh, they're just Ham–lits! Oh, Lord! Peeping through a keyhole!"

.   .   .   .

"?"

"Nikolai Apollonovich . . ."

"Yes?"

"Banged the door going out."

And Apollon Apollonovich Ableukhov was about to ask Semyonych but just worked his mouth and thought:

After all, the old fellow did see Anna Petrovna. . . . Anna Petrovna must have changed, given up, and, I dare say she's gone a bit
gray, and gotten more wrinkled. . . . Should I ask about all that?

Suddenly the face of the sixty-eight-year-old master disintegrated
unnaturally into wrinkles, and his nose receded into the folds.

And a man in his sixties somehow became a thousand-year-old
man. In a strained voice that passed into shrillness, the gray ruin
started to squeeze out a little pun:

"Mm . . . mm . . . mm–Are you . . . mm . . . barefoot?"

"Your Exce . . ."

"No . . . mm—mm—mm . . . I don't mean"—

But he did not succeed in composing the little pun.

"Uh . . . tell me . . ."

"?"

"You have, of course, to be sure, yellow heels?"

Semyonych took offense:

"*I* don't have yellow heels, sir. Chinamen do . . ."

"Hee, hee. . . . Perhaps . . . pink ones?"

"Human ones, sir . . ."

"No, yellow ones!"

Apollon Apollonovich stamped his foot.

Semyonych thought: What's this heel business? And what do heels have to do with it? . . . He himself, the old fool, all last night. . . . And she herself so close by, in an expectant situation. . . . And the son, a regular Hamlitist. . . . And then he carries on about heels! . . . Calls mine yellow . . . why, his own heels are yellow. . . .

But Apollon Apollonovich displayed sheer bullheadedness, as was always the case with his puns. He would get all fluttery, fidgety, plaguey, pestery, like flies that try to get into your eyes just before a thunderstorm on a stifling day, when a grayish blue cloud wearyingly creeps above the lindens. Flies like that are squashed.

"A young lady has . . . hee–hee . . ."

"What does a young lady have?"

"She has . . ."

"What?"

"A pink . . . heel. . . ."

"I wouldn't know. . . ."

"Then why don't you go have a look. . . ."

And without finishing his sentence, Apollon Apollonovich, an actual privy councilor, a professor, pattered off into his room: to take his repose.

And he began helplessly to. . . . Oh, how he had shrunk! Oh, how stooped he had grown! One shoulder seemed lower than the other.

Alarming reports from the provinces. . . . And then, you know—his son, his son! . . . A horrible situation, you know. . . .

No matter! It'll work out!

An uprising, the ruin of Russia. . . . And already they're planning, they've made an attempt. . . . Some student or other.

And to top it all off—gases!

At this point he took a tablet. . . .

·   ·   ·   ·   ·   ·   ·   ·

If you overload a spring with weights it loses its resiliency. In old age the human brain softens and melts.

In his childhood Apollon Apollonovich Ableukhov had frozen, and his gleaming bust seemed sterner, firmer, autoluminiscent, rising above the northern night—until the foul light wind had felled his friend. Of late that wind had developed into a hurricane.†

He had stood, solitary and proud, under the muzzle of the hurricane—cold as ice, firm. But even platinum can be melted. ˙

In one night Apollon Apollonovich had grown bent. In one night he had fallen into ruins, his head had drooped.

And against the fiery background of a Russian Empire in flames stood, instead of a firm, gold-uniformed statesman, a hemorrhoidal old man, unshaven, uncombed, unwashed, in a tasselled dressing gown!

.   .   .   .

Have you ever seen senile but still eminent statesmen who have warded off the blows for half a century?

I have.

At meetings and at congresses they have slowly clambered up to the podium in shiny frock coats, slack jawed, toothless—

—I have seen them—

—from habit they have still gone on trying to move the hearts and minds of men!†

And I have seen them at home.

Bustling like half-wits, dropping sick, obtuse witticisms into my ear in a feeble whisper, they would drag themselves into their studies and would slobberingly boast of a small shelf with their collected works bound in morocco.

I Know What I'm Doing

At precisely ten o'clock Apollon Apollonovich partook of his coffee.

He used to run into the dining room—icy, austere, shaven, diffusing an odor of eau de cologne. Today, his slippers scratching the floor, he dragged himself to his coffee in his dressing gown—unscented, unshaven.

He did not glance at the correspondence, he did not reply to the servants' greetings.

> Beloved Delvig calls for me,
> The comrade of my lively youth,
> The comrade of my youth despondent. . . .

"Listen: do take the dog out of here. . . ."

At half past eleven Apollon Apollonovich, as if remembering

something, began bustling about like a gray mouse; and with delicate little steps he scampered into his room, his drawers showing beneath the open flap of his dressing gown.

The lackey stuck his head in to remind him that the carriage was there.

In astonishment he watched Apollon Apollonovich wheeling a bookcase ladder from shelf to shelf over the velvet runners laid there. And he was climbing the ladder at the risk of his own life. Having clambered up, he was testing for dust on the volumes with one finger.

He called for some dustrags.

The lackeys each took a stearine candle and assumed positions on either side of the ladder.

"Raise the light a bit higher. . . .No, not that way. . . . Not that way either . . . yes that's it . . . higher, a bit higher. . . ."

And out of a dust cloud swirled the mouse-colored skirts, swung the raspberry-colored tassels.

"Your Excellency, why are you troubling yourself. . . ."

Apollon Apollonovich Ableukhov, an actual privy councilor, out of a cloud of dust—you can't be serious! Oblivious to everything in the world, he was flicking a rag over the bindings, and he had a fit of violent sneezing.

"Dust, dust. . . .

"My . . . my! . . .

"Let me have a go at it . . . with a dustrag . . . like this. . . .

"Good!"

The telephone gave an alarmed ring. The Institution was calling. From the yellow house came the answer:

"Yes. . . . He is partaking of his coffee. . . . We will inform him. . . . Yes. . . . The carriage is here."

And again the telephone crackled. To the second call came the answer:

"But we have already informed him. . . . We will inform him. . . ."

To yet a third call came the answer:

"He is occupied with sorting his books. . . ."

.   .   .   .

"Oh, why don't I give these a good dusting! . . .

"Oh, my, my! . . . Just look at them!"

.   .   .   .

The doorbell tinkled again and again. The silence spoke of something forgotten.

And his head turned:

"Do you hear? . . . Listen. . . ."

It could be that scoundrel, Nikolai Apollonovich; it could be Hermann Hermannovich, bringing papers, or Kotoshi-Kotoshinsky, or Count Nolden—mm, mm—even Anna Petrovna.

"Your Excellency, how can we help but hear it? Someone will open, never fear. . . ."

The lackeys reacted to the tinkling.

"I venture to observe that someone is ringing!"

Each lackey extended his candle almost to the ceiling. At the very ceiling a head suddenly protruded from the dust clouds.

"Yes, yes, yes. . .

"You know. . .

"Someone's ringing . . . ringing. . . ."

They sensed something ineffable, and shuddered: hasten—run—hurry!

"That's the mistress!"

"Anna Petrovna!"

Apollon Apollonovich, a mouse-colored heap, eyes darting about, began creeping down the ladder with difficulty, resting his hairy chest against the rungs. He crept down and tapped off in the direction of the staircase, dustrag in hand. He was breathing heavily and taking his pulse.

. . . .

And now, preceded by Semyonych, a gentleman with sidewhiskers, in a uniform with a close-fitting waist and white cuffs, a star on his chest, was ascending the staircase.

Apollon Apollonovich, wrapped up in the skirts of his dressing gown, was peering out from behind the statue of Niobe.

You Will Be Like a Madman

If you have ever been in Petersburg, you know the entryway: oak doors there, with plate glass.

A mace gleamed from behind the panes.

Passersby, for whom all is a dream, dream of a sloping, octogenarian shoulder. A tricorne falls onto the old man's shoulder. The silver-braided doorman gleams as brightly, resembling an attendant in a funeral procession.

And the mace very peacefully rests on his shoulder. He has been dozing for years over *The Stock Exchange Register*. Whether you pass by the door during the day, or in the morning, or toward evening, you will see: the braid, the mace, the tricorne.

And you will come to a stop before this vision. Five years have passed. There has been an uproar of events. Port Arthur has fallen.

That region has been inundated by yellow-faced people. The legends about the horsemen of Genghis Khan have come back to life.

But the vision of times of old is unchanging: the shoulder, the tricorne, the braid, the beard.

Should the white beard stir, should the mace sway and the braid sparkle, you will whirl, like a madman, through the Petersburg prospects.

Listen, listen closely: there is a sound of galloping . . . from the Ural steppes.

It is horsemen.

Frozen immobile for years on end above the entryway of the many-columned building, the caryatid hangs suspended at the entryway: a colossus.

An old, bearded man of stone!

He has been smiling many years: above the noise of the street, above summers, winters, springs—in curlicues of ornamental moulding!

And he has leaned out of timelessness,† over the arrow of the Prospect, as over the line of time. And now and then a crow has settled on his beard. The wet prospect glistens in a play of light; and the flagstones, joylessly illuminated, reflect the greenish faces of the passersby.

·   ·   ·   ·   ·   ·   ·   ·

Oh, what a day!

Droplets began beating, chirring and whispering. A misty felt pressed down, and copy clerks passed by. The doorman opened up for them. They hung their hats on hooks and ran up the red steps through the white marble vestibule; and they walked through the unheated halls to their cold tables. But there was nothing to write. No papers had been brought from the director's office. There was no one there.

Apollon Apollonovich had not made his entrance.

They grew tired of waiting. A bewildered whispering fluttered from table to table. All sorts of dark things were imagined. And the telephone receiver crackled.

"Has he left? . . . It's not possible!"

"Have you informed him? . . . He's still at the table? . . ."

The assistant director descended the velvet steps in a very tall top hat.

Twenty minutes later, ascending the steps, he saw his superior, Apollon Apollonovich Ableukhov, peering out from behind a statue, wrapped up in the skirts of his dressing gown.

"Apollon Apollonovich, so that's where you are. We've been waiting for you, we've been ringing and ringing, telephoning. We've been waiting."

"I . . . mm,—mm," he said, chewing his lips, "I've been putting my library in order. Excuse me," he added, "for being so informally dressed."

And he gestured at the tattered dressing gown.

"Oh, sir, you look all puffed up! You seem swollen."†

The senator now dropped his dustrag on the parquet floor.

"Here's a pretty piece of news: there's a general strike."

"What makes you say that? I . . . mm—mmm. . . ." At this point the old man's face disintegrated into discontented wrinkles.

"Dusting?"

"I've been having a go at it with a dustrag."

The assistant director now bowed respectfully before the ruin, and attempted . . .

But Apollon Apollonovich once again interrupted him:

"Dust, you know, contains microorganisms that cause diseases. . . ."

The gray ruin, who had sat down on an Empire armchair, sprang up, his hand resting on the arm, and buried his nose in the document.

"What is this?"

"I was just reporting to you. . . ."

"No, but allow me . . . ," he savagely fixed on the document.

"Good heavens! Have they all taken leave of their senses?"

"Apollon Apollonovich. . . ."

"How could they even think that. . . . Administrative power is one thing, but a gross violation of lawful procedures is another."

"But Apollon Apollonovich!"

But Apollon Apollonovich began twirling a pencil, tied the tassels of his dressing gown, and said, with trembling jaw:

"I am a man of the school of Plehve. I know what I am doing. . . . Mmm—mmmm. . . . Mm—mmm. . . ."

And he puffed out his cheeks in a balloon.

The career of Senator Ableukhov, which had been built up over the years, was crumbling into dust. Now, after the departure of the assistant director of the Institution, Apollon Apollonovich began pacing back and forth amidst the Empire armchairs. Presently he withdrew, and appeared once more, lugging a heavy file of papers to a small mother-of-pearl table.

A death's head raised itself up out of the Nota Benes, the question marks, the section-markers, the check-marks.

"Just so. . . ."

With a sardonic grin the head raised itself and looked at the fire-place, imagining how that careerist, who had just proposed a deal to him, Ableukhov, was now rushing away from the house through the slush.

"I, gentlemen, am a man of the school of Plehve!"

The sharp little pencil fell onto the paper in huge flocks of question marks: his last official business.

.   .   .   .

The caryatid had not moved: the old bearded man of stone!

The year eighteen hundred and twelve saw him freed from his scaffolding; eighteen hundred and twenty-five saw the seditious December days rage above him; the January days raged and passed: nineteen hundred and five!†

Oh, Bearded Man of Stone!

What he has seen—he will not tell.

The coachman was reining in the horses: and a general in a tricorne was jumping out of a carriage to shouts of "Hurrah!"

And the bearded man concealed his name.

The bearded man knows it, and remembers; but as for telling, he will not tell!

> It's time, my friend, it's time! My heart begs for some peace.
> The days chase on the days, each serving to decrease
> The sum of our own being. Together you and I
> Propose to live some more. But lo! We too shall die.

But the doorman with the mace, dozing over *The Stock Exchange Register*, knew well: Vyacheslav Konstantinovich was still remembered in the Institution, while the Emperor Nicholas of Blessed Memory was not remembered!

> There is no happiness, but there is peace and rest .
> Long since in dreams I've seen a much desired guest:
> Long since, exhausted slave, I have resolved on flight
> To some far-off retreat of work and pure delight.†

.   .   .   .

The bald head raises itself slightly, the faded mouth smiles at the flaring fireplace. The eyes—stony, blue, sunk in green hollows—reflect the flames. All of life is nothing but obfuscation.

"I, gentlemen, am of the school of Plehve . . . I, gentlemen. . . ."

.   .   .   .

In the Institution, whispering fluttered from table to table. Suddenly the door opened:

"Apollon Apollonovich . . . is retiring."

Legonin, the chief clerk, burst into tears. From the assistant director's office came a perspicuous voice, and the crackle of the telephone. The assistant director stood with trembling jaw. Apollon Apollonovich was not head of the Institution.

A Reptile

That place was crowned by a magnificent palace.† The upper part, with its tower stretching into the sky, resembled a fanciful castle: of rosy red, heavy stone! All this did not happen in our day: the crowned head who had lived there was no longer.

Lord have mercy on his soul!†

The upper part of the rosy red palace jutted out of a thicket of leafless branches. Those branches reached out to the sky in mute paroxysms, and as they swayed, they tried to catch the fleeting clouds. A crow shot up, cawing; it soared higher, swayed above the wisps of cloud, and plummeted back down.

A carriage was traversing that place.

And an equestrian statue† stood out black and indistinct against the square. Visitors to Petersburg pay no attention to this statue. A magnificent statue!

The autocrat had raised this statue to his illustrious great-grandfather. He lived in the rosy stone castle. He did not languish long there.† Between flurries of petty tyranny and fits of nobleness, his soul was being torn apart.

Probably the snub-nosed head in white curls appeared in the embrasure of the window more than once. And the snub-nosed head in curls surveyed the spaces beyond the windowpanes. The eyes luxuriated in the fading rosy light of the sky, or rested on the silver seethe and play of the moon's reflection in the thick-foliaged trees. At the entryway stood a sentry in a broad-brimmed tricorne; and he presented arms to a gold-chested general† wearing the order of St. Andrew, as he passed to his carriage decorated in aquarelle. And the coachman in flaming red livery towered from the elevated box, and on the footboard at the rear stood thick-lipped Negroes.

And having cast a glance on all that, Pavel Petrovich again returned to a sentiment-laden conversation with a mannered lady-in-waiting. The lady-in-waiting was smiling; sly dimples and a beauty spot stood out more prominently.

On that night† the silver of the moon poured down, falling on the furniture of the imperial bedchamber and sportively gilding a little cupid. The profile of a recumbent figure was now outlined on a pillow. Chimes were sounding somewhere; and—faint steps were heard. No more than a moment or two passed and the bed was rumpled. The sheets were still warm: the man sleeping there was no longer. A little cluster of white-curled officers, swords heatedly drawn, were inclining their heads toward the empty couch.

People were trying to force a side door, and a woman's voice was lamenting. The hand of a rosy-lipped officer raised the window blind slightly, and from behind the lowered muslin a trembling shadow was outlined in black on the window, in the silver.

Somewhere chimes were sounding and there, in the distance, could be heard the tramping of feet.

.   .   .   .

Nikolai Apollonovich uncomprehendingly surveyed this gloomy place, not noticing how the second lieutenant's shaven physiognomy turned itself on him from time to time. The gaze which Second Lieutenant Likhutin cast upon the victim he was transporting seemed full of curiosity. Their sides kept bumping.

At this point the wind snatched the brimmed Italian hat off Ableukhov's head, and the latter caught it on Likhutin's knees. For a moment he touched Likhutin's fingers, and the fingers trembled in revulsion and fright. Likhutin had the sensation of touching a reptile, the kind that is squashed on the spot.

And Ableukhov's face suddenly looked pinched.

"I would advise you to put your collar up, Sergei Sergeyevich. There's something wrong with your throat. In weather like this it's terribly easy to . . ."

"What, what?"

"Catch quinsy."

"And on a matter involving you," Likhutin suddenly growled.

"?"

"And I'm not talking about my throat. It's that I left the service *on a matter involving you*, that is, not on a matter involving you, but precisely because of you."

"An allusion," Nikolai Apollonovich almost cried out, and once more he caught that glance.

And there was revulsion in that glance: creeping reptiles do not inspire anger. Why, they're squashed, with whatever comes to hand, on the spot.

Something was going to happen. . . . At this point Nikolai Apollonovich grew frightened in earnest. He began fidgeting in his seat and—ten trembling cold fingers clamped on the second lieutenant's sleeve.

"Eh? What? Why are you . . . ?"

At this point a small blancmange-colored house, bordered by rococo curlicues, came into view and moved past.

"Sergei Sergeyevich, I . . . I must confess. . . . Oh, how I regret . . . my conduct was lamentable . . . I acted . . . Sergei Sergeyevich . . . disgracefully . . . I have an excuse, Sergei Sergeyevich . . . I do, I do! You're different from others, Sergei Sergeyevich, you'll be able to understand everything! . . . I didn't sleep at all last night. I'm suffering from insomnia. . . . The doctors have found me . . ." —he stooped to lying—"utter exhaustion of the brain accompanied by pseudohallucinations."

But Sergei Sergeyevich said nothing. He looked at him without indignation. Reptiles do not inspire anger, but are squashed on the spot.

"Pseudohallucinations," Ableukhov kept repeating imploringly, thoroughly frightened, small, clumsy, seeking out the other's eyes with his own.

"I . . . I . . . I . . ."

"Let's get out: we've arrived."

And Second Lieutenant Likhutin stood before the carriage, awaiting the senator's dear son. The latter dillydallied.

"Sergei Sergeyevich, I had a cane with me. . . . Could I have dropped my cane?"

Nikolai Apollonovich kept looking ahead into the mists with leaden, unblinking eyes: he wasn't about to budge!

Sergei Sergeyevich began breathing angrily, impatiently. He grabbed Ableukhov by the sleeve, and began hauling him out of the carriage, like a sack crammed full of merchandise.

And, once hauled down, Nikolai Apollonovich seized Likhutin by the hand: after all, the hand might, perhaps, assume an unseemly position. A gesture might be made, and the Ableukhov stock would be disgraced.

With his free hand, Second Lieutenant Likhutin (wasn't he the rabid one!) grabbed the collar of Ableukhov's mantle.

"I'm coming, Sergei Sergeyevich, I'm coming. . . ."

But he instinctively dug a heel into the side of the entryway step. However, he promptly thought better of it.

The entryway door slammed.

Pitch Darkness[†]

"I . . . stood right here, right here was where I stood . . . I was standing, you know . . ."

"Is that so, Nikolai Apollonovich? . . . Is that so?"

"Having a violent fit of nerves, completely at the mercy of free associations of ideas. . . ."

"Associations?"

"The doctor said. . . . But why are you dragging me along? Don't drag me. I can walk."

"And why are you clutching my hand? Don't clutch at me, please."

"The doctor said . . . the doctor said it's such a rare disorder, very rare. And the domino, and all the rest of it. . . . A disorder of the brain . . ."—came the squeak from somewhere above.

And from somewhere still higher up, a well-fed voice exclaimed: "Ah, hello!"

"Who might that be?" Nikolai Apollonovich asked with relief. He felt the hand which had seized him snatch away.

"I've been standing here ringing and ringing, but nobody answers. And lo and behold! Some familiar voices."

When a match was struck, a bunch of very luxuriant chrysanthemums appeared, and behind them the figure of Verhefden.

"Sergei Sergeyevich?

"You're clean-shaven?

"What! . . . In civilian clothes?

"And you here too, Nikolai Apollonovich? How's your health?

"After the soirée yesterday I must confess I. . . . Were you unwell? You disappeared?"

Suddenly Verhefden was in a hurry:

"Am I in the way? . . . The fact is I just dropped by for a moment. . . . I'm pressed for time. . . . We're up to our neck in. . . . Your father, Apollon Apollonovich, is waiting for me. . . . A general strike is expected. . . ."

An overstarched linen butterfly appeared out of the doorway.

"Please come in, madam is at home."

"No, Mavrushka. Give these flowers to your mistress. It's a debt I owe." He smiled at Sergei Sergeyevich, shrugging his shoulders, the way men shrug their shoulders at one another when they mention a lady.

"A debt I owe Sofia Petrovna, for some 'phoo-phoos.'"

Then he suddenly caught himself:

"Goodbye, old boy. Nikolai Apollonovich, you have an exhausted, nervous look about you."

Footsteps pattered away down the stairs. Then from the lower landing again came:

"You really shouldn't spend all your time with books. . . ."

Nikolai Apollonovich was on the point of shouting:

"Hermann Hermannovich, I also . . . I have to be off. . . . Aren't we going the same way?"

Bang: the door slammed.

Nikolai Apollonovich felt himself grabbed, grabbed right in front of Mavrushka. At this point fright was written all over his face. Openly satanic joy was clearly written on the second lieutenant's face. Drenched in perspiration, he pulled a handkerchief out of his pocket, and with the other hand he squeezed, pressed against the wall, dragged, and shoved the small figure of the student.

But the figure proved supple as an eel, leaping back from the door as it quite naturally tried to defend itself; as it was shoved forward, it shoved back, pushed back.

Nonetheless Nikolai Apollonovich was shoved inside. But in an effort to maintain his last remaining shreds of independence, he observed:

"Actually . . . I'm not dropping in . . . for long. . . ."

With no deference to decorum, Sergei Sergeyevich propelled the broad-brimmed hat straight into the room containing the Fujiyamas. No need to add that under the hat and under the cloak, the owner of the cloak flew in too.

Nikolai Apollonovich was transported through the room containing the Fujiyamas without noticing the traces of plaster on the striped rug (it had been ground underfoot; the rugs had then been cleaned).

A door opened there, and Nikolai Apollonovich caught sight of two eyes in a stream of hair.

A voice exclaimed:

"Oh!"

"Ttrr"—heels dragged across the rug.

Nikolai Apollonovich turned his head, and, catching sight of Sofia Petrovna, shouted at her:

"Leave us alone, Sofia Petrovna, this is a matter for men only"—his cloak flew off and fell like some two-winged creature on the small couch.

"Ttrr"—heels dragged across the rug.

He had a tremendous sense of being shaken up, and, legs twitching, felt himself lifted up and weighed in space, and the broad-brimmed hat, detaching itself from his head, fell with a soft plop. He himself, legs twitching, described an arc and crashed into the door of the little study. The door flew open: he disappeared into the unknown.

The "Solid Citizen"

Apollon Apollonovich stood up.

He tore himself away from the bundles of dossiers placed parallel, from the question marks and exclamation points. The hand holding the little pencil was trembling over the small mother-of-pearl table.

And he understood.

The carriage with the coat of arms would not fly up to the caryatid. The octogenarian shoulder, the tricorne and the mace would not stir to greet him. There would be no getting back Port Arthur. China would rise in uproar, and—the horsemen of Genghis Khan!

Apollon Apollonovich listened closely. There was a distant galloping. No, not a galloping: it's Semyonych walking by. He comes in, walks by.

Apollon Apollonovich did not like the perspectives of the Neva. The clouds scudded by in greenish swarms, and condensed into smoke that clung to the seashore. There the Neva depths beat steellike against the granite. A spire fled into the greenish fog. Apollon Apollonovich started looking around uneasily. Here it was—walls, the domestic hearth. His career had come to an end.

Well?

Snow, not walls! Rather cold. . . . Well? Family life—yes, family life. That is, Nikolai Apollonovich—a really horrible, so to speak . . . and—Anna Petrovna, who in her old age had become. . . .

"Mm-mmm. . . ."

Cerebral play!

It was escaping beyond the bounds of consciousness, and he recalled: Nikolai Apollonovich, small of stature, with his inquisitive glances and with a muddle (one had to be fair) of the most varied intellectual interests.

And he recalled a young girl (some thirty years ago); a swarm of admirers; and a comparatively young man, a state councilor,† her swain.

And—the first night: an expression of disgust, masked by a submissive smile. That night Apollon Apollonovich, a state councilor, committed a vile act sanctioned by set form: he raped the girl. The rape had gone on for years. Nikolai Apollonovich had been conceived between smiles of lechery and submissiveness. Was it surprising, then, that Nikolai Apollonovich had become a composite of disgust, fright, and lechery? They had had to take on the upbringing of the horror they had spawned, humanize the horror.

Instead they had inflated it.

And having inflated the horror as far as it would go, each had run away in horror—Apollon Apollonovich to administer his department, Anna Petrovna to gratify her sexual urge with Mantalini (a singer), Nikolai Apollonovich to philosophy, meetings, and mustaches. Their domestic hearth had turned into a sewer of abomination.

Now he had to return to this very abomination. But instead of Anna Petrovna he would encounter only the locked door leading to her rooms. He had the key. (Only twice had he set foot in that part of the house; he had caught a cold there.)

Instead of his son he would see a blinking, shifty eye of cornflower blue, not exactly that of a thief, not exactly frightened. The horror would conceal itself.

And so on and so on. . . .

On his relinquishment of government service, the formal rooms would be closed up one after the other. The corridor, with rooms for him and his son, would remain; and life would be delimited by the corridor. There he would shuffle about, and there would be: the reading of newspapers, the performing of organic functions, the place that was comparable to no other, the writing of his memoirs just before his death, and the door leading to his son's rooms.

He would peep through the keyhole and jump back; or—no: he would bore a little hole with an awl. His son's way of life on the other side of the wall would be revealed in precisely the same detail as a clock mechanism. And from this observation point he would encounter new interests.

"Papa!"

"Good morning to you, Kolenka!"

And each would go off to his own rooms.

And then, locking the door, he would apply his eye to the little hole, in order to see, in order to tremble now and then at a secret revealed, in order to eavesdrop on how they opened up to one another—Nikolai Apollonovich and the stranger. And at night, throwing off the blanket, he would stick out his head, drenched in perspiration, as he deliberated what he had overheard; and gasping from the jolts of his beating heart, he would run along the corridor . . . to the place that was comparable to no other, slippers slapping.

The life of a "solid citizen"!

.   .   .   .

An irresistible urge drew him into his son's room. The door squeaked and the reception room opened up before him. He stopped on the threshold, so small and old. He worried the raspberry-colored tassels of his dressing gown as he surveyed the hodgepodge: the cage with the green parakeets, the Arabian tabouret of ivory and copper. He saw something absurd: winding down from the tabouret were the folds of a domino that had fallen full on the head of a spotted leopard, which lay sprawled, teeth bared. He remained standing there, chewed his lips, scratched the chin that seemed silvered with hoarfrost, and spat with loathing (after all, he knew the story of the domino). Buffoonish and headless, it spread its satin folds and armless sleeves. Hanging on a rusty Sudanese spear was a half-mask.

To Apollon Apollonovich it seemed stifling. Lead, not air, suffused the atmosphere. It was as if horrible, intolerable thoughts had been pondered here. What an unpleasant room! And what a heavy atmosphere!

There was that grinning mouth full of suffering, there were those eyes of cornflower blue, there was that mass of hair, bathed in light; vested in a uniform with a very slender waist and squeezing a white kid glove in his hand, Nikolai Apollonovich, clean-shaven (perhaps scented), a sword at his side, was suffering from inside the frame. And Apollon Apollonovich looked attentively at the portrait that had been painted the spring just past. He proceeded into the adjoining room.

The unlocked desk struck Apollon Apollonovich's attention: a small drawer had been pulled open. Apollon Apollonovich conceived an instinctive curiosity. He ran up to the desk and snatched a photograph that had been inadvertently left on the desk. He proceeded to turn it this way and that, very deep in thought (his abstraction drew his thoughts away from the contents of the drawer). The photograph depicted a certain brunette lady. . . .

His abstraction stemmed from his contemplation of a certain lofty matter which unfolded into a thought train, which the senator then followed. Then he mechanically lowered his eyes and saw: his hand was no longer turning the photograph but some heavy object, and his thoughts were surveying that type of state functionary who, in colloquial usage, is to be called a careerist.

The object had been extracted by the senator's hand. He mechanically snatched the photograph and came out of his thoughts, now holding an object with rounded ends. Something inside it clanked. What it might be never entered the senator's head (we often drink coffee with cream while suspended above the abyss). With the utmost attention he examined the object with rounded ends as he listened to the ticking of a watch: a clock mechanism! And in a sardine tin?

He did not like the object.

He carried the object into the drawing room for a more detailed examination. With his head bent over it, he resembled a mouse-colored little heap. He was still thinking about that same type of functionary. People of that type always defend themselves with phrases like "as is well known," when nothing is known, or, "science teaches us," when science does not teach.†

Apollon Apollonovich ran over to that end of the drawing room where the long-legged bronze rose up on leonine legs. He set the heavy object down on a small Chinese tray, inclining his enormous bald head, above which spread the circle of the glass lampshade, violet and delicately decorated.

The glass had darkened with time; the delicate painting thereon was darkening with time.

· · · · · · · ·

He Did Not Explain Himself Fully

Nikolai Apollonovich flew into Likhutin's little study, and his heels crashed full weight onto the floor. The concussion spread to the back of his head. He could not help falling on his knees.

He fell and—

> —jumped up, breathing heavily and limping; in his fright he rushed toward the oak armchair, cutting an awkward figure, with his trembling jaw and with visibly trembling fingers, and with a single instinctive urge—to get to the armchair in time to grab on, so that in the event of an attack from behind he could run around the armchair, rushing this way and that to match the movements of his merciless adversary, who would be rushing after him, this way and that.

Or else, arming himself with the chair, he would overturn it and rush as fast as he could to the window (better to crash straight onto the street, shattering the windowpane, than to remain alone with . . . with . . .). . . .

He flung himself at the armchair.

But scarcely had he reached it when a hot breath singed his neck. He had time to glimpse a five-fingered hand about to fall on his shoulder, and the face of the avenger, flushed crimson and with swollen veins. The five-fingered paw would have fallen on his shoulder, but he leaped over the armchair just in time.

And the five-fingered paw fell onto the armchair.

And a crack appeared in the armchair. There was an inhuman sound, the likes of which would never be repeated:

"Because . . . I . . . have involved myself . . . do you understand? . . . in this whole matter . . . this . . . matter. . . . You understand? . . . This matter is no affair of mine. . . . That is, it is my affair. . . . Do you understand? . . ."

The second lieutenant raised his two palms over the cringing little figure, who was awaiting a blow. The little figure, teeth bared, was twisting and bowing, as he tried to protect his cheek with his hands:

"But I understand, I understand. . . . Sergei Sergeyevich, do be quiet, I implore you, quiet, I do implore you. . . ."

He was already on the point of closing up his eyes and stopping up his ears, so as not to see the crimson countenance, so as not to have to listen to the hoarse crowing of that rooster voice.

"A matter . . . in which every decent person. . . . What did I say? Yes, decent. . . ."

A fist slammed into the wall above Ableukhov's head.

Nikolai Apollonovich saw only two legs (they were spread wide; he himself was crouching on all fours). A sudden thought, and—

without considering the consequences, Nikolai Apollonovich quickly crawled between the two legs, jumped up—and without a thought in his head rushed for the door. But . . . two five-fingered paws ignominiously seized him by one skirt of his frock coat: the expensive material ripped.

A piece of the skirt was ripped and flew somewhere to the side: "Stop . . . stop . . . I . . . I . . . am not going to kill you. . . ."

Nikolai Apollonovich was thrown aside. He slammed into a corner. He stood almost weeping from the enormity of it all. An enormous, cold fear made his eyes, normally a dark cornflower blue, look black. He understood that it was not Likhutin raging above him, not an enemy choking with vengeful fury but a violent lunatic, possessed of colossal muscular strength.

The violent lunatic, turning his back, quietly walked up to the door. The door gave a click. Sounds of some kind were heard on the other side of the door—weeping and the shuffling of slippers. Everything fell quiet.

. . . .

She crept up to the keyhole. She looked and saw: a pair of legs and . . . trouser straps. And the legs stamped off into a corner; they were nowhere to be seen. From the corner burst gurgling wheezes, and a throat bubbled, and there was the metallic sound of a lock being clicked shut.

Sofia Petrovna began weeping, and jumped back from the door. She saw Mavrushka, who was weeping:

"What's going on? . . . Oh, my dear madam?"

"What *is* going on? . . . What are they doing, Mavrushka?"

. . . .

And that demented man went on stamping across the room at a diagonal, while from his corner, Nikolai Apollonovich, arms flattened against the wall, went on observing the movements of that demented man.

The demented man was no longer pursuing him. He propped his elbows on his knees, gave a deep sigh and fell into deep thought.

"Oh, Lord!" burst forth.

"Save and have mercy on us!" came a moan.

Nikolai Apollonovich cautiously took advantage of the lull.

A frenzied paroxysm had erupted. Now it was subsiding. And Nikolai Apollonovich, slightly limping, hobbled out of the corner, cutting a rather comic figure in his uniform with its ripped frock coat, wearing galoshes and the muffler he had not removed.

He stopped at a small table, listening to the pounding of his heart, and with an inaudible gesture seized a paperweight.

But there was a treacherous rustle: at this point a little stack of papers scattered. The abating paroxysm erupted once more. His head turned and caught sight of Ableukhov standing armed with the paperweight. Nikolai Apollonovich leaped back with the paperweight.

And Sergei Sergeyevich took up his old refrain:

"Only please have the goodness not to be afraid . . . why are you trembling? . . . I seem to inspire fear in you? . . . I . . . I . . . I . . . ripped the skirt of your coat but . . . I didn't mean to."

"Believe it or not, the domino can be explained by my nervous exhaustion; and it in no way means I have broken my promise. I didn't stand in the entryway of my own free will, but. . . ."

"You will forgive me for what happened to your coat," the second lieutenant interrupted, "the skirt will be sewn up. Yes, why, I'll do it myself. I have needle and thread. . . ."

"Sergei Sergeyevich, that's basically . . . unimportant. . . ."

"Yes, yes, unimportant. . . ."

"It's unimportant with regard to the main topic, with regard to my standing in the entryway."

"But your standing in the entryway is not the point!" The second lieutenant waved his hand in annoyance and again began to pace.

"Well then, is it about Sofia Petrovna?"

"It's not about Sofia Petrovna!"†

"Well, about what, then?"

"Our topic, you see," and the second lieutenant brought his bloodshot little eyes up close to Ableukhov, "you see, our topic is all in the fact that you're locked in. . . ."

"He's gone off his head, he's forgotten everything, his brain functions only by associations. He's actually planning to . . . ," thought Nikolai Apollonovich. But Sergei Sergeyevich hurried on:

"You're safe here. . . . Here's the piece from the skirt of your coat. . . ."

"He's making fun of me," thought Nikolai Apollonovich.

"Here's how it is: you're not going to leave here. . . . But I . . . I'll leave here with a letter dictated by me and signed by you. . . . I'll go to your house, to your room. I was already there this morning, but I didn't see anything. . . . I'm going to turn everything upside down there. In the event that my search proves completely fruitless, I will warn your father because"—he wiped his brow—"it's not a question of your father, it's a question of you, yes, yes, yes indeed—you alone."

He thrust a rough finger into Nikolai Apollonovich's chest and stood, only one eyebrow arched.

"That will never come to pass!"

Playing on the crimson face was:

"?

"!

"!?"

A lunatic!

How strange that Nikolai Apollonovich was listening attentively to this raving. Something inside him shuddered: was this really raving? No, rather—hints, dropped in a disjointed fashion. But hints at what?

"But Sergei Sergeyevich, what are you talking about?"

"What do you mean what? Why, about the bomb."

At this the paperweight dropped. The horrors exceeded all limits: the heavy masses of quintillions turned into gases.

The heavy masses burst into flame. The cobblestones that crammed the body, having turned into gases, spurted through the openings of all the pores, again wound up the spirals of events, but wound them up in reverse order. They also twisted the body into the spiral. Sensation became *zero* sensation. The facial contours took a sharp outline, took on meaning, disclosing in the young man the face of an old man in his sixties.

. . . .

"Sergei Sergeyevich, I'm amazed at you. . . . How could you believe that I, that I . . . how could you ascribe consent to such baseness to me . . . I am no base villain . . . Sergei Sergeyevich, I don't think I'm an inveterate scoundrel. . . ."

Nikolai Apollonovich could not go on.

. . . .

From the shadowy corner stepped a round-shouldered stooping figure, like a swarm come back together, its grinning mouth filled with suffering, its eyes of cornflower blue; and the mass of flaxen-white hair formed what looked like a halo above the very high shining forehead. He stood with palms upturned, indignant, offended, somehow elevated against the background of the wallpaper: it was red.

At this point, Second Lieutenant Likhutin felt that for all his strength, healthiness (he thought he was healthy), and nobleness—he was merely dim obfuscation; and the second lieutenant began to back down perceptibly.

"Yes, I believe you," he waved his hands in perplexity.

"You see, I . . . ," he grew thoroughly embarrassed, "didn't doubt it. . . . Honestly now, I'm. . . . My wife told me. . . . Someone slipped her the note. She went ahead and read it, she opened it by mistake," he lied, blushed, and lowered his eyes.

"Once the note was opened," the senator's son gloatingly seized the opportunity, "then"—he shrugged his shoulders—"then Sofia Petrovna, naturally enough, had every right to tell you, as her husband, what the contents were," Nikolai Apollonovich said through clenched teeth. He continued his attack.

"I . . . I . . . got completely carried away," Likhutin said defensively. His eyes fell on the ill-fated skirt of the coat; he seized on the skirt as a pretext.

"Don't worry, I'll sew it up myself."

But Nikolai Apollonovich fluttered his palms reproachfully in the air.

"You knew not what you did."†

And his dark blue eyes expressed a beautiful sorrow:

"Denounce me, don't believe me!"

And he turned away.

Nikolai Apollonovich wept unrestrainedly. And Nikolai Apollonovich, now freed from raw fear, became utterly fearless. He wanted to suffer. His feelings had been torn apart, as his "I" had been torn apart. And out of his exploded "I" (he was awaiting it) would spurt a blinding torch, and out of there a familiar voice would say unto him, as it always did, would say within him, for him alone:

"You have suffered for me: I stand over you."

But there was no voice. There was no torch. There was darkness. But why was there no reassuring voice saying: "You have suffered for me"? Because he had not suffered for anyone: he had suffered for himself. He, so to speak, was trying to get himself out of the mess of hideous events that he himself had cooked up. That was why there was no voice. In place of the former "I" there was darkness.

He turned away. He wept.

"But honestly," he heard behind his back, in a tone at once reassuring and meek, "I was mistaken, I didn't understand. . . ."

"Taking advantage of your physical superiority, you . . . in the presence of a lady . . . dragged me like. . . ."

Sergei Sergeyevich, hand outstretched, traversed the little study. But Nikolai Apollonovich, in a voice choking from the fury that had engulfed him, and from a sense of amour propre, which had—alas!—come too late, jerked out:

"Like . . . like . . . some little puppy. . . ."

Had Nikolai Apollonovich offered his hand to him, Sergei Sergeyevich would have counted himself the happiest of men. Complete contentment would have played over his face. But his access of nobleness, like his access of fury, was promptly stoppered.

"You wanted to reassure yourself, Sergei Sergeyevich? That I was no parricide? No, Sergei Sergeyevich, no: you should have considered that earlier. . . . But you went ahead and . . . like . . . like a puppy. . . . And you ripped the skirt of my coat. . . ."

"The skirt can be sewed up!"

And before Ableukhov could collect himself, Sergei Sergeyevich rushed to the door.

"Mavrushka! Some black thread! A needle!"

But the opened door almost slammed into Sofia Petrovna, who had been eavesdropping on the other side of the door.

"Oh? . . . Sonechka. . . ."

"Sofia Petrovna!"

"Just imagine . . . Nikolai Apollonovich here . . . you know . . . has gone and ripped the skirt of his coat. . . . It needs to be. . . ."

"Don't worry, Sergei Sergeyevich, Sofia Petrovna. . . ."

And Nikolai Apollonovich, his mouth contorted because of this stupid situation, wiping his eyelashes with his sleeve and limping on one leg, now made his appearance in the room containing the Fujiyamas . . . in a torn frock coat, one of its skirts dangling. He raised his head and, taking note of the damaged ceiling, turned his contorted mouth on Likhutin.

"I did it, Nikolai Apollonovich . . . I was . . . repairing the ceilings. . . ."

But Nikolai Apollonovich, silent, limped as he went out through the hall. Drooping from one shoulder, the fantastic cloak trailed after him. . . .

A Nice Little Game of Solitaire

From an etagere a nice clean little samovar cast a sheen like a mirror, while the samovar bubbling away on the table was unpolished. The newer one was used when there were guests. When there were no guests, the deformed monstrosity was used. Pellets of white bread had been flattened on the spotted tablecloth. A damp spot spread beneath an unfinished glass of sour tea (sour from the lemon); and there was a plate with leavings.

But where were the luxuriant tresses? Only a small braid could be seen.

But of course. Zoya Zakharovna donned a wig (whenever there were guests). In all likelihood she applied makeup shamelessly (we have seen her as a luxuriant-tressed brunette with enamelled, smooth skin; now before us was simply an old woman with a sweaty nose). She was wearing a blouse, and, like everything else, it was dirty (in all likelihood, used as her night jacket).

Lippanchenko was sitting half turned away from the little table, his square stooped back presented to the dirty samovar, in front of a nice little game of solitaire he had laid out, leading one to assume that after supper Lippanchenko had undertaken to pass the evening in his usual way. He had been disturbed, and had torn himself away from the cards. A conversation had taken place, during which solitaire and everything else had been forgotten . . .

And after this conversation Lippanchenko had turned his back: his back on the conversation.

He was sitting with his jacket off. The belt that had been pressing his stomach in was undone, which caused the tail of his uncomfortable shirt to protrude treacherously between his waistcoat and his sagging trousers.

Lippanchenko was pensively contemplating the blot of a cockroach that crawled with a rustle, enormous, black. They were to be found there in abundance.

"Well? . . . What's going on? And why?"

"What?"

"Doesn't a woman who has been faithful, a woman of forty, a woman like me. . . ."

And the elbow of her blouse was torn. Faded skin showed through; there was in all likelihood a flea bite on it.

"What are you babbling about, woman? Speak more clearly. . . ."

"Do you mean a woman like me has no right to ask?"

Lippanchenko turned in his armchair.

Apparently her words had found their mark; and for a moment something like an oppressive pang appeared on his face. He blinked his little eyes. Evidently he wanted to come out with something, and evidently he was afraid to come out with it. He was slowly weighing something.

But these impulses to candor abruptly ended.

"Hmm . . . yes, yes . . . the five on the six. . . . Where's the queen? Here's the queen . . . the jack is blocked. . . ."

Suddenly he cast an inquiring glance at Zoya Zakharovna, and his short fingers, covered with gold-yellow fur, moved one row of cards to another row of cards.

"Well, it's come out."

"What's there to get angry at?"

She now began walking about the room, pressing down hard on her slippers. And a shuffling was heard (the feeler of a cockroach disappeared into a crack).

And, uncorseted stomach protruding, her drooping chin trembled as she walked:

"You would have done better to ask why I'm asking you. . . . Because everyone's asking. . . . They're shrugging their shoulders. . . . So now I think"—she leaned her stomach and breasts on the armchair—"I'd better know."

But Lippanchenko bit his lips and laid out the cards, row after row.

He remembered that the next day—if he could not contrive to throw off the menacing weight of the evidence that had fallen on him—he faced checkmate.

"Hmm! . . . An opening. . . . The king to the opening. . . . You say people are asking?"

"And you thought they weren't?"

Lippanchenko threw down the cards.

"It won't come out, the twos are blocked. . . ."

From Lippanchenko's bedroom came a rattle, as if the window in there were being opened. Who could it be?

Probably Tom, the Saint Bernard.

"But you must understand that your questions"—Lippanchenko got up heaving a sigh—"violate Party"—he took a gulp of the sour tea—"errr, what do you call it, discipline."

Stretching as he walked, he passed through the open door into darkness. . . .

"Why, what does such discipline have to do with me, Kolenka?" —and Zoya Zakharovna lowered her head, as she continued standing over the now empty armchair. "Just stop and think. . . ."

She fell silent, and the chair remained empty. Lippanchenko was pattering off in the direction of the bedroom.

"There have never been any secrets between us," she told herself.

Immediately she turned her head toward the door, and began talking with agitation in his direction.

"But you yourself didn't warn me that, as a matter of fact (Lippanchenko had appeared in the doorway), that you now have secrets."

"It's all right, there's no one in the bedroom," he interrupted.

His mouth gaped in a bored yawn. Unbuttoning his waistcoat, he discontentedly mumbled to himself:

"Oh, what's the point of these scenes?"

"What have I done, Kolenka? . . . Don't I love you? . . . Aren't I afraid for you?"

She twined her arms around his neck.

He saw her porous nose right before his eyes. The pores glistened with sweat. How the skin had lost its freshness! Her eyes were all agoggle as they searched his importunately, they looked like black buttons, there was no light in them.

"Stop . . . enough of this . . . Zoya Zakharovna . . . let me go . . . you're choking me. . . ."

He seized her arms and removed them from his neck.

"You know how sentimental I am and what weak nerves I have . . . I. . . ."

They fell silent.

In the heavy silence, after the long, joyless conversation, when everything had already been said, she washed the glass, the saucer, and the teaspoons.

But he kept on sitting, half turned away from the little table, presenting his square back both to Zoya Zakharovna and to the samovar.

Her anxious eyes began running anxiously over the tablecloth and clambered up onto that fat chest. When he turned, they bored into his blinking little eyes; and—what had time done?

The bright chestnut little eyes which at age twenty-five had sparkled with humor and sly merriment had grown dim and sunken, and were covered with a menacing film. They had been overcast by the smoke of dark yellow, saffron yellow atmospheres. Yes, twenty-five years is no small span of time, but still—to have become so faded, to have become so narrow! And the twenty-five years had pulled the skin into bags beneath the little eyes. The face had yellowed in color, grown oily, completely withered, horrifying in its gray corpselike pallor. And the forehead—it had grown out of all proportion, and the ears had grown bigger. There is such a thing as decent-looking old men. But he was not an old man. . . .

A fair-haired, twenty-year-old student in Paris—the student Lipensky—swelling nightmarishly, had, in the course of two decades, turned into a forty-five-year-old indecent gut: into Lippanchenko.

Inexpressible Meanings

A saltwater pool wrinkled on the sandy seashore.

White-maned strips came rushing in from the gulf out there. The moon illuminated them. Strip after strip foamed up there in the distance, rumbled in the distance, and then broke as it rushed up to the shore in raggedy foam. And it spread over the flat shore, lapping and slicing at the sands, eating away at them. Like the thin edge of a blade it swept over the sands, splashed its way into the saltwater pool, and poured a salt-solution into it.

Then it ran back.

At a certain distance from the sea stretched the branchy arms of bushes. They rose into space, whistling and flapping. Running among them was a tiny blackish hatless figure. From this place rose a gnashing and a groaning. Out of the fog and dampness stretched jagged stumps. A gnarled arm bristling with bare branches, like fur, arched upward.

The tiny figure bent toward a tree hollow, into the shroud of black dampness.

"Oh, my soul, you have departed from me . . . I am so wretched. . . ."†

From his heart welled up:

"Remember me: I am so wretched. . . ."

A bright little dot quivered on the horizon of the sea. It was a commercial schooner approaching Petersburg. Gradually a tiny flame ripened, swelling with light like an ear of grain bearded with the rays of the sun.

Now it turned into a broad strip outlining the dark hull of a vessel behind it, and above it a forest of rigging.

Wooden, bare-branched arms flew up beneath the moon. The head of a bush stretched into space, tossing a network of black twigs. The moon got all tangled up in the network, and now shone there more blindingly. The airy intervals between the branches filled with a phosphorescent glare. They formed into an immense body, glowing phosphorescent, wearing a vitriol-colored cloak which streamed off into the misty smoke. An imperious arm, pointing into the future, stretched in the direction of the light from a small summer-cottage garden, where bushes beat at the latticework fence with supple branches.

The tiny figure stopped, and imploringly stretched out toward the phosphorescent intervals between the branches, which were forming the body.

"But one just can't, on suspicion alone, without any explanation . . ."

The arm was pointing at a window of light.

At this, the figure ran off into empty space, struck its chest against the latticework fence around a small garden, climbed over the fence and slipped soundlessly toward that small gray summer house, its feet catching in the dewy grass.

It stole up to the terrace, and in two leaps was at the door. It pressed against the window: a broad expanse of light there.

They were sitting there—

—Lippanchenko had one elbow propped on the table; the palm of the other hand opened and closed; the fingers were astonishingly stubby, seemed lopped off, were marred by hangnails, had dye under the nails.—

—The tiny figure flew back from the door and wound up in the bushes. It was overcome by a paroxysm of pity.

"Why, one can't just simply. . . ."

Swan Song

Turning his whole torso, Lippanchenko suddenly stretched out his arm—just imagine!—to a violin hanging on the wall.

"You come home to rest, but just look what you find. . . ."

He fetched the rosin. He attacked the piece of rosin ferociously, and with a guilty little grimace, inappropriate to his position in the Party, he set to rubbing his bow against the rosin.

"You're met with tears. . . ."

And he pressed the violin against his stomach and bent over it, resting the broad end on his knees. The narrow end he pushed under his chin. With one hand he tightened the strings, with the other he extracted a sound:

"Plunk!"

And his head bent and leaned to the side as he did this. And he looked at Zoya Zakharovna with a questioning expression, half jesting, half doleful, as if he were asking:

"Hear this?"

She sat down on a chair, a melting expression on her face. She looked at Lippanchenko's finger. The finger was testing the strings, and the strings twanged.

"That's a little better!"

They nodded at each other, he with the renewed ardor of youth, and she with coyness.

"Oh, you're such a . . ."

"Twang-twang. . . ."

". . . big baby, just incorrigible!"

And even though Lippanchenko looked like a rhinocerous, he turned the violin around with a deft movement of the wrist of his left hand; and its broad end now moved into the angle between his shoulder and his inclined head; the narrow end remained in his flying fingers:

"Here we go!"

The hand holding the bow flew up and paused, and then touched a string with a most tender motion. The bow set off, and his entire arm followed the bow; and the head and the fat torso followed the arm. Everything then traveled to one side.

The chair creaked under Lippanchenko, who was straining for all he was worth in a mighty, stubborn effort to produce a tender sound. A somewhat hoarse yet pleasant bass voice unexpectedly filled the room: "Oh, do not te–e–e–mpt . . . ," sang Lippanchenko.[†]

"Meee—without neee . . . ," the violin strings picked it up.

"–eed," Lippanchenko sang off to one side.

In their youthful years they used to sing that old romance for hours on end.

.   .   .   .

"Shhh!

"Listen!

"The window?
"One should go have a look."

. . . .

The moon rose from behind a cloud. Everything around that had been nebulous took separate shape. The skeletons of the bushes emerged black; their shadows fell in shaggy tufts. The airy blots formed into a body, glowing phosphorescent, extending its arm to the window. The tiny figure leaped up to the window. And the window was not latched; as it opened, it gave a slight tinkle.

Shadows stirred in the windows. Someone was coming with a candle behind the curtained windows. The unlatched window lit up. The curtain was pulled aside. A fat figure stood for a moment and looked: a chin seemed to be peering out (the eyes were not visible); two orbits darkled, two hairless arcs above the eyes glistened in the moonlight. The curtain was drawn. Someone fat moved away behind the curtained windows. Soon all was calm. The quaver of a violin and of a voice issued from the summer house.

The tiny figure detached itself from the hollow of the tree trunk and for a second time stole up to the window.

. . . .

"To one who has been disen–cha–a–anted. . . . Are alien cha–a–arms of for–r–rmer days . . . I trust in pro–o–o–mises no longer. . . .

"No mo–re do I believe in lo–o–ove. . . ."

Did he know what he was singing? No, the frontal bone did not know: the forehead was small and creased with wrinkles; it seemed to be weeping.

Thus Lippanchenko sang his swan song.

. . . .

Finally, taking a candle, he set off for his bedroom, but on the threshold he turned indecisively, sighed, and fell to thinking about something. Lippanchenko's whole figure expressed ineffable melancholy.

The candle cut into the room. The pitch blackness was torn apart. Fragments of darkness whirled about the periphery of a flaming, dancing center; and beyond the dark wedges which were the shadows cast by objects was a shadow, an enormous dark fat man, who dashed out from under Lippanchenko's heels, and began moving inside the circle with much fuss and bustle.

The fat man, without shape, without sound, was flung across the space between the wall and the table, broke into sharp angles across the shadow-wedges, and was torn apart in agony.

Thus: the soul, having cast out its body as unnecessary ballast, is at times caught up by the hurricanes of its own movements. They sweep through the spaces of the soul.† Yes, the body is a fragile vessel, sailing off on the ocean of the soul toward a spiritual mainland.

Thus—

Imagine: a rope is wound around your body at the waist, the rope is pulled and you begin spinning with indescribable speed. In ever widening circles you fly head down, back forward. You will fly off into the measureless immensities of the universe, overcoming spaces while becoming spaces.

You are caught up by such a hurricane when the body is cast out as unnecessary ballast.

Just imagine: a point of the body experiences the urge to expand without measure, to expand to a horrible extent (and to occupy a space equal in diameter to the orbit of Saturn). Imagine that you consciously sense not only one point, but all the points. They have all swollen up and have rarefied into a gaseous state. The planets have begun to circulate freely in the voids of your body's molecules. The centripetal sensation has been lost; we are blown to bits; and only the consciousness of shattered sensations remains whole.

What would we then sense?

We would sense that the detached organs are separated one from another by horrible billions of miles. But consciousness knits together a blatant and hideous monstrosity which at the same time lacks wholeness. We feel the seething of Saturn's masses in the spine. The stars of constellations eat their way into the brain. In the center of the seething heart we feel the diseased joltings of the entire heart.† The solar streams of fire, thrown off from the sun, would not have reached the surface of the heart if the sun had moved into this fiery, senselessly beating center.

Were we able to imagine this, before us would rise up the first stages of the life of the soul, which has cast off the body from itself.

Cockroaches

Candle in hand, Lippanchenko stopped. The shadowy wedges stopped along with him. And an immense shadowy fat man (Lippanchenko's soul) was suspended by his head on the ceiling. But Lippanchenko felt no interest in his own shadow. He was interested in a rustling, which was utterly unmysterious.

He felt a revulsion for cockroaches; and now, surprised by the light of the candle, they fled with a rustle into their dark corners.

And Lippanchenko was in a temper.

He stamped over to the corner to get the scrub brush.

He set the candle on the floor. Scrub brush in hand, he clambered onto a chair, and his heavy body jutted above the chair, and his blood vessels were about to burst from the exertion, and his hair was dishevelled. He pursued the fleeing handfuls of insects with the bristly end of the brush. One, two, three!—and there was a crackling beneath the brush: on the ceiling, on the wall.

"Eight . . . ten . . . eleven"—and, with a crackle, the blots fell onto the floor.

Before going to bed, he would crush cockroaches. Having crushed a great pile of them, he set off to sleep.

Now he lumbered into his cosy little bedroom, locked the door with his key, and looked under the bed (this habit had become rooted in him a while ago). He set the guttering candle before him.

He undressed.

Now he was sitting on the bed, hairy and naked, his legs apart. Womanish rounded forms were outlined on his shaggy chest.

Lippanchenko slept in the nude.

Diagonally across from the candle, between the wardrobe and the wall with the window, in a shadowy dark niche, was the intricate outline of hanging trousers. Lippanchenko would try all sorts of places to hang his trousers; and the result was always one and the same: the likeness of someone peering out from there.

And when he blew out the candle, the outline shuddered and stood out more distinctly. Lippanchenko stretched his hand to the curtain on the window and the retreating calico rustled. And the room was radiant with a coppery phosphorescence. Out of the white tin of storm clouds a disc fired a salvo throughout the room, and. . . .

Against the background of the green and vitriol-looking wall appeared a tiny figure in a shabby overcoat; and its white lips smiled, like a clown's. Lippanchenko beat a path to the door, and flattened his stomach and breasts full force against it (he had forgotten that he had locked the door). A jet of boiling liquid slashed along his bare back from his shoulder blades to his buttocks. As he fell he understood: his back had been slit open (this is how the hairless skin of a cold suckling pig with horseradish sauce is sliced). No sooner had he understood this when he felt a jet of boiling liquid beneath his navel.

And from there came a hissing. And some part of him thought that it was gases (his stomach had been ripped open). Bending his head over his heaving stomach, he sank down, fingering the flowing stickiness on his stomach and on the sheet.

This was his last conscious impression of ordinary reality. His consciousness expanded. The monstrous periphery of consciousness sucked the planets into itself, and sensed them as organs detached one from the other. The sun swam in the dilations of the heart; and the spine grew incandescent from the touch of Saturn's masses: a volcano opened up in his stomach.

And the body sat senseless, the head falling onto the chest, the eyes fixed on the cleft stomach. Suddenly it pitched stomach first into the sheet. The arm dangled above the bloody rug, its fur glistening in a rust red play of colors in the moonlight. And the head, with sagging jaw, was flung in the direction of the door. An unblinking pupil gazed at the door. The imprint of five bloody fingers was visible on the white of the sheet. And a fat heel stuck up.

．　．　．　．　．　．　．　．

And in the morning they came in, but Lippanchenko was no more. There was a pool of blood; there was a corpse; and a small figure, with a laughing white face. It had a small mustache, with bristling ends. How strange: the man had mounted the dead body. In his hand he was clutching a pair of scissors. He had extended an arm,† and over his face—over his nose, over his lips—crawled the blot of a cockroach.

End of the Seventh Chapter

Chapter the Eighth
and last

The past unfolds before my very eyes—
Has it been long since it sped by, eventful
And filled with agitation like the ocean?
Silent now it lies in peace and calm,
Not many faces memory has kept,
Not many words now reach me from afar. . . .†

Pushkin

But First of All . . .

—These twenty-four hours!—

—these twenty-four hours of our narrative have expanded and scattered
in the spaces of the soul: the autho-
rial gaze has gotten all tangled up
in the spaces of the soul.

Cerebral, leaden games have plodded along within a closed-in horizon, in a circle that has been traced by us—

—in those twenty-four
hours!

The news of Anna Petrovna had come fluttering along from
somewhere or other. We forgot that Anna Petrovna had returned.

Those twenty-four hours!

That is, an entire day and night: a concept that is relative, where
an instant—

—or—something that can be defined by the amplitude of
events in the soul is an hour, or a zero: experience grows
apace, or is absent: in an instant.

The arrival of Anna Petrovna is a fact, and a tremendous one.
We, the author, had forgotten about Anna Petrovna. And as usual,
the heroes of the novel—following our example—had forgotten about
Anna Petrovna.

But nonetheless . . .

Anna Petrovna had returned. But she had no inkling of the events.
Only one thing that happened troubled her: there had been no
notes or messengers for her. Neither Nikolai Apollonovich nor
Apollon Apollonovich had paid any attention to what had happened.

.   .   .   .

The deluxe hotel was confining her in one of its smallest rooms. And for hours on end Anna Petrovna sat on a chair staring at the patterns of the wallpaper. They assailed her eyes, and she shifted her eyes to the window. And the window looked out on an olive-hued wall where there was smoke instead of sky. All that could be seen in a window over there, diagonally opposite, were piles of dirty dishes and a washtub.

And she would ring. And some whirligig of a girl would appear. And Anna Petrovna would vouchsafe to ask for:

"Thé complet."

A lackey in a black tailcoat would appear, in starched shirt front and glistening tie, with a huge tray set on his palm and shoulder. He would run his eyes over the tiny room, the ineptly mended dress, the cheap Spanish clothes lying on the double bed, and the battered little suitcase. He would jerk the huge tray off his shoulder, and the "thé complet" would descend precipitously. And the lackey would withdraw.

And—no one, nothing. Just the same loud laughter and racket from the next room, and the conversation between two maids in the corridor. She would shift her eyes to the window, and the window looked out on the olive-hued wall where there was smoke instead of sky—

> —(suddenly there came a knocking at the door; and Anna Petrovna gave a start and splashed her tea on the napkins on the tray)—

> > —in the window over there, diagonally opposite, piles of dirty napkins and a washtub could be seen.

The maid handed her a calling card. Anna Petrovna half rose from behind the small table. She made a quick gesture of her hand as she patted her hair.

"Where is the gentleman?"

"In the corridor."

"Ask him in."

And there could be heard—the racket from the next room, the conversation between the two maids in the corridor, a piano, and steps rapidly running toward the door. Apollon Apollonovich Ableukhov, not stepping across the threshold, kept straining to make something out in the half-twilight. The first thing he saw was an olive-hued wall, visible beyond the window, and smoke instead of sky. In the window over there, diagonally opposite, piles of dirty dishes and a washtub could be seen.

·   ·   ·   ·   ·   ·   ·   ·

The first thing that struck him were the meager furnishings of the tiny room. A room like this in a first-class hotel?

Well, what of it? There's nothing to be surprised about. All first-class hotels in all first-class capital cities have tiny rooms like this. Yes, indeed: "Premier ordre—depuis 3 francs."† And heaven help you if you take it!

There was a bed, a table, and a chair. And on the bed, in disarray, were a little reticule, straps, a black lace fan, a small cut-glass Venetian vase, wrapped—just imagine—in a stocking (of purest silk), more straps, and something made of lemon-colored fabric rolled into a ball. All these were souvenirs of Granada and Toledo—

—so the three thousand silver roubles, recently dispatched to Granada, must not have been received; how embarrassing for a lady of her position to be carting these old rags around.

A silhouette took shape. His heart was wrung. On a chair

—but no, not on a chair!—he saw Anna Petrovna, sunken, grown heavier, with gray in her hair; the first thing he understood was the fact that her chin now protruded from behind her collar and a rounded stomach now protruded; the two azure-filled eyes of the once beautiful dear face glistened there as before.

Apollon Apollonovich was crushing his hat in his hand. He let his eyes run around the room, where straps, a black lace fan, a stocking, something made of extremely bright lemon yellow fabric rolled into a ball, Spanish, no doubt, lay scattered.

. . . .

Two and a half years had changed him. Two and a half years earlier, she had seen before her (during their last conversation), above a small mother-of-pearl table, a face carved from stone. But now on the face was a complete absence of features.

Two and a half years ago Apollon Apollonovich had been an old man, but there had been something ageless about him. He had looked like a statesman. Now? Where was the iron will, where was the stony gaze? No, the old man in him outweighed everything. She was struck by his emaciation. She was struck by his stooped figure, his trembling jaw and fingers, and by the color of his coat. When she was there, he had never had coats of this color made.

Finally Apollon Apollonovich raised his head and said haltingly: "Anna Petrovna!"

Her features lit up; it was as if all of her surged toward him. But all the same: she did not budge from the spot.

But Apollon Apollonovich ran toward her, in his coat, hat in hand. The surface of his immense skull, bare as a baby's knee, and his two protruding ears reminded her of something, and his lips touched her hand.

And when he straightened up, what stood out about his small figure were his little trousers, his little coat, and his tiny wrinkles. His two bulging eyes did not look like stone.

Apollon Apollonovich was searching for the right way to address her:

"I, you . . . ," he wondered for a moment whether to add "my dear," but instead finished, "know . . ."†

"?"

"I have come to pay my respects. . . ."

And Anna Petrovna caught a confused, mild, sympathetic glance —of cornflower blue.

"We have . . .

"A strike on our hands. . . ."

It Swayed above a Heap of Objects . . .†

At this point the door flew open.

Nikolai Apollonovich found himself in the vestibule, out of which he had run in such haste. On the walls glittered a display of antique weapons: here were rusting swords, there, halberds fixed at an angle. Nikolai Apollonovich seemed beside himself. He tore off the Italian brimmed hat with an abrupt sweep of the hand. When he fell into thought for a moment, the lines of his white countenance stood out dry and cold and sharp, iconlike, as he directed his gaze to the spot where beneath a rusty green shield the spike of a Lithuanian helmet glittered and the cruciform hilt of a knight's sword sparkled.

Suddenly he flushed. Limping slightly, still in his rumpled cloak, he flew up the steps of the carpeted staircase. He was panting and shaking with fever. In point of fact he had been standing too long in the rain. The most curious thing of all was that the cloth had been ripped on the knee of the leg on which he was limping, and a scrap of cloth was flapping about. Between the two skirts of his frock coat—one intact, the other torn—the half-belt danced about, for it was sticking out. And Nikolai Apollonovich looked lame and hunchbacked, with a little tail, when he flew full speed up the soft steps of the staircase, a thatch of flaxen white hair streaming, past the walls where a pistol and a battle mace hung at a tilt.

Not himself at all, he flew into his varicolored room, and the green parakeets set up a despairing shriek in the cage, and began flapping their wings. The shriek interrupted his flight. For a moment he stared straight ahead, and he saw the spotted leopard with gaping jaws at his very feet. He began rummaging in his pockets (trying to find the little key to the desk).

"Eh?

"Damn it all . . .

"Have I lost it?"

And he began rushing helplessly about the room looking everywhere for the traitorous key he had forgotten, pawing through the bibelots, seizing the three-legged gold censer while muttering to himself: Nikolai Apollonovich, like Apollon Apollonovich, talked to himself.

He hurtled into the next room—straight to the desk. He caught his foot on the Arabian tabouret and it crashed to the floor. He was staggered to find the desk unlocked; and the drawer was sticking out traitorously. It had been pulled open half way. His heart sank: how could he have forgotten to lock it? He tugged at the drawer. . . . And—and—and. . . .

No, it could not be!

Objects lay in disorder in the drawer. The photograph of cabinet size. No sardine tin. The lines of his countenance stood out above the drawer, and set off something like eyes, black: from dilation of the pupils. Thus he stood between the armchair and the bust of— but of course, it stands to reason—Kant.

He pulled out the drawer. Papers and packets of letters lay in order there. Everything went onto the top of the desk. But . . . there was no sardine tin. His legs buckled under him. Still wearing his Italian cloak and his galoshes, he fell on his knees, letting his burning head drop into his sweat-dampened hands. In this position he froze. The thatch of hair had a strange deathly look, like a blot in the half-twilight of the room.

Up he leaped! Straight for the bookcase! And the bookcase flew open. And objects began sailing onto the carpet. There was no sardine tin. He began rushing about the room like a whirlwind, his precipitous movements calling to mind His Excellency, his papa. Fate was having its little joke. From the bed (here he rummaged under the pillows)—to the fireplace. He got his hands all smudged up. Then—to the lower rows of the bookshelves. He thrust his hands between the books; many volumes tumbled down with a rustle.

There was no sardine tin.

And his face, smudged with soot and dust, swayed absurdly above the pile of objects that had been flung into a heap and pawed through by long spidery fingers that seemed independent of his hands. His hands, protruding from the Italian cloak, crawled all over the floor. Trembling and sweaty, he would have reminded anyone of a fat-bellied spider, a devourer of flies. Thus, when an observer tears a very delicate spider web he sees the following sight: the immense insect, which has been quivering on a silvery thread, is disturbed and begins running back and forth from the ceiling to the floor.

Nikolai Apollonovich was taken unawares:

"Nikolai Apollonovich!"

Nikolai Apollonovich, still sitting on his haunches, turned. Seeing Semyonych, he covered the heap of objects with his cloak, and so resembled a hen sitting on her eggs.

"I venture to report . . ."

"As you can see, I'm busy!"

With his mouth stretched from ear to ear, he looked just like the head of the leopard on the floor, teeth bared.

"As you see, I'm sorting my books."

And Nikolai Apollonovich mechanically half rose to his feet. His countenance was smudged with ashes, dust, and soot. At this point a blush flashed like lightning across his face, and Nikolai Apollonovich cut a comic little figure, in a student's frock coat with only one skirt and with a half-belt dancing about.

"Mama? Anna Petrovna?"

"She's in there with Apollon Apollonovich, in the drawing room, sir. She has graciously asked that. . . ."

.   .   .   .

In this room, not so very long ago, Nikolai Apollonovich had grown into a self-contained center, into a series of logical premises that flowed from the center and predetermined everything: the soul, thought and this very armchair. Not so very long ago he had been the sole center of the universe here. But ten days had gone by, and his self-awareness was now getting disgracefully stuck in the heaped-up pile of objects. Thus does a fly, freely running around the edge of a plate on its six legs, suddenly get hopelessly stuck by one leg and wing in sticky thick honey.

.   .   .   .

"Psst! Semyonych, Semyonych, listen!" Here Nikolai Apollonovich quickly scampered out through the doorway, overtaking Semyonych. He leaped across the overturned tabouret and clutched at the old man's sleeve (oh my, how those fingers do clutch!).

"Did you happen to see anywhere around here . . . the fact of the matter is that . . ." He got all tangled up in his words, and crouched a bit as he dragged the old man away from the door leading to the corridor. "I left it. . . . Did you happen to see a certain object here? Here in the study. . . . This kind of object, a toy . . ."

"A toy, sir?"

"A child's toy . . . a sardine tin. . . ."

"A sardine tin?"

"Yes, a toy, shaped like a sardine tin, it's heavy, the kind you wind up, also it's ticking. . . . I put it in here, it's a toy. . . ."

Semyonych slowly turned, freed his sleeve from the clutching fingers, fixed his eyes on the wall for a moment (on the wall hung an African shield, made from the armor of a rhinocerous that had once fallen), thought for a moment and disrespectfully snapped out:

"No!"

Not even "No, sir," just "No."

"All the same I thought you might . . ."

Can you beat that! Good fortune, joy in the family at last; why, the master himself, the *minister*, is beaming on such an occasion. . . . And would you look, here he's going on about a sardine tin that's . . . heavy . . . that you wind up . . . a toy. And he himself's running around—with one skirt ripped!

"So may I announce that . . ."

"I'm coming, I'm coming . . ."

And the door closed. Nikolai Apollonovich stood here, without understanding where he was, by the overturned dark brown tabouret, in front of the hookah. Hanging on the wall in front of him was an African shield made from the thick hide of a fallen rhinocerous, with a rusty Sudanese spear suspended on one side.

Without understanding what he was doing, he hastened to exchange the traitorous frock coat for a frock coat that was brand new. But first he washed the soot off his hands and face. As he washed and dressed he kept saying to himself:

"How could this have happened, what's going on? . . . Really now, where could I have hidden it? . . ."

Nikolai Apollonovich was not as yet fully aware of the magnitude of the horror that had fallen upon him, and that stemmed from the accidental disappearance of the sardine tin. Luckily it had not yet entered his head that: *they had been in his room in his absence, had discovered the sardine tin with horrible contents, and had considerately carried off the sardine tin.*

The Lackeys Were Astonished

And exactly the same kind of houses rose up there, and the same kind of gray human streams of people passed by there, and the same

kind of yellow-green fog hung there. Faces ran by there in preoc-
cupation. The sidewalks conversed in whispers and shuffled beneath
the gang of stone giants—the houses. Prospect after prospect flew to
meet them. And the spherical surface of the planet seemed embraced, as in serpent coils, by blackish gray cubes of houses. And
the network of parallel prospects expanded into the abysses of the
universe, in surfaces of squares and cubes: one square per "solid
citizen."

But Apollon Apollonovich was not looking at his favorite figure:
the square. He did not lapse into an unthinking contemplation of
the stone parallelepipeds and cubes. Gently rocking on the soft seat
cushions of the hired carriage, he stole an occasional agitated glance
at Anna Petrovna, whom he himself was taking to the lacquered
house. What it was they had talked about there, over tea, in the
hotel room, forever remained an impenetrable mystery to all. It was
after this conversation that they decided Anna Petrovna would
move to the Embankment the very next day. But today Apollon
Apollonovich was taking Anna Petrovna for a reunion with her son.

And Anna Petrovna was all flustered.

They did not speak in the carriage. Anna Petrovna kept looking
out the windows of the carriage. She had not seen these gray prospects for two and a half years. There, beyond the windows, the
numeration of the houses was visible. And the circulation went on.
There, from there, on clear days, from far, far away, came the
blinding blaze of: the golden needle, the clouds, the crimson ray of
the sunset. There, from there, on foggy days—no one, nothing.

With unconcealed pleasure Apollon Apollonovich was slumped
against the walls of the carriage, cut off inside the closed-in cube.
He let his eyes flit about. Only now and then did Anna Petrovna
catch a baffled and bewildered look and—just imagine—a look that
in a way was mild, and nothing more: blue, very blue, childlike,
even blank (could he be lapsing into his second childhood?).

"I have heard, Apollon Apollonovich, that you're to be made a
minister?"

But Apollon Apollonovich interrupted:

"Where have you just come from, Anna Petrovna?"

"Why, I've come from Granada. . . ."

"I see, I see, I see . . . ," and, blowing his nose, he added: "Well,
you know, things have come up, unpleasant things, you know, at
the office . . ."

And—what was that? He felt a warm hand on his own hand. His
hand had been stroked. . . . Hm, hm, hm: Apollon Apollonovich
got all discomfited, disconcerted, even somehow frightened. He
even felt a certain unpleasantness. Hm, hm: no one had acted this

way toward him for fifteen years . . . why, she had actually stroked him. . . . That, he had to admit, he had not expected from this person . . . hm, hm . . . (after all, these past two and a half years Apollon Apollonovich had regarded this particular person as . . . a person . . . of easy . . . virtue . . .).

"As it happens, I'm retiring. . . ."

The hurtlings, the thunderings of quivering carriages! The melodic cries of automobile roulades! And a detachment of policemen!

There where nothing but pale gray misty haze hung suspended, at first appeared the dull outline and then the full shape of the dingy blackish gray St. Isaac's Cathedral. . . . And it retreated back into the fog. And an expanse opened: the depths, the greenish murk, into which a black bridge stretched away, where fog draped the cold, many-chimneyed distances and whence rushed a wave of onrushing clouds.

. . . .

In point of fact, the lackeys were indeed astonished!

This is how it was later told by the young lad Grishka, who had been on duty in the vestibule:

"Here I'm sitting and counting the days† from the Feast of the Protection of the Mother of God to the Feast of the Nativity of the Mother of God. . . . And so that makes . . . from the Feast of the Nativity of the Mother of God to the Feast of St. Nicholas it's. . . ."

"What are you talking about, the Feast of the Nativity of the Mother of God!"

"So it adds up to, as I figure. . . . Somebody drives up. I go to the door. So I throw the door open, and, oh heavens! It's the master himself in a hired carriage with a lady up in years, with a cheap waterproof on her."

"Not a waterproof, you little scamp, they don't wear waterproofs any more."

"Well then, in a coat. And the master jumps out, and gives his hand to the mistress, and renders every service real cavalier-like."

"How 'bout that!"

"Him doing it!"

"Sure enough, they haven't seen each other for two years," chimed in several other voices.

"Well, sure. So the mistress gets out of the carriage, only the mistress isn't looking her old self. She grabs herself under the chin. She's got unmended holes in her gloves. Maybe they don't mend 'em in Spain."

"Enough of that!"

"And our master, Apollon Apollonovich, drops some of his dignification. There he's standing by the carriage, in a puddle, in the rain—Lord o'mercy! And when the mistress leaned right on his arm, you should have seen how our master's legs buckled. Well, I says to myself, how could he hold up someone as heavy as her!"

"Don't go weaving yarns like that!"

"I'm just telling the way it was, but what's the use of talking? Mitry Semyonych here will tell us all about it!"

"Well?"

"She's aged some. . . . First off I didn't even recognize her, and then I recognized her because I still remember how she'd give me little treats to eat."

.   .   .   .

Indeed!

Anna Petrovna and Apollon Apollonovich had both been agitated by their little talk. And on entering the lacquered house they did not exchange any outpourings of feelings. Apollon Apollonovich began to blow his nose . . . and, under the rusty halberd, to snort into his sidewhiskers. Anna Petrovna graciously vouchsafed to answer the bows of the lackeys. She embraced Semyonych and looked as though she wanted to shed a tear or two, but . . . she did not take out her handkerchief.

Apollon Apollonovich maintained an air of indifference: nothing special had happened! Everything was just fine, thank you!

However, there was a lackey here who remembered the manner in which the mistress had made her departure abroad—with just a travelling satchel in hand. On the eve of her departure she locked herself in, wouldn't admit the master. *That what's-his-name with the mustache* was there in her room—oh, what was his name?— Almondini.† He used to sing at their house, "tra-la-la. . . ." And he never tipped.

Now they were in the hall. There was rarely any heat here, for Apollon Apollonovich mostly stayed to himself in his study. And now he realized that he was not alone: he would stroll about here . . . with Anna Petrovna, across the small echoing high-gloss squares of floor.

Rarely did Apollon Apollonovich stroll across the small squares with Nikolenka: almost never!

Bending his arm like a pretzel, he escorted her through the hall. Anna Petrovna soon stopped him, pointing at a painting in pale tones.

"Do you remember this fresco, Apollon Apollonovich?"

"Why, of course!"

"Where?"

The remembrance of the misty lagoon, and of an aria sobbing in the distance overwhelmed him: it had been some thirty years earlier. Remembrances overwhelmed her as well. They divided into two parts: some thirty years earlier, and—Kolenka. . . .

"Kolenka. . . ."

At this point they stepped into the drawing room. Cabinets with porcelain baubles and tiny leaves of incrustation—mother-of-pearl and bronze—leaped at them.

"And Kolenka is fine . . . just fine . . . getting along fine"—he ran off somewhere to the side.

"Why didn't he come to see me?"

"He, Anna Petrovna . . . mmm . . . was, in his turn, very very"— the senator, strangely enough, got all tangled up in his words, took out his handkerchief, and blew his nose at length.

"He was overjoyed."

A silence fell. The bald head began swaying under the long-legged bronze.

Semyonych appeared in response to the bell.

"Is Nikolai Apollonovich at home?"

"Yes he is, sir. . . ."

"Mm . . . listen, tell him that Anna Petrovna is here!"

"Perhaps we should go to him ourselves"—Anna Petrovna grew agitated, but Apollon Apollonovich turned to Semyonych and interrupted:

"Mmm . . . Semyonych, let me tell you. . . ."

"Yes, sir!"

"What is a hussar's wife called?"†

"A hussaress, sir. . . ."

"No, a hussy!"

.   .   .   .

"Hee, hee, hee. . . ."

.   .   .   .

"Kolenka is acting . . . now don't be alarmed . . . acting . . . now don't be alarmed . . . strangely."

"?"

Golden pier glasses standing between the windows swallowed the drawing room in mirror surfaces.

"Kolenka has become somehow secretive . . . kh, kh"—and seized by a fit of coughing, Apollon Apollonovich drummed his finger on a small table, remembered something, frowned, and began rubbing the bridge of his nose with his hand. However, he quickly collected himself, and with exaggerated gaiety, he cried out:

"But really, no, it's nothing . . . just a trifle. . . ."

There Was Utter Meaninglessness

Nikolai Apollonovich, trying to ignore a stabbing pain in his knee joint (that was quite a bump he'd gotten), was limping slightly: he was running down the corridor.

Whirlwinds of thoughts and meanings raged within him. Or not even whirlwinds of meanings, but of meaninglessness. If someone should stop the swirling whirlwind in Ableukhov's head only for an instant, then meaninglessness would vest itself in thoughts.

Here they are:

The thought of the horror of his situation; a horrible situation has now been created (as a result of the disappearance of the sardine tin): the sardine tin, that is, the bomb has disappeared; and therefore, someone has carried off the bomb; and he will be arrested; but that is not what really matters: the bomb has been carried off by Apollon Apollonovich himself; carried off just at the moment when accounts have been settled with the bomb; and he knows everything.

Everything—what does that mean? Absolutely nothing has happened. There is no plan for a murder. Nikolai Apollonovich denies it categorically: it's a vile slander, this plan.

The fact of the bomb remains.

Since his father is summoning him, since his mother—no, he can't possibly know: he's not the one who has removed the bomb from the room. As for the lackeys. . . . The lackeys would long since have discovered it. But no one's said anything. No, they don't know about the bomb. But where is it, where? Did he really put it away in the desk? Maybe he stuck it somewhere under a rug, without thinking, by accident.

He often did things like that.

In a week it would come to light by itself. . . . But no: it would announce its presence tonight—with a really horrible thundering roar (the Ableukhovs could not endure thundering roars).

Maybe—under a rug, under a pillow, on a bookshelf, it would roar and burst. And—the bomb has to be found, but there's no time to look—Anna Petrovna's here.

Oh, everything was in a muddle: whirlwinds of thoughts swirled with inhuman velocity and howled in his ears, so that there were no thoughts at all.

And with a meaningless boiling liquid in his head, Nikolai Apollonovich ran, limping slightly on his right leg, the one with the painfully aching knee joint.

Mamma

The first thing he saw was . . . was. . . . But what is there to say at this point: the face of his mother. It had aged, and her hands were trembling (in the lacework of light from the golden street lamps that had just been lighted outside the windows).

"Kolenka, my very own, my darling boy!"

He could not hold back; he rushed to her.

"Is it really you, my boy? . . ."

He could not hold back. Sinking on his knees before her, he threw his arms around her. He pressed against her knees and broke into racking sobs—why, he did not know. His broad shoulders began heaving (he had received no affection these last few years).

"Mamma, it's you. . . ."

And he wept.

Apollon Apollonovich stood there, in the half-twilight of a niche, a finger lightly tapping a small porcelain doll, a Chinaman. The Chinaman was bobbing his head. Apollon Apollonovich emerged from the half-twilight of the niche, making soft little sounds of surprise. He moved forward in tiny steps, and unexpectedly boomed:

"Calm yourselves, my friends!"

To tell the truth, he could not have expected such feelings from his cold, secretive son, on whose face, these two years past, he had seen nothing but little grimaces, a mouth rent from ear to ear, and downcast eyes. A concerned Apollon Apollonovich ran out—to fetch some object or other.

"Mamma, it's you. . . ."

"My darling boy."

.   .   .   .

The touch of fingers on his arm brought him to:

"Here, Kolenka, have a little sip of water."

And when he raised his tearstained countenance from her knees, he saw the childlike gaze of an old man of sixty-eight. Apollon Apollonovich was standing here in a little jacket, holding a glass of water. His fingers were dancing, and he was more trying to pat than actually patting Nikolai Apollonovich on the back, the shoulders, the cheeks. Suddenly he stroked his flaxen white hair with his hand. Anna Petrovna was laughing; she was adjusting her collar with her hand, although there was no reason to do so.

And Nikolai Apollonovich raised up slightly from his knees:

"Excuse me, mamma, I'm not myself . . . I'll be all right in just a minute. . . ."

He drank some water.

Here Apollon Apollonovich set the glass of water on the small mother-of-pearl table. Suddenly he burst out in senile laughter, the way little boys laugh at the antics of a jolly older man.

"I see. . . .

"I see. . . ."

Apollon Apollonovich was standing there by the pier glass which was crowned with the wing of a cute little gold-cheeked cupid; and beneath the cute little cupid laurel wreaths and roses were being gored by the heavy flames of flambeaux.

But then came the sudden slash of memory! The sardine tin! †

A paroxysm burst within Nikolai.

"Just a moment, I'll . . . I'll be back. . . ."

"What's wrong with you, my dear?"

"Let him be, Anna Petrovna. . . . I advise you, Kolenka, to be alone with yourself . . . for five minutes or so. . . . And, you know. . . . And then come back. . . ."

And, faintly simulating a paroxysm of the kind that had just occurred, Nikolai Apollonovich staggered, letting his face fall, in a rather theatrical manner, into his fingers. And the thatch of hair had a strange deathly look there.

Staggering, he exited.

. . . .

"Yes, yes. . . . Strictly speaking, I didn't recognize him. . . . These . . . these, so to speak, feelings"—and Apollon Apollonovich darted from the mirror to the windowsill—"these, these . . . paroxysms . . ."—and he patted his sidewhiskers.

"They demonstrate . . . ," he turned abruptly and raised the toes of his shoes, balancing himself on his little heels, and then brought his whole weight down on the rapidly falling toes of his shoes.

"Demonstrate . . . ," he put his hands behind his back (beneath his little jacket) and turned one hand round and round behind his back (which made his little jacket wag). And Apollon Apollonovich seemed to be running about the drawing room with a little wagging tail.

"They demonstrate a naturalness of feeling, and, so to speak"— he shrugged his shoulders—"the good qualities of his nature . . . I didn't expect it at all."

A snuffbox lying on the small table abruptly struck the attention of the eminent statesman. Wishing to impart a more symmetrical appearance to its position on the table vis-à-vis the tray lying there, Apollon Apollonovich walked up to that small table and from the tray snatched . . . a calling card, which he began turning between his fingers. At this instant he was visited by a profound thought, which unfolded into a retreating labyrinth of irrelevant discoveries. But Anna Petrovna, who was still sitting in the armchair, noted:

"I always said. . . ."

"Yes, you know, my dear. . . ."

Apollon Apollonovich rose and ran from the small table to the mirror.

And said in a more formal tone: "You know . . ."

From the mirror—into the corner.

"Kolenka really surprised me. And I must admit his conduct has reassured me"—he wrinkled his brow—"with regard to . . . with regard to. . . ." He took his hand from behind his back, and began drumming his fingers on a small table:

"Hm, yes! . . ."

He interrupted himself:

"It's nothing."

And he fell into thought.

And the Thunder of a Roulade

Nikolai Apollonovich entered his room. He stared at the Arabian tabouret, and let his eyes follow the incrustation of ivory and mother-of-pearl. He slowly went up to the window, which opened expanses: there the racing river, and a rocking barque; and the splashing stream. From the drawing room, from somewhere in the distance, cascades of roulades filled the silence. They had been played in just this way before: he used to fall asleep to these same sounds.

Nikolai Apollonovich stood over the heap of objects, and agonized:

"But where is it? . . . How could it have happened. . . . Where in fact did I put it?"

He could not recollect.

And—shadows, shadows. And out of the shadows there, green patches of armchairs; and emerging from the shadows there—the bust of—it stands to reason—Kant.

Only now did he notice a piece of paper folded over twice. Visitors who do not find their host at home leave such pieces of paper on a table. He mechanically took the paper in his hand. He saw the handwriting: familiar, Likhutin's. Yes, of course: he had completely forgotten that in his absence Likhutin had been here, rummaging and digging around.

He had rummaged through the entire room.

A sigh of relief broke from him. Everything was explained: Likhutin! Of course, of course: he had been rummaging around here, he had searched and found it. And having found it, he had carried it off. He had seen the unlocked desk, and he had looked into the desk. And he had been struck by the sardine tin, by its weight, by its appearance, and by its clock mechanism. The second lieutenant had gone and carried the sardine tin off. There was no doubt.

He sank into an armchair with relief. Flying cascades of roulades filled the silence. And so it had been before: roulades had come from there, some nine years ago and some ten years ago: Anna Petrovna now and then used to play Chopin (never Schumann). It now seemed to him that no events had taken place. Everything had explained itself so simply: the sardine tin had been carried off by Second Lieutenant Likhutin (who else but him, unless you assumed, but—why assume that!). Alexander Ivanovich would take care of everything else (at this very same time, we would remind the reader, Alexander Ivanovich Dudkin was having his little talk with the late Lippanchenko at the summer house). No, absolutely no events had taken place.

There, beyond the windows, Petersburg pursued, with cerebral play and with plangent expanse. Onslaughts of damp cold wind attacked. Enormous nests of diamonds were shrouded in mist beneath the bridge. And—no one, nothing.

And the racing river; and the splashing stream; and a rocking barque; and the thunder of a roulade.

A Watermelon Is a Vegetable . . .

After two and a half years a dinner was held.

The cuckoo clock cuckooed. A lackey brought in a steaming soup tureen. Anna Petrovna beamed with contentment, while Apollon Apollonovich—by the way, as recently as today, as recently as this morning, had you taken a close look at the decrepit old man, you would not have recognized this ageless statesman who was now invigorated and erect, and who took up his napkin with a supple movement. They were having the soup course. At this point the side door squeaked. Nikolai Apollonovich, lightly powdered, clean-shaven, spruce, hobbled over to join the family, wearing a student's frock coat with a very high collar (calling to mind the collars of the age of Alexander I).

"Mon cher," Anna Petrovna affectedly jerked a pince-nez up to her nose, "you are limping, I see."

"Ah?" Apollon Apollonovich threw a glance at Kolenka and—seized the pepper box. "Indeed you are," and he began overpeppering his soup.

"Ah, maman, I tripped. And my knee aches."

"Shouldn't you apply some Goulard's extract?"

"Ah, Kolenka," Apollon Apollonovich, raising a spoonful of soup to his mouth, looked out from under his brows, "bruises of the knee joint are not to be trifled with. Bruises can lead to complications."†

And he swallowed the spoonful of soup.

"Maternal feelings . . ." and Anna Petrovna's big childlike eyes were now agoggle, and her head was pressed into her neck ". . . but it's surprising; after all, he's grown up now, and I'm still worrying about him. . . ."

And, very naturally it had slipped her mind that two and a half years earlier it had not been Kolenka that she had been worrying about. Kolenka had been overshadowed by a long-mustachioed man with eyes like two prunes. Daily she had knotted the violet silk tie of a stranger, there, in Spain. She would give him a laxative, Hunyadi-Janos.†

"Maternal feelings, you remember, when you had dysentery. . . ."

"Exactly."

"It would seem that you are still suffering from," Apollon Apollonovich rumbled out of his plate, "the consequences of dysentery?"

"I hasten to say, sir . . . berries . . . are still bad for . . . the young master," came Semyonych's voice at this point. From time to time he peeped through the door; he was not serving at table.

"Berries!" boomed Apollon Apollonovich's bass, and he unexpectedly turned full face toward Semyonych.

"Berries," he began chewing his lips.

The lackey who was serving (not Semyonych) gave an anticipatory smile, looking exactly as if he wanted to announce to everyone:

"Here it comes!"

"Tell me, Semyonych, is a watermelon a berry?"

"A watermelon, Your Excellency, is not a berry, but a vegetable."

But Apollon Apollonovich turned full face, and let fly with—oh, oh, oh!—an impromptu:

> Good for you, Semyonych,
> Aren't you something great!
> Look at what you figured
> With your bald old pate!

. . . .

After dinner he strolled through the unlighted hall. And the hall gave off a very faint gleam, both from the moon and from the lacework cast by the street lamp. Apollon Apollonovich strolled across the little squares of floor here, and with him was Nikolai Apollonovich. They kept stepping out of shadow—into the lacework of light cast by the street lamp; they kept stepping out of this bright lacework—into shadow. Head bent low, Apollon Apollonovich was talking—half to his son, half to himself—in a mild and confiding manner quite unusual for him:

"You know . . ." he then said, less formally: "You know, son: being a servant of the state is a difficult position."

They retraced their steps.

"I kept telling them all: no, promoting the import of American haybalers is no laughing matter. There's more humanitarianism in it than in expansive speeches. . . . Public law teaches us . . ."

They walked back across the echoing little squares of parquet floor. They kept stepping out of shadow into the glittering wedges of moonlight.

"All the same, we need humanitarian principles, and humanism is a great concept, which has been arrived at through the suffering of such minds as Bruno, as . . ."†

For a long time they continued to wander here.

Apollon Apollonovich spoke in an extremely cracked voice. Now and then with two fingers he took his son by the buttonhole of his frock coat and brought his lips right up to his ear.

"They're a bunch of windbags, Kolenka, humanitarianism, humanitarianism! There's more humanitarianism in haybalers. We need haybalers!"

With his free arm he grasped his son by his slender waist, drawing him over to a window—into a corner. He was mumbling and shaking his head. They no longer took him into account, he was not needed.

"You know, they've bypassed me!"

Nikolai Apollonovich did not dare believe his ears. Yes, it had all happened so naturally—without a little talk, without a stormy scene, without confessions—this whispering in the corner, this affection.

Why, then, for all these years, had he. . . .

"So then, Kolenka, my dear friend: let's you and I be more open with each other."

"What? I can't hear. . . ."

Past the windows flew the mad, piercing whistle of a small steamboat. A flaming lantern on the stern vanished at an angle into the fog, and rings spread, ruby red. Thus, head bent low, Apollon Apollonovich was talking in a mild and confiding manner, half to his son, half to himself. They kept stepping out of shadow into the lacework of light cast by the street lamp. They were stepping out of this bright lacework—into shadow, into shadow.

.   .   .   .

Apollon Apollonovich—small, bald and old—faintly illuminated by the flickerings of the dying embers, began laying out a game of solitaire on a small mother-of-pearl table. He had not laid out any games of solitaire for two and a half years. This is how he had been imprinted on Anna Petrovna's memory. That had been two and a

half years ago, just before their fateful conversation. And the little
bald figure had been sitting at this very same small table and at the
very same kind of game of solitaire.

"The ten. . . ."

"No, my dear, it's blocked. . . . And in the spring, you know
what, Anna Petrovna? Why don't we go to Prolyotnoe?"† (Prolyotnoe was the Ableukhov estate; Apollon Apollonovich had not
been at Prolyotnoe for some twenty years.)

Beyond the ice, the snows, the jagged line of the forest he had
nearly frozen to death out there, by a stupid accident, fifty years
ago. While he had been freezing to death, someone's cold fingers
had stroked his heart. An icy hand had beckoned. And behind him,
the ages stretched into immeasurable expanses. Ahead of him, an
icy hand revealed immeasurable expanses. Immeasurable expanses
flew to meet him. An icy hand!

And now it was melting.

For, now that Apollon Apollonovich was freeing himself from
his official duties, he remembered for the first time: the orphaned
distances of the provinces, the wisps of smoke from tiny villages,
and the jackdaw. He suddenly wanted to see the wisps of smoke
from the tiny villages, and the jackdaw.

"Let's go to Prolyotnoe. There are so many flowers there."

But Anna Petrovna, once more carried away, was talking about
the vivid beauty of the palaces of the Alhambra. But in her trans-
port of ecstasy she forgot, truth to tell, that she was lapsing, all the
same, into an unsuitable tone, that she was saying "we" instead of
"I"—"we," that is, Almondini and "I" (or "Mantalini," whatever
his name was).

"We arrived in the morning in a darling little carriage drawn by
burros. The harness had pompons as big as this on it, Kolechka.
And you know, Apollon Apollonovich, we got used to . . ."

Apollon Apollonovich listened and kept shifting the cards around,
and finally gave up. So he did not finish the game of solitaire. He
sat hunched, stooped, illuminated by the bright purple of the embers. Several times he grasped the arm of the Empire armchair, as
if making ready to jump up. He realized just in time that it would
be tactless to interrupt her torrent of words, and he would fall back
into the armchair, yawning from time to time.

Finally he noted affectionately:

"I really must admit I'm tired."

And he shifted from the armchair into the rocker.

· · · · · · · ·

Nikolai Apollonovich volunteered to escort his mother to her
hotel. As he left the drawing room, he turned full face toward his

father. He caught (or so it seemed to him) an ever-saddening gaze directed at him from the rocker. Yes, Apollon Apollonovich was sitting in the rocker and rocking the rocker by nodding his head and moving his foot. That was his last conscious perception; strictly speaking, he never saw his father again. And at sea, in the mountains, in cities, in the blinding halls of major European museums, that look came to mind. And it seemed to him that Apollon Apollonovich had consciously been taking leave of him back there, by nodding his head and moving his foot. The old face and the quiet creaking of the rocker, and—that look, that look!

The Watch

He escorted his mother to her hotel. Afterwards, he turned onto the Moika. There was gloom in the windows of the little apartment. The Likhutins were not there. Nothing to be done: he turned and went home.

He hobbled into his bedroom. He stood for a while in the darkness: shadows, shadows and—the lacework of light cast by the street lamp. From habit he took off his watch and looked at it: three o'clock.

At this point everything rose up anew.

He understood that his fears had not been mastered. The certainty that had gotten him through the evening now collapsed and disappeared somewhere. And everything grew unsteady. He wanted to take a bromide, but there was no bromide. He wanted to read in "Revelation"; there was no "Revelation." Just at that time an unsettling sound reached his ears: a soft tick-tick, tick-tick: the sardine tin?

This thought grew in intensity.

He was not tormented by it, but by something else: that old, delirious something that had been forgotten in the course of the day, and that had arisen in the course of the night.

"Pepp Peppovich . . . Pepp. . . ."

Bloating into an immensity, out of the fourth dimension, very likely, it was penetrating the Yellow House, and it was rushing through the rooms. Its surfaces were sticking to his soul, and his soul was becoming the surface of a huge, rapidly growing bubble, which had swollen into Saturn's orbit. Oh, oh, oh! Chills ran through Nikolai Apollonovich. Winds wafted into his forehead. Everything—was bursting.

Nikolai Apollonovich was reaching toward the sound that plagued him. He was searching for the location of the sound. Shoes faintly creaking, he would creep toward the desk, that tiresome something would grow more distinct, but when he reached the desk—it would vanish.

The watch was ticking.

"Tick-tick" was softly coming out of the shadowy corner; and he crept back away from the desk into the corner. Everywhere were shadows and more shadows, and the silence of the tomb.

Nikolai Apollonovich was panting as he rushed about, outstretched candle in hand, amidst dancing shadows. He kept trying to catch the flitting sound (thus do children chase after a little yellow butterfly).

Now he had found the true direction. The strange sound was disclosing itself, and the ticking could be distinctly heard. An instant more and he would take it by surprise (the butterfly would not get away).

Where, where, where?

And when he began an even more dogged search for the point from which the sound emanated, he instantly found the point: found it in his own belly. In point of fact: an enormous heaviness was weighing on his stomach.

He saw: he was standing by his night table, and on a level with his belly, on the surface of the table was ticking . . . the watch that he had taken off; he looked at it distractedly: four o'clock.

He moved back into his old frame (yes, yes, Second Lieutenant Likhutin had carried off the accursed bomb). And the feeling of delirium was disappearing, and the horrible heaviness in his stomach was disappearing. He threw off his suit. He unbuttoned his starched linen—collar and shirt—with pleasure. He pulled off his drawers, revealing the leg where the knee had become swollen; and the legs disappeared into the snowy white sheets. But he fell into thought, propping himself up on one arm.

And the candle went out.

But the watch went on ticking. Total darkness surrounded him. And in the darkness the ticking again began to flit about like a little butterfly taking wing from a flower: now here, now there. And his thoughts were ticking. All the thoughts began pulsing in various areas of his inflamed body: in the neck and in the throat, in the arms, in the head, even in the solar plexus.

And lagging behind the body, they were outside the body; they formed a conscious contour on all sides of him, a foot away, and more. He understood: it was not he who was thinking, that is, it was not his brain that was thinking, but this conscious contour outlined and pulsing outside the brain. In the contour, pulses, and projections of pulses—all, all—were turning into thoughts thinking themselves up. Yes, yes: a stormy life was raging in his eyeballs.

The ordinary points of light now flared up in sparks; they leaped from their orbits into space, and they began dancing about, forming a tiresome tinsel, a swarming cocoon of lights, a foot away and more. This is what formed the pulsation. It flared up.

"But it's ticking, it's ticking. . . ."

Another one raced past. . . .

Thought affirmed that situation which the brain denied and with which it stubbornly struggled: the sardine tin is here. Yes, the sardine tin is here. The hand is running around it; the hand is tired of running: and when it runs to that fateful point (that point is already near). . . . Flitting pulses of light madly scattered in all directions as the sparks of a bonfire scatter if you give the bonfire a powerful whack with a cudgel. They suddenly scattered: an azure insubstantiality was bared beneath them. The sparkling center instantly pierced the perspiration-covered head of the person who had lain down here, its prickly and quivering lights resembling a gigantic spider that had run here from other worlds, and being reflected in the brain—

> —an unendurable roar will resound, which you perhaps may not even have time to hear because before it strikes your eardrum your eardrum will be shattered (as will a few other things)—

>> —the azure insubstantiality disappeared; and with it the sparkling center beneath the onrushing tinsel of light; but in a mad movement Nikolai Apollonovich now flew out of bed: the flow of thoughts being thought not by him instantly turned into pulses; the pulses began beating in the temple, in the throat, in the neck, in the arms . . . not outside the organs. . . .

He stamped off in his bare feet, but landed up—in a corner.

It was getting light.

He pulled on his drawers and stamped off into the dark corridor. Why, why? Oh, he was simply afraid. He was gripped by an animal instinct for life. He did not want to go back out of the corridor, and he did not have the courage to look into his rooms. For he no longer had the strength to try to find the bomb. And everything was in a muddle. He did not remember the minute or the hour: after all, every minute could prove fateful.

And going off into the corner, he squatted on his haunches.

And instants were slowly ebbing away within him; and minutes seemed hours. Many hundreds of hours flowed by. The corridor turned deep blue; the corridor turned gray: broad daylight was near.

Nikolai Apollonovich was becoming convinced that the thoughts thinking themselves were nonsensical. The brain prevailed. And when he decided that the allotted time had long since elapsed, then the version that the sardine tin had been carried off by the second lieutenant was somehow diffused all about in vapors of blissful images. Nikolai Apollonovich remained squatting on his haunches in the corridor—whether from a feeling of security, whether from fatigue—except, except: he dozed off.

Something slippery touching his forehead brought him to. And when he opened his eyes he saw—the slobbering muzzle of the bulldog. The bulldog was wheezing and wagging its little tail. He pushed the bulldog away with an indifferent hand. He was on the point of wanting to resume what he had been doing, to continue something or other. He wanted to bring the whirling vortices to a halt in order to make a discovery. When suddenly—he understood: why was he on the floor?

Why was he in the corridor?

He dragged himself back to his room. While approaching the bed, he was bringing the sleepy whirling vortices to a halt. . . .

    —A thundering roar: he understood everything.

    .   .   .   .

On long, long winter evenings thereafter, Nikolai Apollonovich repeatedly returned to that dull, heavy roar. It had been a special kind of roar, comparable to no other in any way, deafening and hollow, with a metallic, bass, oppressive quality. And then everything had fallen silent.

    .   .   .   .

Presently voices, the thud of bare feet, the soft howling of the bulldog were heard. And the telephone began crackling. He opened his door a bit, and streams of cold wind poured in. Lemon yellow smoke filled the room. In that stream of wind he stumbled, incongruously, over something splintered: over the piece of a shattered door.

There—a heap of cold bricks, there too—shadows running out of the smoke, and charred tatters of rugs: how had they gotten there? Then one of the shadows barked at him rudely:

"Hey, what are you doing here? Can't you see some terrible misfortune's happened in the house!"

He heard someone saying:

"Oh, these bastards, they should all be . . ."

"It's me," he tried to say.

But here he was interrupted:

"A bomb. . . ."

"Oh!"

"That's right . . . it blew up. . . ."

"?"

"In Apollon Apollonovich's . . . study. . . ."

"?"

"Well, thank heavens!"

Let us remind the reader: Apollon Apollonovich had absent-mindedly and quietly carried the sardine tin into his study; and he had forgotten about the sardine tin. It stands to reason that he was in a state of ignorance about the contents of the sardine tin.

Nikolai Apollonovich ran up to the place where there had just been a door. There was no door: there was a huge gap from which smoke billowed. Had you looked into the street, you would have seen that a crowd was gathering, that a policeman was pushing them back off the sidewalk, and that gawkers, heads thrown back, gaped at the sinister yellowish-lemon clouds pouring out of the black gaps of the windows and out of a fissure that cut across the house.

.   .   .   .

Nikolai Apollonovich, not knowing why himself, began running back, away from the gap. And not knowing where he was going, he found himself—

> —on the bed (right on the very pillow!) sat Apollon Apollonovich, his naked little yellow legs pressed to his chest; he was in his undershirt; grasping his knees with his arms, he was bawling; he had been forgotten in the general din; there was no one to comfort him; all alone, by his lonesome . . . bawling his head off, making himself hoarse . . .—
>
>> —Nikolai Apollonovich rushed to the helpless little body, the way a wet nurse rushes to a three-year-old toddler who has been entrusted to her, whom she has forgotten about, and who has fallen down; but the helpless little body—the toddler—seeing who was running toward him—up and jumps from the pillow and—up and waves his arms in indescribable horror and with a sprightliness that was anything but childlike.

And off he bolts, out of the room, leaping into the corridor!

Nikolai Apollonovich, shouting "stop him," set out after him, after the little figure. Both rushed into the depths of the corridor (something or other on fire was being extinguished there); and the sight of the flickering little figures, yelling strangely, was eerie; and the shirt was fluttering in flight; and their heels tapped and flickered along; and Nikolai Apollonovich set off in pursuit, hopping and limping on his right leg; with one hand he clutched at a leg of his falling drawers, and with the other he strove to grab the fluttering hem of his father's shirt.

He ran and shouted:

"Wait . . .

"Where are you going?

"But stop!"

Having reached the door leading to the place that was comparable to no other, Apollon Apollonovich, with a cunning that passed all understanding, caught hold of the door; he found himself in that place: into that place he had made his getaway.

For an instant Nikolai Apollonovich recoiled from the door. And engraved on his mind were: the turn of the head, the sweating brow, the lips, the sidewhiskers and the eyes like molten stone. And the door banged shut. Everything disappeared: he had made his getaway into that place.

Nikolai Apollonovich desperately pounded on the door and implored, shouting his head off, making himself hoarse:

"Let me in. . . ."

And—

"Aaa . . . aaa . . . aaa. . . ."

He fell before the door.

And he flung his head into his hands. At this point he fainted. The lackeys thudded up at a run. They dragged him into his room.

And—here we put a full stop.

.   .   .   .

We will not try to describe how the fire was extinguished, how the senator, heart furiously pounding, later had a little talk with the police. After this talk, the doctors went into consultation. The doctors found that he had dilatation of the aorta. Yet all the same: during the entire period when the strike was in progress, he appeared in chancelleries, offices, and ministerial residencies—exhausted, emaciated. The mighty little bass thundered forth persuasively in chancelleries, offices, and ministerial residences—with a hollow, oppressive quality. We can tell you that he managed to prove a thing or two. Someone or other was arrested and then released; important connections were brought into play here, and the matter was squelched. No one was touched. While all this was going on, his son was laid up with attacks of nervous fever, completely unconscious. When he finally came to, he saw that he was with his mother. There was no one in the lacquered house. Apollon Apollonovich had moved to the country. He spent the entire winter amidst the snows, without stirring, having taken indefinite leave, and having gone directly into retirement from leave.† And for his son he arranged a passport to travel abroad, and money. One Ableukhova, Anna Petrovna,† accompanied Nikolenka. She returned only the following summer. Nikolai Apollonovich did not return to Russia until the demise of his father.

End of the Eighth Chapter

Epilogue

A February sun is on the wane. Shaggy cactuses are scattered here and there. Soon, very soon sails will fly toward the sandy shore from the gulf. Here they come: sharpwinged, rocking. A small cupola is lost among the cactuses.

Nikolai Apollonovich, in a blue gandurah and a bright red Arabian chéchia, squats motionless on his haunches. An extraordinarily long tassel dangles from the chéchia. His silhouette is distinctly etched against the flat roof. Below him is a village square and the sounds of a tom-tom: they strike the ears with a hollow, oppressive quality.

Everywhere are the white cubes of hovels. There a bellowing Berber urges on a little donkey with shouts; and a heap of branches gleams silver on the little donkey. The Berber is olive skinned.

Nikolai Apollonovich does not hear the sounds of the tom-tom, he does not see the Berber. He sees Apollon Apollonovich before him—bald, small, old—sitting in a rocker, rocking the rocker by nodding his head and moving his foot. He well remembers that movement.

In the distance is the pink of an almond tree.† That jagged mountaintop is bright violet-amber. That mountaintop is Zaghouan; and the cape—Cape Carthage. Nikolai Apollonovich has rented a small house from an Arab in a coastal village near Tunis.†

.   .   .   .

Fir branches bent under the weight of snow: shaggy. Up ahead was a five-columned wooden building. Snowdrifts had leaped over the terrace railings and formed mounds. On them, the delicate pink reflection of a February sunset.

A tiny stooped figure in felt boots and mittens passes by, leaning on a cane, fur collar raised, fur hat pulled down over his ears. He makes his way along a cleared path. He is supported under the arms. A warm lap robe is in the hands of the figure supporting him.

Enormous spectacles had appeared on Apollon Apollonovich in the country. They steamed up in the frost, and neither the jagged gray forest distance, nor the wisps of smoke from tiny villages, nor the jackdaw could be seen through them, but only the glittering wedges of moonlight and the little squares of parquet floor. Nikolai Apollonovich—gentle, attentive, sympathetic—head bent low, kept stepping out of shadow—into the lacework of light cast by the street lamp. He kept stepping out of this bright lacework—into shadow.

Of an evening the old gentleman sits at the table in his room surrounded by oval frames. In the oval frames are portraits: of an officer in tight leather breeches, and an old lady in a bonnet; that officer—yes, that's his father; and the old lady in the bonnet—his late mother, née Svargina. And the old gentleman is penning his memoirs which are to see the light in the year of his death.

And they have seen the light.

They are most witty memoirs: all Russia knows them.

.   .   .   .

The flame of the sun assaults you. It suffuses your eyes with crimson. You turn away, and it beats at the back of your head in a frenzy. It makes the desert seem greenish and deathly. However, life *is* deathly. How good it would be to remain here forever!

Wearing a thick pith helmet with netting, Nikolai Apollonovich sits on a pile of sand. Before him is an immense moldering† head that is on the verge of collapsing into sandstone thousands of years old. Nikolai Apollonovich is sitting before the Sphinx.

He has been here for two years now. He is doing research in the museum at Bulaq.† Yes, yes, the commentaries on "The Book of the Dead" and the writings of Manetho† are incorrect. Yes, yes, Nikolai Apollonovich has been engulfed by Egypt. He foresees the fate of Egypt in the twentieth century. Culture is a moldering head: everything in it has died; nothing has remained. There will be an explosion: everything will be swept away.†

Oh, it's good that he has work to occupy him. At times he tears himself away from his abstract schemes and gets into it deeply. And it seems that not everything has died. There are sounds of some kind; there is a roar in Cairo; a special kind of roar; it reminds him of that same sound: deafening and hollow, with a metallic, bass, oppressive quality. And Nikolai Apollonovich is drawn to mummies. He has been brought to mummies by "chance." What about Kant? Kant is forgotten.

Evening has begun to fall. The large piles at Gizeh† stretch menacingly into the dawnless twilight. Yes, yes: everything is expanded in them, everything expands from them; and dark amber lights now go on in the dust suspended in the air. And it is stifling.

And he has leaned, deep in thought, against the dead side of a pyramid. He is himself a pyramid, the summit of a culture which will crash into ruins.†

.   .   .   .

In a soft armchair, in full sunlight, an old gentleman sat motionless. Now and then he looked at a little old lady with his huge cornflower blue eyes. His legs were wrapped up in a lap robe (they were paralysed). Fragrant bunches of lilacs had been placed on his lap. And the old gentleman kept leaning toward the old lady, his whole torso slipping out of the armchair:

"You say he's finished it? That he's coming?"

"He's putting his papers in order."

Somewhere in Egypt Nikolai Apollonovich had brought his monograph to completion.

"What's the title?"

The old gentleman beamed:

"The monograph is entitled . . . me–emme . . . 'On the Letter of Dauphsekhrut.' "† Apollon Apollonovich was forgetting absolutely everything: the names of ordinary objects. But he definitely remembered the word Dauphsekhrut. Kolenka was writing about Dauphsekhrut. He had only to throw his head back to see the gold of still-green leaves raging and storming there, and the azure, and the fleecy clouds. And a little wagtail running along the path before him.

"You say he's in Nazareth?"†

What a thick carpet of bluebells! The bluebells opened their lilac maws. A heavy movable chair stood in the solid mass of bluebells. Sitting in the chair under a sailcloth umbrella was a wrinkled Apollon Apollonovich, unshaven, stubble showing silver on his cheeks.

.   .   .   .

In 1913 Nikolai Apollonovich still continued for days on end to roam the fields, the meadows, and the forests, observing the work in the fields with gloomy indolence. He went about in a visored cap, and he wore a camel-colored sleeveless peasant coat. His boots creaked. A golden spade beard changed his appearance, and a lock of silver stood out in his thatch of hair. The lock had appeared suddenly. His eyes had begun to trouble him in Egypt and he had taken to wearing dark blue spectacles. His voice had grown harsher, and his face was sunburned. His quickness of movement had disappeared. He lived all alone. He never invited anyone, and never visited anyone. He was seen in church. Of late he had been reading the philosopher Skovoroda.†

His parents had died.

The End

Notes

The main purpose of these notes is to provide the reader with as much "factual" data as we deem necessary to an understanding of the novel. The quotes from Baedeker and from various histories, the references to real-life people, and the comments on Russian manners and mores are not meant to suggest that we are dealing with a "realist" novel in any of the accepted senses of the term. As our Introduction indicates, we are well aware that *Petersburg* is a work of Symbolist fiction. Bely takes pains to create an aura of "reality" which he undercuts at the same time. The reader is caught in a field of tension between the "real" and the "unreal." P. M. Bitsilli's observation on the art of Vladimir Nabokov could apply equally well to *Petersburg*: "All art, like all culture in general, is the result of a strenuous effort to *free oneself* from actuality; using empirical data as *material*, the artist tries to rework them so as to touch another, ideal world" (*Sovremennye zapiski*, No. 68, 1939). For this technique to work, the reader must of course know the "material," whether geographical, cultural, historical, or literary. Bely takes for granted that his Russian reader has such knowledge. The English reader most likely does not.

Another purpose of these notes is to discuss some textological matters and some problems of translation. However, they are not meant to provide a systematic critical "reading" of the novel but merely to point the way.

Complete bibliographical data are furnished for sources when they are cited. The following four books constitute an exception. Because they are frequently referred to throughout the notes, only title or author and page numbers are given after first mention:

Karl Baedeker, *Russia, with Teheran, Port Arthur, and Peking. A Handbook for Travellers* (1914; facsimile edition reprinted by Arno Press/Random House, 1971);

Annie Besant, *Man and His Bodies* (Ninth Edition, 1947);

Michael T. Florinsky, *Russia. A History and an Interpretation in Two Volumes* (New York, 1947);

The Oxford Dictionary of the Christian Church, ed. F.L. Cross (London, 1957).

Readers will note that the transliteration system in citations often differs from our own (this is particularly true of Baedeker); we could not, of course, change this. Also, Russia before 1918 used the Julian ("Old Style") calendar, which was thirteen days behind the Gregorian ("New

Style") calendar. Therefore, all dates before 1918 are given in Old Style, although sometimes the New Style equivalent is indicated in parentheses.

We also provide a map of Petersburg on which the principal streets, bridges, public buildings, monuments, etc. mentioned in the text are marked. There is no indication of where the characters live: that is a matter Bely himself deliberately makes ambiguous (see our Introduction).

Prologue

In his rambling and often bumbling address to the reader the narrator imitates the beginning of Imperial proclamations which listed all the official titles of the Emperor: "We, Nicholas the Second, Emperor and Autocrat of All the Russias, Moscow, Kiev, Vladimir, Novgorod; Tsar of Kazan, Tsar of Astrakhan, Tsar of Poland, Tsar of Siberia, Tsar of Tauric Kherson, Tsar of Georgia; Ruler of Pskov and Grand Prince of Smolensk, Lithuania, Volhynia, Podolsk and Finland; Prince of. . . ." The list continues for paragraphs. It concludes with "et cetera, et cetera, et cetera."

"Great Russia" comprises what most foreigners traditionally think of as "Russia," i.e., the territory of European Russia stretching east from the borders of Poland (then part of the Empire) to Siberia. Within this land mass lie "Little Russia," or the Ukraine as it is now officially known, in the south, and "White Russia" (or Belorussia) in the west. Although both are now republics of the Soviet Union and even have their own representatives to the United Nations, neither was ever really a separate political entity. Until their absorption into the Russian state, parts of both belonged to a variety of East European powers, including Poland and Lithuania. Their "borders" were as flexible as their political fortunes. Both, however, have a linguistic identity: Ukrainian and White Russian are, like Russian, separate East Slavic languages.

"White Russia" and "Red Russia" had political overtones during the Bolshevik revolution and later, but not at the time this novel was written. Here "Red Russia" is the standard translation for the Russian *Chervonnaya Rus'*. In his *A History of Russia*, Volume II: *Kievan Russia* (New Haven, 1948, p. 59) George Vernadsky writes: "He [Vladimir] marched upon the Poles and took Peremyshl, Cherven, and a number of other west Ukrainian towns (981), since known as the 'Cherven cities.' The name Cherven was later understood as the old Russian adjective meaning 'red' and consequently this region was eventually spoken of as 'Red Russia' (*Chervonnaia Rus'*)."

Rus (or Rus' or Russ) is the oldest designation for territory deemed Russian. In later chapters of the novel the narrator, following a Russian literary tradition, sometimes employs "Rus" as a kind of lyrical contraction for "Russia."

Downgraded: There is no accepted equivalent for the term *zashtátnyi górod*. Because we wished to avoid littering the text with untranslated Russian words and phrases we have rendered it as "downgraded." In the bureaucratic language of the time (which the Prologue in part mimics), the term meant a town which had ceased to be the administrative center of a district.

Moscow . . . Kiev: Formulaic expressions. Kiev was the chief city of what is known as Kievan Rus from approximately the eleventh to the early thirteenth centuries. It then passed to the control of the Mongols, and later to Poland, becoming part of the Russian state only in the middle of the seventeenth century. As the political, cultural, and spiritual center of the first state that could be considered Russian, it was often called the "mother of Russian cities," or the "Jerusalem of Russia," because of its many places of religious pilgrimage.

From the fourteenth to the seventeenth centuries, Moscow (or Muscovy) rose to domination over all other Russian city-states. It was displaced as the capital when Peter the Great moved the seat of government to the recently founded Petersburg in 1712, but it remained "Holy Moscow," the second city of the Empire, the place to which every tsar returned to be crowned, and the symbol of all that was truly Russian, as opposed to the "un-Russian" and "Western" city of Petersburg. The symbolic and actual rivalry of the two cities became a major theme of nineteenth-century Russian literature. The narrator alludes to this rivalry in the last five paragraphs of the Prologue.

Petersburg: The city was founded in 1703 by Peter the Great. Its first official name was the Russian form of the Dutch for "Saint Peter's City"—Sankt Pieter Burkh—which became Sankt-Peterburg. Russians, however, have always associated the city with its founder, not his patron saint, and have called it simply Petersburg or, more colloquially, Pieter. The Cyrillic version of this transliterates as Piter, but we have used the Dutch spelling to emphasize foreignness, for even the popular form "Piter" is not Russian. (See also p. 304.) With the outbreak of World War I, the name was russianized to Petrograd; and in 1924, it was once again redubbed, as Leningrad.

Tsargrad is the old Russian name (meaning the city of Caesar) for Byzantium. Konstantinograd is the Russian equivalent of the Greek Constantinople, i.e., the city of Constantine (Russian: Konstantin).

With the fall of Constantinople to the Ottoman Turks in 1453 and the collapse of the Byzantine Empire, Russia became the most powerful Orthodox state. The Grand Princes of Moscow regarded their capital as the new center of Orthodoxy and saw themselves as the protectors of all Orthodox Christians. From this evolved the seductive notion of Moscow the Third Rome. (The first had fallen under the control of the Papacy, the second, Constantinople, to the no less abhorrent infidel Turks.) There were extrareligious factors at work too. The last ruler of Byzantium, Constantine Paleologue, had died fighting on the walls of his capital. In 1472, his niece Zoe (rechristened Sofia) Paleologue married Grand Prince Ivan III of Moscow; official ideologues cited this union to bolster dynastic claims: if the power and authority of the Caesars had passed from Rome to the Byzantine Emperor, where but to Moscow was that power to pass now that Byzantium had vanished?

Thenceforth the Grand Princes of Moscow adopted the title "Tsar" (derived from Caesar) and the regalia and rituals of the vanished Byzantine court. The dream of "recapturing" Constantinople for Orthodoxy endured for centuries. When the Turks were expelled from the northern shores of the Black Sea in the eighteenth century, Catherine the Great ordered one of her grandsons christened Konstantin in honor of both the founder of Constantinople and the last Paleologue, in anticipation that he would sit on the throne of a new Byzantium (under Russian protection, of course).

Nevsky Prospect: The main street of the capital and its most famous and fashionable thoroughfare. In the eighteenth century, what Baedeker (*Russia. A Handbook for Travellers*, 1914; reprinted in 1971, Arno Press) calls "streets of the first class" (p. 101) were known as *pershpektívy* ("perspectives"); later they became "prospects." We have retained "prospect" instead of the technically more accurate "avenue" not only because this form has become standard in translations of Russian literature, but also because the word connotes space, in Russian as in English. Indeed, the narrator plays on the idea of space here, and throughout the novel, through recourse to words containing *pro-*: *prospékt*, prospect; *prostránstvo*, space; *rasprostranyát'sya*, expatiate; and others.

"numbered houses": Streets in Petersburg were given names only in 1737, and houses were given numbers (a Western innovation) much later. Both practices were adopted in Moscow still later.

"houses . . . for the public": The narrator realizes that his "logic" has brought him perilously close to the Russian expression for a brothel, "public house" (*publíchnyi dom*), and so says "houses *for* the public."

"rectilineal prospect": "Nevski Prospekt is 115 ft. wide and 2¾ M. long, . . . the longest street in St. Petersburg. From the Admiralty it runs in a *straight line* [to] Znamenskaya Square, where it trends slightly to the S. and runs through a poorer quarter to the Alexander Nevski Monastery . . . it is the busiest street in St. Petersburg" (Baedeker, p. 103; italics ours). Petersburg was laid out according to the most up to date Western theories of city planning; perfectly straight streets are characteristic. In the much older Moscow, the streets grew up to connect scattered living sites around the Kremlin, and they therefore wind and twist; some of the major thoroughfares even form circles (or "rings").

"Other Russian cities . . .": Peter the Great desired his new city to be of stone, like the Western European capitals he had visited. In the early years, however, most buildings in Petersburg were of wood covered with stucco to imitate brick and stone.

"a million-and-a-half": In 1905 the population of Petersburg was 1,635,100, with 49,177 births and 42,935 deaths. By 1914 it had risen to 2,217,500 (*Ocherki istorii Leningrada*, III, Leningrad, 1956, p. 105). The standard history of Moscow (*Istoriya Moskvy*, V, Moscow, 1955, p. 15) gives that city's population as 1,174,673 in 1902 and 1,345,749 in 1907.

"swarms the printed book": The image of the "swarm" (*roi*) recurs throughout the novel. In the 1935 edition, "printed book" was changed to a plural, presumably by Bely himself.

Chapter the First

The epigraph is the last five lines of the Introduction to Pushkin's long poem "The Bronze Horseman" (1833), and is the first of many allusions in the novel to this work. Interestingly enough, when this Introduction was first published separately in 1834, it bore the title "Petersburg. A Fragment of a Long Poem." Russian writers and critics seem to like to quote literary works from memory. Bely was no exception. The resulting errors range from the trivial to the horrendous. The error here is of the first variety: "*O nei*" ("Of it") instead of Pushkin's "*Ob nei*" (same meaning).

The first paragraph evokes the eighteenth-century novel, as do the chapter subtitles and the titles of the chapter divisions. Cf., e.g., *Tom Jones* or the opening of Daniel Defoe's *The Life, Adventures and Piracies of the Famous Captain Singleton* (1720): "As it is usual for great Persons whose Lives have been remarkable, and whose Actions deserve Recording to Posterity, to insist much upon their Originals, give full Accounts of their Families, and the Histories of their Ancestors: So, that I may be methodical, I shall do the same, tho' I can look but a very little Way into my Pedigree as you will see presently." Our Russian narrator can look very far and very fancifully indeed; this fabulous genealogy is not unlike those concocted for tsars in the late sixteenth century. There is, of course, no mention of "red-skinned peoples" in the Biblical account of Shem's ancestors (Genesis, 10:21–31). "Hessitic" is listed in no encyclopedia or dictionary, Russian or otherwise; it is sheer invention, a Gogolian flaunting of non-existent knowledge—and should not, therefore, be rendered as "Hittite," as some translators have done.

"the Kirghiz-Kaisak Horde": In the eighteenth century Central Asia did not yet belong to the Russian Empire. (It was acquired through a series of conquests in the nineteenth century.) What we know as Kazakhstan was inhabited by the nomadic Kirghiz, descendants of the Mongols who had once dominated Russia. They "were divided into three hordes —the eldest, the middle, and the youngest. Pressure from the Kalmyks forced them to seek aid from the Russians [in the eighteenth century]" (George Vernadsky, *A History of Russia*, New Haven, 1930, p. 97). Ab-Lai (or Ablai, 1711–1781) was a sultan of the Middle Horde and Khan after 1771. He became a Russian subject in 1740, the last year of the reign of Empress Anna (reigned 1730–40; daughter of Ivan, i.e., Ioann, Peter the Great's half-brother), and did much to further the development of peaceful relations with Russia.

For centuries it has been fashionable for Russian nobles to trace their ancestry to real or imagined Mongol dignitaries. The great eighteenth-century poet Derzhavin did so, for example, and recently Nabokov (in

Strong Opinions, New York, 1973, p. 119) wrote of ". . . Genghis Khan, who is said to have fathered the first Nabok, a petty Tartar prince in the twelfth century who married a Russian damsel in an era of intensely artistic Russian culture."

Mirza (the Tartar murza, a variant of the Persian mirza) was a title preceding the names of Tartar noblemen.

Ukhov: *úkho* is the Russian for "ear."

No Ninth Department actually existed.

"my senator": The Emperor himself appointed senators from the three highest ranks in the civil and military service (see note on Table of Ranks, p. 300); they thereby became members of the Senate, a body founded in 1711 by Peter the Great. Originally it was the highest administrative, legislative, and judicial organ of the state, but gradually its powers eroded until, by Apollon Apollonovich's time, it functioned mainly as the highest court of appeal. The uniform worn by senators consisted of white trousers and a jacket resplendent with gold (see the description of Apollon Apollonovich's uniform in the third chapter).

"Thus had he . . . been portrayed," etc.: In creating Apollon Apollonovich, Bely drew on several "real-life" persons and on one major literary antecedent, even flaunting the fact. The main prototype was Konstantin Pobedonostsev (1827–1907), the chief procurator of the Holy Synod and one of the most hated reactionaries of the time. Though small in stature, like Apollon Apollonovich, he was one of the most powerful figures during the reign of Alexander the Third and his son Nicholas the Second, whose tutor Pobedonostsev had been. Like Apollon Apollonovich, he adamantly opposed any attempt to change the status quo, whether through liberal reform or of course outright revolution. Several unsuccessful attempts were made on his life. As a fanatical anti-Semite, he did everything in his power to block measures to alleviate the plight of the Jews. The prominent role played by Jews in the revolutionary movement makes it easy for a conservative like Apollon Apollonovich to identify all the radical press as Jewish. In a widely reproduced caricature of 1905 Pobedonostsev was shown in the same posture as Apollon Apollonovich: a puny figure with enormous ears and bat's wings, perched on the sleeping figure of a woman in Russian national dress. Bely himself invoked the image of Russia kept in the sleep of reaction in a 1905 essay entitled "The Green Meadow" ("Lug zelënyi").

In Bely's mind Petersburg was synonymous with the huge bureaucratic apparatus that controlled Russia. (Baedeker, p. xv, describes the capital as "a political city swarming with officials.") It is therefore not surprising that one of his heroes is a major force in that bureaucracy. The mention of ears is meant to recall one of the most famous bureaucrats in Russian literature, Tolstoy's Alexei Karenin. When Anna returns to Petersburg from Moscow in the novel (*Anna Karenina*, Book One, Part One, Chapter XXX), the first thing she notices about her husband is his ears ("'Oh, mercy! why do his ears look like that?' she thought, looking at his frigid and imposing figure . . ."). For her, these ears become emblematic of their oppressive relationship, and she leaves him for a more romantic figure (as does Apollon Apollonovich's wife, also named Anna). Unlike Anna Karenina, however, the Anna in *Petersburg* returns rather shamefacedly to her husband.

Bely takes care to be vague about just what office is held by Apollon Apollonovich. We first see the senator (Chapter I, the section entitled "The Writing Table Stood There") dealing with a case involving the clergy. This would lead us to believe that he works in the Holy Synod, like Pobedonostsev. But his daily ride to the office takes him in the direction of the Ministry of the Interior, which is far from the head-quarters of the Synod. However, we cannot identify him with that Ministry either. All we really know is that he is head of the Government Institution of "Oh, uhhh, what was its name?"—an "identification" meant to recall the opening of Gogol's story "The Overcoat."

The first name Apollon (the Russian form of Apollo) also suggests Apollonius, the Antichrist in Vladimir Solovyov's "A Short Story of the Antichrist," the concluding portion of his *Three Conversations* (1899–1900), as well as Apollyon, the corrupter and destroyer in *Revelation* (9:11). Any Russian reader of the time would immediately associate Apollo (and his counterpart Dionysus) with Nietzsche's *Birth of Tragedy* (1872). Of course Bely had read the book too. Many traces of it are to be found in *Petersburg*, e.g., specific mentions of Dionysus later in the novel or, more subtly, the embodiment in Apollon Apollonovich of the theme of a carefully controlled surface covering Dionysian chaos.

Semyonych: "The patronymic instead of the Christian name is used in the case of faithful household plebians whose age entitles them to respect" (*Pushkin's Eugene Onegin*, trans. by Vladimir Nabokov, Volume 2, Princeton, 1964, p. 273).

Actual Privy Councilor: The second highest rank in the so-called Table of Ranks, which was instituted by Peter the Great and lasted until the Romanov dynasty fell in 1917. Three branches of state service were distinguished—court, military, and civil—and each was divided into fourteen ranks, the fourteenth being the lowest. (The complete Table of Ranks is given in English in the Modern Library Giant edition of the *Collected Tales and Plays of Nikolai Gogol*, New York, 1964.) Apollon Apollonovich, as we learn shortly, is himself an Actual Privy Councilor.

"a white Petersburg night": Because of its extreme northern location (59° 57′ N. lat. and 30° 20′ E. long.), Petersburg experiences very long days and short nights during the summer solstice, when a kind of eerie half-light persists even after the sun has set. These are the famous "White Nights." "The early summer (middle of May to middle of June, O.S.) is to be recommended for a visit to St. Petersburg; during this part of the year the environs of the city . . . can be seen . . . in the glorious illumination of the 'white' summer nights. On June 21st the sun does not set at St. Petersburg till 9.22 p.m., and it rises at 2.43 the next morning" (Baedeker, pp. xv–xvi). It is a traditionally "romantic" time in the city.

Count W.: He is called Count Doublevé (the French for "W"). See note on Witte (p. 328).

"having things cold": The late Soviet scholar Boris Vasilievich Mikhailovsky has suggested in an essay on *Petersburg* (in his *Izbrannye stat'i o literature i iskusstve*, Moscow, 1968, p. 450) that Bely may have based the senator's passion for coldness on the ideas of the brilliant conservative thinker Konstantin Leontiev (1831–1891), who advocated "freezing" Russia, i.e., fixing its stage of development for all time at autocracy. The motif of coldness and frigidity also figures in Tolstoy's portrait of Karenin.

"a harrowing experience": The moronic word play in the Russian turns on the senator's hearing a resemblance between the word *barón* (baron) and *boroná* (harrow, pronounced *baraná* in standard Russian). In his memoirs Bely wrote that such puns were a favorite game of his own father, Nikolai Bugaev, a brilliant mathematician and one of the most distinguished professors of Moscow University, who was noted for eccentric behavior.

"An icy drizzle": This is probably as good a place as any to comment on the weather conditions in the novel, about which Bely is very precise and accurate. Baedeker (p. 102) characterizes the climate of the city in general as "raw, damp, and very unsettled; woolen underclothing is the best protection against chills." Of more particular interest is Kaigorodov's (see also page 322) description of late September and early October in the city (under the heading "Autumn Weather," in the Petersburg daily newspaper *Novoe vremya*, October 7 [20], 1905): "For the last few days the weather has been extremely changeable and irregular. . . . Rain, sometimes mixed with snow, has often fallen; the sun from time to time has looked out for a brief period; rather stormy winds have been blowing from the southwest." Kaigorodov could have written an identical report on the basis of the descriptions in the novel. Also: "During the night of October 3 the first snow fell, mixed with rain" (*Novoe vremya*, October 6 [19], 1905).

"rain, influenza, and grippe": The hostility of Petersburg's climate has been a traditional theme in literature about the city ever since Pushkin's "The Bronze Horseman" and, especially, Gogol's "The Overcoat."

"the embankment": The granite-faced banks of the Neva and its branches (see below) that run through the city are known as the Embankments (or Quays). At this point in the novel the Ableukhov house is situated on the English Embankment (see map), one of the most fashionable sections of the city.

"the islands" (sometimes "the Islands"): "The Nevá, 42 M. long, flows out of Lake Ládoga, reaches the town at the Alexander Nevski Monastery, and farther on takes a sharp turn to the W. and (now 650 yards in breadth) divides into three branches: the *Great* or *Bolshaya Nevá* . . .; the *Small* or *Malaya Nevá*; and the *Great* or *Bolshaya Névka*, from which two arms diverge, enclosing the 'Islands' " (Baedeker, p. 99). Bely means not only the Kamenny, Krestovsky, and Elagin Islands with their parks and summer houses, but the large Vasilievsky Island (see below), Aptekarsky Island and the so-called Petersburg Side of the city, which is also an island.

Nikolaevsky Bridge: "The *Nicholas Bridge* [Nikolaevsky Bridge] which leads from the English Quay to Vasíli Ostrov [Vasilievsky Island], is a granite and iron structure resting on seven piers, and was built in 1842–50 by Kierbedz. At the N. end is an opening for ships (1.15–2.15 a.m. and 5.15–6.15 a.m.). At the farther end of the bridge is a small *Marble Chapel* erected in 1854 and dedicated to St. Nicholas, containing a mosaic portrait of the saint after an original in Bari" (Baedeker, p. 111). The Ableukhov house must virtually face the bridge, one of several in the novel on which crucial events occur.

"a yellow house": The institutions and private houses lining the English Embankment are painted a pale yellow color. Because state-owned buildings were often painted that color, "yellow house" became a euphemism for an insane asylum; in fact, for Russians this is the primary meaning of the expression. Yellow is the dominant color used in descriptions of Petersburg by many Russian writers, especially the Symbolists, for whom the color in this urban setting has a malevolent and sinister overtone.

Vasilievsky Island is located directly opposite the English Embankment. It was inhabited mainly by the middle and lower classes. The main public buildings on its Embankment (facing the Neva) include, proceeding east, the Mining Academy, the Academy of Arts, the University, the Academy of Sciences and the Stock Exchange which sits on its eastern tip, called the "Strélka" (lit., "small arrow," "pointer"). (See map.)

St. Isaac's Cathedral: For nearly two centuries the height of buildings in Petersburg has been regulated by statute. Most are only four or five stories high. However, this remarkably horizontal profile is interrupted and accentuated by three prominent vertical features, all of which appear as major leitmotifs throughout the novel. They are St. Isaac's Cathedral, the spire of the Admiralty, and the spire of the Cathedral of Peter and Paul in the Fortress of the same name.

Least successful of them all from an architectural point of view is the enormous "*St. Isaac's Cathedral, or Cathedral of St. Isaac of Dalmatia*, the largest church in St. Petersburg, built in 1819–58, in the place of an earlier church, after plans by the French architect, Ricard de Monferrand. The cost of the building amounted to more than 23,000,000 rb.—The cathedral, built of granite and marble with a lavish disregard of cost, is in the shape of a cross 364 ft. long and 315 ft. wide, and is *crowned by an enormous gilded dome, visible at a great distance*"

(Baedeker, p. 109; italics ours). "The inner height of the dome from the floor is 269 ft. (St. Peter's in Rome 404 ft., St. Paul's in London 225 ft.); the height of the whole building to the top of the cross is 333½ ft." (Baedeker, p. 109; see map).

"equestrian monument of Emperor Nicholas I": Apollon Apollonovich's ride to his office takes him past St. Isaac's Cathedral south into the Marie Square, in the center of which, facing the Cathedral, stands the "*Monument of Emperor Nicholas I* by Baron Klodt, 49 ft. high and erected in 1859. The Tzar, in the uniform of the Chevalier Guards, is represented on a prancing horse. The pedestal is adorned with bronze trophies, and four reliefs depicting events in the Tzar's life. At the corners are figures of Justice, Strength, Wisdom, and Faith (portraits of the Tzar's wife and daughters)" (Baedeker, p. 110; see map). A soldier stood honorary guard at each of the major monuments to previous rulers. Apollon Apollonovich's carriage would then turn east in the Square at the Monument and travel up the Morskaya to Nevsky Prospect.

"the carriage": Bely always uses the "neutral" word *karéta* (carriage) for the senator's equipage. Given the description of it in the next paragraph and elsewhere, it most closely resembles the English brougham: "1. a four-wheeled, boxlike, closed carriage for two or four persons, having the driver's perch outside" (*Random House Dictionary of the English Language*, unabridged, New York, 1966).

". . . the termination of life's journey": An oblique reference to the large number of high officials, from close relatives of the Tsar to ministers and heads of government agencies, who were assassinated by terrorists between 1901 and the end of 1907, when radical terror in Russia, which had previously claimed many victims (among them Tsar Alexander II himself in 1881), reached unprecedented dimensions.

"the gold needle": The prominent gold spire of the Admiralty (see map) is known as the "Admiralty needle" (*admiraltéiskaya iglá*), the term Pushkin uses in "The Bronze Horseman." Of course it is architecturally a spire (and this is the last dictionary meaning of *iglá*, marked "rare"); but to translate it that way would be to delocalize geography: in the context of Petersburg, "needle," to a Russian, automatically and exclusively refers to the Admiralty.

The Admiralty was one of the first buildings erected in Petersburg (1705). It served as the headquarters of the fledgling Russian navy and as a shipyard well into the nineteenth century. The original building was replaced in 1806–23 by a magnificent neoclassical structure of massive but graceful proportions after the designs of A. D. Zakharov. The tower is "230 ft. high, ending in a tapering gilded spire, and surmounted by a weather-vane in the form of a crown and ship" (Baedeker, p. 108). The Admiralty marks the center of the architectural plan of the left-bank section of the city. Three main streets, among them Nevsky Prospect, converge at this point.

As early as 1907 a Symbolist journal announced that Bely was at work on a novel, set in the Petersburg of Pushkin's time, called the

"Admiralty Needle." Nothing came of it, but Bely at one point did consider using the title for what eventually became *Petersburg*.

the Flying Dutchman: Peter the Great was not only a passionate sailor but a great admirer of the seafaring Dutch. He spent many months in Holland, numbered several Dutch citizens among his closest friends and advisers, gave his new city a Dutch name (see also p. 296), and modelled it on Amsterdam, another city of canals.

Bely identifies Peter with the Flying Dutchman, the legendary sea captain and hero of the Wagner opera. (For a time Bely was a fervent admirer of Wagner, like most Russian intellectuals.) Peter appears in several later sections of the novel in the guise of a Dutch sailor or sea captain. If the city was founded by the Flying Dutchman, it must partake of the curse he bears. Thus Bely finds a new way of linking Petersburg with the Russian tradition of the city as an accursed place. In fact, the 1916 version of this passage twice repeats the word "hellish" (*ádskie*).

The German Sea: In Bely's time what we call the North Sea was known in Russian either as *Nemétskoe móre* (the German Sea) or *Sévernoe móre* (the North Sea); now only *Sévernoe móre* is used. We have translated literally because of the Flying Dutchman associations in this passage.

"delusion," etc.: Bely ties his conception of the city to another aspect of the tradition: the city as a locus of delusion, as in Gogol's "Nevsky Prospect," and of illusion, as in Dostoevsky's novel *The Raw Youth* (or *The Adolescent*).

"the general census": The only comprehensive census ever taken in Imperial Russia was in January, 1897.

"as in serpent coils": The image suggests the mystical symbol of the Ouroboros, the serpent swallowing its own tail, usually interpreted as a symbol of eternity. The Ouroboros is sometimes a dragon or, in China, two dragons biting each other's tails. Both dragon and serpent figure prominently in the Apocalypse.

"solid citizen": There is no real English equivalent for the Russian *obyvátel'*. Originally the word meant nothing more than "resident," or the constant inhabitant of a certain place, which is the primary meaning in this instance. By Bely's time it had taken on disparaging overtones, which suggested a person of limited views, self-satisfied mediocrity, and lack of concern with larger social or class issues; "philistine" comes close in this respect, but fails to imply, as does the Russian, that the person is from the middle class as well. "Solid citizen" may catch some of the irony and contempt.

"gray human streams": In a 1909 essay entitled "Symbolism" Bely wrote: "We live in a twilight world, neither light nor dark—a gray half-darkness" (*Arabeski*, Moscow, 1911, p. 242). Later, commenting on the "color tonality" of *Petersburg*, he noted that it "corresponds to the tragicomedy (black-yellow) of obfuscation (gray)" (*Masterstvo Gogolya*, Moscow, 1934, p. 308). "Obfuscation" (*mórok*): see page 311.

"shadows": Here, as throughout the novel, Bely uses the word *ten'*, meaning both shadow and shade (i.e., ghost). The English "shadow" contains both meanings, but the second (shade, ghost) is probably less present to the mind of most modern speakers. We considered translating *ten'* in some cases as "shadow," and in others as "shade"; however, there were simply too many instances in which *both* meanings were operative at once or in which ambiguity of meaning was Bely's point. Therefore, we decided to use "shadow" only. Interestingly enough, in this particular sentence Bely must have decided that a reader might take the word *ten'* to mean someone's actual shadow only; he changed the word to "specter" (*prizrak*) in the 1928 edition.

the Seventeenth Line: On Vasilievsky Island "every street consists of two *Lines*, the right side of the street . . . being denoted by even numbers (Line II, IV, etc.), the left side by uneven" (Baedeker, p. 101). The stranger's residence is thus on the left side of the street which comprises the Sixteenth and Seventeenth Lines (see map).

"the memory of Petrine Petersburg": Peter's original plans for Petersburg called for the main part of the city to stand north of the Fortress of Peter and Paul on the so-called Petersburg Side. Then Vasilievsky Island was chosen for this distinction, and a grid of parallel Lines intersected at right angles by three prospects was laid out by the French architect Le Blond. But the rapidly growing city soon jumped the river to the mainland, i.e., the left bank of the Neva, which had originally been intended for naval shipyards (the Admiralty) and military installations. This became the administrative, business, and cultural center.

"Peter's line turned into the line of a later age," etc.: Bely gives a capsule history of the major architectural styles which shaped the city: the relatively simple north European baroque of Peter's reign, the flamboyant rococo of the Empress Elizabeth's times, the sober but elegant neoclassical style of Catherine the Great and her grandson, Alexander I.

"small Petrine houses": The architect Tressini's "ability to design small, practical dwellings, and to construct them in wood and brick, plastered and painted in imitation of stone, was just what Peter and his gentry required in these first years, when more monumental building was beset with difficulties. This sensible, utilitarian style appeared in his designs for houses for the various classes of citizens . . . almost all traces of the earliest urban architecture have disappeared . . ." (George Hamilton, *The Art and Architecture of Russia*, Baltimore, 1954, p. 169). If Western models were followed in the design of these and subsequent structures, at least one native Russian tradition asserted itself in the bright colors with which the buildings, from palaces to the most humble cottages, were painted.

"Don't let the crowd . . . in from the islands!" etc.: The bridges across the Neva can be drawn to allow ships to pass or, in case of civil emergencies, to control the flow of people from one part of the city to another.

"upstart intellectual": There is no English equivalent of the Russian *raznochínets* (plural, *raznochíntsy*). In his *History of Russia* (New Haven, 1930, p. 163), Vernadsky writes: "The revolutionary idea was chiefly current among the 'Raznochintsi'—that is, individuals of no definite class: the children of peasants and merchants having received secondary or higher education; the children of the clergy who did not desire to enter the church; the children of small civil servants who did not desire to continue the vocation of their fathers; and the children of impoverished nobles. These Raznochintsi rapidly formed a new social class, the so-called 'intellectuals,' which included many members of the nobility." "Intellectual" alone will not do as a rendering of *raznochínets*; the Russian *intelligént* serves for that, but as Vernadsky points out, the intelligentsia included many nobles. Since the point of view is almost always that of Apollon Apollonovich, whenever the word *raznochínets* is used in the novel, we decided on "upstart intellectual": to him such men are not members of the nobility, yet were playing an ever more prominent role in Russian society, loudly, often violently opposing the existing social order which Apollon Apollonovich (a nobleman) represents and upholds. See also Christopher Becker's "Raznochintsy: The Development of the Word and of the Concept," *American Slavic and East European Review*, No. 1, 1959, pp. 63–74.

"stream of vehicles": Literally "a stream (or flow) of *prolyótki*" (plural of *prolyótka*). We have found no exact English equivalent for this distinctive Russian vehicle—a light, low-slung one-horse carriage for two people, with a raisable top. Typically, Bely combines two of the most prominent images of the novel into one phrase: flowing water and flight (the word *prolyótka* is formed from the Russian root meaning "to fly"). Elsewhere we translate the word as "fast carriage." We considered using the now archaic English "fly": although not exactly the same type of carriage, it at least has the same root as the Russian. But "hemmed in by a stream of flies" creates a misleadingly surrealistic image completely absent in the Russian text.

"bearded caryatid": In English, a caryatid is a columnar *female* figure used to support a balcony (e.g., the Erechtheum on the Acropolis). In Russian, the word is feminine in gender (*kariatída*), as are the pronouns that match it. Some Russian dictionaries define it as "only" a female figure, some as "primarily" female; but in *Petersburg* it is first called a "bearded caryatid," then "an old, bearded man of stone," and we are informed that it has the torso of a satyr. We have retained "caryatid" throughout (instead of resorting to a word like "telamon") in keeping with Bely's own strange usage, which seems part of his technique of undermining "normal" language, and which also may point to the theme of androgyny that occurs elsewhere in the novel.

The Stock Exchange Register: One of the most widely read Petersburg daily newspapers, *Birzhevye vedomosti*. Bely uses the colloquial name for its second (or evening) edition: "*Birzhovka*."

"turmoil in China, and Port Arthur had fallen": European nations, including Russia, had been squabbling for decades about spheres of in-

fluence in China. Japan took an equally strong interest. Chinese reaction to these humiliating actions culminated in the Boxer Rebellion
in May, 1900, but that did not deter the foreign powers. In 1898 Russia
had extracted from China a twenty-five year lease on the Liaotung
Peninsula which contained Port Arthur, and soon turned this year-
round port into its main stronghold in the Far East. In July, 1900, Russia occupied the remainder of Manchuria. "Russian Far Eastern policy
during this period," Michael Florinsky remarks in his *Russia. A History
and an Interpretation* (New York, 1947, Volume 2, p. 1267), "offers a
nearly perfect example of shameless duplicity." One of the results was
Russia's bumbling into a major war with Japan in January (February,
New Style), 1904. After a long and bloody siege, Port Arthur fell to
the Japanese on January 1, 1905. It was but one of the major blows to
Russian arms and prestige in the disastrous war.

countess–counter: The "pun" in the Russian is between *grafínya* (countess) and *grafín* (decanter). The Russian for count is *graf*.

Girl Students: Bely uses an endearing diminutive (*kursístochka*) of *kur-
sístka*, for which there is no exact English equivalent. They were young
women who had finished high school and who were attending various
extension courses of higher education. "College girl" or "coed" will
certainly not do!

"Ab–lution is not the sol–u–tion . . .": There is no way to translate literally and convey the important phonic play in this passage. The stranger
overhears a drunken lovers' quarrel in which one party shouts "Just
you try spilling acid on me!" The phrase in Russian begins with "*Abl
. . . éika.*" We have substituted a phrase hinting at some of the mystical
nonsense commonly bandied about in discussions of the impasse reached
by Russian society and methods of breaking through it.

"Prov–ocation": Again no literal translation will do. The stranger hears
the end of the conversation, which in Russian is "*Porá* ("time to be
off") . . . *právo* ("true enough")." *Právo* is pronounced "práva," which
matches the pronunciation of the first two syllables of *provokátsiya*,
i.e., provocation.

"At noon . . .": To this day a cannon-shot fired from the Peter and Paul
Fortress signals noon in Leningrad.

Presumably Grand Duke Konstantin Konstantinovich (1858–1915),
grandson of Nicholas I, president of the Academy of Sciences, and a
poet, playwright and translator who published under the initials "K.R.,"
i.e., Konstantin Romanov. In normal speech the "ovich" ending of Russian patronymics is commonly slurred into "ych." This occurs throughout the novel; for example, "Ivanovich" often appears as "Ivanych."

"He's gone . . .": While climbing the stairs to his office Apollon Apollonovich sees a portrait (cf. following note), and through his mind flashes
a line from Pushkin's unfinished "Lyceum" poem "There was a time
. . ." ("Bylá porá: nash prázdnik molodói," 1836).

Whenever possible, every year on the nineteenth of October Pushkin would meet with his school chums from the first graduating class of the exclusive Lyceum at Tsarskoe Selo to celebrate its founding. He regularly wrote a poem to mark the occasion. Those school years had been the happiest, most carefree time of his life and his closest friends had all studied there with him.

The portrait is of Vyacheslav Konstantinovich von Plehve (or von Pleve), the hated reactionary Minister of the Interior from 1902 until July, 1904, when he was assassinated by a terrorist's bomb. Von Plehve had been appointed to replace D. S. Sipyagin, who himself had been assassinated. Plehve is presented in the novel as Apollon Apollonovich's closest friend and protector in the bureaucracy; like Apollon Apollonovich, he was an implacable foe of Sergei Witte.

"My turn has come . . .": Apollon Apollonovich next thinks of the first two lines of the fourth stanza from another "Lyceum" poem of Pushkin, "The more often the Lyceum celebrates . . ." ("Chem cháshche prázdnuet litséi"), written in 1831. The poet Anton Delvig (1798–1831), Pushkin's closest friend, died before this reunion. Thus Delvig calls Pushkin from beyond the grave to a "crowd of shadows."

"And o'er the earth . . .": The concluding lines (the last incomplete because the poem was never finished) of Pushkin's 1836 "Lyceum" poem described three notes up. By Apollon Apollonovich's time such nature imagery invariably served as a code for revolutionary activities in general, and for the revolution which most people sensed as being imminent.

"the deacon Zrakov's pupil": The Russian text reads literally "The dossier on deacon Zrakov." The name Zrakov contains the Slavic word *zrak* meaning "eye," from which the Russian *zrachók* ("pupil of the eye") is formed. Apollon Apollonovich makes the association and remembers the eyes of the stranger.

"opened the door": This is one of the rare instances in the novel when a door is simply opened. As in Dostoevsky, they usually fly or swing open (or shut) with some violence.

Kólenka, Nikólenka, and Kólya are all diminutives of Nikolai.

St. Panteleimon or Pantaleon, Martyr (died c. 305). The name means "the All-merciful" (or "the All-compassionate"). His feast day is July 27. A physician himself, he was honored in the West during the Middle Ages as one of the patron saints of physicians. His cult is much more popular in the Orthodox Church, where he is venerated as a *Velikomúchenik* (literally, Great Martyr) and wonderworker. Prayers are addressed to him to aid those suffering from demonic possession and insomnia. He is also invoked in the Orthodox Church when water is blessed. Even more interestingly, given the context of Bely's novel, his large eyes are emphasized on icons and he carries a small box (for his medical equipment) which looks very much like a small bundle.

"out of his head": According to legend, the goddess Pallas Athena was born when Zeus, suffering from a frightful headache, split his own head open (or had it split open), and out stepped the goddess, full grown. At the end of this section in the 1916 version, we are told that Apollon Apollonovich is suffering from a migraine.

Millionnaya Street (see map) leads from Palace Square to the Field of Mars. It passes the Hermitage, crosses the Winter Canal, and then runs by a series of palaces, elegant private dwellings, and barracks for several elite regiments of the Imperial Guard.

   According to L. K. Dolgopolov, there was such a low-class restaurant on the Millionnaya at the time. ("Andrei Belyi v rabote nad 'Peterburgom,'" *Russkaya literatura*, No. 1, 1972, 162.) The street is now named in honor of the terrorist Khalturin, who tried to assassinate Alexander II by placing a bomb in the Winter Palace.

"suddenly": Compare an early Chekhov story, "The Death of a Government Clerk" ("Smert' chinovnika," 1883): "But suddenly. . . . This 'but suddenly' is often met with in stories. Authors are right: life is so full of the unexpected!" Chekhov, of course, is poking fun at one of the favorite devices of the pulp fiction of the time. The word occurs frequently in Dostoevsky too.

Secret police: In 1880 the "Third Section" was reorganized as a department of the Ministry of the Interior; from 1881–1884 it was headed by von Plehve. The Okhrana ("security police"), designed to combat any activity in the Empire (or among Russians living abroad) that was considered subversive, had become thoroughly compromised long before 1905. It not only infiltrated but even sponsored revolutionary parties, terrorist groups, and labor organizations. Many of its officers were double agents, responsible for planning and implementing the assassinations of several government officials, among them von Plehve himself. In 1905 its headquarters were located in the house on the Moika (No. 12) where Pushkin had died (now a Pushkin museum), only a few steps from the Winter Canal and "our" restaurant on the Millionnaya.

"the spire of Peter and Paul": The Cathedral of SS. Peter and Paul was founded at the same time (1703) as the Fortress of the same name (see map) which it dominates. The Cathedral served as the burial church of all Russian rulers from Peter the Great on. "The extremely slender gilded spire, which is one of the highest in Russia (394 ft.), is crowned by an angel bearing a cross 23 ft. in height" (Baedeker, p. 173). The spire throws the rest of the building out of proportion, and "was an aggressive assertion of Peter's wish that the horizon of St. Petersburg should be the antithesis of the rounded, bell-like aspect of Moscow. Such pointed spires were unknown in earlier Russian architecture and were certainly suggested to Peter during his travels abroad . . ." (George Hamilton, *The Art and Architecture of Russia*, Baltimore, 1954, p. 171).

The name Lippánchenko is formed from the root *lip*-, meaning "sticky." (It is tempting to suppose that Bely may also have been thinking of *lípovyi*, a slang term for "fake" or "counterfeit," which is widely attested in literature by the 1920s.) As a double agent Lippanchenko has as many names as his real life "counterpart," the infamous Evno Azef, whom Bely acknowledged using as a model. Azef was one of the masterminds of the Terrorist Organization of the Socialist Revolutionary (SR) Party (see page 321) and simultaneously an agent of the secret police. He helped plan the assassination of von Plehve, among many others. After being exposed in 1908, he managed to escape to Berlin. In the final section of his memoirs (in *Literaturnoe nasledstvo*, Vol. 27–28, Moscow, 1937, p. 454), Bely insists he did not know that Azef used the pseudonym Lipchenko while living abroad; the sounds "l-p-p," he says, rang in his ears as the phonic equivalent of chaos and they determined the creation and use of the names Lip*p*anchenko and A*poll*on A*poll*onovich. However that may be, he could not have been unaware of the details of the Azef affair (the sensation of 1908) when he made the name Lippanchenko (whose "real name" in the novel is Lipensky).

"His lips . . . pieces of sliced salmon": One might recall that Azef's real patronymic was Fishelevich, probably formed from the German *Fisch*, i.e., fish. There is also the German *Lippe*, i.e., lip.

"all over the walls": Alexander Ivanovich puns, in the Russian, on the similarity of the words "both of us" and "wallpaper" (*"bylo by s námi s obóimi"*).

"What is Man?": In the Russian one man asks "What is truth?" The other replies with a play on words: "Truth (*ístina*) is what you eat" (the nonexistent noun *éstina*, formed from the verb meaning "to eat" [*est'*]). Our Feuerbachian English ("You are what you eat") honors the moronic spirit of the Russian original.

"evoked the memory of a fateful face": Bely himself later pointed out that the mysterious "eastern" face that appears on the wall of Dudkin's garret is a version of the oriental-featured moneylender in the painting that hangs in Chartkov's room in Gogol's "The Portrait" (Bely, *Masterstvo Gogolya*, Moscow, 1934, p. 303).

"All words with 'sh' . . .": This passage is the second instance of the way sounds create their own reality for the stranger. In the Russian, the contrast is between two vowels, *y* and *i*. By using the consonants *sh* and *s* we had to change words only very slightly to capture the word play here. A literal translation would, of course, have produced gibberish.

"student uniform": The original states only that Nikolai would appear in a uniform; this might have led Western readers to assume that he was in the military. Compare Baedeker (p. 101): "Nearly one-tenth of the male population of St. Petersburg wear some kind of uniform, including not only the numerous military officers, but civil officials, and even students, schoolboys, and others."

"abandoned the family hearth," etc.: Anna Karenina leaves her bureaucrat husband for Vronsky, an aristocratic military officer; but he has an "artistic nature" and takes up painting while he and Anna are living in Italy.

Domino: "A masquerade costume, consisting of a robe with a hood adjustable at pleasure and including a light half mask" (*Webster's New International Dictionary of the English Language*, Second Edition, Unabridged). Anyone who has attended a performance of Mozart's *Don Giovanni* or Verdi's *A Masked Ball* has seen them.

Bely uses *másochka*, the diminutive of *máska*. This could mean "a small mask," but presumably he means a mask covering the eyes and nose, with a long lace beard dangling from it.

"a spire": The Fortress of SS. Peter and Paul with its Cathedral (see page 309) is located in that part of the city, north of the Neva, called the Petersburg Side (see map).

"the great black bridge": Presumably the Troitsky Bridge (see map and page 319).

"two lions . . .": A recent Soviet guidebook to Leningrad states: "One of the most outstanding architectural details is the stone or bronze sculpture of the lion, recumbent or rampant. It stands on the embankments and porches and occasionally even on the staircases of apartment houses" (Yelena Doroshinskaya and Vadim Kruchina, *Leningrad. Guidebook*, Moscow, no date, p. 11).

The Moika (see map) is a river emptying into the Neva. Faced with stone, it cuts through the left-bank area of the city, as do several canals. Bely is describing the segment of it that lies north of Nevsky Prospect, where it is lined (as it is for most of its course) by fashionable houses and government buildings. Much of the novel's action takes place in this section of the city.

"Obfuscation" renders one of Bely's favorite words, *mórok*. No single English word captures all its meanings. Like *mrak*, it denotes darkness and gloom, but it also connotes anything that darkens the mind, including phantoms. Obfuscation comes close, but is more abstract than the Russian.

"apples of electric lights": In Russian this is *yábloki elektrícheskikh svétov*. This is not only a picturesque way of describing the bulbs that light the Nevsky Prospect, but also is phonically suggestive of the surname of the man responsible for the original system of illumination: Pavel Nikolaevich Yáblochkov (1847–1894); his last name is formed from *yáblochko*, the diminutive of *yábloko*, "apple." Among his inventions was the so-called "Yablochkov candle" (1876), a kind of arc lamp, which was first used in 1878 to light the streets of Petersburg.

Hemorrhoids have been the occupational hazard of government officials and clerks in Russian literature at least since the time of Gogol's "Overcoat" (1842).

"bat": See page 299. In the 1916 version, Apollon Apollonovich's nickname among the clerks is "the bat" (*netopyr'*).

1812 was, of course, the year of the Napoleonic invasion of Russia. In December, 1825, a group of young army officers from the nobility attempted a coup d'etat in Petersburg during the interregnum following the death of Alexander I. This Decembrist uprising, as it is known, was quickly suppressed by the new Emperor, Nicholas I.

"you'd better do it," etc. We have had to modify these statements somewhat in order to avoid the "thee and thouing" so unnatural in English but so common in Russian. The absentminded Apollon Apollonovich addresses his secretary in the familiar or impolite second person singular rather than the proper second person plural. At several other places in the novel we have made similar changes.

COLD FINGERS: In the 1916 version, the section titles ("Wet Autumn," "Apollon Apollonovich Recalled," etc.) are almost always taken from a sentence that follows in the text. This is not always the case in the 1922 version, simply because Bely often cut just those sentences that supply the titles. "Cold Fingers" represents a special case. Despite the emphasis on the coldness of the Ableukhov house, nowhere in either the 1916 or 1922 version is mention made of "cold fingers." In an article on the textual problems of the novel, Ivanov-Razumnik explains that in one of the early drafts of the novel, Bely placed the description of how Apollon Apollonovich once almost froze to death in the countryside (where "cold fingers" stroked his heart) at this point in the novel. He then moved the passage to the second chapter (see "Beloved Delvig Calls For Me"), but neglected to remove the title "Cold Fingers" ("K istorii teksta 'Peterburga,'" *Vershiny. A. Blok. A. Belyi*, Petrograd, 1923).

"wearing a coat . . . with a turned-up collar": The Russian text has only "wearing a coat." In the 1916 version the puzzled servant then replies that all Nikolai's visitors wear coats, to which Apollon Apollonovich adds "a coat with a turned-up collar." This triggers the servant's memory. With this latter part of the exchange carelessly cut from the 1922 text "wearing a coat" becomes quite meaningless. Therefore we have restored the detail of the collar.

Niobe: "Like Niobe, all tears," Hamlet observes of his mother's mock grief over his father's death (Act One, scene II). In Greek mythology the seven sons and seven daughters of Niobe, daughter of Tantalus, were killed by the arrows of Apollo and Artemis, the only children of Leto, after Niobe had boasted to Leto of her reproductive superiority. Niobe wept for her slain children until she turned into a column of stone from which the tears continued to flow.

"Something awful, something sweet": Cf. Gogol's story "Viy," whose hero, Khoma Brut, experiences just such a sensation as he is ridden through the air by the mysterious old woman: "He felt a somehow exhausting, unpleasant, and yet sweet sensation." "Sweet" has overtones of "voluptuous."

The short Winter Canal (see map) leads from the Moika to the Neva. Millionnaya Street crosses one of the two stone bridges which arch it, and the Palace Embankment the other. The Canal separates the Hermitage on the west and the Imperial Hermitage Theater (often used at the time for court festivities) on the east. Behind the theater, and facing the Millionnaya on its northern side, were the Barracks (No. 33) of the First Battalion of the elite Preobrazhensky Regiment. Part of this building also abuts the Winter Canal. The Winter Canal serves as one of the central locales of the novel's action.

"the four-storied palace": One would assume that Bely meant the Winter Palace, but it has only three stories resting on a low basement. Furthermore, the scene is set by the Winter Canal, which is separated from the Winter Palace by several large buildings. There is a four-story building on the Winter Canal, but it is the Barracks mentioned in the preceding note. Bely, who was a Muscovite and not a Petersburger, may have mistakenly assumed that this building, standing so close to the other buildings of the Palace, was part of it too. The adjective "smooth" (*gládkii*), used in the 1916 version (but cut from the 1922 text) to describe the side of the "four-storied palace," would certainly apply to the building housing the Barracks, but hardly to the highly ornamented rococo Winter Palace. The use of the word palace with "four-storied" may also be an example of that device of "exact inexactitude" Bely employs to describe the city. Certain details give the appearance of reality, but readers familiar with the city realize that something is wrong, i.e., that this is only an illusion. Another example is the "three-storied five-columned building" on the Moika which is always mentioned when the Likhutin's apartment house appears: no such building actually existed, but Bely took details from real Petersburg buildings (none of them, however, on the Moika) to create his composite structure, thus creating a deliberately illusory "reality." (See also the Introduction and L. K. Dolgopolov's article "Obraz goroda v romane A. Belogo 'Peterburg,'" *Izvestiya Akademii Nauk* [Seriya literatury i yazyka], Tom 34, No. 1, 1975.)

Liza: Here and throughout the novel the reference is to the heroine of Tchaikovsky's opera *The Queen of Spades* (1890), which was based on the Pushkin story (1834) of the same name. Opera conventions of the late nineteenth century could not admit the ironic tone of the Pushkin tale, which ends with the hero, Hermann (Germann), in a madhouse and the heroine, Liza, apparently suffering no ill effects from Hermann's actions. Having comfortably married, Liza is in a position to put her young ward, a poor relation, through the same misery she herself suffered at the hands of her late protectress, the old Countess. The opera treats the fate of the hero and heroine very differently. In the final act, the climactic confrontation of the two lovers takes place at the Winter Canal, under the arch which connects the Hermitage and the Hermitage Theater. There Liza finds out that Hermann, in learning the secret of the three cards that will make his fortune at gambling, really did cause the old Countess's death, as she had feared. Liza also realizes that Hermann has lost his mind. But she loves him still, and tries to persuade him to flee with her; the mad Hermann, obsessed with his secret, pushes her away and rushes off to a gambling house. In despair Liza runs to the Palace Embankment and throws herself into the Neva. Hermann, after losing everything on his third and final card, kills himself.

Dolgopolov ("Andrei Belyi v rabote . . .," op. cit., pp. 161–162) remarks that with the first performance of the opera in 1891, it "promptly captivated its listeners. . . . At the beginning of the century the images and motifs of the opera entered into the life of a wide spectrum of the artistic intelligentsia of Petersburg. Drawings and decorations and paintings were based on the theme of the story and the opera."

"the yellow house on the Gagarin Embankment": The Ableukhov house is now definitely placed on the Gagarin (or French) Embankment, which stretched from the Fontanka to the Liteiny (or Alexandrovsky) Bridge. The house has "shifted" earlier in the chapter from its English Embankment location: Dudkin, who is taking his bundle to the senator's son, would have crossed the Nikolaevsky Bridge and found himself at the Ableukhov house immediately. Instead he is on the Nevsky when he meets the senator's carriage. This, of course, makes sense only if the Ableukhov house is on the Gagarin Embankment, which lies in the opposite direction from the English Embankment (see map). Likewise, in the Second Chapter, when Dudkin is making his way home from the Ableukhov house, he goes west, in the direction of the Winter Palace, the Admiralty and Senate Square where the Bronze Horseman stands. After pausing by the statue, Dudkin crosses the bridge to Vasilievsky Island and home. This is possible only if the Ableukhov house is on the Gagarin Embankment.

"the Square": This is the Palace (or the Alexander) Square bounded on the north by the Winter Palace and on the south by the crescent-shaped building of the General Staff. The statues mentioned are those which adorn the roof of the Winter Palace (the 1916 text says that the statues stand above "dark-red walls"; in 1905 the Winter Palace was in fact painted dark red).

"The entryway door," etc.: It is questionable how well this passage —which initially baffled us and everyone to whom we showed it—works in Russian or in English. How can a person go through a door and yet have that same door close in front of him? Everyone assumed that "in front of" was a misprint for "behind," but this is not the case. The locution is possible if the point of view is that of a shadow, not the possessor of the shadow. And here we have "the shadow of a woman." (In Russian *pered nei* means both "in front of it" and "in front of her," because the word *ten'*, shadow, is feminine.) Observe yourself entering a completely dark space with a light at your back; your shadow is thrown in front of you, and as the door closes behind you, it appears to close in front of your shadow; when the door closes completely your shadow disappears, if the room you are entering is dark. This is what happens here, after which the woman herself finally "appears" in the darkness as the "black little lady."

"caped greatcoat": Bely uses the word *nikoláevka*, the popular form of *Nikoláevskaya shinél'* (i.e., a "Nicholas greatcoat"). This style of coat came into fashion during the reign of Nicholas I, and was still being worn in 1905. It allows Bely a nice play on the first name of his hero, Nikolai.

Chapter the Second

The epigraph is taken from the seventh stanza, lines 1–4, of Pushkin's unfinished long poem "Ezersky" (1832–33). Pushkin abandoned the work when he began writing "The Bronze Horseman." The translation of lines 3–4 is very free; literally they read: "I am a bourgeois, as you well know / And in that sense a democrat." Pushkin uses the word *meshchanín*, which in his time was an equivalent of the French "bourgeois" or the German "Bürger." By 1905, the word had taken on derogatory overtones; it might best be rendered as "middle-class type" (and we have done so later).

The Comrade: A "left-wing" newspaper published at the time in Petersburg. By "the most recent type of newspapers" Bely means the anti-government periodicals which were being printed and sold in Russia at this time when governmental authority was collapsing. A section of the Manifesto of October 17, 1905 (which helped end the revolution of 1905) guaranteed a free press in Russia. This guarantee was not always honored literally, but many radical periodicals were openly printed and sold.

"the disappearance of some writer or other," etc.: A reference to Daryalsky (specified by name in the 1916 version), the hero of Bely's novel *The Silver Dove*. Bely originally planned *Petersburg* as a sequel to this novel, but he subsequently abandoned that plan. Only a few minor details like this link the two novels.

The Chernyshev Bridge (see map) crosses the Fontanka, and gives onto a square of the same name, on which were located the Ministries of the Interior and Education.

Dust imagery, prominent throughout the novel, is a common apocalyptic motif in Russian Symbolist writing. This can in part be traced to the cataclysmic volcanic eruptions at Krakatoa (1883) and Martinique (1902), the dust from which created spectacular red sunsets all over the world.

Sofia Petrovna: Sofia (Sof'ya) is the Russian form of Sophia. She will also be called Sophie, Sonya, and Sonyushka. Petrovna means "daughter of Peter."

"A special feature of the Eastern Church is the doctrine of Heavenly Wisdom (*Sophia*). The concept of a personified 'Heavenly Wisdom' is first to be found in Late Judaism. . . . [In Eastern Orthodox theology] the Mother of God and Heavenly *Sophia* were two separate entities. In iconography, too, the distinction was maintained. Heavenly Wisdom is usually represented together with her three daughters: Faith, Love and Hope. . . . In modern Russian religious philosophy, and chiefly in the works of Vladimir Soloviev, Pavel Florensky, V. N. Ilyin and Sergei Bulgakov an elaborate Sophiology has been developed" (Ernst Benz, *The Eastern Orthodox Church. Its Thought and Life*, New York, Anchor Paper, 1963, pp. 62–63). Both the Sophiology and the late apocalyptic writings of the philosopher Vladimir Solovyov (or Soloviev; 1853–1900) profoundly influenced the young Bely and his generation of Russian Symbolists. For some, like Bely and Blok, Sophia was primarily the incarnation of the Eternal Feminine. At one time Bely even believed that she was embodied in a flesh and blood woman (Blok's wife). That Bely gives the name Sofia to the woman with whom Nikolai is infatuated and the last name Solovyova (the feminine form of Solovyov) to the foolish frump who loves Nikolai is typical of his clowning with ideas he held very dear. Self-mockery is one of the most notable features of his personality.

There is another Sofia Petrovna in Russian literature who comes to mind: the heroine of Chekhov's story "Misfortune" ("Neschast'e," 1886). She enjoys her power over her would-be lover and torments him by her indecision. She is both attracted to sensual gratification and afraid of its results. The story has been seen as a parodic treatment of *Anna Karenina*.

"the extraordinary luxuriance of her hair": With this detail Bely parodically links the heroine with Anna Karenina; Anna's "mark" in Tolstoy's novel is the "willful little tendrils" of her curly hair.

The entire description, however, points to another "model," Grushenka in *The Brothers Karamazov*: "She had a full figure, with soft, as it were, noiseless movements, softened to a peculiar over-sweetness, like her voice . . . her sumptuous black dress . . . she was twenty-two years old. . . . She was very white in the face, with a pale pink tint on her cheeks. . . . Her upper lip was thin, but the slightly prominent lower lip was at least twice as full, and looked pouting. But her magnificent, abundant dark brown hair, her sable-coloured eyebrows and charming grey-blue eyes. . . . There was a child-like look in her eyes, a look of childish delight. . . . It was that softness, that voluptuousness of her bodily movements, that catlike noiselessness. . . . Connoisseurs of Russian beauty could have foretold with certainty that this fresh, still youthful, beauty would lose its harmony by the age of thirty, would 'spread'; that the face would become puffy . . ." (Book Three, *The Sensualists*; Chapter X, "Both Together"; Garnett translation). This tendency to point simultaneously to at least two models is characteristic of Bely's parodic techniques throughout the novel.

Peri: "1. *Persian Myth.* An imaginary being, male or female, like an elf or fairy, descended from fallen angels, excluded from paradise till penance is accomplished. They were originally regarded as evil, but later as benevolent and beautiful. 2. A fairylike or elflike creature; hence, by extension, a very beautiful person, esp. a woman" (*Webster's New International Dictionary of the English Language*, Second Edition, Unabridged). The Russian has the same meanings.

Hokusai: One of only two instances in the novel when Bely himself supplies a footnote. Among the most celebrated works of the Japanese painter and print designer Katsushika Hokusai (1760–1849) are the series of color prints entitled "Thirty-Six Views of Mount Fuji" (1834–35). Around the turn of the century, Japanese art was extremely fashionable in Russia and also in Western Europe, where Japanese prints made a great impact on the Impressionists.

Verhefden: The Hermann Hermannovich of Chapter One (in the section "The Writing Table Stood There").

"Dun-CAN and Ni-KISCH": Arthur Nikisch (1855–1922) was a famous conductor, whose posts included the Leipzig Opera and Gewandhaus Orchestra, the Boston Symphony Orchestra, and the Berlin Philharmonic. He conducted often in Petersburg, and was a champion of the music of Tchaikovsky and Wagner.

The American dancer Isadora Duncan (1878–1927) arrived in Petersburg in December, 1904, and not on the morning in January, 1905, when the funeral for those killed in the Bloody Sunday massacre was taking place, as she herself—with her flair for the dramatic—would have it in her memoirs. News of her "conquests" of Western European capitals had preceded her, and her first appearance in Petersburg, on December 13 (26), 1904, attracted considerable attention. She was quickly taken up by the cultural elite of the city and even exerted some influence (still a matter of debate) on the Russian ballet, especially on Mikhail Fokine. She danced in Russia many times thereafter and in the 1920s was married to the poet Sergei Esenin. Angel Peri would quite naturally share this enthusiasm and would also quite naturally trivialize it. For although Duncan danced the leading Grace in the Bacchanal ballet section of Wagner's *Tannhäuser* at Bayreuth in 1904, she admired the German composer too much to think of dancing his other works.

The block capitals in each name indicate the syllable on which Angel Peri places the stress (actually, Bely uses acute accents). Unquestionably she is wrong in the case of Nikisch (it should be NIK-isch). For "Duncan," however, the normal stress *in Russian* today does fall on the second syllable, and Angel Peri therefore seems to be correct. Bely's point is made in translation, but what is he driving at from the viewpoint of the Russian reader? Either he is simply careless, or he is reflecting the fact that no standardized pronunciation of the name had yet been agreed on in Russian.

"Meloplastics" renders *meloplástika*, a word Bely invented, no doubt to suggest Angel Peri's confusion of the word *metalloplástika* with Duncan's revolutionary ideas of "liberating" the body from the "constrictions" of classical ballet by imbuing the freedom of gymnastics with the "spirit of the dance." (*Metalloplástika*, literally "metalloplastics," was a popular "artistic" pastime among Russian schoolgirls: heating a special needle, they would trace designs on treated metal plates that came in kits.)

Bely may also have in mind the word *mimoplyáska* ("mime-dance"), which Nikolai Vashkevich coined in a 1908 article on the "state of the dance" (Vera Krasovskaya, *Russkii baletnyi teatr nachala XX veka. 1. Khoreografy*, Leningrad, 1971, p. 47). For Vashkevich, *mimoplyaska* was the last word in choreography, and Duncan its model. Bely certainly would have known Vashkevich, who had close ties with the Moscow publishing house "Skorpion," which put out the Symbolist journal *Vesy* (*The Balance*) which Bely helped edit, and where many of his works appeared.

"copper collection box": It was *tin* only a few paragraphs earlier. We cannot decide whether this (and similar instances later in the novel) is a careless slip on Bely's part, or whether he deliberately pokes fun at the inconsistencies so common in many of the long Russian nineteenth-century novels.

"*Man and His Bodies*, by Madame Henri Besançon": Angel Peri merges the name of the influential French philosopher Henri Bergson (1859–1941) with that of Annie Besant (1847–1933). Bergson's "vitalistic" theories were well known in Russia by 1905. Besant, a famous "free thinker" and social reformer in Victorian England, was converted to theosophy in 1889 after reading Madame H. P. Blavatsky's *The Secret Doctrine*. After Blavatsky's death in 1891, she became the most prominent proselytizer of the Theosophical Society and in 1907 was elected its international president, an office she held until her death. *Man and His Bodies*, first published in 1896, was her best known work and was translated into many languages. Bely himself took a keen interest in theosophy and "converted" to Rudolf Steiner's anthroposophy, one of its offshoots, while at work on *Petersburg*.

"yet another visitor . . . her husband," etc.: Readers familiar with Chekhov's story "The Grasshopper" ("Poprygun'ya," 1892) may already have noticed a parodic resemblance between husband, wife, and milieu there, and the Likhutins here.

"Ukrainian type": Bely uses the tautological *khokhól-maloróss. Khokhol* is the pejorative term for a Ukrainian; *maloross* means Little Russian, i.e., Ukrainian.

"Gr–gorian Regiment of His Majesty the King of Siam": Foreign monarchs allied to Russia, friendly with her, or related to the Imperial family were sometimes made honorary "patrons" of Russian Army units as a mark of special favor. The detail can also be seen as one of the many "Eastern symbols" in the novel.

"a cross between a Semite and a Mongol": In the two Soviet editions of the novel (1928 and 1935) the word Semite is cut and replaced by *khokhol* (see note above, beginning "Ukrainian type").

"Ooo": This is not a long "o" but the "oo" of buff*oo*n, and the "u" of Able*u*khov. It also occurs in the Russian for "monster" (*uród*), "frog" (*lyagúshka*), "buffoon" (*shut*) and "doll" (*kúkla*). Bely often builds whole paragraphs around it, but a translation can, of course, only hint at this. Throughout the novel it is associated with revolution (and occurs in the word itself: *revolyútsiya*).

Petersburg Bridge: Because the Troitsky Bridge, which crosses the Neva at its greatest width (645 yards), led to the Petersburg Side of the city it was often known as the Petersburg Bridge. "This iron bridge was constructed in 1897–1903 as a memorial of the silver wedding of the Tzar Alexander III and the Tzarina Marie Feódorovna. It is supported by six piers and cost upwards of 5 million rubles" (Baedeker, p. 173). It is the largest bridge near the Likhutin apartment, and it would seem to be the "iron bridge" which figures so prominently in the novel; there Nikolai almost commits suicide, there he makes his "fateful promise." This may, however, be "particularizing" the novel too much, for Bely often seems to have a "mythic" bridge in mind, not any real one.

The Ciniselli Circus, on the Fontanka (see map), was not far from the Likhutin apartment. "Performances in winter only" (Baedeker, p. 95). Angel Peri might have seen the following at the Circus as well as a bearded lady: "Today a large troupe of African savages, negroes, acrobat-gymnasts is arriving by ship from England. This troupe has appeared with success under the name 'the blac skins fellows' [sic!] for over a year at the London Hippodrome. The first appearance of these black-skinned daredevils will be on the second half of today's (October first) program at the circus" (*Birzhevye vedomosti*, October 1 (14), 1905, "Theater" section, under "Ciniselli Circus").

"Sudanese spears with massive hafts": The Russian calls these "*strély*," i.e., arrows, but the rest of the description makes "spears" more appropriate in English.

"spring was coming": The expression "political spring" came into vogue to describe the brief administration of Prince P. D. Svyatopolk-Mirsky, a comparatively liberal and enlightened man appointed in August, 1904, to fill the post of Minister of the Interior left vacant by the assassination of the hated von Plehve. Mirsky resigned after the "Bloody Sunday" incident (January 9, 1905), when workers peacefully assembled in front of the Winter Palace to petition the Tsar for reforms were fired upon by the authorities with heavy loss of life.

"the master's colonnaded house": The age-old reaction of the peasants to oppression during times of disorder was to march on the landowner's manor house to plunder and burn. Such disturbances occurred with great frequency in the late spring and the summer of 1905, and troops often had to be summoned to put them down. The conflagrations—known in Russian as the "red cockerel" (*krásnyi petúkh*)—claimed many lives and millions of rubles.

"the fields of bloodstained Manchuria": Manchuria was the primary battleground in the war between the Japanese and Russia (see page 307). Russian losses were extremely high. Many of the wounded and deserters who made their way back to the cities joined the revolutionary elements there, having seen bungling, disorganization, and even chaos in the Russian General Staff. The Browning handgun was the

most popular weapon in the revolutionary arsenal and virtually became a symbol of revolution. Troops and police were often fired upon
by individuals in the protesting crowds.

Liteiny Bridge: The popular name of the Alexandrovsky (or Alexander)
Bridge (see map), which led from Liteiny Prospect, on the left bank
area of the city, to the Vyborg Side, one of the major working-class
sections of the city. The industrial areas were placed as far from the
administrative center as possible. Such areas did indeed "ring" the city.

"railway station": Nevsky Prospect, as noted before, runs in a straight
line from the Admiralty as far as Znamenskaya Square, in which is
located the Nikolaevsky (or Moskovsky) Railway Station, with trains
for Moscow, Tver, Novgorod, etc.

"He's gone": See note on p. 307.

"My turn has come," etc.: The complete fourth stanza of the 1831 Lyccum
poem mentioned in note on p. 308. There is one mistake in Bely's citation of the final line: *ushédshii* instead of *utékshii*.

"napkin": When the bundle is first mentioned in Chapter One, it is said
to be wrapped in a napkin (*salfétka*). Now the Russian has it wrapped
in a *poloténtse*, which is usually translated as "towel." We decided to
use napkin here as well, following Webster's second meaning for napkin: "Hence, any little cloth or towel" (*Webster's New International
Dictionary of the English Language*, Second Edition, Unabridged).

"mice": One of the earliest names for Apollo is the "mouse god" (Smin-
theus); later in the novel Apollon Apollonovich is sometimes likened
to a mouse in various ways. For example, his dressing gown is described
as being of a mouse-gray color. We should note too that the common
Russian for bat (to which Apollon Apollonovich has been compared
earlier) is *letúchaya mysh'*, i.e., "flying mouse." The mousetrap "clicks"
at the moment when the bundle is given to Apollon Apollonovich's
son, Nikolai.

"Behind Nikolai Apollonovich's back": Here and elsewhere we have
translated the Russian phrase *za spinói* literally as "behind the back"
(although normally it simply means "behind") because of the importance of "back" imagery in the novel.

"the history of gnosticism": A dropped comma after gnosticism in the
1922 edition (uncorrected in the 1928 and 1935 editions) produced the
nonsensical "the history of gnosticism of Gregory of Nyssa." There
is no such work.

St. Gregory of Nyssa (c. 330–c. 395), Bishop of Nyssa, one of the Cap-
padocian Fathers, and the younger brother of St. Basil the Great. "St.
Gregory of Nyssa was a thinker and theologian of great originality
and knowledge, acquainted esp. with Platonist and Neo-Platonist spec-
ulation, as well as an outstanding exegete, orator, and ascetical author.
. . . His ascetical works include treatises on virginity, in which he
develops the thought that by virginity the soul becomes a spouse of
Christ. . . . He was an ardent defender of the Nicene dogma of the

Trinity. . . . In his eschatology he is influenced by Origen, with whom he holds that ultimately both the souls in hell and the devils will return to God. In his account of the Atonement he employs, prob. for the first time, the simile of the fishhook by which the devil was baited" (*Oxford Dictionary of the Christian Church*, London, 1958, p. 588). Dudkin later uses a variant of the fishhook image in the Sixth Chapter, in the section entitled "Petersburg."

St. Ephraem Syrus (c. 306–73), Syrian Biblical exegete and ecclesiastical writer. The style of his works, "characterized by repetitions and the accumulation of metaphors, is repellent to modern readers. . . . One of his favourite subjects was the Last Judgement, which he described in terrifying colours" (*Oxford Dictionary of the Christian Church*, pp. 455–56).

The vision of St. John the Divine is entitled *Apocalypse* (*Apokálipsis*) in the Slavic Bible; in the Russian translation it is *Revelation* (*Otkrovénie*). Bely uses both titles interchangeably in the novel.

Harnack, Adolf (1851–1930), German Church historian and theologian. "In the range of his achievements Harnack was prob. the most outstanding Patristic scholar of his generation." Dudkin may know the name because of the controversy which surrounded Harnack's name due to his critical attitude to traditional Christian dogma or because of his famous series of lectures delivered in the winter of 1899–1900, and widely publicized, which stressed "the moral side of Christianity, esp. the claims of human brotherhood, to the exclusion of all that was doctrinal" (*Oxford Dictionary of the Christian Church*, p. 609).

Yakutsk was the capital of a region in northeastern Siberia to which many political exiles were sent. They routinely escaped and made their way back either to the major urban areas of European Russia or to Western Europe.

Boris Mikhailovsky (see page 301) points out that Bely took this detail of the stranger's escape from the biography of G. A. Gershuni, one of the leaders of the Terrorist Organization (*Boeváya organizátsiya*; literally, "fighting organization") of the Socialist-Revolutionary Party (SR's). Although no political parties legally existed or performed constitutional functions in Russia until October, 1905, there were underground organizations, like the Populist-tinged SR's (or the Social-Democrats, Lenin's party) which used the name "party." The SR Party was officially founded in 1900 and its much feared Terrorist Organization in 1901. "Shrouded in secrecy, and acting under the orders of the central committee, it [the Terrorist Organization] devoted itself to the perpetration of political murders. Similar terroristic units were established by local socialist revolutionary groups. From 1902 until 1907 . . . the country was swept by waves of political assassinations carried out by socialist revolutionaries" (Florinsky, II, pp. 1153–54). The famous Azef (see page 310) was another of the leaders of the Organization.

Nietzsche: In Russia, enthusiasm for the German philosopher was not confined to modernist literary circles like the Symbolists. The cult of the "superman" and the exaltation of the individual ego above the "inert masses" struck a responsive chord in several of the anarchist and terrorist organizations as well. The anarchist Emma Goldman, for example, wrote in her autobiography: "Nietzsche was not a social theorist but a poet, a rebel and innovator. His aristocracy was neither of birth nor of purse; it was of the spirit. In that respect, Nietzsche was an anarchist, and all true anarchists were aristocrats" (cited in Paul Avrich's *The Russian Anarchists*, Princeton, 1967, p. 172).

Dudkin's interest in Nietzsche and mysticism and his intimate knowledge of modernist literature (see his comments on literature in Chapter Six) find a parallel with another leader of the Terrorist Organization of the SR Party. Boris Savinkov, who with Azef planned the murder of von Plehve, Grand Duke Sergei Alexandrovich (the Tsar's uncle), and many other high officials, was a "terrorist of immense daring, imagination, and resourcefulness" (Florinsky, II, p. 1154). He published two successful novels under the pseudonym "V. Ropshin" and later numbered several prominent Russian modernist writers, most notably the poet Zinaida Gippius, among his friends.

"keyboard," etc.: The metaphor is drawn not from Nietzsche (as Bely well knows), but from the rantings of Dostoevsky's hero in "Notes from the Underground" (near the end of the eighth section of Part One). Dostoevsky himself had in mind the image of harmony in the writings of the French Utopian Socialist François Fourier (1772–1837).

"universal space": Bely uses *mirovóe prostránstvo*, which the German *Weltraum* translates almost perfectly. It contains the idea of the space of the universe, even outer space.

"A Semite": Throughout this paragraph, as earlier (see page 318), Semite is deleted in the two Soviet editions of the novel.

Helsingfors: The Finnish capital, Helsinki. Until the proclamation of Finnish independence in December, 1917, the Grand Duchy of Finland was part of the Russian Empire and the official name of the city was the Swedish Helsingfors.

Kaigorodov: The noted Russian botanist Dmitry Nikiforovich Kaigorodov (1846–1924) wrote widely on Russian forests, flowers, mushroom hunting, birds, and butterflies. Beginning in 1888, he published in the Petersburg daily newspaper *Novoe vremya* a regular column and occasional bulletins on the nature and seasons in Petersburg and its immediate surroundings (see also page 301). The book Apollon Apollonovich refers to is Kaigorodov's famous *From the Kingdom of the Birds* (*Iz tsarstva pernatykh*, 1892).

"a gloomy building," etc.: Presumably the University (see map). On October 1, a mass meeting of workers and students (2000 people) took place at the Polytechnical Institute. It was followed by an even larger meeting (more than 5000) at the Mining Institute; finally, on October 5, a mass meeting was held at the University which was attended by more than 12,000 people. (*Birzhevye vedomosti*, in its issue of October 7 (20), 1905, wrote that such mass meetings had been held at the University every day from September 30 to October 6.) These unprecedented demonstrations were widely reported in the press, especially the mass meeting at the University.

"A surprise law of August 27, 1905, granted autonomy to the universities. Irresistible outside pressure and the broad interpretation put on this loosely worded enactment by university authorities (now elected by academic corporations) turned the lecture halls into public forums where freedom of speech and of assembly blossomed immune from police intervention. Revolutionary oratory flowing from the rostrums deserted by the professors inflamed the imagination of eager audiences in which university students mingled with government officials, tradesmen, artisans, factory workers, soldiers, *starry-eyed society matrons*, housewives, and even children" (Florinsky, II, p. 1176; italics ours).

"A bad smell hung in the air": This sentence was cut from the two Soviet editions of the novel.

"gray coat": "The *Gorodovóis* or policemen are clad in a black uniform with green facings, the officers in grey" (Baedeker, p. 101).

Ivanov, Puzanov: Ivan Ivanovich Ivanov is the Russian equivalent of Everyman; Puzanov is a comic name suggesting a pot belly; they betoken the spread of revolutionary unrest to every element of Russian society, even those normally identified as supporters of the regime. The merchants in Russia formed a very distinct class. The wealthiest were included in the "first guild," established in 1724 when Peter the Great divided the urban population of Russia into three groups or "guilds." This system was revised in the 1785 Charter of the Cities when the urban population was divided into six groups. The merchants constituted the second of these groups and this merchant group was further subdivided into three "guilds," with the wealthiest merchants in the first.

"Bodies . . . everywhere," etc.: In its report on the October 5 mass meeting at the University, *Birzhevye vedomosti* (October 7 (20), 1905) noted that the crowd had become so large that the meeting broke up into groups which filled every available lecture room and auditorium.

"Strike": "One speaker after another, primarily workers, mounted the lecture podium. The words 'political strike' were in the air and escaped the lips of almost every speaker." (*Birzhevye vedomosti*, October 7 (20), 1905, on the October 5 mass meeting. The newspaper reported that the meeting lasted until after midnight.)

"the glittering bridge": The "temporary" (although it stood on the spot for decades) Dvortsovy or Palace Bridge (see map) which led from Peter (or the Senate) Square to Vasilievsky Island. This bridge-on-boats was later replaced by the new Palace Bridge, slightly to the west of the Winter Palace.

"the enigmatic Horseman": Standing in the center of Peter Square is the most famous monument of Petersburg, the equestrian statue of Peter the Great, known as the Bronze Horseman from Pushkin's long poem of that title ("Mednyi vsadnik"). "The Tzar, riding up a rocky slope,

has his face turned to the Nevá, and points with his right hand towards
the scene of his labours. The horse is balanced on its hind-legs and tail,
while its hoofs trample on a writhing snake. The statue is 16½ ft. high.
The sculptor *E. M. Falconet* (1716–91) made the model in 1769 and
supervised the work of casting it (1775). . . . The monument was un-
veiled on August 7, 1782, and cost 425,000 rb." (Baedeker, p. 108).
Catherine the Great commissioned the monument, in which the Tsar is
crowned with a laurel wreath. The abortive Decembrist uprising (see
page 312) took place in this square, around the monument. (The square
is now known as Decembrist Square.)

"Finnish granite": The pedestal for the Bronze Horseman is an enormous
block of Finnish granite "46 ft. long, 19½ ft. wide, and 16½ ft. high"
(Baedeker, p. 108). This great rock was known to the peasants in the
area where it was found as the "thunder stone" because it had supposedly been split by lightning. According to legend, Peter used to
mount the stone to observe the building of his city in the distance.

This long section beginning with "Russia, you are like a steed" and
concluding with "Arise, oh Sun!" is the only extended passage in the
entire novel in which Bely made not a single change when he revised
the 1916 text. That is indicative of how important the passage was to
him, and how carefully he crafted it.

This prophetic meditation on Russia's destiny deliberately recalls the
following lines from the second part of Pushkin's "Bronze Horseman,"
which precede the description of Evgeny's challenge to the statue (see
page 334): "Where are you galloping, proud steed, and where will
you set down your hooves? Oh, mighty master of fate! Was it not thus
that you, on the very brink of the abyss on high, reared up Russia with
your iron bridle?" Here both Bely and Pushkin raise the central problem posed by Peter and his Westernizing innovations for generations
of Russian intellectuals: had Peter, by opening his window to the
West, detached Russia from her native traditions ("soil," the Russian
póchva), divided her in two (the peasants on the one hand and the new
Westernized elite on the other), and set her on an unknown course
which would inevitably lead to ruin and destruction? This "Westernizing" decision has been called the first true Russian revolution (to be
sure, many historians now dispute this, but it was a common notion in
Bely's day), and Peter Russia's first great revolutionary. The "arisen
Peter" will later call the revolutionary Dudkin "my son."

"bronze": The title of Pushkin's long poem "Mednyi vsadnik" has traditionally been translated into English as "The Bronze Horseman," although the adjective *médnyi* properly means "copper." We have decided to preserve this translation, but readers should be aware that some
of the novel's symbolism (the play on things "coppery") in later
chapters may be obscured as a result. Bronze (*brónza*, or *brónzovyi* in
the adjectival form) is, of course, an alloy of copper and tin.

Nizhny (or Nizhny-Novgorod), Vladimir, and Uglich are towns northeast of (and much older than) Moscow. They are rich in events and
associations in medieval Russian history. Bely seems to have forgotten

that Vladimir is situated high on a bluff overlooking the Klyazma River.

"yellow hordes of Asians": Russians have always felt that by serving as a buffer between Asia and Europe, they spared Western nations the devastation and enslavement the Mongol Hordes visited on medieval Russia. Late in the nineteenth century there was much talk of the "Yellow Peril" (see p. 327). Vladimir Solovyov's poem "Panmongolism" (1894) predicted a new invasion of Russia by Asiatic hordes as retribution for Russia's "sins." This poem, as well as the concluding portion of Solovyov's *Three Conversations* (1899–1900), an apocalyptic tale entitled "A Short Story of the Antichrist," exerted a powerful pull on Bely's fervid imagination, with its account of the "final days," when worldwide conflicts between the races would usher in the Second Coming of Christ.

Tsushima; Kalka: For those ready to see evidence of the Yellow Peril everywhere and apocalypse around the corner, the terrible defeat of the Russian Navy in the Straits of Tsushima on May 27, 1905 (New Style) could only confirm their worst fears. The Japanese annihilated a large Russian squadron in a few hours, thereby creating the impression that Imperial Japan was a world power to be reckoned with.

The battle on the river Kalka (1223), in which the invading Mongols (also known as Tartars) crushed a Russian army and its Cuman allies, and then executed many captive Russian princes, must have produced a similar impression on the medieval Russian mind. (Florinsky, I, p. 55, notes that to the Old Russian chroniclers, this event in particular and the Mongols in general were seen as an emanation of the Unclean Spirit, i.e., the Devil.) The disastrous defeat was just the prelude to the great Mongol invasion and the subsequent conquest of Russia.

Kulikovo Field: On September 8, 1380, a Russian force led by Grand Prince Dmitry of Moscow routed the Mongols under Khan Mamai in a great battle on Kulikovo Field, on the River Don. The distinguished nineteenth-century historian Sergei Solovyov (father of the philosopher) called this first major victory of Russian arms over the Mongols "a sign of the triumph of Europe over Asia," and the battle has been seen as marking the beginning of the end of the so-called Tartar yoke. Actually, the Mongols effectively maintained their control of Russia until well into the fifteenth century. In the apocalyptic terms of this passage, the invocation of Kulikovo Field indicates that the narrator awaits the end of yet another cycle of Russian history and the beginning of a new one signalling Russia's rebirth.

"the two goddesses above the arch": Presumably the figures of Justice and Piety atop the arch connecting the buildings of the Senate and the Holy Synod on Peter Square. There are also two winged female "genii" on the facade of the arch.

"Mongol mugs": The Japanese delegation to formalize the peace treaty between Russia and Japan was then in Petersburg. (See page 329.)

Kolpino: "As soon as the immediate environs of St. Petersburg are left behind us, the scenery becomes dreary and desolate. . . . 24 V. [versts; Kolpino is approximately 3½ miles south of Petersburg] *Kólpino*, a town of 20,200 inhab., situated on both banks of the Izhóra, and containing an iron-foundry belonging to the Admiralty" (Baedeker, pp. 261–262).

"kicked out": Because of famine and the depressed state of the rural economy, thousands of peasants had fled to join the urban proletariat. A common method of getting rid of such workers who had become too radical was to fire them summarily and order them back to their villages.

Morzhov, the porter: "*Dvórniks* or yard-porters . . . combine the functions of the French concierge, the American chore-man, the English hall-porter, and a subordinate police-official" (Baedeker, p. 101). The name Morzhov is comic because it is derived from the word *morzh* ("walrus") and also because it suggests an obscene Russian expression.

"a bottle appeared," etc.: Shoemakers and cobblers are traditionally drunkards in Russian literature. The name Bessmertny means "immortal."

"Styopka kept talking," etc.: This conversation and the character of Styopka (also referred to by his formal given name Stepan) are among the few items that connect *Petersburg* with *The Silver Dove* (see page 315), where a dissident Russian religious sect awaits the birth of a Savior to one of its members, the carpenter's wife Matryona. The 1916 version, however, is more detailed at this point: much of the plot of *The Silver Dove* is referred to, its hero Daryalsky is mentioned by name, and Styopka conceals the fact that he has attended the orgiastic rites of the sect ("the Doves"), where he picks up his apocalyptic fervor and the appropriate imagery.

"his little booklet": In the 1916 edition Styopka gives the title of the "little booklet." It is Tolstoy's first published play, *The First Distiller* (1886), a dramatization of his temperance-tract story "The Imp and the Crust." The first distiller is the Devil himself. The semiliterate Styopka never quite knows what to call printed material; thus he resorts to *tsidúli* for the revolutionary leaflets being passed out at the Kolpino factory where he worked. This is a substandard form of *tsidúly*, which in Bely's time meant "notes" or "short letters," and which in earlier usage had more official overtones (e.g., written exchanges between provincial governors). We render it as "notations" a few paragraphs earlier in an effort to suggest Styopka's misusage.

"the souls of the slain," etc.: Styopka means the souls of the thousands of Russian seamen who drowned at the battle of Tsushima and who thus died without benefit of the last rites of the Church.

"The Chinese are putting up some heathen temple or other": No such building was being erected in or near Petersburg in 1905. However, between 1909–1915 a Buddhist temple was built (according to the plans of the architect G. V. Baranovsky) in Staraya Derevnya, a suburb of

Petersburg, at the initiative and with the support of the Dalai Lama. The project provoked heated controversy in the Russian press.

Both this "piece of writing" and the final paragraphs of this chapter were cut unmercifully in the two Soviet editions of the novel, to remove all references to Solovyov, a new infant, and the Second Coming of Christ. Bely missed "prophesying" the death of Stalin (1953) by only one year, and the great Sino-Soviet quarrel by not many more.

Church of Philadelphia: "A city of the Roman province of Asia. It was the seat of one of the 'Seven Churches of Asia,' addressed in Rev. 2–3, and was there commended for its faithfulness and given promises for the future (3:7–13). The circumstances in which this Church was founded are unknown" (*Oxford Dictionary of the Christian Church*, p. 1060).

Solovyov and Sophia: See note on pages 315–16.

"There's a certain prophecy," etc.: Styopka's "prophecy" and his previous speech are a mixture of Biblical imagery and the half-baked apocalyptic notions that were in the air at the time in Russia. But his language is so elliptical and so illiterate that not all specific referents can be confidently determined. It is clear, though, that "the crown" refers to the Japanese victory in the war with Russia; and that the "Prooshan Imperor" is Kaiser Wilhelm II who coined the phrase "the Yellow Peril" (*die gelbe Gefahr*) to describe the rising Japan as a major Far Eastern power after she had defeated China in the war of 1895. This was widely and favorably reported on in the Russian press, and met with great sympathy among many Russian intellectuals. Vladimir Solovyov saluted the statement in a well-known poem of 1900, "The Dragon (To Siegfried)," where the Dragon of the Nibelungen legends (and Wagner's setting of them) becomes China, and the new Siegfried is the militarist but Christian Kaiser, heir to the Crusaders, for he alone "understood: the cross and the sword are one."

"Even so, come, Lord Jesus!": The last sentence of the next to the last verse in the Book of Revelation.

Chapter the Third

The epigraph is taken from stanza fifteen (lines 6–9) of Pushkin's "Ezersky." In quoting line 6, Bely's memory either betrayed him or he used a text that is no longer considered standard; the accepted version now reads "Although he was no military man" (*"Khot' chelovék on ne voénnyi"*). Every edition of *Petersburg* but the first contains a misprint in the second line of the epigraph: "But" (*No*) instead of "No" (*Ne*). Don Juan, a demon, and a gypsy are all characters in Pushkin's own works.

A HOLIDAY: October 5 was the Saint's Day of the Tsarevich Alexei, heir to the throne. *Novoe vremya* (October 7 [20], 1905) reported that Petersburg was decorated with flags for the holiday and that special services were held in all the city's churches. On October 4, according to the same newspaper, a review of the Imperial Guard was held in Petersburg, in the presence of the Emperor himself, by way of preview of the next day's festivities. On October 5, the Emperor was back at Peterhof, his summer residence outside the city. Bely seems to have merged these two events into one day.

"all aglitter and ashimmer": Yet another Gogol reference, and of a peculiar kind: in the story "Viy" the naked waternymph who appears to the "philosopher" Khoma Brut is described in exactly these words (Bely: *blesk i trépet*; Gogol: *iz bléska i trépeta*).

"smart carriage": Bely uses the word *likhách*, which Baedeker (p. 90) describes as "superior one-horse cabs with pneumatic tyres, [which] are not bound by the tariff and usually charge 1 rb. for a short drive." The word is derived from the adjective *likhói*, meaning dashing or jaunty. *Likhách* itself, now obsolete in these meanings, could apply either to the carriage or to the horse and driver.

"the staircase": Apollon Apollonovich is ascending the magnificent Grand (or Ambassadorial or Jordan) Staircase which led to the Imperial State apartments in the Winter Palace, and was used for great ceremonial and state occasions. Visitors to the Hermitage in Leningrad (which now occupies the Winter Palace itself, as well as the former museum premises) enter the museum collections by this staircase.

Count Witte: In the 1916 edition he is not identified by name (because of the censorship), but is called Count Doublevé (French for "W"; see page 301). The character of Sergei Witte (1849–1915), who numbered both conservatives and liberals among his close friends, has long puzzled historians. He served as one of the closest advisors to the reactionary Alexander III; for years only Pobedonostsev rivalled his influence both on Alexander and his son Nicholas II. He held the powerful office of Minister of Finance from 1892 until August, 1903, when he was relegated to the honorary position of president of the Council of Ministers because of his vehement criticism of Russia's Far Eastern policy. In the summer of 1905 he was recalled from semiretirement to head the Russian peace delegation to the Portsmouth (New Hampshire) conference convened to end the Russo-Japanese War (see page 329).

In September, 1905, Theodore Roosevelt, who met Witte at Portsmouth, wrote: "I suppose Witte is the best man that Russia could have at the head of her affairs at present. . . . I cannot say that I liked him, for I thought his bragging and bluster not only foolish but shockingly vulgar when compared with the gentlemanly restraint of the Japanese. Moreover, he struck me as a very selfish man, totally without high ideals" (cited in Florinsky, II, pp. 1260–1261). Yet in the crisis of 1905 he was felt by all sides to be the one man capable of saving the Romanov dynasty, and he persuaded Nicholas to sign the liberal Manifesto of October 17, which he had written. Nicholas never forgave him. Witte's career ended in April, 1906, when he resigned all his offices.

Apollon Apollonovich, as the protege of von Plehve, would hate Witte, who was von Plehve's implacable enemy and rival.

"a certain treaty": The Portsmouth Treaty, which ended the Russo-Japanese War. Witte, the head of the Russian delegation, managed to win favorable terms for his side. He was rewarded on his return to Petersburg in September, 1905, by being made a Count. His reputation and influence were then at their peak. One may suppose that Apollon Apollonovich, like Witte's other enemies, called him the "Count of Portsmouth" or "Count Half-Sakhalin" (Russia had to cede one-half of the island to Japan in the settlement).

Peace had been declared at Portsmouth on August 23 (September 5, New Style), but final arrangements had been made only on October 1, as Nicholas' Proclamation of October 5 (signed at Peterhof) announcing the Treaty and the official conclusion of hostilities specified. The Russian public read the Imperial Proclamation in the newspapers of October 7 (20).

"there": The 1916 edition specifies that the review was held on the Marsovo Pole (the Field of Mars), which stretches to the southeast of the Marble Palace as far as the Moika (see map). Such reviews were one of the most spectacular sights of the capital. "The mounts of each of the regiments of the household cavalry are all of one colour (Horse Guards black, Gatchina Hussars dapple-gray, Chevalier Guards chestnut, etc.)" (Baedeker, p. 116).

"the steel bristle:" A quote from Pushkin's well-known saber-rattling poem "To the Slanderers of Russia" ("Klevetnikam Rossii," 1831).

OFF TO A MASS MEETING: The 1922 text actually says "At a Mass Meeting" (Na mítinge); the 1916 version contains the correct Na míting: "Off to a Mass Meeting."

"My devachanic friend": In Man and His Bodies Besant writes: "Devachan or Devaloka, the land of the Gods, the happy or blessed land, as some translate it . . . is a specially guarded state, into which positive evil is not allowed to intrude, the blissful resting place of man in which he peacefully assimilates the fruits of his physical life" (Ninth edition, 1947, p. 66). Devachan to theosophists is a part of the "mind world."

Cohen's Theorie der Erfahrung: Hermann Cohen (1842–1918) was the founder and head of the Marburg School of Neo-Kantianism, whose best-known latter-day advocate is perhaps Ernst Cassirer (1874–1945). Cohen's theories of logic were rather well known in Russia toward the end of the nineteenth century; in their social aspects, they figured prominently in the views of the so-called Legal Marxists. For two centuries, the University of Marburg had attracted young Russians. Cohen's most famous Russian student was Boris Pasternak; for an account, see Pasternak's autobiographical Safe Conduct. The full title of the work mentioned in the text is Kants Theorie der Erfahrung (Kant's Theory of Experience, 1871).

Comtianism, Kantianism: Only the vowel differentiates Kant (Kant) from Comte (Kont) in Russian. Amusingly enough, this confusion was accidentally foreshadowed in Bely's first collection of essays (Simvo-

lízm, 1910): the first item in the list of misprints specifies that "Kant" should be corrected to "Kont."

Mill's *Logic*: John Stuart Mill's (1806–1873) influential *System of Logic* was published in two volumes in 1843. It soon became known in Russia, where, along with certain other of his writings, it exerted a considerable influence on social thought.

Sigwart: Christoph von Sigwart (1830–1904), a professor at Tübingen University, who was in some respects a follower of John Stuart Mill (the favorite philosopher of Apollon Apollonovich). His books included a study of Giordano Bruno (also admired by Apollon Apollonovich), but his most important work was a two-volume *Logic* (*Logik*, 1873 and 1878).

"professor of the philosophy of law": In the early 1860s Pobedonostsev began his long career as a jurist, and coauthored the reform of the law courts.

"Gazing at the rays . . .": The opening lines of A. A. Oppel's romance "You forgot" ("Zabyli vy"), set to a poem (1888) by Pavel Alexeyevich Kozlov (1841–1891). It was one of the most popular Russian songs of the late nineteenth and early twentieth century. The Angel intentionally changes (or misremembers) the second line, which reads not "You stood," but "We stood." In the song a woman "who swore to love the poet to the grave" fails to carry out "her sacred vow." The final (third) stanza reads: "But death is near, near too my grave. / When I die, my voice, like the quiet rustle of the grass / Will sound and will say to you with melancholy: / He lived only for you . . . and you forgot him!"

The Queen of Spades: See page 313. Judging by the rhythm of the "tu-tum: tum, tum" etc. the Angel is humming the first bars of the agitated orchestral opening to the Winter Canal scene in the opera. Like so many other of Tchaikovsky's "divine harmonies," it was fated to end up as an American pop song, entitled "I Must Go Where the Wild Goose Goes."

Hermann: The obsessed hero of Tchaikovsky's opera *The Queen of Spades* (see page 313).

"you will not be at the ball": Likhutin's precautions may also be prompted by schoolboy memories of the description of balls in Pushkin's *Eugene Onegin*, Canto One, XXIX: "there is no safer spot for declarations / and for the handing of a letter. / O you, respected husbands! / I'll offer you my services" (*Pushkin's Eugene Onegin*, trans. by Vladimir Nabokov, Volume 1, Princeton, 1964, p. 109).

"I will go," etc.: With her imagination fixated by Tchaikovsky's opera, the Angel's defiance may in part result from the fact that one of the opera's scenes takes place at a masquerade ball where the hero and heroine arrange to meet for what proves to be a fatal rendezvous.

"a fist smashed the dressing table in two": Perhaps a parody of the reaction of another husband to the defiance and the adulterous behavior of his wife, namely Pierre in Tolstoy's *War and Peace* (Book Four, Chapter Six), who smashes the marble top of a large table by flinging it onto the floor.

Chapter the Fourth

The epigraph is the opening line of one of Pushkin's most personal lyrics (1833; untitled), which was never published during his lifetime. It exists in several English translations.

THE SUMMER GARDEN (see map): This public park on the Palace Embankment was laid out by Peter's command in 1712, and "forms a long rectangle about 37 acres in area" (Baedeker, p. 116), "with avenues of crow-haunted shade trees (imported elms and oaks) and noseless statues of Greek deities (made in Italy)" (*Pushkin's Eugene Onegin*, trans. by Vladimir Nabokov, Volume 2, Princeton, 1964, p. 41). Tchaikovsky's opera *The Queen of Spades* opens there.

"The statues each stood hidden beneath boards": Because of the damp climate in Petersburg and the rapid changes in temperature, the seventy-odd marble statues by eighteenth-century Venetian artists which adorn the Garden are displayed only in the summer; at other times they are encased in wooden boxes.

"that garden had grown emptier," etc.: In the eighteenth century the Summer Garden was considerably larger than in Bely's day or the present. It had "a hothouse for exotic plants, an aviary for rare birds, a grotto laced with mother-of-pearl and a 'hall for glorious celebrations'. . . . Peter the Great was especially fond of the labyrinth with dozens of fountains. . . . The storm and flood of 1777 caused great damage to the Summer Garden. Its pavilions, arbours and fountains were destroyed. . . . The ruins and debris were cleared up, but the buildings and fountains were not reconstructed" (Y. Doroshinskaya and V. Kruchina, *Leningrad. Guidebook*, Moscow, no date, pp. 172–173). Gradually the Field of Mars encroached on some of its area.

"Peter himself had planted this garden," etc.: Bely drew the entire description in these paragraphs, down to the smallest details, from Chapters Three and Four of M. I. Pylyaev's *Staryi Peterburg* (Petersburg, 1887), a delightfully whimsical and informative compilation of the most varied facts and legends about the life, people, customs, and places of interest in the capital during the first hundred years of its existence.

The description of the "musicians in bright red huntsmen's garb" refers to the famous "horn orchestra" which provided music for festivities in the Summer Garden in the eighteenth century. There is a picture of the players and their bizarre instruments on page 75 of Pylyaev's book.

"Peter's small house": The Small House (*Domik*) or Summer Palace of Peter the Great is "an unpretentious two-storied building erected in 1711" (Baedeker, p. 116) in the "Dutch style" by Trezzini. It stands in the Summer Garden, hard by the Fontanka, a river which took its name—*fontán* means fountain—from the fact that it supplied the water for the Garden's many fountains.

Solovyova: See pages 315–16.

"The leaves stirred," etc.: cf. Kaigorodov's description of autumn in Petersburg (see page 301): "In general, the fall of leaves in Petersburg and its near surroundings is ended by October 1. In the gardens, parks and public squares leaves still remain only on poplars, willows, and also on a few larch and shrubs. The landscape has taken on its late-autumn character, and autumn has entered its second and final phase."

"And why Pompadour?": Perhaps in part because the French favorite of Louis XV is mentioned in the monologue of the old Countess in Tchaikovsky's *The Queen of Spades.*

Krafft and Ballet: Two of the most elegant confectioners in the city, Krafft at Italyanskaya No. 10, and Ballet at Nevsky No. 54.

"rust red Palace"; Rastrelli: "The *Imperial Winter Palace*, the imperial winter residence, finished in 1764 from a design by Rastrelli, was partly burned down in 1837 and restored by the beginning of 1839. The building, which is 499 ft. long, 384 ft. wide, and 92 ft. high, is painted a brownish red and faces the Nevá on the N. and the Palace Square on the S." (Baedeker, p. 112).

   Count Bartolommeo Francesco Rastrelli (1700–1771), the chief architect of the Empress Elizabeth (Elizaveta) Petrovna (reigned from 1741–1762), is credited with creating the style known as "Elizabeth's Rococo." In the eighteenth century the palace was painted turquoise blue, as it is again now. Elizabeth could have looked from it at the Neva only in its unfinished state, for she died before the palace was completed and never lived there.

"zemstvo official": This is the only instance where we have followed the practice of the historians and retained the Russian because there is no equivalent phenomenon in English-speaking countries. The term *zémstvo* is derived from *zemlyá* ("earth"), and describes the regional assemblies that were established by an 1864 law by way of promoting more local self-government after the emancipation of the serfs three years earlier. Zemstvos existed on both the district (*uézd*) and province level, spread throughout much of European Russia, and had considerable success in tackling such problems as public health and education, despite constant harassment by higher authorities. They involved the participation of three classes: the nobility, the wealthier towndwellers, and the peasantry, though matters were weighted in favor of the nobility. "Immediately before and during the 1905 Revolution they emerged as a prominent political force on the side of liberalism through the new device of All-Russian Congresses. . . . They had great popularity among the liberals and the professional classes in general, but little appeal outside of them. They were the indispensable element in the process . . . of transforming tsarism into some kind of modern monarchy" (B. H. Sumner, *A Short History of Russia*, New York, 1949, pp. 69–70).

"a professor of statistics": Many professors were active in the drive to establish a liberal party, which began in the summer of 1905 and culminated in the creation of the Constitutional-Democratic Party (the so-called Cadets) in October, 1905.

"the latest banquet": "The liberals, although lacking an agreed program, were in a fighting mood. In October, 1904, the Union of Liberation adopted a threefold plan of action . . . [one of whose points was] to carry on political agitation at banquets organized on the pretext of celebrating the fortieth anniversary of the reformed law courts" (Florinsky, II, p. 1170). Such banquets became a familiar feature of the liberal campaign for a constitution in 1905 as well. "The coming spring": see page 319.

"Who are you . . .?": This quatrain resembles stanzas in Bely's 1908 poem entitled "The Masquerade Ball" ("Maskarad"), included in his verse collection *Ashes* (*Pepel*, 1909). That poem, in which a red domino (death) appears at a masked ball and announces to the guests that they are fated to perish, prefigures the scene in the novel in several particulars. Both episodes may perhaps be related to Edgar Allan Poe's "The Masque of the Red Death."

"his heart racing": Bely uses the expression *serdéchnyi pripádok*, which now means "heart attack." In the early twentieth century, however, the expression was used to cover a gamut of physical sensations, from a shock which made the heart beat faster to an actual heart attack. Apollon Apollonovich does suffer from heart trouble, but he is not having a heart attack here in our modern understanding of the term. We have had to translate the expression in different ways throughout the novel depending on the context.

Taxil, Palladism: Léo Taxil, whose real name was Gabriel Antoine Jogand-Pagès (1854–1907), was among the most notorious and often fined anticlerical writers in France. In 1885 he announced his conversion to Catholicism. He began publishing a series of works "exposing" Freemasonry and in particular the Satanism and devil worship with which he claimed it was closely connected. The most famous of these works was the "memoirs" of "Diana Vaughn," arch-priestess of the "Palladium," supposedly the highest secret order of Masonry. This Palladium involved devil worship; Vaughn, destined to be the spouse of the demon Asmodeus, rebelled against it, clung to virtue, and was tormented by angels and devils until she decided to confess these horrors to the world. The gullible seized on this "exposé" and used it to attack the liberal Masons. In 1896–97, the imposture was revealed; Taxil admitted that he had invented the whole business and that Diana Vaughn was the name of his typist. He was subsequently excommunicated by the Vatican.

A SCANDALOUS UPROAR: Bely uses the word *skandál* (usually translated as "scandal"). Such noisy riotous outbursts regularly disrupt the novels of Dostoevsky, most notably in *The Devils* (or *The Possessed*) during the "benefit" held at the local governor's house.

"glued himself": Russian *prilíp*, a play on the name Lippanchenko (see pages 309–10).

The row of dots preceding this sentence in the 1922 text replaces the section title "The White Domino" of the 1916 edition.

"the metallic Horseman had started up in pursuit": Evgeny, the hapless hero of Pushkin's "The Bronze Horseman," can trace his lineage to an old noble family, but has been reduced to the level of a humble clerk in the huge bureaucracy of the capital, and has lost his young fiancée in the disastrous flood of 1824. As he wanders the city, demented, he passes the statue of Peter the Great—the Bronze Horseman; he raises his fist and curses the emperor who built a city on this accursed site. The Horseman then gallops down from his crag and pursues Evgeny through the streets of the city. As a figure of cosmic retribution, the Bronze Horseman pursues many of the characters in *Petersburg*.

"the islands are on fire": In Dostoevsky's *The Devils*, a fire breaks out in the suburb across the river after the governor's wife's benefit for the young governesses. (It is a case of deliberate arson to "cover" a murder.) In Fyodor Sologub's novel *The Petty Demon* (1907), the masked ball, which has turned into a scandalous riot, is ended when the building in which it is being held is put to the torch by the mad hero, Peredonov.

Kazan Cathedral: Built in imitation of St. Peter's in Rome, the Kazan Cathedral (see map), with a large semicircular square opening on the Nevsky, was the site of a large student demonstration which was broken up by Cossacks, with heavy casualties, on March 4, 1901.

"The convulsive twitchings," etc.: Despite vigorous efforts for its abolition, the death penalty (by hanging) still existed for acts of terrorism against the state. The morning issue of *Birzhevye vedomosti* for October 14 (27), 1905, contained a lengthy article on the movement for the abolition of the death penalty throughout the Western world and Russia. The article also contained excerpts from an interview with Senator I. Ya. Foinitsky who stated his strong opposition to capital punishment for any crime.

"once the liberal son of a priest": Many of the most famous *raznochíntsy* (see page 306) of the nineteenth century were the sons of priests. The editor has followed the usual course of becoming a liberal, but has then turned to reactionary politics.

"a mirror": In Dostoevsky's *The Double*, whenever Golyadkin's double seems to appear he is usually emerging from a doorway or from what the "real" Golyadkin takes to be a mirror.

"the province of Ploshchegorsk": An invented province with a comically oxymoronic name: *plóskii* (whence *plóshche*) means "flat," while *górskii* (whence *gorsk*) means "mountain, highland." It also resembles the standard Russian word for "plateau" (*ploskogór'e*), but suggests that the plateau is even flatter (*plóshche* is the comparative degree of the adjective *ploskii*).

"These are critical times": Added from the 1916 edition. By cutting the line Bely made Apollon Apollonovich's "Yes, you are right" meaningless.

"Suddenly everything was illuminated," etc.: During this "dawn of reconciliation" a rosy red or pink color predominates. In *Man and His Bodies* (p. 44) Besant writes "if he [man] feels love, rose-red thrills through it [the astral body]."

"pale red:" Every edition of the novel contains the neologism *blednokovróvyi* here, which would mean "pale-carpeted," certainly a bizarre color. We presume this to be a misprint (as noted before, many misprints in the 1916 edition were never corrected and appear in every subsequent edition of the novel) for *blednokrovávyi*. Only a check of the original manuscript might clear up this point. (Neither word appears in a list of all the colors used by Bely in his prose fiction, which was compiled by the author's widow, Klavdiya Nikolaevna Bugaeva, in 1944 [the unpublished manuscript is in the archives of the Saltykov-Shchedrin Library in Leningrad].)

"*One hundred million?* Or more?": "According to the 1897 census, the total population of Russia, exclusive of Finland, was 125.6 million. . . . The census data were published in 1905, eight years after the census was taken" (Florinsky, II, p. 1235).

"From the cold cliffs of Finland to fiery Colchis": A line from Pushkin's "To the Slanderers of Russia" (1831). Colchis was the Greek name for the east coast of the Black Sea.

The first four lines (misquoted) of a well-known Pushkin lyric of 1834 (untitled). Pushkin seems to have written it in June, 1834, when he tried unsuccessfully to secure permission to retire from the civil service and move to the country.

"Toward him ran," etc.: Compare the conduct of Raskolnikov in *Crime and Punishment*, Part One, Chapter IV, when he saves a young girl from a would-be seducer.

Chapter the Fifth

The epigraph is the four opening lines of the elegy which Lensky, a young poet (or, as T. S. Eliot would say, a young man who wrote verse), composes the night before his fatal duel with his neighbor and former friend Onegin in *Eugene Onegin*, Canto Six, stanza XXII. (There is a small error in Bely's citation of the third line.) Here Pushkin pokes fun at the Romantic cliches of his time; yet when set to music by Tchaikovsky in the opera *Eugene Onegin*, the elegy became one of the most famous tenor arias in Romantic music. Bely parodically compounds this nice paradox by applying the lines to Nikolai's ridiculous situation.

"some kind of giant," etc.: The description evokes Peter the Great, who was a giant of a man (nearly seven feet tall), with a small nose and mustache. He loved to spend long hours drinking, smoking, and carousing with simple seamen whom he always invited to state receptions and banquets. He was no mean sailor himself.

"A–baaate," etc.: The opening lines of one of the most beautiful songs—"Doubt" ("Somnenie," 1838)—by Mikhail Glinka (1804–1857), set to a poem by the all but forgotten Nestor Vasilievich Kukolnik (1809–1868). Several fine recordings have been made of it, perhaps the best by the late Jennie Tourel.

"a hulk—of stone": The giant of the previous section, Peter the Great, is now associated with the Stone Commendatore, that emblem of retribution and doom, of the Don Juan legend. A huge stone funerary figure of the man the Don has killed, he leaves his grave at the Don's defiant challenge and drags him down to Hell. Like Molière, Mozart, and others, Pushkin made use of the legend, in his short play *The Stone Guest*.

"the psychological method": This grotesque early version of encounter therapy has an obvious parodic connection with the meetings between the police inspector Porfiry Petrovich and Raskolnikov in *Crime and Punishment*. Earlier in this section Bely has alluded to another Dostoevsky novel as well: the conversation between Ivan Karamazov and the bastard Smerdyakov about their parentage in *The Brothers Karamazov*.

"on a September night I too," etc.: The autobiographical aspect of the novel derives from the fortnight Bely spent in Petersburg in September, 1906, when he was at the height of his painful involvement with Lyubov Dmitrievna Blok, the wife of his best friend, the poet Alexander Blok. In the chapters "Domino" and "Skvoznyaki prinevskogo vetra" ("Gusts of Neva Wind") in the third volume of his memoirs (*Mezhdu dvukh revolyutsii*, Leningrad, 1934, pp. 89–100) Bely describes how he had aimlessly wandered the streets of Petersburg in virtual mental collapse and had often contemplated suicide. He writes that he not only planned to appear before Blok's wife wearing a red domino, but that he actually sat in a cheap restaurant on the Millionnaya, talking to a "sweating coachman" (paralleled by the scene in Chapter One of *Petersburg*: "Why Don't You Keep Quiet!"). In the final installment of his memoirs, commenting on his work on *Petersburg*, Bely confirmed the connection: "I must say that I worked intensively on the subjective experiences of the senator's son, into which I put something from my own previous personal experiences" (*Literaturnoe nasledstvo*, Vol. 27–28, Moscow, 1937, p. 454).

"The square": The Peter Square, bounded on the east by the Admiralty, on the south by a garden behind which looms St. Isaac's Cathedral, and on the west by the buildings of the Senate and Synod (see also page 325).

"Fiery pigments," etc.: This verse fragment—with "pigments" (*kráski*) changed to "grains" (*zërna*)—appears as the epigraph to the sixth section of Marina Tsvetaeva's seven-part poem-cycle "To Mayakovsky" ("Mayakovskomu," 1930). Tsvetaeva does not identify Bely as the author, but no doubt he is.

"slipped the messenger twenty copecks": "*Commissionnaires . . .* The charge for an ordinary message or parcel is 20 cop., for long distances 40 cop.; at night double those rates" (Baedeker, p. 93).

"blob . . . bounce about": At one point, Porfiry Petrovich, the police interrogator in *Crime and Punishment* who "works on" Raskolnikov, is described as a bouncing ball.

Lessing: We have had to supply this last name in order to hint at the word play several lines below. The child feels himself becoming spherical, like the little fat man, while his German governess grows smaller and smaller. The child is "zeroing–zeroing–zerooo . . ." (in Russian: "*nólilos'–nóllilos'–nolll . . .*"; *nol'* means zero). *Karolina Karlovna* "*kárlilas': kárllilas', karlll.*" *Karlilas'*, etc., is a morphologically plausible neologism formed from the noun *kárlitsa*("female dwarf"), which would be identical in sound with the nonexistent infinitive form *kárlit'sya* ("to become dwarfish").

"convivial bowl": There is no English equivalent for the term *bratína*, a kind of communal bowl or pitcher, usually of wood, used in peasant households in old Russia. The paperweight is an appropriate object for the senator's study: one of the articles of ultraconservative faith was a belief in the absolute devotion of the Russian common people to the Tsar.

"just you wait!": This is one of the rare instances where Bely added something significant to the 1922 revision of the earlier text. The "just you wait!" (*uzhó* in Russian) is the defiant challenge (*uzhó tebé!*) that Evgeny flings at the Bronze Horseman in the Pushkin poem (see page 334). The typesetter of the 1922 text obviously misread the *uzho* for the adverb *uzhé* (already). The misprint was corrected in the 1928 edition.

"the logic of Dharmakirti," etc.: Nikolai (like Bely himself) has read *Nyayabindu; Buddiiskii uchebnik logiki sochinenie Darmakirti i tolkovanie na nego Nyayabindutika sochinenie Darmottary, tibetskii perevod izdal s vvedeniem i primechaniyami F. I. Shcherbatskoi* [*Nyayabindu; Buddhist Treatise on Logic by Dharmakirti and Explanation (Nyayabindutika) by Dharmottara; Tibetan Translation; ed. with Introduction and Explanation by F. I. Shcherbatskoy*], published in Petersburg by the Academy of Sciences in 1904 as volume VIII of the Bibliotheca Buddhica. (Shcherbatskoy published the Sanskrit original in 1918.) The Nyayabindu of Dharmakirti, with its commentary by Dharmottara, is the only major work of Buddhist medieval (seventh century) logic to survive in the original Sanskrit. When the Huns ravaged the centers of Buddhist learning in India, most manuscripts were destroyed. Therefore, we know them only from Chinese and Tibetan translations. One suspects that Bely, despite his own interest in Buddhism, used the names here as much for their exotically euphonious sound as anything else. (He also mentions this same work in his long poem "The First Encounter" ["Pervoe svidanie," 1921].) Dharmakirti saw three phases in logic: 1) sense perception 2) inference–indirect judgment and 3) syllogism.

THE LAST JUDGMENT: Soviet censorship forced Bely to make drastic cuts and "revisions" throughout this section. Among them, "The Last Judgment" became "Judgment."

"astral journey": Bely uses the term in a theosophical sense. Like many other creative artists of the time (Yeats, for example), Bely took a profound interest in theosophy and knew its writings well. The dreams in the novel in no way conform to any theosophic (or anthroposophic —see page 339) formula, but a few citations from Besant's *Man and His Bodies* might be pertinent here. For the theosophist, the astral body and the astral world are composed of "astral matter"; the more developed the man, the more his astral body can move about freely during sleep and "with immense rapidity at any distance, without causing the least disturbance to the sleeping body on the bed" (p. 52). "When a person 'goes to sleep,' the Ego slips out of the physical body, and leaves it to slumber and so to recuperate itself for the next day's work. The dense body and its etheric double are thus left to their own devices, and to the play of the influences which they attract to themselves by their constitution and habits. Streams of thought-forms from the astral world of a nature congruous with the thought-forms created or harboured by the Ego in his daily life, pass into and out of the dense and etheric brains, and, mingling with the automatic repetitions of vibrations set up in waking consciousness by the Ego, cause the broken and chaotic dreams with which most people are familiar" (pp. 29–30). This might also be related to Dudkin's belief that "you bring home with you what you have experienced on the streets," the experiences dragging after you "like a tail" (see p. 64 of the novel) or his reaction to his terrible nightmare (see p. 212 of the novel). Compare also the following from Rudolf Steiner's (see page 339) *Knowledge of Higher Worlds and its Attainments* (London, 1963): "Even though these images are faint during life in the physical world, they are none the less present, following the individual as his world of desire, in the way a comet is followed by its tail" (p. 119).

Chronos (or Cronos) was one of the Titans in Greek mythology. He rose against his father Uranus, who had kept his children confined in the nether world after their birth, and castrated him. Chronos, in turn, had been warned that one of his own offspring would overthrow him, so he swallowed them at birth. Zeus, however, was saved by a ruse of his mother and eventually defeated him. The Romans identified Chronos with *Saturn*.

"paradise apples": The Russian *ráiskie yábloki* can be read both as the apples of paradise and as a variety of small apple (compare the English "paradise apple" too: "*Hort.* A dwarf type (*Malus sylvestris paradisiaca*) of the common apple, used primarily as grafting stock"; "paradise" in *Webster's New International Dictionary of the English Language*, Second Edition, Unabridged).

Turanian: A member of any division of a supposed nomadic people who preceded the Aryans in Europe and Asia but were neither Aryan nor Semitic. As an adjective it is applied loosely to a "family" of languages of Asiatic origin which are also neither Aryan nor Semitic. In Steiner's anthroposophy (see note headed "There was no Earth," below), logic was invented during the periods when the Mongols and Turanians were predominant.

Saturn: To the Romans the god Chronos. As a planet it shines with yellowish light. It was the most remote planet known in the ancient world. In astrology it is the earthy, masculine planet, and symbolizes *coldness* and *dryness*, as well as melancholy (hence the adjective "saturnine"). In alchemy it is *lead* (compare the frequent use of "leaden atmosphere" in the novel).

"There was no Earth," etc.: This and the following paragraph were completely cut from the two Soviet editions (1928 and 1935) of the novel.

Until now we have largely ignored the anthroposophical dimension of the novel. Bely, like Vasily Kandinsky, Paul Klee, Christian Morgenstern, Bruno Walter, and, most recently, Saul Bellow, was an adherent of anthroposophy, an offshoot of theosophy founded by Rudolf Steiner (1861–1925), who elaborated a "scientific method" for studying the world of the spirit. Bely spent several years as a member of the Steiner entourage and his "conversion" to this "science of the spirit" coincided with the writing of *Petersburg*. But he was not writing an anthroposophical tract, and not even the most intimate knowledge of anthroposophical teachings will provide a definitive explanation of his novel. He borrowed images from Steiner's writings, and occasionally made use of some of its general principles, but, as with Russian literature, the myth of Petersburg, and other sources, Bely bent everything to his own purposes. The metaphors he created to describe the spiritual world are very much his own, as is the vision of history.

Still, the influence of Steiner is particularly evident in Nikolai's dream. Of anthroposophy in general, the *Oxford Dictionary of the Christian Church* (p. 61) writes: "A religious system evolved by R. Steiner from neo-Indian theosophy, but placing man instead of God in its centre. It aims at leading man by a certain discipline of 'concentration' and 'meditation' towards an 'intuition' in which the lower ego receives the vision of the higher self. Anthroposophy teaches a highly elaborated and fantastic doctrine of the origin of the world, the various epochs of mankind, the 'sun being' ('Sonnenwesen') Christ, reincarnation, and 'Karma.' "

A belief in reincarnation and metamorphosis (with the notion of multiple bodies: the physical, the etheric, and the astral, a simplification of theosophy's teaching of seven bodies to three) is an essential part of anthroposophy. This figures obviously in Nikolai's dream. The second essential principle of Steiner involves an infinite evolution of "body" in which "spirit" is ever more developed and refined. Here Steiner drew not only on Indian religion, but on the writings of Ernst Heinrich Haeckel (1834–1919), who believed in the essential unity of organic and inorganic nature, and thought that the development of the individual recapitulates the development of the entire species. Steiner took this quite literally. Life and Death form a circle, the "wheel of birth," in which birth opens into "life" and Death into "other life." As we pass through the evolutionary spiral or gyre of the reincarnation cycle, we gain experience. The goal of life becomes the development of one's spiritual faculties to their utmost.

Steiner's cosmology taught that Saturn was the first stage of cosmic evolution. (This Saturn is not to be confused with the present planet which was also, for Steiner, undergoing its own evolution.) In the beginning—the Saturn stage—the earth was fire and the physical body began. To each of the stages he assigned an animal or insect; the butterfly belongs to the first. In the second embodiment (Sun), earth is Air and the etheric body appears. The bee belongs here. In the third stage (Moon), earth is Water, the body astral; this is the fish. In the last stage (Earth), land emerges from water and the Ego appears; this stage is the snake. Then the cycle begins anew with the Saturn stage (now called Venus). And so the cycle moves in seven stages of cosmic evolution, manifesting greater and greater spirit, each stage recapitulating the former, but on a higher level. (See especially the fourth chapter, "The Evolution of the World and Man," in Steiner's *An Outline of Occult Science*, first published, in German, in 1909.)

Thus Nikolai's dream draws on two major sources: 1) the images generated by the novel itself, and 2) a freely interpreted vision of Steiner's theory of the development of the spirit, imaged here as a journey, or as the cycle of spirit after death in which all human bodies except the physical pass on to higher worlds. (Steiner believed that once we leave the physical body and enter the astral world, the sense of time is lost: one second can contain all of time or can contain a moment expanded forever.) When we enter the astral realm, the body becomes incandescent (much like the robe here). Motion goes outward, around the stars, but in the direction of Saturn. As the etheric body floats into space, we sift experiences in search of moral consequences. We "age" ourselves so that when reincarnated, our spirit will be on a higher level. We begin with our most recent experiences and go backwards to childhood (as happens in the dream, where time moves backwards), until we enter, as pure spirit, into cosmic levels and establish communion with all stars, spirit bodies, etc. At this stage the astral body expands, and at the culmination, spirit will absolutely understand the Ego (at this stage the sun is dominant). Yet Ego has a longing for reincarnation, and starts its descent into bodies. It chooses its parents, and is reborn, picking up qualities of both its parents. Also, in various stages we are reincarnated now as a male, now as a female (which may have something to do with the androgynous nature of the major characters).

Chapter the Sixth

The epigraph is taken from the Second Part of Pushkin's "The Bronze Horseman." See page 334.

"dried raspberries": Russians either add them to tea or make an infusion from them as a sudorific.

Serafim (or Seraphim) of Sarov: "The first and greatest of the *stártsi* ["elders"—plural of *stárets*] of the nineteenth century was Saint Seraphim of Sarov (1759–1833). . . . Entering the monastery of Sarov at the age of nineteen, Seraphim first spent fifteen years in the ordinary life of the community. Then he withdrew to spend the next thirty years in seclusion. . . . This was his training for the office of eldership. Finally in 1825 he opened the doors of his cell. From dawn until evening he received all who came to him for help, healing the sick, giving advice. . . . Seraphim was extraordinarily severe to himself (at one point in his life he spent a thousand successive nights in continual prayer, standing motionless throughout the long hours of darkness on a rock), but he was gentle to others, without ever being sentimental or indulgent. Asceticism did not make him gloomy . . ." (*The Orthodox Church*, Timothy Ware, Penguin paperback, 1964, pp. 130–131). The 1916 edition specifies that the image in Dudkin's room represents the saint's thousand nights of prayer. See also G. P. Fedotov's *A Treasury of Russian Spirituality* (New York, 1948) for a study of the saint and a translation of his famous conversation with Nicholas Motovilov.

"the organ of a general body": Here Bely cut "the organ of a general body," in the 1916 text, to "the general body," in the 1922 version. This destroys the comparison, and so we have restored the 1916 reading. In the next sentence we have added the adjective "individual" to modify "thought" in the interests of more effective metaphor, again following the 1916 edition.

"beyond the railway," etc.: The turn in Nevsky Prospect at Znamenskaya Square (see notes on pages 297, 320). The Morskaya is a major street running off Nevsky Prospect near the Admiralty.

"Dionysian": The word was cut from the 1928 and 1935 editions. Soviet ideologues (and censors) have never felt comfortable with Nietzsche.

"the Apocalypse": In the 1928 and 1935 editions, cuts were made here and in the next paragraph to remove all references to the Apocalypse.

"in research into the occult": Cut from the two Soviet editions.

"Don't confuse allegory with symbol": This paragraph and the opening of the next long paragraph were altered beyond recognition in the editions of 1928 and 1935.

"as Plato describes it": Dudkin has in mind the following passage in Plato's *Phaedo* (69 C), where Socrates says: "True virtue in reality is a kind of purifying from all these things; and temperance, and justice, and courage, and wisdom itself are the purification. And I fancy that the men who established our mysteries had a very real meaning: in truth they have been telling us in parables all the time that whosoever comes to Hades uninitiated and profane will lie in the mire, while he that has been purified and initiated shall dwell with the gods. For 'the thyrsus-bearers are many,' as they say in the mysteries, 'but the inspired few.' And by these last, I believe, are meant only the true philosophers." (Quoted from the F. J. Church translation; the·"thyrsus-bearers," of course, are the Bacchantes.) Besant, in *Man and His Bodies*, writes that after death "The Ego quickly shakes off the etheric double, which, as we have seen, cannot pass on to the astral plane, and leaves it to disintegrate with its lifelong partner [the physical body]" (p. 31). Both theosophy and anthroposophy teach a variety of spiritual exercises to their initiates. These exercises are designed to develop the organs of supersensible perception believed present in all men. In the 1916 edition Dudkin says that he is aware of all this because a "very close friend" who studied at such schools told him about it.

"momentous events were rumbling": All but one of the incidents mentioned in this paragraph were reported in the Russian press at the time. The exception is the "event" in the town of Ak-Tyuk. We have been unable to find any such place in the standard reference sources; apparently it is an invention of Bely's. In the 1916 redaction, the "event" is described at some length: a worker quarrels with a policeman at a railway station, grabs a bank note from him, swallows it, and is forced literally to cough it up by being given a vomative. The Gogolian touches contrast too sharply with the matter-of-fact tone of the remainder of the paragraph, which may explain why Bely cut this from the text. One line was also cut from the account of the "event" in the theater at Kutais (a town in the Caucasus, of some 50,000 people, and capital of the province of the same name): "The public shouted 'Citizens!'" In its evening edition of October 8 (21), 1905, *Birzhevye vedomosti* reported that on the evening of October 7, during a performance at the theater in Kutais, "a voice cried out 'Citizens! Let us honor the memory of Prince S. N. Trubetskoy!' The whole audience rose as one man." Trubetskoy, the first elected rector of Moscow University and a widely admired liberal, had died on September 29. The authorities tried, with little success, to prevent demonstrations in his memory.

The same issue of *Birzhevye vedomosti* carried a dispatch from Tiflis reporting that on October 7, at 10:00 A.M., a terrorist threw a bomb at a local Tiflis policeman named Sanikidze, who had recently discovered a bomb factory in a village near the city. Sanikidze and several passersby received only minor injuries. (The same story can also be found in the October 8 issue of *Novoe vremya*).

The October 8 issue of *Birzhevye vedomosti* also reported the closing of the public library in Odessa on October 7, by order of the Ministry of the Interior, and the closing of the "Motor" factory at Reval that same day by order of its administrators because of revolutionary agitation and unrest among the workers who had run up red flags and had tried to seize the factory. When police were called in to remove the flags, one of the factory inspectors was seriously injured by pieces of iron thrown at him by the strikers.

Every issue of *Birzhevye vedomosti* and *Novoe vremya* in early October carried reports of unauthorized mass meetings and political rallies being held in major universities and educational institutions throughout Russia. Classes virtually came to a standstill. Both newspapers also noted that street demonstrations and mass meetings demanding governmental reforms had gotten so out of control in Perm that Cossacks had to be called in. This in turn provoked demands that the Cossacks be removed.

"a strike had already begun," etc.: *Novoe vremya* on October 8 reported that all passenger service on the Moscow–Kazan railway line had ceased on October 7, when engineers on passenger trains began a strike. Within a few days this strike "spread to the entire network, engulfed the telegraph and telephone services and paralyzed practically all industry" (Florinsky, II, pp. 1176–1177). It was the greatest general strike in Russian history and helped precipitate the governmental crisis that Apollon Apollonovich is called on to help deal with in the final chapter of the novel.

Sympathy strikes had been organized by the shipyards and the typesetters in Petersburg on October 4 and 5 in support of demands made in Moscow late in September by striking typesetters, always among the most radical of the workers, in Russia and elsewhere. As a result, no newspapers appeared in the capital on either of those days (See *Novoe vremya* for October 7 (20), 1905.) The Petersburg newspapers suspended publication on October 14, and most did not resume until the crisis eased in November. The lead editorial in *Birzhevye vedomosti* for October 14 (27) opened with the statement that "The disorganization of Russian life has reached unheard of limits and will soon reach impossible ones." By then the Neva Shipbuilding Factory had been completely shut down for several days, as had the Alexandrovsky Factory, one of the oldest factories in Petersburg, whose workers were among the most revolutionary.

"Oh, had he the strength!" Added from the 1916 edition.

"a consumptive . . . even a Bulgarian": Insarov, the hero of Turgenev's novel *On the Eve* (1860), is a Bulgarian nationalist committed to liberating his country from Turkish domination. He dies of consumption at the end of the novel.

"Shemakha . . . he was almost killed in the massacre at Isfahan": Shemakha is a town in Azerbaidzhan, about eighty miles west of Baku. It had been a major cultural center in ancient times, but never recovered from the effect of invasions by Mongols, Turks, and Persians. In 1805 it became part of the Russian Empire. By the turn of the century it had grown into a major silk manufacturing center, with a population that was about eighty percent Moslem. It was also the scene of rather frequent earthquakes, most recently (as of the time of *Petersburg*) one in 1902 which devastated the town.

By the late nineteenth century, the despotic government of Persia (Iran) had allowed both England and Russia to carve the country up into monopolies, concessions, and spheres of influence in return for large sums of money which went straight into the pockets of the ruling family. Opposition to this situation existed in the form of a growing nationalist movement, which culminated in outright revolutionary activity between 1905 and 1909. This activity was further encouraged by the Russian revolution of 1905, especially in Azerbaidzhan. There Persian revolutionaries came into contact with revolutionary workers in places like Shemakha and Baku. There were many varieties of revolutionaries and nationalists (for example, the Babis), but there was no Young Persia movement as such. (Bely forms it on the model of Young Italy, Young Egypt, Young Germany, etc.) Shishnarfiev can be identified with none of the groups. By the massacre in Isfahan Bely may mean the terrible riots in Isfahan and Yazd in the summer of 1903 when mobs, incited by the authorities, tortured and killed any Babis who fell into their hands (see Edward G. Browne, *The Persian Revolution of 1905–1909*, London, 1910).

Young Persia: See previous note.

"Had one raised their lids": The literary reference is to Gogol's story "Viy." Here the monster, Viy, has eyelids so long that they reach the ground. He commands his creatures to raise them so that he can see the hero, Khoma Brut, and when Khoma looks into the eyes, he is destroyed.

"Abracadabra," etc: This sentence is added from the 1916 edition.

"The tracks of the railway rush onward," etc.: In the chronicle section of the issue of October 6 (19), 1905, *Novoe vremya* reported on a major railroad disaster with heavy loss of life along the Moscow–Petersburg main line at 4:00 A.M. on October 4. Parts of the song strikingly resemble the newspaper account: "As a result of an improperly shunted switch, the train rushed onto a siding where it smashed into a barrier and knocked it down. After moving for some distance over the embankment, the locomotive tumbled into a ditch, dragging the cars of the train with it. . . . The catastrophe found the passengers sound asleep. Awakened by the crash of the coaches being smashed, many of the passengers, in panic-stricken terror, leaped onto the tracks where they saw the sight of the destruction with their own eyes."

"the Fortress": The Fortress of SS. Peter and Paul contained the State Prison where many political prisoners were interrogated and incarcerated.

"false passport"; Pogorelsky: Here Dudkin is given the name of a well-known early nineteenth-century writer, A. Pogorelsky, the pseudonym of Alexei Alexeyevich Perovsky (1787–1836). It is not immediately apparent why Bely chooses this writer, who is distinctly inferior to the mainstays of the novel (Pushkin, Gogol, Dostoevsky, etc.). Perhaps it is because Pogorelsky was famous in his time for stories that combined ordinary, even sordid life, with elements of the fantastic that drew heavily on German Romanticism, especially the works of E. T. A. Hoffmann. (See, for example, his collection of stories, *The Double, or Evenings in Little Russia*, 1828.) Perhaps Bely wishes to suggest the whole question of paternity and legitimacy which figures so prominently in the novel: Pogorelsky himself was the illegitimate son of Count Alexander Kirillovich Razumovsky; when Shishnarfiev addresses Dudkin as Gorelsky, instead of the proper Pogorelsky, he may be suggesting that Dudkin is illegitimate by employing the common Russian practice of referring to the illegitimate sons of prominent men by dropping the first syllable of the father's name (so Repnin becomes Pnin, etc.). More significantly, Alexei was the name of Peter the Great's son and heir, whom he had executed in 1718.

Like most Russians, Dudkin was obliged by law to carry an internal passport (as distinct from one issued for travel abroad). The internal passport system was extremely complicated by this time, but it had been in effect, in various forms, since at least the reign of Peter the Great—and it remains in effect to this day in the Soviet Union. Forged papers and revolutionary pseudonyms were stock in trade in the revolutionary movement.

"back staircase": The Russian *chërnaya léstnitsa* means both "black staircase" and "back staircase, service entrance."

"the necessity of destroying culture": Many anarchists and several of the leading Russian modernist writers (taking their cue from Nietzsche, among others), called for the "destruction of culture" or eagerly awaited the holocaust. Valery Bryusov's poem "The Coming Huns" ("Gryadushchie gunny") is typical of the mood: the poet longs for the coming of the barbarians, who will burn the libraries and defile the temples of the old world. The 1916 version is more specific about this "period of healthy barbarism." Among the "lower strata," Dudkin finds "hooliganism and the riotous behavior of Apaches"; among the "aristocratic upper strata," a "love for primitive culture," in addition to the points cited in the 1922 text. Among the bourgeoisie the examples include "Eastern ladies' fashions and the cakewalk—a Negro dance."

Prayer Book, etc.: Bely uses the word *Trébnik*. These volumes contained prayers used in the various rites of the Orthodox Church, which are celebrated in Church Slavic, not Russian. Dudkin's memory has confused the title of the prayer with something from Vladimir Solovyov, whom he has obviously been reading. "Admonitory prayer to demons" is closer to the subtitle ("An Admonitory Word to Sea Devils") of Solovyov's 1898 poem "Das Ewig-Weibliche" than to Basil the Great's "Prayer of Exorcism for those Suffering from Demons" in the *Trebnik*.

"It's you *they're* looking for": There is no way to convey the deliberate ambiguity of the Russian here: *oní* means both "he" and "they." When speaking of a member of a class above themselves, peasants used the plural (i.e., "they" really means "he"); but Stepan is also repeating the sinister phrase which haunts the paranoid Dudkin, so "they" does mean "they" as well.

"Petersburg is built on a swamp": This is a statement of fact. During construction, parts of the swamp had to be drained (one reason for some of the canals) and piles had to be driven to support the weight of the buildings. Thousands of lives were lost in the harsh climate. The Neva takes its name from the Finnish *newa* or *newo*, meaning "swamp."

"And in vodka": Considering that Dudkin is conducting a conversation with himself (or his own double, which will soon vanish), one might note the following from Besant's *Man and His Bodies*: ". . . the etheric double is peculiarly susceptible to the volatile constituents of alcohol" (p. 29).

"with water you swallow germs," etc.: Baedeker (p. 102) italicizes the following warning to visitors to Petersburg: "*Unboiled water should on no account be drunk*." Tea (not vodka) is recommended as a substitute.

Both *Novoe vremya* and *Birzhevye vedomosti* frequently reported outbreaks of cholera in European Russia during October, 1905. For instance, the October 9 (22) issue of *Novoe vremya* contained the following suggestive notice in the column "Notes on the Capital": "Throughout the spring and summer of this year all city and local public agencies have been actively and energetically preparing for the battle against an expected cholera epidemic. The danger then threatened only from without, *primarily from Persia*" (our italics). Petersburg enjoyed the deserved reputation as the most unhealthy capital city of Europe.

the Farce Theater: In 1905 the Farce Theater (Winter Season) was located at Ofitserskaya No. 39. It usually offered programs of French farces and light comedies.

"registered there": Any Russian citizen not only needed an internal passport (see page 345) but had to have it registered and stamped for it to be valid in a city. This is still true in the Soviet Union.

"*Enfranshish*": In the second chapter of the novel we are told that the "meaningless word *enfranshish*" comes into Dudkin's memory from "the devil only knows where." Dudkin repeatedly mentions that his garret is infested with insects, among them bedbugs. In revising the 1916 version, Bely cut from the first section of the sixth chapter a sentence stating that Dudkin had been battling the bedbugs with insect powder (Baedeker, p. xiv, recommended insect powder for all visitors to Russia). Insect powder in Russian is *persídskii poroshók*, literally "*Persian* powder." Omry Ronen of the Hebrew University in Jerusalem can recall seeing advertisements in the Russian press of the time for such insect powder and, printed on the containers, in Roman letters, the words "*En franchise*." We may suppose that Dudkin, who probably does not know French, also has seen this "meaningless word," transposes it into Cyrillic letters and comes up with enfranshish, and its reverse, the "Persian" Shishnarfne, as a result. Ronen's suggestion seems convincing. The reverse of "sh" in English is of course "hs," but in Cyrillic "sh" is a single letter, making the mirror effect possible. *Shish* is also a vulgar Russian word for "nothing" and the name of a vulgar gesture where the thumb is thrust between two closed fingers.

"The floor is thickly strewn with earth": This was a primitive but effective form of insulation.

"the forts of Kronstadt": The naval base of Kronstadt guards the sea approaches to Petersburg. "*Cronstadt*, a fortified town with 65,000 inhab. and the station of the Baltic fleet, lies upon the island of *Kotlin*, which is 7¼ M. in length and 1¼ M. in width. Its batteries, built upon piles, and looking as if floating on the sea, command the entrance to Nevá bay. The original fortifications on the island were made [by Peter the Great] in 1703" (Baedeker, p. 184).

Pushkin: The second (and last) author's footnote in the novel. "Weightily sonorous" (*tyazheló-zvónkoe*) appears in Pushkin's "The Bronze Horseman," where it describes the galloping (*skakán'e*) of the Horseman through the streets of Petersburg.

"anagram": The 1916 text has "shorthand report" (*stenográmma*), not "anagram." While the Shishnarfne/Enfranshish doubling is not strictly an anagram, the 1922 version makes as much sense as the 1916 version.

"the destinies of Evgeny": The hero of Pushkin's "The Bronze Horseman" (see page 334).

"Petro Primo Catharina Secunda": The inscription on the granite block on which the Bronze Horseman stands. Characteristically, Bely misspells part of it ("Catherina" instead of "Catharina"). The same inscription, in Russian, appears on the other side of the pedestal. Catherine the Great commissioned the monument (see pages 323–24).

"the Metallic Guest": Again Bely alludes both to "The Bronze Horseman" and to *The Stone Guest* of Pushkin (see page 336).

"start seeing a Green Dragon": Bely uses the normal Russian expression for drinking oneself into delirium tremens: *dopít'sya do zelënogo zmíya*. In the context of this passage, however, the expression also takes on apocalyptic overtones (the Dragon of Revelation 12 who threatens the "woman clothed with the sun" is rendered in the Slavonic Bible as *zmíi*), which Bely emphasizes by capitalizing the words *Zelënyi Zmíi*. Hence our literal translation.

"white . . . woman": Here Bely plays with a normal Russian expression, which he imbues with apocalyptic overtones. In the context a Russian reader would expect the word "fever" (*goryáchka*) to follow "white" (*bélaya*), inasmuch as the expression as a whole (*bélaya goryáchka*) means delirium tremens. Instead, Styopka substitutes another feminine noun, *zhénshchina* ("woman"), thereby conjuring up the apocalyptic image of the "woman clothed with the sun" of Revelation 12:1.

"a Finnish . . .": Dudkin is about to ask for a "Finnish knife," a kind of switchblade very common in Russia at the time. To have had him ask in English for a "switch . . ." would have eliminated an evocation of the "Finnish theme" in the book (e.g., Dudkin's sojourn in Helsinki, the block of Finnish granite on which the Bronze Horseman stands, etc.).

Chapter the Seventh

The epigraph is the opening line and the first half of the second line of the 1834 Pushkin lyric quoted earlier (see page 335). Bely's misquotation of the first half of the first line is certainly deliberate.

Gaurisankar: A mountain 23,450 feet high in the Himalayan chain, near Mount Everest.

"Wer reitet," etc.: The opening lines of Goethe's ballad "Erlkönig" ("The Elfking"), also well known as a Schubert song. Bely then cites these two lines and the final line of the same poem in the standard Russian translation by Vasily Zhukovsky (1783–1852).

CRANES: One wonders if a Zhukovsky association is at work here. Another of his famous translations from the German is of Schiller's ballad "Die Kraniche des Ibykus" ("The Cranes of Ibycus"), a retelling of the Greek legend of the murder of the lyric poet Ibycus. "According to tradition, he was murdered by robbers near Corinth, and called on a flock of passing cranes to bear witness. Shortly afterward, during the performance of a play in a Corinth theater, one of the murderers, at sight of some cranes flying overhead, involuntarily exclaimed, 'the avengers of Ibycus.' Suspicion was aroused and the murderers identified. Hence the 'cranes of Ibycus' became a proverb for the belief that 'murder will out' " (*The New Century Classical Handbook*, New York, 1962, p. 584).

"I am sick . . .": Nikolai melodramatically sees himself as a Biblical sinner who will fall down before Christ to ask for peace (the Russian *uspokói* which is used here is always rendered in the King James as to "give rest" or "refresh"). He hopes to hear Christ's "Arise . . . Go . . . Sin no more." (Bely merges two different Gospel scenes here: the "Arise" is Jesus' command to the palsied man in Matthew 9:5, while "Go and sin no more" is addressed by Jesus to the "woman taken in adultery" in John 8:11.)

"wrap it all up . . . into the Neva with it": A parodic reference to the barber's "solution" of how to get rid of the incriminating nose in Gogol's "The Nose."

"about shaving": Both the 1916 and 1922 texts have "about my neck" at this point, but in the 1916 version Nikolai has just been babbling away about the fact that Likhutin's neck is wrapped up. By removing this part of the conversation Bely robbed the remark of meaningful context; our change of "neck" to "shaving" (which Nikolai has just mentioned) restores the context.

"prayer service": Bely uses the word *akáfist*. The Acathistus is a liturgical hymn in set form in honor of Christ, the Mother of God, etc. The most famous, in honor of the Mother of God, is sung on the Saturday of the Fifth Week of Lent.

"(we know what Lippanchenko was thinking)": "We know what" is added from the 1916 version for greater clarity.

"earthen vessel": Because of the Biblical reference (for example, 2 Corinthians 4:7) we have rendered *skudél'nyi sosúd* in the manner of the King James Bible, rather than as "weak vessel."

"Section-marker": The sign is as follows: §

"bank notes": Literally "credit notes"; compare Baedeker (p. xiv) "paper-money (the so-called credit-notes) consists of notes of 1,3,5,10, 25,50,100, and 500 rb."

"Creeper/creaker" is an attempt to convey the pun *vereshchít/véresk*, where the sound of the verb describing the clerks' quill pens moving over paper (*vereshchít*, literally "squeaks") suggests to Bely's ear the sound of the noun *véresk*, the plant Erica s. Calluna vulgaris. (Usually rendered as "heather," the plant spread quickly and could choke growth in forests, much in the same way the bureaucracy itself spread.) This pun is phonologically and even morphologically plausible inasmuch as *shch/sk* is a regular consonant alternation in Russian. It is set in motion by Bely's use of the word *list* which means both the leaf of a plant and a sheet of paper (the plural forms are different).

Kozlorodov, etc.: The names are invented; the situation (described at greater length in the 1916 edition) betokens the collapse of central authority in the period of revolutionary disturbance. Local officials took advantage of the chaos to settle scores with enemies in the bureaucracy. "Ivanchi-Ivanchevskys" seems to indicate that our narrator is afflicted with a nervous stammer.

Phlegethontic waves: Phlegethon (or Pyriphlegethon, "the fiery"), one of the rivers of Hades. In Plato's *Phaedo*, Socrates states that its waters torment parricides and matricides. The metaphor (much more developed in the 1916 version) is yet another of the literary references: to Pushkin's 1824 lyric "Prozerpína" ("Persephone").

"Ham–lits": There is no way of capturing the wordplay Bely puts into the mouth of the illiterate Semyonych. He calls his masters *khamléty*, a melange of *kham* ("boor," "lout") and "Hamlet" (although the Russian word is pronounced "Gamlet," he may well have heard the English version in the highly educated family he serves). He carries the sound association into the next sentence, when he calls them *khímiki*, a foreign word usually meaning chemists, but in vulgar speech having the meaning of scalawags or rascals.

Avgiev, etc.: The column "In the Streets of Petersburg" ("Na ulitsakh Peterburga") in the Friday, October 7 (20) issue of *Birzhevye vedomosti* contained numerous reports of increased criminal activity in the city. Gangs of thugs, taking advantage of the fact that the police were occupied almost exclusively with civil unrest (strikes, rallies, illegal parades, etc.), were roaming the city robbing, looting, setting fires, assaulting passersby, and terrorizing ordinary citizens. For Russians, the name Avgiev suggests the "Augean Stables" (*Avgievy konyushni*).

"did not notice Semyonych": The "not" of the 1916 text was accidentally dropped from the 1922 edition; this mistake was never corrected in subsequent editions. The passage makes sense only if it contains "not."

"Of late that wind had developed into a hurricane": Added from the 1916 edition. At the time, the image of wind (or of various other natural phenomena) commonly denoted revolutionary unrest. In the opening paragraph of his 1917 essay *Revolution and Culture* (*Revolyutsiya i kul'tura*, Moscow, 1917) Bely himself compared the March Revolution to a hurricane.

"to move the hearts and minds of men": The Russian text contains the expression *udaryát' po serdtsám* (literally "to try to strike at the hearts [of men]") which entered the language from Pushkin's 1831 poem "An Answer to an Anonymous Author" ("Otvet anonimu") and became a cliché. We have chosen an equivalent English cliché.

"timelessness": Bely uses the word *bezvrémen'ye*, literally "timelessness," but figuratively "hard times" or any period of social stagnation. In this last meaning it was often used to describe the period following the Revolution of 1905. From the context it is clear that Bely intends the word to be understood literally here, but for any Russian reader the word carries the other meanings as well.

"You seem swollen": In Russian "*Otelkí.*" The 1916 edition reads "*Otyóki,*" i.e., edema.

"The January days raged and passed: nineteen hundred and five!": The terrible Bloody Sunday massacre of January 9, 1905 and the widespread unrest that followed served as a kind of prelude to the full outbreak of revolution in the autumn of 1905.

"There is no happiness," etc.: The last four lines (slightly misquoted) of the 1834 Pushkin poem whose first four lines appear above it in the text (see page 335).

"a magnificent palace": The Mikhailovsky (or Michael) Castle (*Zámok*; see map), "built in a medieval style in the reign of Paul I between 1797 and 1800, probably by Brenna from a design of Bazhénov, on the site of a summer-palace occupied by the Empress Elizabeth" (Baedeker, p. 118). In 1822 it was made the Engineering Academy and was thus called the Engineer's Castle (*Inzhenérnyi zámok*). The young Dostoevsky lived and studied there.

    Because of his fear of assassination or coup d'etat, Paul (Pavel) the First made the palace a veritable citadel with massive walls of granite, and with a deep moat all around. (Now it is bordered on two sides by canals.) Normally it was filled with specially chosen guards; each access was protected by gun emplacements and by a drawbridge, raised when the Tsar retired for the night. All precautions proved useless (see below).

The tower stretching to the sky is the spire of the chapel inside the palace.

"Lord have mercy on his soul!": Cut from the editions of 1928 and 1935.

"an equestrian statue": To the south of the Mikhailovsky Castle stands an equestrian statue of Peter the Great, "cast in the reign of Elizabeth from designs by Rastrelli the Elder, and set up under Paul I. The inscription on the marble pedestal runs 'To the Great-Grandfather by the Great-Grandson 1800'" (Baedeker, p. 119). Visitors to Petersburg, eager to see the more famous Bronze Horseman, might indeed ignore it.

"He did not languish long there": Paul lived in the new palace for only forty days. He was a man of highly unstable character, felt by many to have been mad; his behavior swung from acts of capricious cruelty and tyranny to sober, well-intentioned acts of generosity and kindness. His family and court lived in fear of his unpredictable outbursts, which could easily end in disgrace and exile for the targets. The epithet "snub-nosed" accurately describes Paul's most prominent physical feature. The final sentence of this paragraph was cut from Soviet editions of the novel.

"a gold-chested general": Bely probably means Count Peter Pahlen, military governor of Petersburg and leader of the plot against Paul. The mannered lady-in-waiting is the Emperor's mistress, Princess Gagarina.

"On that night," etc.: On the night of March 11 (23), 1801, a group of conspirators, intent on the overthrow of Paul, managed to gain access to his bedroom in the Mikhailovsky Castle. Accounts vary widely as to what happened next. Some say that during an argument with the Emperor, who resisted demands for his abdication, the conspirators (most of whom were drunk) grew alarmed by the sound of approaching footsteps, and strangled Paul on the spot. Other accounts suggest that the assassination was deliberately premeditated and carried out in a singularly brutal manner. Equally debatable is the extent to which the Emperor's son, who ascended the throne as Alexander I, was involved. There is no doubt that he knew of the conspiracy and gave his assent to it. Some historians argue that he believed his father would merely be deposed and sent under guard to some distant place of exile; others insist that he must have realized the plot would inevitably end in murder. At any rate, Alexander, while professing contrition, visited no severe punishment upon the murderers. His life and reign were clouded by rumors that he was a parricide. Thus we have a historical parallel to Nikolai's behavior.

PITCH DARKNESS: The Russian expression *t'ma kroméshnaya*, which Bely uses here, means "outer darkness" in its Slavic Biblical usage, but absolute or pitch darkness in modern Russian. In the 1916 edition the expression is applied ironically and comically to the complete darkness of the outer entryway to the building in which the Likhutin apartment is located. By cutting this portion of the text Bely rendered the "joke" pointless. Therefore, we chose the neutral term "pitch darkness."

"a state councilor": Fifth from the top in the Table of Ranks (see page 300).

"as is well known"; "science teaches us": *Kak izvéstno* and *naúka nas úchit* were two of Stalin's favorite phrases.

"It's not about Sofia Petrovna": Inexplicably dropped in the 1922 text and restored by us.

"You knew not what you did": Compare Christ's words from the cross: "Father, forgive them; for they know not what they do" (Luke 23:34). Throughout the encounter between Nikolai and Likhutin Bely makes parodic references to the events surrounding the trial and crucifixion of Christ (the weeping women, the rent garment, etc.), for Nikolai would like to see himself in the role of an "innocent martyr" who has suffered for others.

"I am so wretched": In Russian *bédnyi ya*. Compare Romans 7:24: "O wretched man that I am!" (In Russian: *Bédnyi ya chelovék!*)

"Oh, do not tempt . . .": The opening line of another of Glinka's most famous songs, set to the poem "Dissuasion" ("Razuverenie," 1821), by a contemporary of Pushkin, the poet Evgeny Baratynsky. Lippanchenko sings the first, third, fourth, fifth (misquoted), and sixth lines of the song. Apollon Apollonovich could sing it with perhaps better reason.

"They sweep": A misprint in the 1922 text makes this read "It sweeps." The 1916 edition has "Hurricanes sweep."

"of the entire heart": The 1916 edition reads "of an enormous heart." The 1928 version reads "of the whole sun." The later revision does not make the passage much clearer.

Dudkin's small mustache "with bristling ends" and his pose astride the dead Lippanchenko mimic the Bronze Horseman.

Chapter the Eighth

The epigraph is taken from the monk Pimen's monologue in Pushkin's verse tragedy *Boris Godunov* (Act One, "Night. A Cell in the Chudov Monastery" [Scene V], lines 19–24) of 1824–25.

Given the subsequent description of the senator's ride with Anna Petrovna back to their house (once again on the English Embankment), the "first-class hotel" in question is the very fashionable Hôtel de l'Europe (the Evropeiskaya) on the corner of Nevsky Prospect and Mikhailovskaya Street (see map). According to Baedeker, rooms without bath started at three rubles.

"I, you . . .": Another instance in which Apollon Apollonovich hesitates between using the familiar form of address (*ty*) or the polite form (*vy*).

"ABOVE": The 1922 text reads "below," but we have restored the "above" of the 1916 edition, mindful of the fact that the words of the title with "above" appear in the text proper.

"counting the days," etc.: The three religious holidays mentioned are all "fixed feasts." The Feast of the Protection of the Mother of God falls on October 1 (14). Sometimes called "The Protecting Veil of the Mother of God" (from the Slavic *Pokróv*), the feast has no counterpart in the Western Church. The Nativity of the Mother of God, one of the Twelve Great Feasts of the Orthodox Church, falls on September 8 (21). The Feast of Saint Nicholas the Wonderworker falls on December 6 (19) for which reason it is called *Zimnii* ("Winter") in Russian.

Almondini: His name, as we know, is Mantalini, but the servants, unaccustomed to foreign names, call him "Mindalini," from the Russian *mindál'*, almond. Because Bely specifically mentions an almond tree in the Epilogue we thought it better to render the "joke" as Almondini, rather than Mindalini.

"hussar's wife," etc.: Literally, Apollon Apollonovich's idiotic joke goes: "Who is the wife of a Chaldean?" (*khaldéi*), the answer being the vulgar *khálda* (a coarse, insolent woman, i.e., a brazen hussy), which makes "sense" only because *khaldéi* can also mean in colloquial speech a coarse, insolent fellow.

"But then came," etc.: In the 1916 and 1922 texts the phrase "But then came the sudden slash of memory! The sardine tin!" is not set off as a separate paragraph and the sentence which follows says only "A paroxysm burst within *him*." A reader would conclude that all this is taking place in the mind of Apollon Apollonovich, not Nikolai, which is clearly impossible in the context. When making some revisions for the 1928 text Bely tried to solve the problem (which he obviously recognized) by changing *Apollon* Apollonovich in the preceding paragraph to *Nikolai* Apollonovich, which is preposterous, inasmuch as Nikolai is still standing by his mother and it is Apollon who has been darting back and forth. The confusion is easily dispelled by substituting *Nikolai* for *him* and making the sentence "But then came," etc., a separate paragraph.

"Bruises can lead to complications": Apollon Apollonovich's comment to his son is very similar to the remark reportedly made by Paul I to his son Alexander the day before his assassination: "You should always deal with indispositions at once, in order to prevent them from becoming serious illnesses." (Quoted in K. Waliszewski's *Paul the First of Russia*, London, 1913, p. 443.)

Hunyadi-Janos: Mineral waters bottled at this Hungarian town were widely sold as a laxative. We cannot resist quoting the Cournos translation of this sentence: "[she] called him a pet name."

Bruno: The Italian philosopher Giordano Bruno (1548–1600) was burned at the stake by the Inquisition in Rome. He was a warm admirer of

Copernicus, and in the latter half of the nineteenth century he was held up as a hero by anticlerical elements throughout Europe. Given Apollon Apollonovich's own views of the clergy, Bruno is an appropriate object of admiration here.

Prolyotnoe: The name of the Ableukhov estate is derived from the word *prolyót*, i.e., flight past, flight by, suggesting an inhospitable place to be passed by quickly.

"gone . . . into retirement": Apollon Apollonovich is forced to retire from the service when his personal life becomes enmeshed in the public mind with the revolutionary events of October, 1905. Pobedonostsev was removed from his post as chief procurator of the Holy Synod (a job he had held since 1880) in October, 1905, by his one-time ally Witte.

"One Ableukhova, Anna Petrovna": The style mimics a passport entry.

Epilogue

"almond tree": See page 353.

"a coastal village near Tunis": Bely and Asya Turgeneva (although never married by the church, they lived as man and wife) spent the closing weeks of 1910 in Tunis, then the capital of the French Régence de Tunis (Tunisia). In January, 1911, they rented a small Arab house in Rades, a nearby village, where they lived for almost two months. Baedeker (*The Mediterranean*, 1911, p. 363) describes Rades as a "picturesque little town which is a favorite summer residence of the wealthy Moslems of Tunis" and which affords a fine view of the hills of Carthage and the bay of Tunis. Bely and Asya then travelled, via Malta and Port Said, to Cairo, where they spent most of March.

"moldering": We have restored this word, which was inexplicably dropped from the 1922 version. Without it, Bely's deliberate parallel between the Sphinx and culture (in the next paragraph) is destroyed. The following, from a recent short biography of Bely, is an excellent statement of what Bely intends by such a parallelism: "He conceived of cultural achievements as the external manifestation of man's internal process of imbuing the chaotic objective world with meaning. Bely took nothing for granted; there was to him no such thing as given reality. The world outside man is chaotic, meaningless, and therefore hostile, until it is transformed in the human mind, and this idea was not an abstract philosophical conviction, reached as a result of study, but the product of a real and inescapable way of perceiving the world. To Bely, then, a period or a culture is defined by the way in which it creates form out of chaos. An architectural shape cannot be fully described in terms of material and function, but is to be seen as the tangible expression of a certain psychic disposition" (John Elsworth, *Andrey Bely*, Letchworth, England, 1972, p. 72).

The museum at Bulaq: The famous Egyptian Museum, founded in 1857 by Auguste Ferdinand François Mariette (1821–1881), French Egyptologist and author of the scenario on which Verdi's *Aida* is based. It now stands in the main square of Cairo, but at the time of Nikolai's visit, the Museum was still located in its original building at Bulaq, a section of Cairo, and its director was the well-known Egyptologist Sir Gaston Maspero (1846–1916). The excellent library contained many rare manuscripts.

"The 'Book of the Dead' is a modern name. In Egyptian it was called 'Spells for Coming Out by Day,' and it is a compilation, apparently made somewhat previously to the New Kingdom, of over 150 magical spells, to be recited by the dead man to protect himself from injury, demons and the 'second death,' to enable him to emerge from his tomb, to accompany the gods, to secure acquittal at the Judgment, and for other purposes" (*Introduction to Egyptian Archeology*, Ed. by R. Engelbach, Cairo, Imprimerie de l'Institut Français d'Archéologie Orientale, 1946, p. 197).

"It is to *Manetho* that we owe the word *dynasty* as applied to Egyptian history. Manetho of Sebennytos (Samannûd) was an Egyptian, probably a priest of Heliopolis, who lived in the Ptolemaic Period, about 300 B.C., and who wrote in Greek three books of 'Egyptian Memoirs' in which he grouped the kings, from Menes to Nectanebo II, into 30 dynasties, which correspond to the various royal houses that ruled Egypt successively or, at certain periods, simultaneously. Manetho's works have been lost, but fragments of them, corrupted through successive copyings, have been preserved by Josephus, Eusebius and others" (Ibid., p. 12).

"There will be . . . swept away": This sentence is one of the few instances in which Bely added something for the 1922 text. It is obvious why.

"large piles at Gizeh": These are, of course, the famous pyramids outside Cairo. Bely's own initial reaction upon seeing them was "madness and horror" (*bezúmie i úzhas*; in an unpublished letter to A. S. Petrovsky).

"He is himself a pyramid . . . crash into ruins": Bely added the last sentence of this paragraph for the 1922 edition.

"On the Letter of Dauphsekhrut": "The Instruction of Duauf" (the name is transliterated in several different ways) is among the best-known documents of early Egyptian writing. Dating to a time between the Old and the Middle Kingdoms, it contains the instructions of Duauf to his son. An edition was prepared by Gaston Maspero (see above). An English translation can be found in *The Ancient Egyptians. A Source Book of Their Writings*, Ed. Adolf Erman; trans. A. M. Blackman (Harper Torchbooks, 1966; this is a reprint of the translation from Erman's 1923 German original, *Die Literatur der Aegypten*, first published in English in London in 1927 under the title *The Literature of the Ancient Egyptians*).

"Nazareth": Bely and Asya Turgeneva spent several weeks in and around Jerusalem on their return from the Near East to Russia in late March and early April, 1911.

Skovoroda: Grigory Skovoroda (1722–1794), the Ukrainian philosopher, theologian and poet, often called the "Russian Socrates." In his difficult philosophic dialogues he criticized "pure empiricism and developed a dualistic Platonic metaphysics with a mystical and pantheistic coloring" (*Dictionary of Russian Literature*, Ed. William Harkins, 1956, p. 289). Alexander Lavrov has traced Bely's own interest in Skovoroda, whom he undoubtedly knew through the writings of Vladimir Ern (1881–1917). In a 1912 monograph on Skovoroda, Ern attacked the rationalist philosophy which he claimed had brought about a crisis of European thought, and he accused rationalism of having renounced nature, which had been turned into a "soulless mechanism" (Lavrov, "Andrei Belyi i Grigorii Skovoroda," *Studia Slavica* [Budapest] XXI, 1975).